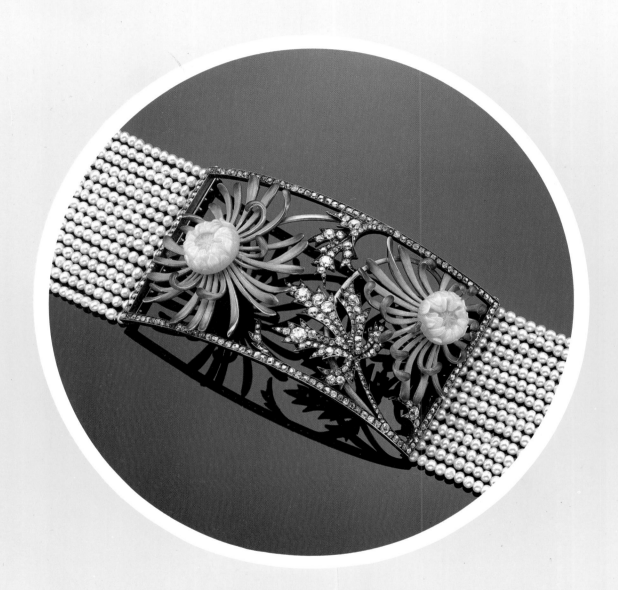

A hardstone and diamond corsage ornament by Boucheron, set with carved lapis lazuli, coral and jade, and suspended with a turquoise drop. This impressive piece, made for the Paris Exposition des Arts Décoratifs of 1925, was designed by Lucien Hirtz and mounted by Bisson; the lapidary work had been carried out by Brethiot.

Boucheron Collection. Photograph by courtesy of Boucheron.

Understanding
JEWELRY

David Bennett
and Daniela Mascetti

Antique Collectors' Club

First published 1989
© 1989 David Bennett and Daniela Mascetti
World copyright reserved

Reprinted 1990, 1991
Revised edition 1994
Reprinted 1996, 2000

ISBN 1 85149 361 1

The right of David Bennett and Daniela Mascetti to be identified as
authors of this work has been asserted by them in accordance with
the Copyright, Designs and Patents Act 1988

British Library Cataloguing in Publication Data
A catalogue record for this book is available from the British Library

Printed in England on Consort Royal Satin from Donside Mills, Aberdeen,
by the Antique Collectors' Club Ltd., Woodbridge, Suffolk, IP12 1DS

ANTIQUE COLLECTORS' CLUB

The Antique Collectors' Club was formed in 1966 and quickly grew to a five figure membership spread throughout the world. It publishes the only independently run monthly antiques magazine, *Antique Collecting*, which caters for those collectors who are interested in widening their knowledge of antiques, both by greater awareness of quality and by discussion of the factors which influence the price that is likely to be asked. The Antique Collectors' Club pioneered the provision of information on prices for collectors and the magazine still leads in the provision of detailed articles on a variety of subjects.

It was in response to the enormous demand for information on 'what to pay' that the price guide series was introduced in 1968 with the first edition of *The Price Guide to Antique Furniture* (completely revised 1978 and 1989), a book which broke new ground by illustrating the more common types of antique furniture, the sort that collectors could buy in shops and at auctions rather than the rare museum pieces which had previously been used (and still to a large extent are used) to make up the limited amount of illustrations in books published by commercial publishers. Many other price guides have followed, all copiously illustrated, and greatly appreciated by collectors for the valuable information they contain, quite apart from prices. The Price Guide Series heralded the publication of many standard works of reference on art and antiques. *The Dictionary of British Art* (now in six volumes), *The Pictorial Dictionary of British 19th Century Furniture Design*, *Oak Furniture* and *Early English Clocks* were followed by many deeply researched reference works such as *The Directory of Gold and Silversmiths*, providing new information. Many of these books are now accepted as the standard work of reference on their subject.

The Antique Collectors' Club has widened its list to include books on gardens and architecture. All the Club's publications are available through bookshops world wide and a full catalogue of all these titles is available free of charge from the addresses below.

Club membership, open to all collectors, costs little. Members receive free of charge *Antique Collecting*, the Club's magazine (published ten times a year), which contains well-illustrated articles dealing with the practical aspects of collecting not normally dealt with by magazines. Prices, features of value, investment potential, fakes and forgeries are all given prominence in the magazine.

Among other facilities available to members are private buying and selling facilities and the opportunity to meet other collectors at their local antique collectors' clubs. There are over eighty in Britain and more than a dozen overseas. Members may also buy the Club's publications at special pre-publication prices.

As its motto implies, the Club is an organisation designed to help collectors get the most out of their hobby: it is informal and friendly and gives enormous enjoyment to all concerned.

For Collectors — By Collectors — About Collecting

ANTIQUE COLLECTORS' CLUB
5 Church Street, Woodbridge, Suffolk, IP12 1DS, UK
Tel: (01394) 385501 Fax: (01394) 384434
Email: sales@antique-acc.com Website: www.antique-acc.com
——— *or* ———
Market Street Industrial Park, Wappingers' Falls, NY 12590, USA
Tel: (914) 297 0003 Fax (914) 297 0068 ORDERS: (800) 252 5231
Email: info@antiquecc.com Website: www.antiquecc.com

To Diana, Livia and Merle
and to Philip

Contents

Foreword

It is always useful, when setting out to write a book on a given subject, to have a particular reader in mind. In recent years many works have been published on jewellery, most of which have contributed to the body of knowledge, and some have shed new light on a specific aspect, maker or field. Acknowledging the existence of such books, we have set out to provide a 'primer' for the reader who is perhaps embarking upon a career in the jewellery trade, or collectors who are looking for a practical base on which to build their knowledge.

For anyone infatuated with a particular specialist field in the fine or decorative arts, working for a great auction house such as Sotheby's is a privileged position, not least in respect of the sheer volume of pieces that pass through one's hands in any year. In our case this has encompassed not only the celebrated collection of the Duchess of Windsor and legendary stones such as the Ashoka diamond, but also the paste brooches and 'insignificant' trifles that give so much insight into the lives of people in the past. The section on gemstones needs its own special caveat. The modern synthetics represent daunting problems even for the qualified gemmologist. We have attempted to outline the basic methods of determining the nature of a given stone, where this is possible and within the scope of the amateur and the limited range of instruments available. Nevertheless, it should be stressed that particularly where an expensive purchase is contemplated, impartial expert advice should be sought. We hope that anyone reading this section will at least be aware of some of the myriad problems that present themselves.

The notes on sale room prices given at the end of this book are intended only to provide perspective on comparative values of pieces. Obviously, retail values are higher and in any event time soon erodes the accuracy of such figures. This should therefore not be taken as a 'buyer's guide'.

Finally, we have found it impossible to avoid some value judgements appearing in the text. We make no apology for this since jewellery is intensely personal.

1994 Reprint — A Note

One of the phenomena of the end of the twentieth century is the speed at which styles and fashions return. Already by the late 1980s, when the first edition of this book was published, jewellery of the 1950s was enjoying a renaissance as collectors and fashion leaders rediscovered and reassessed the aesthetic criteria within which it has been designed.

Since then the same reappraisal has taken place with 1960s jewellery, and very recently the 1970s. This new edition, therefore, includes chapters devoted to these interesting decades of design.

They were years when new forces appeared in the market, and the jewellery industry, as a result of political and economic changes of international importance, began to take the shape it holds today; no longer were Europe and the Americas the main markets as the burgeoning economies in the Middle East and Asia began to make their presence felt.

Acknowledgements

We are grateful to Dr Edward Gübelin, C.G., F.G.A. for allowing us to reproduce some of the exceptional photomicrographs of inclusions in gemstones published in his book *Photoatlas of Inclusions in Gemstones,* Zürich, 1986 (plates 1-24), and to Mr A.P.C. Lamont of De Beers for allowing the reproduction of the photographs of diamond cuts (plates 27-32).

With very few exceptions all the jewellery in this book has appeared at auction at Sotheby's and has been photographed in our photographic department. We would therefore like to thank Eddie Edwards, Michael Oldford and their colleagues, both past and present, for having made this book 'visually' possible.

We also would like to thank all those who lent us their jewels for study and photography and all our colleagues in the jewellery department at Sotheby's who put up with us while writing this book.

GEMSTONES

Introduction
The Tools of the Trade

Unfortunately, a knowledge of gemstones is not easily acquired without access to a great number to study, and a daunting array of sophisticated instruments. It is assumed that the reader can satisfy neither of these conditions, but nevertheless wishes to pursue the subject as far as a modest budget will allow.

Pocket Lens
If one buys nothing else, a x10 pocket lens must be considered absolutely vital. This particular magnification is chosen since it is at this power that the presence of flaws in a diamond is judged; it is also a useful magnification for the study of inclusions in other stones. The lens should also, by preference, be achromatic (colours are unchanged when viewed through the lens) and aplanatic (corrected for linear distortion). Such lenses are not expensive, and are in the range of £5 to £35.

Microscope
A microscope is vital where higher magnifications are required, although a power beyond x40 is rarely used. A simple school laboratory instrument can serve the purpose and may be purchased cheaply, secondhand. A separate light source, able to be focused if possible, or transmitted by means of a fibre optic, will prove invaluable.

Refractometer
A summary of the operation and construction of the instrument is given in Appendix A, together with a brief introduction to the refraction of light. All gem materials have a refraction index (RI) associated with them. This is expressed as a number, or a range of numbers, many of which are readable on this instrument with a little practice. On the face of it, this instrument would appear to answer all the problems of gem testing; sadly this is not the case. A synthetic sapphire will have the same reading as a natural sapphire, stones in settings are notoriously difficult to read and cabochon stones are virtually impossible. Couple this with the fact that many materials have indices very close to one another and it will be understood why the instrument has not been placed at the head of the list. Nevertheless, it is of great use in pointing one in the right direction; if the blue stone under test has an RI of 1.72 it cannot be a sapphire, and is probably a spinel, either natural or synthetic.

Chelsea Colour Filter
This little instrument, scarcely larger than a pocket lens, merits inclusion if

only because of its low price. It should not be relied upon as being diagnostic, simply as a quick reference particularly useful in the case of emeralds, pastes, demantoid garnets and synthetic blue spinels.

Other Instruments

Most other instruments would be ruled out by the amateur on the basis of cost. The spectroscope is a useful diagnostic tool but is very difficult to use, particularly for stones which exhibit absorption lines at the extreme ends of the visible spectrum. The polariscope is of use for quickly identifying stones which crystallise in the cubic system from stones with a differing crystal structure (e.g. ruby from garnet and red spinel). The dichroscope is a useful back-up when testing birefringent (see Appendix A) gemstones, though like the spectroscope it is not easy to use, and is really only applicable to unmounted stones.

The Stones

Diamond

So much has been written generally about the history and occurrence of diamond over the years that there is little need to add much more, other than to refer the reader to the bibliography. In particular are recommended Eric Bruton's excellent work simply entitled *Diamonds,* and for a glimpse of the exotic, Ian Balfour's exhaustively researched book *Famous Diamonds*.

Before setting out elementary ways by which diamond may be tested, it may prove useful to outline the principles of valuation. Unlike other stones, most diamonds are valued for their absence of colour (coloured diamonds will be dealt with separately). Very few diamonds, however, have a complete lack of colour, most having some tinge of yellow or brown. Those that are colourless are called 'white' yet even this term is open to degree. The colour (or lack of colour) of diamonds may be graded, usually by close comparison with a set of master stones. The most highly respected body for carrying out this procedure is at present the Gemmological Institute of America (GIA); their system of alphabetical grading, which has international acceptance, starts at 'D' for the finest white or colourless stones and descends through the alphabet to 'Z' colour, beyond which a diamond will be sufficiently yellow to begin to be valued as a 'fancy colour' stone. 'D', 'E' and 'F' colour are all graded as colourless, or 'white', diamonds, and the difference between them will be barely perceptible to the untrained eye, even by comparison. Nevertheless, even though the visual difference is small, the price differential is vast. For example, if a well-cut/brilliant 'D' colour of 5 carats and internally flawless is worth y thousand dollars per carat (dollars are the international currency when valuing diamonds); an 'E' colour stone of similar weight and purity might be worth in the region of 70% of that price per carat; an 'F' colour stone 50%;

and 'L' colour stone only 17%. Clearly, buyers are willing to pay a large premium for the best.

Absence of flaws is measured or gauged by examining the stone under a magnification of ten times (x10). A stone that has no visible flaws at this magnification is graded 'internally flawless' (IF). The presence of minute flaws would mean the grading was lowered to VVS, either 1 or 2. Slightly larger flaws and the stone is graded VS, either 1 or 2. The next category SI would be visible to the naked eye, although still extremely small. Beyond that the stones are graded imperfect (I). In this case the flaws have become so pronounced that they begin to inhibit the brilliance of the stone. Surface damage, however small, would also mean the stone could not be graded IF, although the certificate may mention the fact that the stone is 'potentially flawless' with small loss of weight by re-cutting. As with colour, value is also substantially affected by the presence of flaws: using the same example of a brilliant-cut stone of 5 carats with a grading of 'D' colour, internally flawless worth y thousand dollars per carat, a similar stone but VVSI might be worth 70% of the price per carat, and an SI stone 32%.

Cut is also an important factor when pricing diamonds (see plates 27-32): 'old mine', bulky brilliant-cut stones from the nineteenth century, might be worth 25% less than a modern stone of good manufacture. The 'fire' or brilliance of diamond is best exhibited when a brilliant-cut stone achieves 'total internal reflection'; this is best explained by imagining the back facets of the stone acting as mirrors, in this way all the light which enters the front of the stone is bounced across these facets and back out again, splitting up on the way into the colours of the spectrum. Early this century cutters began to understand that this effect was achieved only when the proportions of a brilliant-cut diamond, and the angles between its facets, were of certain dimensions. Sadly, the new cuts meant a loss of weight-yield from the rough crystal, and since most 'old mine' diamonds are re-cut this explains whey they are worth less per carat. Matters are complicated further when one considers the 'fancy' shapes such as emerald (or step) cuts, pear shapes (or archaically 'pendeloque') and marquises. Here the proportions of stones of the same weight vary greatly, as indeed may quality of manufacture. Premiums will be paid for 'well laid out' stones, or 'good models'. Fancy cuts are also subject to fashion. In larger diamonds, over 20 carats, many prefer step, marquise or pear shaped to brilliant-cut stones; a 40 carat brilliant-cut would be difficult to wear as a ring while an emerald-cut might look sensational. In smaller diamonds under 10 carats, fancy cuts might be worth less than brilliants.

Finally, weight needs to be considered: a stone weighing 0.99 carats will be worth very much less than a stone of 1.10 carats; a diamond of 1.00 carats exactly will be difficult to sell since even minor abrasion of the facet edges, which often occurs through wear, will result in a stone of less than 1 carat after repolishing. A 2 carat stone of a certain colour and purity will be worth more per carat than a similar quality 1 carat stone, depending on market forces, the same for a 3 carat stone, and so on. Once over 10 carats, the rarity of the material pushes the value up even further. In short, valuing 'white' diamonds is a balancing act between the 'four C's': colour, clarity, cut and carat.

Diamonds occur in nature in a range of colours (see plate 36). Shades of yellow and brown are the most common. Diamonds that are 'off colour' fall into this category, and are stones where the colour is not sufficiently pronounced for them to be called 'fancy' as the colour is merely tinged. Brown fancy-coloured diamonds, sometimes called 'cognac' or 'cinnamon', are the least valuable of the colours, though this may change with fashion since they can be very attractive. Fancy yellow diamonds, often called 'canary', are highly sought after, the most attractive is a strong daffodil yellow. Blue and pink diamonds are extremely scarce and even when the colour is faint they attract very high prices. Ideally, blue diamonds should have no grey in the colour, pink diamonds no brown. Recently the Argyll mines in Australia have been producing small quantities of deep pink, sometimes purple, stones of great beauty; though these stones are seldom over 1 carat in weight, they have been attracting large sums of money. Green and red diamonds are the rarest of all, and owners of these stones can ask virtually any price they like: the mere appearance of one of these stones on the market causes a sensation. The highest price ever paid at auction to date per carat for a diamond was for a red stone weighing only 0.95 carats which fetched the staggering sum of $880,000 ($926,315 per carat), some 100 times more than the finest white diamond of the same size.

There are people who collect only coloured diamonds, and have the financial resources available to match their search for what are arguably the rarest of all earth's treasures.

Early this century it was discovered that diamonds buried for a time in radium salts would turn green. Sadly, however, these stones remained radioactive afterwards and horrific stories are told of these early treated diamonds causing skin carcinomas on the hands of unwitting purchasers. With the passage of time processes improved and diamonds are now being produced via nuclear reactors in a variety of colours without, of course, residual radioactivity. The methods of detecting artificial colouration of diamonds are complex and restricted to the laboratory. Nowadays, no fancy-coloured diamond should be offered for sale without a certificate from a recognised gemmological laboratory stating that the colour is natural.

Diamond or Imitation?
Diamond poses special problems for the gem tester; its RI at 2.42 is off the scale of the refractometer, and the qualities of 'fire' and brilliance that make the stone so attractive are just the qualities the amateur is unable to test. Similarly the hardness for which the stone is justly famous is not a characteristic that can be tested in such a way as to form the basis for a firm identification; the popular idea that if a stone scratches glass it must be a

diamond is dangerously false for most gemstones in common use are harder than glass and will scratch it!

Those who deal a lot with unmounted diamonds might well find it useful to have a specific gravity liquid made up to a density of 3.52; in such a liquid diamond would remain suspended whereas all other stones would either sink or float. Due to the often noxious quality of these liquids, and the fact that most stones encountered will be mounted, this is the only instance where it is considered that the purchase of 'heavy liquids' is justified.

Recently, several instruments have come on to the market specifically designed to test diamonds and to spot the large number of synthetic materials used as imitations (although diamond itself has been produced synthetically, the cost of the process at present renders large scale production commercially unjustifiable, but unfortunately this is unlikely to remain the case for very long). The majority of these instruments test the relative thermal conductivity of the materials. In practice, the instruments are easy to use, if the instructions are followed with care, but since errors can occur they are best used for proving what is not a diamond rather than for confirming what is. More sophisticated, and diagnostic, methods of testing, such as absorption spectrum and relative transparency to x-rays, are beyond the scope of the amateur.

Nevertheless, there are certain simple clues which should lead one to be suspicious of any colourless stone purporting to be diamond:

a) All good quality pastes are relatively soft and susceptible to abrasion. In many cases even the particles of dust in the atmosphere will abrade the surface. Diamond is the hardest substance known to man, and can only be scratched by another. Thus if any stone appears (under a magnifying glass) to be scratched, and this usually happens along the facet edges, then this should be a strong cause for suspicion. It is worth remembering, however, that diamonds which have been stored together loosely in a jewel box can exhibit the same surface damage. Pastes were normally placed in closed settings; it is always worth turning the jewel over to see if the backs of the stones are visible. Closed settings for diamonds are unusual after 1800, apart from rose diamonds.

b) Diamonds crystallise in the cubic system and are thus singly refractive (see Appendix A). Close examination should therefore be made of the back facets with a pocket lens viewing through the table of the stone; any doubling of these facets would be a very strong indication that the stone is not a diamond (n.b. in certain rare cases, diamond can exhibit anomalous double refraction due to stress characteristics within the stone).

c) Under magnification, the facet edges of some diamond imitations, such as cubic stabilised zirconia (CSZ), appear as though moulded and less well defined than those found on diamond. It will take some practice, however, before such subtle differences can be picked up.

    d) Diamonds fluoresce in a variety of ways. If under ultraviolet stimulation all the stones in a brooch either fail to fluoresce or all fluoresce in the same way this would be a very strong indication that the stones are not all diamond.

Stones commonly used to imitate diamond

Natural	white sapphire
	white topaz
	rock crystal (quartz)
	white beryl
	white zircon

Synthetic	CSZ (cubic stabilised zirconia)
	spinel
	strontium titanate
	GGG (gadolinium gallium garnet)
	lithium niobate

Of the natural stones, only white zircon will be off the scale of the refractometer. If it is thought that a stone might be diamond and an RI is obtained, no further test are necessary for it is not diamond. Failing to obtain an RI, however, *cannot* be used as an indicator that the stone might be 'right', because: (a) it is often difficult to get a reading even though the stone under test is well within the range of the instrument; (b) many of the synthetic stones mentioned above are off the scale of the refractometer, including the alarmingly diamond-like CSZ.

Ruby

Among the coloured gemstones, ruby is by far the most valuable, exceeded in price per carat only by the rarest pink, blue and green diamonds. Yet at present it is only ruby from one small area of the world that is so highly prized.

    The town of Mogok in Upper Burma is remote and inaccessible and has been for hundreds of years; recently the government has restricted visas to foreigners which now allow for only the shortest of stays. For centuries the finest rubies in the world have come from this small area of a few square miles, but it was not until the British annexed the region in the late nineteenth century that the deposits could be mined effectively, under the auspices of Edwin Streeter, the Bond Street jeweller. Nevertheless, the number of gem-quality stones over 5 carats that emerged during the period of British ownership was relatively small, and further mining has virtually ceased since the departure of the British just before the Second World War.

    To appreciate why Burmese rubies have been so highly sought for centuries a little more must be understood about the stone itself. Ruby is a variety of

Plate 1. *Microscopic examination of the interior of gemstones can reveal clues to their origin. Characteristic of Burmese rubies are crystals of calcite which can be recognised by their marked cleavage planes. Where such crystals are present it is a pretty foolproof guide that the stone is not only natural but also from Burma. (Magnification x 25.)*

Plate 2. *'Silk', which is actually a mass of minute hair-like crystals of rutile, is one of the most striking of all inclusions and is found in many rubies and sapphires. In Burmese rubies the 'silk' is usually short and intersects at 60 and 120 degrees. (Magnification x 40.)*

Plate 3. *The 'silk' in this ruby from Sri Lanka is typical in that it stretches from one side of the stone to another; compare with plate 2. (Magnification x 60.)*

Plate 4. *A characteristic view of the interior of a ruby from Thailand; lace-like fluid haloes surrounding quest crystals. (Magnification x 32.)*

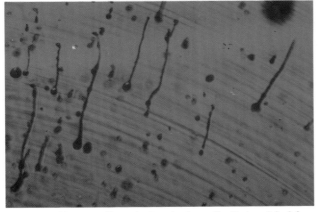

Plate 5. *This verneuil synthetic ruby is easily distinguished from natural stone by the curved bands, or striae, and the irregularly shaped gas bubbles.*

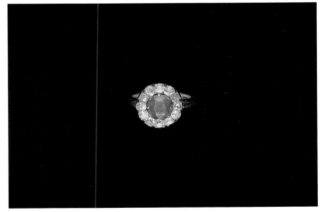

Plate 6. *A fine red spinel in a diamond cluster ring of about 1900. Spinels of this quality can imitate ruby very closely and are probably equally rare.*

the mineral species known as a corundum. Sapphire is a member of the same family and shares its chemical composition and crystal structure: aluminium oxide, crystallising in the trigonal system. It has an RI of 1.76 to 1.77, a double refraction of .008 and a specific gravity of around 4.00. In its pure form corundum is colourless (white sapphire). In the case of ruby, the red colour is due to small amounts of chromic oxide (and in some cases iron). The rubies from Burma are mainly coloured by chromium giving them the distinctive blood red hue (often called pigeon blood) with which the finest stones have always been associated. The presence of chromium as a colouring agent in a gemstone often gives rise to a strong fluorescence. In the case of Burmese stones this fluorescence will exhibit itself even by artificial light which, being strong in the red end of the spectrum, causes the stone to 'sing' or appear greatly improved; very often the stone will appear to be almost internally illuminated, glowing magnificently like a hot coal. As a result, never be tempted to buy a ruby by artificial light but always insist on seeing the stone in daylight, you may be astounded by the change that can occur; a deep red stone may appear a totally washed out pink when viewed in the street. However, luckily for poor quality rubies, most jewellery is worn at night. Typically, rubies from Sri Lanka appear to be more often pink than a true blood red. Nevertheless, stones from this location are often very attractive, and because they share the same fluorescence characteristics as Burmese stones can appear remarkably transformed at night.

Perhaps the most common location for rubies used in jewellery these days is Thailand. These stones can appear very deceptive, and, curiously enough, this deception most often occurs in the light of day. Thai rubies owe much of their colour to the presence of iron and where this is the case the stones have a brownish tinge, somewhat similar to a garnet, yet the colour is often very saturated and in good examples can approximate to the blood red of a Burmese stone. Iron inhibits fluorescence, however, and as a result a Thai stone will not normally exhibit the characteristic 'fire' of the Burmese or good quality Sri Lankan material. In daylight, however, this difference is not so apparent, yet the difference in value can be enormous: a gem-quality Burmese ruby of 5 carats can be worth ten times as much as a similar quality ruby from Thailand.

Yet not all rubies from Burma are valuable. Ruby is not, relatively speaking, a rare gemstone. Some Burmese stones could be worth as little as $20 per carat, others perhaps as much as $200,000 per carat. As with most gemstones, the value is a balance between the richness and beauty of the colour (or absence of it in the case of white diamond), and the degree of purity, or lack of flaws. A cynic might suggest that the rarity of the material is also important. There can be little doubt, however, that if presented with the choice between a fine ruby from Burma and another from Thailand, one would pick the former on grounds of beauty alone, without hesitation. How often is it, however, that the amateur has the benefit of a stone as comparison? Other locations for ruby are East Africa (Kenya and Tanzania) and Pakistan. All three of these sources are relatively new and the stone can be very effective. In the last few years another new source of fine quality rubies has appeared on the market — Vietnam. These stones are often very similar in appearance to Burmese rubies being strongly fluorescent and chrome-rich. For stones of fine colour, good purity and fair size, the importance of location to value cannot be too strongly stressed. For smaller stones and rubies of inferior quality, the fact that they are from Burma or some other location is of far less significance, except perhaps in the case of a Victorian jewel, where the presence of African rubies would make one immediately sceptical that the piece were genuine.

Sadly, the ability to pick out the Burmese stones from a parcel of rubies from various locations is not easily acquired and is beyond the scope of this book. Much of it lies in a thorough knowledge of the type of inclusions and flaws associated with a stone from a certain area, e.g. Burmese rubies often have well-formed crystals of calcite, which taken into consideration with other features of the stone, can pinpoint the origin of the stone. The calcite is derived from the host rock out of which the stone is mined, which in the case of Burmese rubies, is calcite schist. Several excellent works on gemstone inclusions will be found in the bibliography.

In recent years a number of laboratories which specialise in gemmological identification have begun to issue certification which not only testify to a stone's natural origin but also to the geographical location where it was mined. Perhaps the most prestigious and highly respected of these laboratories for coloured stones is at present that run by Professor Edward Gubelin in Switzerland. These days virtually every important coloured stone that appears on the market would be expected to carry with it its 'pedigree' in the form of a gemmological certificate. This in itself can be a further trap for the amateur; occasionally rubies appear on the market with little to recommend them as gemstones, other than the fact that they have a Burma certificate. It cannot be stressed too strongly that the word 'Burma' is not a guarantee of quality in ruby.

Other red stones sometimes confused with ruby

Natural red spinel can be a very attractive and effective gemstone, but it is relatively rare in jewellery, and can be differentiated from ruby quite easily by means of a refractometer (spinel having an RI of 1.72) (see Appendix A). Where the use of this instrument is impossible, perhaps by reason of a protruding setting, the fact that the stone crystallises in the cubic system, and is therefore singly refractive, will prove useful; unlike ruby, it will display no dichroism through a dichroscope, and will remain unchanged when revolved under a polariscope. The colour of red spinel is usually more strawberry rather than the characteristic raspberry of ruby (remember this is purely a generalisation), indeed many people have described the spinel colour as 'sweet' or 'sugary'. Like most Burmese and Sri Lankan rubies, spinels are often highly fluorescent. The phenomenon known as 'silk' is common to many Burmese,

Plate 7. *This illustration shows the danger of buying some sapphires; although from the top this stone appeared of good colour, this view from the side shows the large 'window' through the stone where the colour disappears. In addition the stone is very bulky; most of the weight of the stone is accounted for by the depth. This sapphire is from Sri Lanka.*

Plate 8. *The blue of a Kashmir sapphire is truly exceptional. It is characteristic to discover colour or growth bands within the stone. (Magnification x 20.)*

Plate 9. *As in rubies, so in Burmese sapphires the 'silk' is characteristically short. (Magnification x 10.)*

Plate 10. *Folds of 'feathers' — liquid-filled inclusions — are commonly found in Burmese sapphires. (Magnification x 32.)*

Plate 11. *This Burmese sapphire shows typical dense concentrations of titanium oxide 'dust' forming growth lines which follow hexagonal directions. (Magnification x 60.)*

Plate 12. *Red crystals of uranium pyrochlore are commonly found in sapphires from Pailin in Cambodia. (Magnification x 50.)*

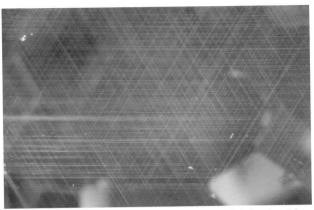

Plate 13. A view of 'silk' in a sapphire from Sri Lanka. Note, as in rubies from the same locality, the needles are exceptionally long. In this case, if the 'silk' is sufficiently well-defined it will form a star. (Magnification x 45.)

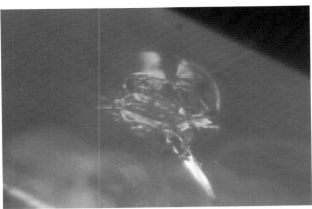

Plate 14. Crystals of zircon, often found in Sri Lankan sapphires, are usually surrounded by a 'halo' where the radioactive elements within the zircon have destroyed the host crystal. (Magnification x 50.)

Plate 15. The curved bands so characteristic of Verneuil synthetic corundum are usually more easily seen in sapphire than ruby, due to the suspension of minute gas bubbles. (Magnification x 20.)

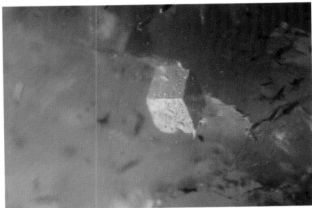

Plate 16. A rhomb of calcite (accompanied by slender brownish prisms of parisite) form a fingerprint of origin in this Colombian emerald from the Muzo mine. (Magnification x 25.)

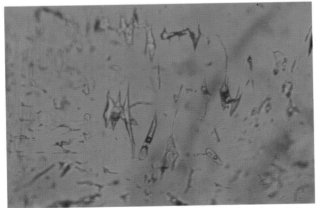

Plate 17. Typical of Colombian emeralds are these jagged three-phase inclusions (containing a liquid, a gas and a crystal). (Magnification x 50.)

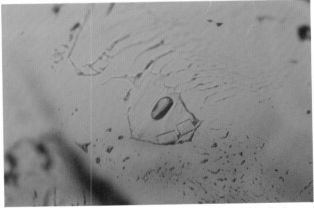

Plate 18. Another example of a three-phase inclusion so characteristic of emeralds from Colombia: the crystals and gas bubbles are clearly visible. (Magnification x 50.)

Vietnamese and Sri Lankan rubies. To the naked eye this appears as a whitish sheen within the stone which catches the light as the stone is tilted, and is due to minute filaments of the mineral rutile. 'Silk', which is a common feature of both natural ruby and sapphire, is perhaps the first indentifiable inclusion the student gemmologist is aware of; its presence in a red stone is a pretty good indication that the stone is a ruby, though it can be induced in some synthetics (see below). Perhaps the most characteristic inclusions in red spinel are crystals that closely resemble bubbles, and often lead the amateur to mistake the stone for red paste.

Red tourmaline is often cited as a material which may be confused with ruby. Fine red tourmalines are known as 'rubellites', but they seldom approximate to the true red of ruby, and can easily be differentiated by means of the refractometer (tourmaline has an RI of 1.62-1.64 and has a double refraction of .018). Unlike ruby it is never fluorescent. Perhaps confusion would only occur in stones where the quality is very low and the price difference minimal. Familiarity with the particular pinkish red common in tourmaline, however, should make even these confusions unlikely In fact the commonly-seen and characteristic whitish inclusions, combined with the typical body colour, remind one most of those raspberry flavoured boiled sweets!

Garnets are perhaps most easily confused with ruby, and since they have an RI which spans that of ruby it makes the usual use of the refractometer dangerous. Luckily they are singly refractive and will show no dichroism through the dichroscope (it should be remembered, however, that this instrument is awkward to use and is only really useful for unmounted stones). Perhaps of more use is the fact that they remain unchanged when revolved under the polariscope. The relatively rare pyrope garnets can approach the blood red of fine rubies but have a lower RI, between 1.74 and 1.75. The more common almandine garnets are coloured by iron, unlike pyropes which are coloured by chromium, and are therefore not fluorescent. Unfortunately they can be confused with Thai rubies, and where a confusion does occur, perhaps the easiest way of resolving it is by using a pocket spectroscope. Although this instrument is difficult to use in most cases, the three distinctive broad absorption bands of the almandine are distinctive and easily seen, even by the amateur (see also section on garnets). Red pastes can be spotted in the usual way using a pocket lens; look out for gas bubbles (n.b. red spinel), and swirls of colour, etc.

Synthetic ruby, as is the case with all synthetic materials, shares the same crystal structure and chemical composition as its natural counterpart. As a result the instruments normally used for testing stones, such as the refractometer, are inapplicable. Synthetic rubies and sapphires have been around since the turn of the century when the French scientist Verneuil perfected a special furnace where pure alumina, and small amounts of metallic colouring agents, were passed through an oxy-hydrogen flame to crystallise in 'boules' (which looked rather like those small gas cylinders used to recharge soda syphons). This process can produce synthetic material of great size in a very short space of time; luckily it is the very speed of the process that gives rise to the easiest method of detection. The synthetic corundum is deposited in curved bands which are often seen through the stone after it is cut. In addition, small bubbles of gas are often visible, trapped within the stone. As soon as the new synthetic material appeared on the market, it was adopted by jewellers. Some years ago, Sotheby's sold a fine historical revival necklace by Giacinto Mellilo, the celebrated Italian jeweller; on inspection the small rubies in the piece turned out to be synthetic, and there was no evidence that they had been replaced. One wonders whether Mellilo himself knew the difference when the piece was made just before the First World War!

Fortunately, even small rubies are seldom free of flaws; in sizes over 1 carat it is virtually unheard of, yet large synthetic rubies are quite common since they are so cheap to produce; in addition the colour will almost immediately arouse suspicion, appearing 'too good to be true'. In short, any ruby over 1 carat that is virtually flawless and of fine colour should be tested. Since most synthetic rubies are coloured exclusively by chromium they will exhibit a spectacular fluorescence by artificial light and especially ultraviolet stimulation. Careful examination with a pocket lens or miscroscope will usually reveal the curved colour bands and small gas bubbles that make the diagnosis conclusive. Perhaps a simple awareness that synthetic rubies exist will be sufficient to deter the amateur from being taken in by sizeable stones. Where smaller stones have been employed, say less than a third of a carat, in a piece of jewellery, the problem is greater. The practice of using synthetic rubies and sapphires as part of the design in jewels such as brooches and bracelets made during the period 1920-1950 is not uncommon. Though natural rubies and sapphires of this size are relatively cheap, so that the greatest expense may well be in the cutting, buyers should be aware that a jewel set with synthetics will be very difficult to resell simply because the word 'synthetic' will put off many buyers. In small synthetic stones the curved lines and gas bubbles may well be virtually invisible and the amateur may have to rely on his eye: it is extremely rare for a parcel of small natural rubies to share exactly the same hue, for the cost of the stones may well have made the tedious task of selecting the stones impractical. Yet with synthetics this problem seldom arises. Thus, if under a lens all the stones share the same colour, and appear flawless, buyers should be suspicious. In the end the quality of the jewel will give a clue: look at the colour and purity of the diamonds and other stones, for example, examine the fineness of the setting, the metal and workmanship and so on. Cartier, to illustrate the point, would never have employed synthetics.

Sadly, the march of science has meant that new methods of producing synthetic stones have appeared. The recent 'Kashan' rubies have posed many problems, even for the gemmologist. It is not within the scope of this book,

Plate 19. One of the most distinctive inclusions in emerald are these rod-like crystals of tremolite found in emeralds from the Sandawana mine in Zimbabwe. (Magnification x 20.)

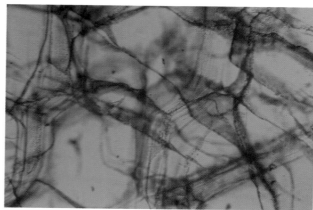

Plate 20. These intricate wispy 'veils' and 'feathers' are characteristic of flux-grown synthetic emeralds. (Magnification x 15.)

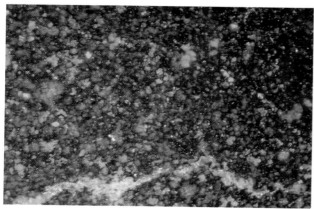

Plate 21. This 'treated' Australian opal has had the background darkened by sugar and sulphuric acid to enhance the flashes of colour. Under magnification the opals have a 'pepper-like' character. (Photomicrograph by J.I. Koivula.)

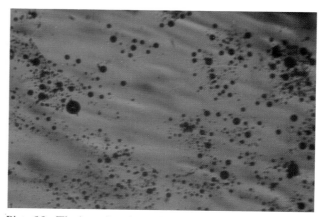

Plate 22. The irregular size and shape of the air bubbles within a swirly flow structure mark this green paste imitation. (Magnification x 20.)

Plate 23. Sometimes swirls and strings of bubbles in green pastes can imitate the complex inclusions of natural emerald. (Magnification x 6.)

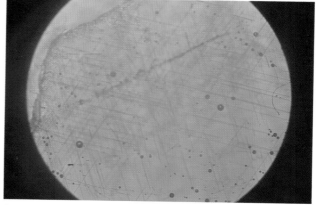

Plate 24. A close-up of a garnet-topped doublet (green paste bottom), viewed through the table. The rutile needles are clearly visible in the almandine garnet top, which also displays a jagged edge. Note the tiny air bubbles in the cement layer. (Magnification x 10.)

Plate 25. A collection of garnets in a 1930s brooch: the green stones are demantoids; the red ones almandines and pyropes; the yellow examples on the right hand edge are hessonites.

however, to discuss all these developments and the complicated methods necessary to detect them. It should be of some comfort to note that encountering these new synthetics in jewellery before 1960 is extremely rare. Unfortunately this is unlikely to remain the case for long, because the financial gain for the unscrupulous, in replacing stones in period settings and selling them as the real thing, is great. It is to be hoped that buyers, aware that such stones exist, take advice, and more importantly, demand a detailed receipt before embarking on a substantial purchase, to protect themselves from fraud. (Composite stones, such as doublets, are discussed in Appendix C.)

Sapphire

Many people believe sapphire to be the most beautiful of all gemstones, even though it may not be the most valuable. The finest Burmese rubies are worth $150,000 per carat, or more, but the most a fine sapphire could attain (at the time of writing) would perhaps be in the region of $80,000 per carat, though for highly important and rare examples, of whatever material, the price is finally governed by how much anyone is prepared to pay to buy the best.

Like ruby, the origin of a sapphire is vitally important to value. As Burma is to ruby, so Kashmir is to sapphire, and, as in Burma, few stones are still being mined in Kashmir. The colour of a gem-quality Kashmir sapphire is astounding, the most perfect velvety mid-blue, often accompanied by a characteristic sea green dichroism when light is transmitted through the stone. The epithet 'sleepy' is often ascribed to these stones, the colouring appearing slightly milky, due to minute liquid filled cavities or crystals within the stone which are often difficult to see, even under a high powered microscope. What is often easier to see is a characteristic phenomenon known as 'zoning' (see plate 8), where the colour appears to be concentrated in parallel bands. In addition, Kashmir sapphires lose none of their colour in artificial light, which is rare in this stone. It is important to point out however that not all Kashmir sapphires are fine. Buyers should remember that a gemmological certificate stating Kashmir origin is not in itself a guarantee that the sapphire is of good quality.

Unlike ruby, large sapphires weighing over 50 carats are not excessively rare, though a Kashmir stone of this size would be extremely uncommon; once over only 10 carats, sapphires from this region command very high prices. From the buyer's point of view there is some comfort to be drawn from the fact that the true cornflower blue of a fine Kashmir sapphire, once seen is not easily forgotten; quite simply it is so unlike the run-of-the-mill stones seen in jewellers' windows. Sadly, many years could be spent in the lower end of the jewellery trade without ever seeing one, and yet it is only through a comparison with these stones that the colour of other fine sapphires can be judged.

Burmese sapphires can also be of superb quality: the colour is more commonly saturated, tending towards an ultramarine blue, and, even in large examples, fine quality stones can be found, perhaps fetching as much as $40,000 per carat or more. Sapphires from Sri Lanka, in general, tend to be paler, some stones being virtually colourless. The best Sri Lankan stones can resemble the blue of Kashmir but would probably fetch less than $15,000 per carat. Both Burmese and Sri Lankan sapphires are associated with inclusions, which exhibit themselves as fine white needles, similar to those associated with ruby, which catch the light when the stone is rotated, and liquid-filled feathers (see plate 10). In Burmese stones the 'silk' (the general term for these inclusions) is usually composed of short clusters of needles when viewed under a lens, and angled at 60 or 120 degrees to one another (see plates 9 and 11). In Sri Lankan stones the 'silk' is generally longer, often stretching from one side of the stone to another, and generally in one or two directions only (see plate 13). Presence of 'silk' in a stone is a pretty foolproof guide to the fact that the stone is genuine and not a synthetic; it must be pointed out, however, that conspicuous 'silk', which is readily visible to the naked eye, will considerably reduce the stone's value except where it is so pronounced as to produce a 'star' (see plate 37). 'Silk' can, however, also be produced in synthetic star sapphires. Another fingerprint of Sri Lankan sapphires is inclusions of zircon, indeed zircon is often found with sapphires in gem gravels in the area. Zircon is a mildly radioactive material which as a result tends to destroy the crystal lattice in the host material in its immediate vicinity, creating the distinctive 'halo' (see plate 14).

Thai sapphires are generally very deep in colour and often resemble a blue spinel. The deepest coloured sapphires, and consequently the least valuable, come from Australia. Some Australian stones are so saturated in colour that they appear black (probably due to excess iron as a colouring agent), unless the stone is held up to the light. Such stones are scarcely worth setting in jewellery. Some good sapphires are mined in Cambodia, especially at a place called Pailin (see plate 12). During the latter part of the nineteenth century mines were opened in Montana, USA, the stones being known as 'new mine' sapphires. These stones have a characteristic pale electric blue colour and are often seen in jewellery made before the First World War.

Heat treating of sapphires has been common for some time. The process can remove the 'silk' from stones and more importantly lighten the colour of deeply saturated examples. It is no surprise that the process is applied to a great proportion of the sapphires mined in Australia; since the process is carried out in Thailand it is difficult to tell what proportion of the sapphires that emerge from Bangkok are actually of Thai origin. Commercially heat treatment of both sapphires and rubies is generally accepted though difficult to detect; where an important gem has been found to be heat treated, the value may be substantially reduced. Gem testing laboratories are beginning to issue certificates which state, where possible, if a stone has been subjected to heat treatment or not, and suggest a country of origin.

Mention has already been made of the fact that it is rare for the colour of sapphires not to deteriorate by artificial light (the standard electric light bulb is strong in the red end of the spectrum). The most marked examples of this

Plate 26. *Carved amber beads, mostly of Chinese workmanship, probably originating from Burma.*

Plate 27. *The brilliant-cut diamond.*

Plate 28. *The step- or emerald-cut diamond.*

Plate 29. The marquise diamond.

Plate 30. The pear-shaped or pendeloque diamond.

Plate 31. The heart-shaped diamond.

Plate 32. The oval-shaped diamond.

colour change are seen in some types of Sri Lankan sapphires which will turn a deep purple at night due to the presence of chromium within the stone; indeed when viewed under a Chelsea colour filter (which cuts out all wavelengths other than red) these stones often appear to glow like a ruby. Colour change like this in a sapphire is not considered desirable and will reduce the value of the stone. When purchasing a sapphire it is always useful to carry a small pocket torch with which to view any colour change that may occur; even the fine deep blue of a Burmese stone may appear inky or purplish in these conditions. In short, remember that jewellery is mostly worn at night.

Other blue stones sometimes confused with sapphire
Sapphire is often a relatively flawless gem species, so where obvious inclusions are not present, it is important to remember the possibility that the stone may be synthetic. The method of detecting the most commonly encountered synthetic sapphires is precisely the same as that for detecting synthetic ruby (see plate 15), if anything the curved lines and gas bubbles are more easily seen. It must be remembered that recent innovations will render the job of detection more difficult, but have yet to penetrate the jewellery market. Small synthetic sapphires, when set in the body of a jewel, can be more difficult to detect and, as in the case of synthetic ruby, occur with alarming frequency in jewels manufactured between the wars. This is one of the few cases where the amateur will find an ultraviolet light source useful; these instruments may be either hand held, or are available fitted to a box into which the jewel is placed and viewed through an aperture. Under short wave ultraviolet stimulation most synthetic sapphires glow with a palish green hue that appears to emanate from the surface of the stone like a sort of dust, due to an excess of titanium, which with iron accounts for the colour of sapphire. It is extremely rare for a jewel to include both natural and synthetic sapphires when used in large numbers and small sizes (except of course where a natural stone has been lost and replaced with a synthetic), so this quick test can be very useful as natural sapphires are almost always inert under short wave ultraviolet.

Recently a new material known as 'tanzanite' has appeared on the market. This is a blue form of the mineral zoisite and the finest examples may resemble a sapphire quite closely. Even these good examples, however, have a blue that is not quite true to sapphire, characteristically tinged with red. A quick test on a refractometer will reveal the difference as tanzanites have an RI in the region of 1.70, and sapphire 1.76-1.77.

Blue spinel can resemble sapphire, though since the colour is usually very dark and inky only poor quality sapphires could be mistaken for it. Again a quick RI test would prove useful, for spinel is 1.72 and singly refractive. Synthetic blue spinel is rarely coloured to resemble sapphire (more often aquamarine) and will appear a bright red under a Chelsea filter. It also has a distinctive absorption spectrum due to the presence of cobalt as a colouring agent. Pastes and composite stones are dealt with in Appendix C.

Emerald

The last in the series of 'precious' stones, like ruby and sapphire its value is greatly determined by the area where it is mined. To ruby the catchword is Burma, to sapphire Kashmir, to emerald it is Colombia, in particular those stones from a mine at Muzo, not far from Bogota, an area which has yielded emeralds of the most beautiful rich grass green colour.

Most emeralds are badly flawed, much more so than sapphire and even most rubies. Many emeralds are virtually opaque, having merely a green body colour but no life. Moreover emerald occurs in large quantities; some crystals have been found many metres long travelling through the host rock. (A man once presented us with a suede pouch containing an emerald crystal some eight inches in height, three inches in girth and weighing several hundred carats. Though genuine emerald, the object more closely resembled a large lime-flavoured boiled sweet than a precious stone. Although of some interest to a collector of minerals, the object would have best served as a paperweight. Needless to say, its owner was very crestfallen after our interview.)

Emeralds have undoubtedly been highly valued for thousands of years. Some of the best examples are purported to have come from India, but it now seems that the most likely explanation is that they were traded by the Spanish who had opened up mines in South America in the sixteenth century. Much is talked in jewellery circles of 'old material'; in general this refers to the particularly saturated deep green of the stones that appear on the market only rarely and seldom through a new source via a mine. It is this material that is most highly prized; at the time of writing large particularly fine examples might command prices of up to $100,000 per carat if sufficiently free from flaws. It should be stressed that emeralds of this quality and size are as rare as fine Burmese rubies and seldom appear on the market.

Emerald is a silicate of beryllium and owes its colour, in the majority of cases, to small traces of chromium, the same element that gives rise to the fine red of Burmese rubies. When viewed through a Chelsea filter (which absorbs all colours other than red) the majority of emeralds will appear red to brown owing to the presence of chromium. This is a useful quick test, ruling out most other green stones and pastes, but it cannot be relied upon since some emeralds, particularly those coloured by vanadium, will still appear green, and most synthetic emeralds will also show up red when viewed in this way. Emerald is relatively soft (having a hardness of 7 on Mohs scale, see Appendix B), the surface is easily abraded and the edges chipped. Examples have been seen which have spent so long in the jewel box in company with diamonds, sapphires and rubies, that as a result have appeared almost opaque due to the lack of lustre brought about by constant rubbing with harder materials. One such stone looked so poor that its owner had been offered only £500. After we had repolished it the value of the stone had increased tenfold.

Typical inclusions of Colombian emeralds are 'three phase'; these look like jagged flat cavities which are liquid filled and also contain a crystal and a bubble of gas (see plates 17 and 18). Muzo emeralds often have small crystals

Plate 35. A fine topaz and diamond brooch, mid-19th century. The colour of the topaz is absolutely typical, and the beautiful setting shows the esteem with which these stones were held at the time.

Plate 33. An Australian black opal set in a diamond cluster ring. The lack of red flashes in the stone reduces the value considerably. A Mexican fire opal set in a diamond brooch, c.1910. Note the characteristic slightly domed table to the stone which makes taking a refractive index difficult.

Plate 37. A natural star sapphire showing characteristic asterism.

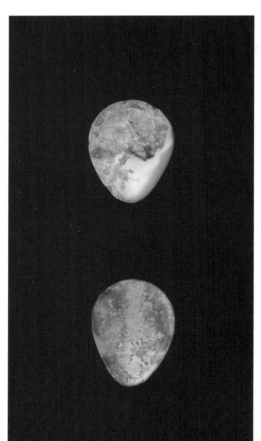

Plate 38. A natural blue spinel showing the typical 'bubble-like' inclusions that may lead it to be confused with paste.

Plate 34. A fine Australian black opal showing a good play of colour. Note the reverse of the stone shows where the sandstone matrix has been roughly cut away. This opal weighed nearly 19cts. and sold for £6,600 at auction in 1985, despite its irregular shape.

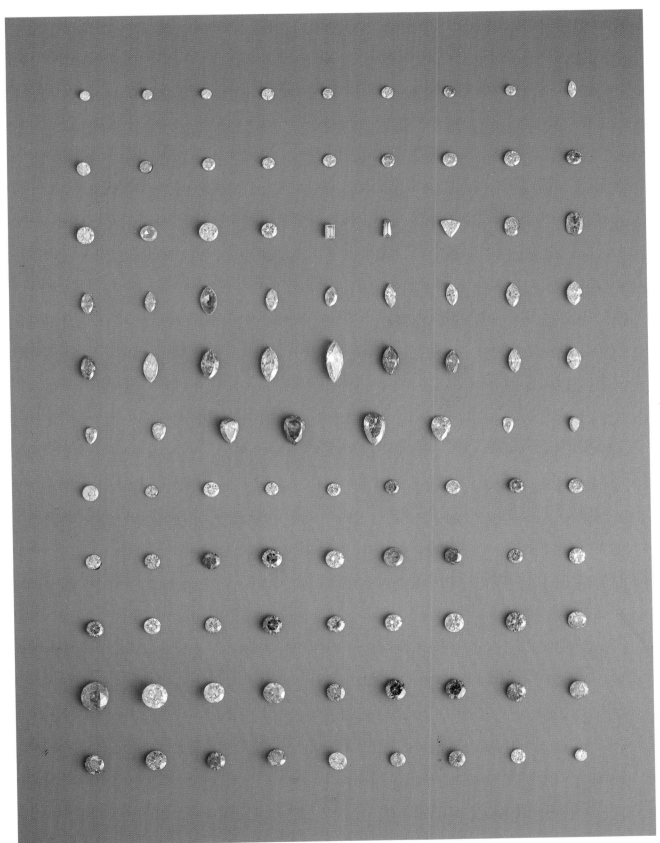

Plate 36. A collection of diamonds showing the wide range of colours in which they are found.

of calcite, similar to those found in Burmese rubies (see plate 16). Chivor mine emeralds (which also may be of fine quality) often have small metallic crystals of iron pyrites. Of other emerald localities the most important are Siberia, East Africa, the Transvaal, India and Pakistan. Each location had inclusions associated with it; in particular emeralds from the Sandawana mine in Zimbabwe, which first appeared on the market in the late 1950s. Good examples from this area exhibit a good deep green body colour which can resemble Colombian material quite closely. To add to the confusion, they are often relatively free from flaws and so run the risk of being passed off as valuable 'old material'. In comparison, however, the colour of these stones may be seen to be almost blackish, too deep and saturated, and consequently lacking in life. Fortunately, Sandawana emeralds have characteristic inclusions which are associated with tremolite, the host rock from which they are mined (see plate 19). Under magnification, tremolite crystal inclusions appear as numerous fibres, rather like hair, which weave in and out of one another within the stone. Once seen, these inclusions, which are so unlike most other emerald 'flaws', are not easily forgotten. Moreover, Sandawana emeralds of over 5 carats are rare. Nevertheless, buyers have paid absurdly high prices for these Zimbabwean stones thinking they were fine Muzo emeralds; this is another example which illustrates the importance of taking professional, preferably independent, advice, before embarking on a costly purchase.

Not all emeralds make claims to being anything other than what they are. Viennese and Hungarian jewellery of the second half of the nineteenth century is often set with pale opaque emeralds which make no attempt to hide their origin, mainly because their value is so low. Characteristically these stones came from Habachtal in the Austrian Tyrol and so have a local flavour. The colour of the stones was often enhanced, quite legitimately, by placing green reflective foil behind the stone in a closed setting. This practice was also common in India. Buyers should obviously beware of paying a sizeable sum if they cannot see the back of the stone.

Other green stones often confused with emerald
Compared with sapphires and most rubies, synthetic emeralds pose far greater problems. The streets of Bogota, the 'emerald capital' of Colombia, are teeming with bogus gem dealers who will sell you a synthetic which even the gifted amateur will have difficulty differentiating from the real thing. Often we meet people returning from Colombia, Brazil or the Far East, who have bought stones either from reputable dealers, or in a back street, thinking that because they had purchased these stones in the area where they were mined they must have a bargain. At best they will have purchased a stone at virtually the same price as in Europe or the USA, at worst they will have acquired a poor example, a synthetic, or a paste. The gem market is international and the majority of gem dealers, whether they be in Bangkok or New York, are aware of the value of their merchandise. (South Africa is one of the most expensive

places in the world to buy diamonds.) The range and complexity of synthetic emeralds take them beyond the scope of this book, but it should be remembered that the processes used in the production of these stones are constantly under revision, and new types are being produced, posing unique and challenging problems for the gemmologist (see plate 20).

The practice of 'oiling' emeralds is not well documented and yet occurs frequently enough for it to be of some concern. In this process the stone is immersed in oil, often with a green pigment, which is taken up through minute fissures which extend to the surface. This can not only increase the colour of an emerald but can also cover up unsightly blemishes on the surface. Microscopic examination will usually reveal where this process has taken place, and cleaning methods, notably ultrasonic immersion, will prove that the process is reversible! Synthetic emerald has also been bonded to the surface of poor quality stones to enhance their appearance, although this practice is relatively rare.

Of the natural stones which can resemble emerald only fluorspar has proved to be a problem. Luckily this mineral will only resemble poor quality emerald but it can exhibit remarkably emerald-like inclusions under a magnifying glass, notably the three-phase inclusions associated with Colombian stones. To complicate these matters, fluorspar will appear red under a Chelsea filter like most emeralds, both natural and synthetic. An RI test will quickly reveal the difference as fluorspar shows a single line around 1.43 and emerald is doubly refractive with a mean RI around 1.58. In addition, as the name would suggest, fluorspar is strongly fluorescent (violet under ultraviolet stimulation) and is very soft for a gemstone, only 4 on Mohs scale, and thus nearly always has rubbed or scratched facets when set in jewellery. Tourmaline, jade, peridot, green sapphire and zircons are almost invariably so unlike the green of emerald as to pose few problems, and all have RI's higher than emerald. It is interesting to note that should one have purchased a jade (which is at best translucent) in mistake for an emerald, of what could only be poor quality, the jade would be far more valuable.

Emerald is also open to imitation. Doublets (see plate 24 and Appendix C) have been produced in various guises, the most confusing being emerald on emerald. In this case the stone will have natural seeming inclusions and natural constants such as RI and SG. The bonding layer in these cases is usually at the girdle of the stone and to make matters worse, with a layer of green dye associated with the adhesive. Other forms of doublet will respond to a simple RI test for identification as well as most pastes. A word of caution here because the green glass often used to imitate emerald is typically of poor quality and often appears to have emerald-like inclusions to the naked eye (see plates 22 and 23). Under magnification, however, these are seen to be chains of bubbles, or cracks, within the stone, which is another good reason to carry a pocket lens when buying stones! Some purchasers may be put off buying emerald for fear of buying a fake, but synthetic emeralds are rare and seldom encountered in jewellery until recently. In most countries buyers are protected by some form of consumer act which would enable them to return a stone which proved false. An itemised receipt should always be requested and where a stone is being purchased for a large sum of money one can ask for a certificate from a reputable gem-testing laboratory; even paying for the certificate may well be worthwhile.

Topaz

Of the semi-precious stones, topaz is a personal favourite. The finest stones are a glorious orange-red, the colour of quince jelly, and are extremely rare, yet this rarity is not reflected in their value, for the most a good topaz could be expected to fetch would be perhaps $5,000 per carat (see plate 35). Topaz, until the advent of the Trades Description Act, has been subject to an important (and costly) case of mistaken identity as the name was also used to describe the yellow forms of quartz, correctly known as citrine. This practice is still, sadly, relatively common today and is a perfect example of the jewellery trade trying to make their geese into swans. Citrine is an abundant and therefore cheap gemstone which resembles only the poorer forms of topaz.

Topaz is a splendid gem material, which is hard (8 on Mohs scale) and lustrous, and takes a particularly fine polish. Its colours range from white, through yellow and reddish browns to blues. Pink varieties are usually reddish brown stones which have been heat treated. In terms of value, the orange-red varieties are highly prized, the blues, which resemble aquamarine, are of lower value and have their colour improved artificially, and white examples, in common with other colourless stones other than diamonds, are relatively cheap. The RI of the fine stones, and the pink stones derived from them, is 1.63-1.64, while blues and whites are lower, 1.61-1.62. Typically the 'quince jelly' colour stones show an orange fluoresence under long wave ultraviolet stimulation.

The cut of topaz, particularly in early jewellery, is often characteristically a long oval or oblong table which has been cut along the length of the crystal. Also characteristic, since topaz cleaves easily and perfectly parallel to the base of the crystal, are cleavage planes within the stone which commonly are at right angles to the table of the gem. It should be remembered that it is easy to induce cleavage in topaz so the stone should be treated with some care, lest it be dropped.

Stones confused with topaz

The colour of quince topaz, once seen, is distinctive. Nevertheless, synthetic sapphires have been produced to closely resemble them and an RI test is useful here. The yellow and brownish yellow forms resemble citrine. Quartz is softer than topaz and does not take such a high polish, moreover the colour of a citrine can only approximate the richer, subtler colours of topaz. Again an RI will quickly reveal the difference (citrine 1.54-1.55). It is worth noting that colourless topaz, since it has a relatively high dispersion, has been used to imitate diamond.

In summary, practice has shown that a quick RI test is usually sufficient to detect topaz, and luckily no synthetics have been produced commercially.

Aquamarine
As ruby is to sapphire, so aquamarine is to emerald. Both are forms of the mineral beryl. Aquamarine is appropriately named and in its finest forms should be a perfect sea blue. Specimens that have traces of green are far less highly valued.

Unlike emerald, aquamarine can be virtually flawless and yet still be of only moderate value. The most distinctive inclusion is aptly called 'rain', being small needle-like crystals or cavities running parallel to the main axis. The more intense and perfect the blue, the more valuable the stone becomes. In practice, fine aquamarine might fetch as much as $3,000 per carat. Most stones, however, are worth considerably less, the average being perhaps $300-$500 per carat, for an attractive example of over say 5 carats.

Stones confused with aquamarine
The cheapest and most common imitation of aquamarine is synthetic blue spinel, but like other synthetic spinels, spherical bubbles are usually present, moreover, under a Chelsea filter, synthetic blue spinels that are used in jewellery, turn red due to colouration by cobalt. This dichroism can be detected by a trained eye in artificial light. Blue topaz, which can occur in large sizes, can also resemble aquamarine quite closely and, being less valuable, it is important to check all stones with a refractometer as the RI of blue topaz is considerably higher (aquamarine 1.57-1.58, blue topaz 1.61-1.62). Blue topaz is also more lustrous and lively than aquamarine (one may well ask why the latter is more valuable!). Blue zircon has even greater fire and lustre than blue topaz and also has the characteristic strong double refraction which is readily seen as a doubling of the back facets when the stone is viewed with a lens through a table. Blue pastes are easily detected by the same means mentioned above (see Appendix C).

Chrysoberyl, alexandrite and cat's-eye
Chrysoberyl is an interesting mineral that provides an attractive range of stones varying from transparent yellow, greenish yellow and yellowish brown, to the rare colour changing alexandrite. Also found is the precious cat's-eye, which is always cut en cabochon and is usually of a semi-opaque rich honey colour. The phenomenon which gives these stones their name is due to minute rod-like crystals, or cavities, which display a thin band of light, parallel to the direction of these inclusions, radiating over the surface of the stone as it is turned. A similar effect can be seen in a reel of cotton. Chrysoberyl cat's-eye can be stunning in appearance and fine examples, where the 'eye' is well-

defined and the body of the stone of an attractive honey colour, are rare and worth a great deal of money, some $5,000-$20,000 depending on size. Far more common, however, are quartz cat's-eyes (see section on quartz family) and since these are of small value it is important to be aware of the difference. In general, quartz cat's-eyes are far more opaque and tend to a more greyish green body colour or pale brown. In addition, since the 'eye' in quartz is due to relatively large filaments of asbestos, the 'eye' is normally not as well-defined as in chrysoberyl. Detecting the difference between poor chrysoberyl and good quartz cat's-eye can present a problem, especially if the stone is mounted where a specific gravity test is impossible. A simple test is not available to the amateur since 'distant reading' methods of detecting RI (chrysoberyl 1.74-1.75, quartz 1.54-1.55) in stones cut en cabochon are extremely difficult. Here is a good case where the amateur should obtain a specifically worded receipt (stating the stone to be chrysoberyl if a high price is involved) to protect from fraud, intentional or otherwise. Crocidolite, a mineral which produces the popular 'tiger's-eye', is sufficiently like chrysoberyl cat's-eye to be worth a mention here; luckily, however, this common and inexpensive gemstone once seen is not easily forgotten. Chrysoberyl also yields highly lustrous and attractive pale yellow stones which have been known in the past as chrysolites. These stones were particularly popular during the eighteenth century and the first half of the nineteenth century, particularly in Portugal which imported large quantities from its colonies in Brazil. The high degree of fire exhibited by these stones, many of which could be near colourless, recommended them to jewellers as a diamond substitute. A quick RI reading will readily identify them (1.74-1.75).

Alexandrite is the most valuable form of chrysoberyl. The most important thing for the amateur to know about these stones is that they are extremely rare and consequently very expensive. Fine examples exhibit a good green body colour in daylight which changes to a rich burgundy by artificial light (other than fluorescent). Perhaps the most notorious error in gemstones is the confusion between colour changing synthetic spinels and corundums, and alexandrites. Unscrupulous gem dealers in Egypt used to sell these synthetics as the real thing to unwitting customers, on the mistaken assumption that they were mined at, and took their name from, the city of Alexandria. The fact that they paid a mere few shillings for these stones instead of many thousands of pounds was not enough, it seems, to make them suspicious. Often, to their astonishment, we have been able to divine the past of the owners of these stones with the question 'Were you in Egypt during the war?'

The value of true alexandrite is dependent on the strength and attractiveness of the colour change. In poor examples, where the colour change is to a slight muddy brown (most commonly associated with stones from Sri Lanka) the value may by only a few hundred pounds a carat. In fine examples, where the colour change is distinct and deep red, the value will be many thousands of pounds a carat (traditionally associated with stones from Siberia); in addition rare cat's-eye forms are found.

The simplest test for alexandrite is an RI (1.74-1.75); alexandrite (which owes its colour change to chromic oxide like ruby) should also show dark absorption lines in the red end of the spectrum through a spectroscope. This will be difficult for the amateur and again, advice should be sought from a reputable jeweller, and a specified receipt obtained. For some, alexandrite is really a gemmological curiosity, and does not stand up well beside the beauty of other gemstones. Finally, as a word of caution, it should be remembered that some true synthetic alexandrites have reached the market, although, it must be said, none have yet been encountered by us.

Spinel

In jewellery, it is really only the red and blue varieties that need concern us. Red spinel is an extremely attractive and relatively rare gemstone that in fine examples rivals ruby, sharing chromium as the same colour source. (The famous stone in the Imperial State Crown known as the 'Black Prince Ruby' was discovered to be a spinel.) In practice, the colour of spinel, to the trained eye, tends towards a strawberry red (often described as a 'sweet' red) as opposed to the blood red (pigeon's blood) of a fine ruby. Nevertheless, good red spinels can be spectacular stones, and though only a handful of examples over 5 carats have been seen, their value is still in the low thousands of pounds per carat — a value multiplied 30 or 50 fold for the equivalent Burmese ruby. The methods for distinguishing ruby and spinel are described in the ruby section. Blue spinel is usually greenish or inky in colour, but can resemble sapphire; the methods of determining which is which are dealt with in the sapphire section (see plate 38).

Synthetic spinels, which are common, resemble both ruby and sapphire. It is important here to note the RI of spinel (1.72). It is also worth remembering that colourless synthetic spinel has also been used to imitate diamond since it crystallises in the cubic system and is therefore, like diamond, singly reflective.

Zircon

It is only since the First World War that the most commonly seen variety of zircon, the blue, has appeared in jewellery. Indeed, most people who have heard of zircons think that all are blue, but in fact their colour is due to heat treatment, usually to the orange-brown stones discovered in the Mekong Delta. As with most heat treatment (see sapphires) the centre of operations is Bangkok. Sadly, the colour of heat treated blue zircons is not stable and can fade.

The most characteristic aspect of zircon, other than green and most brown varieties, is that they have a high degree of double refraction. This phenomenon is so well marked in zircon that to demonstrate the doubling of the back facets to a novice one could not choose a more useful stone. Coupled with this is a high degree of dispersion, giving the stone great 'fire'. Both these aspects of zircon are fortunate since its RI is off the range of the refractometer. Those who possess a spectroscope will also see a distinctive absorption spectrum composed of narrow evenly spaced lines spanning all colours due to the presence of radioactive elements.

Colourless, or white zircons, known formerly as 'jargoons', were often used to imitate diamond because of their high dispersion, particularly in Indian jewellery, since Sri Lanka is the major source of the material. Diamond, of course, being singly refractive, is easily distinguished from zircon through a lens.

The presence of radioactive elements in zircon, as in other minerals, can result in the breaking down of the crystal structure of the stone. Technically such stones are known as 'metamict'; where the process is complete the stone is usually green and does not show the characteristic double refraction, moreover they may have a readable RI as low as 1.78. It is a complex process and it should be remembered that not all green zircons are metamict and many zircons have intermediate properties. Commercially, however, it is only the blues, and to some extent the orange-brown stones, that need concern us — all of these will exhibit the 'high state' properties: high dispersion, strong double refraction, no readable RI, and in addition a high lustre.

Tourmaline

A widely-distributed and varied colour gem material, it is mainly the green and red varieties that are encountered. A good green tourmaline is a handsome stone, which takes a high degree of polish and has a deeply saturated colour tending towards a blackish green. As with all tourmalines, they are strongly dichroic (two coloured) and the two shades of green, typically bluish and yellowish, are usually easily seen as the stone is revolved. Moreover, if stones are viewed along their length the colour is often so intensified that they appear black. Red tourmalines can be good enough to imitate poor rubies to the untrained eye and are often known as 'rubellites'. Here again the strong dichroism should give a clue as to their origin coupled with the fact that the red is characteristically raspberry in colour.

The majority of tourmalines are heavily flawed, the most characteristic inclusion being liquid filled cavities which often appear black through a lens or microscope. Pink tourmalines can be confused with the more costly pink topaz and care should be taken with the refractometer (tourmaline RI 1.62-1.64) and note taken of the fact that tourmaline is strongly doubly refractive.

Blue, brown and black varieties also occur, as well as the unusual 'watermelon' coloured stones which shade from pink to green. Tourmaline is only 'semi-precious' and even the finest examples would struggle to reach $1,000 a carat, most stones being below $100 a carat. Recently some very attractive specimens from Mozambique have been seen, including some rare peridot-green stones and fine blue examples. With the rise in value of precious stones, tourmalines may become a force in the market, as the Japanese are already strong buyers.

Peridot

Formerly called 'olivine', since it is a gem variety of that mineral, the name peridot has been adopted for many years to avoid confusion with demantoid garnets, which used to bear the same name. Peridot offers perhaps the least problems to the amateur, for its distinctive olive or yellowish green colour is scarcely imitated in nature and where pastes present themselves, the strong double refraction of the stone (easily visible through a lens) makes identification relatively simple. It has an RI of 1.65-1.69 which is usually easily readable in cut stones.

The classic source of peridot is the romantic sounding Island of St. John in the Red Sea (a place no student gemmologist ever forgets). Fine stones also come from Burma and Arizona. In jewellery, peridot is most associated with the 1830s and 1840s, and, like demantoid, at the turn of the century, was greatly admired by the Arts and Crafts movement.

It is worth mentioning, purely as a point of detail, that a brown sub-species is also known, called 'sinhalite'.

Garnets

The name garnet does not refer to a single stone but rather to a group of minerals (see plate 25) which share similar chemical compositions and crystallise in the same system (cubic). Most garnets encountered in jewellery will be in shades of red or brownish red, which are not valuable stones but can be attractive. The best examples, coloured by chromium and known as 'pyrope', can approximate to the red of ruby. Even so, few jewellers will bother to differentiate between 'pyrope' and 'almandine', or other forms, since there is little commercial advantage to be gained.

The red garnets are seldom imitated since no natural red stone is as cheap. Sometimes red pastes might be mistaken for garnet but the use of red glass (paste) is usually with the intention of imitating ruby. It is worth pointing out that garnet is most often quite heavily flawed or included with a variety of crystalline material. The constants, RI and SG, of the garnet family are quite widely spaced and do not prove very helpful as a means of identification for the amateur and, moreover, like pastes, they are singly refractive.

Green garnets, however, are rare and valuable. The beautiful demantoid garnet, a variety of andradite, is a spectacular gemstone having a dispersion higher than diamond giving it great life and fire. Its colour, in fine examples, is a brilliant grass green, yellower than emerald, and this combined with its brilliance makes confusion unlikely. Green garnets, which first appeared on the market during the second half of the nineteenth century, were mined in the Urals, and are particularly common in jewels dating from about 1895 to the First World War. Good examples may be worth several thousand dollars a carat but rarely exceed 5 carats in size, most stones being quite small.

Characteristic inclusions are aptly called 'horse's tails' and are brownish filaments of asbestos. Most examples will show this distinctive trademark, which is fortunate for the RI of demantoid (1.89) is off the scale of the refractometer. In practice there are few stones which can imitate the distinctive bright green of demantoid; peridots may resemble pale examples but they are strongly double refractive and have a readable RI at around 1.67. It should be remembered, however, that certain synthetic garnets (YAG) have been coloured by chromium to imitate demantoid, but these are invariably flawless and not yet encountered in a period jewel. Recently, attractive green forms of grossular garnet have been discovered in Kenya in the Tsavo National Park, which have a good leaf green colour but lack the fire of demantoid and are relatively soft, making them prone to abrasion. The value of such stones is widely varied. On a recent trip to Kenya, a fine 2 carat example was purchased for $300, despite the fact that they are marketed in the USA under the trade name 'Tsavorite' for prices in excess of $1,000 per carat. Their RI of 1.74 makes them readily identifiable.

Pearls

Unique amongst gem materials in that it is manufactured by a mollusc, pearl may also be one of the oldest materials used as a gemstone by man since it requires no further attention by human hand. For many generations fine pearls commanded legendary prices but the price domination ended with the advent of cultured pearls on to the market in the 1920s and 1930s.

The formation of a pearl within the oyster sac begins as the oyster's reaction to an irritant, usually a shell-boring parasite. In a series of successive layers, the oyster deposits crystals of aragonite (calcium carbonate) in an organic material called conchiolin around the source of irritation. Successive layers are gradually built up until the pearl is formed, rather like the layers inside an onion. The crystals of aragonite lie rather in the fashion of slates on a roof and account for the unique lustre of pearl.

In cultured pearl, a small mother-of-pearl bead is used as the nucleus around which the oyster then builds successive layers of natural pearl. X-rays will reveal the mother-of-pearl bead nucleus and are the surest method of identification. Good cultured pearls have a relatively thick nacreous layer, but poor ones will only have a thin film deposited on the bead. Cultured pearl necklaces have been seen where the beads are so badly worn that the mother-of-pearl is clearly visible. The layers of natural pearl deposited on cultured pearls may vary from perhaps 0.5mm to 3mm.

It is not of great use to the amateur but worth stating, that once familiar with pearls one gets used to the particular characteristics of each variety, which is, after all, only of importance if one is offered a natural specimen. Pearls should be of good colour and lustre, the best show a sort of rosy bloom, and the 'skin' should be as near perfect and unblemished as possible. Poor cultured pearls are often waxy in colour and show imperfections rather like worm casts on the surface. The higher the colour and lustre, the greater the value. Large natural pearls of fine colour, lustre and skin, and of good shape, are still extremely valuable. Large, regular shaped, cultured pearls of good colour and skin, over say 10mm in diameter, are also rare and valuable. Necklaces of exceptional quality cultured pearls have been sold at auction for more than $1 million.

'Baroque' pearls are misshapen pearls and can be of natural or cultured origin and in either case of far lesser value than round or pear-shaped examples. 'Blister' pearls are cut from the shell of the oyster and take the form of a cabochon. Double blister pearls cemented together can imitate a large round pearl if the junction layer is disguised by the setting. 'Jap' or 'Mabé' pearls are blister pearls with a mother-of-pearl disc and plug cemented to the back: all blister pearls are of small value.

'Imitation' pearls are usually glass spheres to which a coating of 'essence d'orient', made of fish scales, has been applied, or a hollow glass bead where the same substance is used to coat the interior. The age-old practice of rubbing the 'pearl' against the front teeth applies here since a natural or cultured pearl will appear gritty, and an imitation pearl smooth.

Pink pearls, which closely resemble coral, are produced in the conch and show a characteristic 'flame-like' surface when viewed under a lens and a silvery sheen. Fine examples can be valuable, into the low thousands of pounds.

Freshwater pearls, or river pearls, which tend to have less lustre and are sometimes found in jewellery of the nineteenth and early twentieth century, are notably from the Tay in Scotland and the Mississippi in the USA. Non-neucleated cultured pearls are mainly produced in Lake Biwa in Japan; these are lighter than ordinary cultured pearls, are whiter, and commonly oval-shaped. Once seen they are readily identified and their value is low.

Natural black pearls are rare and valuable. Cultured pearl may be stained with silver nitrate to represent black pearl, the colour induced is darker and more uniform. Natural black cultured pearls have also been produced and if of good size then their value can be considerable.

For the amateur, identification of natural pearl is probably best left to an accredited gemmological laboratory with recourse to X-ray equipment, but in any case, the buyer of natural pearl is entitled to ask for a testing certificate to confirm the origin.

Jade

The name jade is used for two distinct minerals: jadeite, a precious variety, and nephrite, also known as 'New Zealand' jade or greenstone, which is far more extensively found and, to most eyes, less attractive. It is important to know that this subdivision exists, especially since fine jadeite bead necklaces have been sold for hundreds of thousands of pounds, whereas a good nephrite bead necklace may be purchased for less than a thousand.

Jadeite of finest quality is a luscious apple to grass green, translucent and magnificent. This rare form of the stone is known as 'imperial jade', which term refers to the particular colour and translucency. The first time we encountered a bead necklace of this material, unaware of what it was, we took it to be a sort of stained green chalcedony of exceptional beauty. Luckily time was taken to study it carefully. In addition to other more elusive qualities, it exhibited the characteristic 'orange peel' polish (minute specks where the polish has not taken, which is so characteristic of jadeite). This identification was fortunate indeed, since the single row of beads sold twenty years ago for £50,000! Other colours of jadeite are far less valuable and more common. 'Lilac' jade of pale mauve tint is an attractive material and a bead necklace has been known to fetch many thousands of pounds (beware, however, that staining of pale jade to imitate lilac jade is common). Least valuable is the ubiquitous and aptly named 'mutton fat' variety, which was often carved by the Chinese.

Nephrite can never imitate the exceptional, almost emerald green, of jadeite. Most green nephrite is a deeper green, more the colour of an ivy leaf, and takes a finer, more oily polish which is quite unblemished.

Distinguishing between jadeite and nephrite is not an easy task for the amateur. Where the back of a cabochon presents a flat surface an RI reading may be possible (jadeite in the area of 1.65-1.66, nephrite 1.61-1.63). Where facilities are available an SG test will prove conclusive (jadeite 3.33, nephrite 2.95). In practice, nephrite is seldom passed off as fine jade; Few 'imperial' jade necklaces are sold in Europe, most finding their way to the more educated market in Hong Kong where the material is valued above almost all others.

Care should be taken when buying a fine jade cabochon set in a ring since the colour may be enhanced by a closed setting, by staining (though this is uncommon), and by forming a sort of doublet with a darker material at the back.

Turquoise
The colour of fine turquoise, traditionally, should be the pure blue of a summer sky. It is important that this is understood since many turquoises, particularly from Arizona, are a bluey green with which the name turquoise is more commonly associated.

Sadly, turquoise is an extremely difficult material to test since because it is often apparently flawless and is at best translucent, its internal features are hidden. In addition it is almost always cut en cabochon and thereby virtually inaccessible to the refractometer and thus a real problem is presented to the gemmologist. For the amateur, who does not have recourse to tests of SG and a spectroscope, the problem is virtually insurmountable. Beware of the possibility that turquoise has been powdered and bonded with resins and other substances, dyed to improve colour, and may be imitated by a variety of substances such as glass and porcelain. A relatively rare simulant odontolite, or fossil ivory naturally stained, is worth mentioning since it has been encountered on only one occasion, set in a piece of fine diamond jewellery from the 1830s. Once identified, its rarity in a piece of jewellery probably enhanced its value far beyond that of turquoise (a virtually infallible test is the application of a minute drop of acid which will effervesce due to the presence of calcium carbonate).

Lapis lazuli

Unlike other materials used in jewellery, lapis is best described as a rock, for it is a complex mixture of many materials; lazurite, haüyne and sodalite impart the blue colour, flakes of pyrites the characteristic spangling, and calcite is largely responsible for the white areas visible in poorer quality specimens. The best examples will be of uniform deep blue associated with the ancient mines of Afghanistan. The most common imitator of lapis is a form of stained jasper known commercially as 'swiss lapis'.

Beads of lapis are difficult to test on a refractometer, but where a flat surface presents itself the RI of lapis at around 1.50 may be useful, though vague. 'Swiss lapis', generally a poorer blue, tending towards green, which when polished takes a much higher lustre, will also show areas of transparent quartz where the stain has not taken. Synthetic spinel has also been produced to imitate lapis and, as in most varieties, is coloured by cobalt. The manufacturing process causes the synthetics to exhibit a granular structure (not unlike lapis), and the characteristic spangles of natural lapis are imitated by specks of gold. This material has not been seen employed as beads, but more usually as stones for signet rings, etc. Where a flat surface is available a reading may be obtained at 1.72.

Sodalite has often been used as a material in earrings and is sometimes confused with lapis. In general it exhibits a paler blue with larger areas of white. (Purely as a point of detail it has an RI around 1.48.)

Quartz family

Quartz is the commonest of all minerals, but its hardness and lustre make it ideally suited to use as a gemstone. In its crystalline form it yields two (semi precious) varieties that need concern us here: amethyst and citrine. The latter has been dealt with under topaz since it is often confused with this more precious mineral. It should be understood that citrine is a widespread and therefore common gemstone which can be attractive in shades of yellow and yellowish brown. A simple RI test will distinguish it (RI 1.54-1.55) from topaz, as will its distinctive shade of yellow. Brown forms are known as 'smoky quartz', or 'cairngorms' due to their common occurrence in Scotland.

Amethyst is the purple or violet form of crystalline quartz. The finest examples, traditionally from Siberia, have a rich saturated colour and are very beautiful gemstones, which were popular in the mid-nineteenth century. Nowadays Brazil is the major source. A common inclusion in amethyst is often described as 'tiger stripe' or 'finger print', consisting of liquid filled fissures within the stone. Colour zoning is generally also present and helps to distinguish it from paste. A fine amethyst of say 6 or 7 carats may be worth several hundred pounds. It is interesting to note that most citrines are derived from poor quality amethyst through heat treatment. Rose quartz is a pale pink variety that is seldom if ever flawless but may be confused with pink tourmalines, where a quick RI test should reveal the difference.

Cryptocrystalline quartz (which does not display a crystal structure) yields a wide variety of gem materials, all of which are merely ornamental and of low value. When the material is translucent it is known as 'chalcedony', which is often dyed green to represent jade, but also blue, pink, etc. The RI of all cryptocrystalline quartz is slightly lower, around 1.53, though in practice the need to test this material is rare since its value is so small. Also included in this group are onyx, a black variety banded with white (note the pale green mineral, known mistakenly by the same name, which is in fact a variety of alabaster); jasper; sardonyx (brown banded with white, often used for hardstone cameos); bloodstone (green flecked with red) and agates.

Amber

Amber has always been a tricky material since it is so easily and effectively imitated by plastic. Amber is simply fossilised resin (the insects so often found trapped within it inhabited the planet some forty million years ago); in colour it ranges through yellow, the colour of acacia honey, that of Baltic amber, through reddish-brown, to the brown of Oloroso sherry, associated with the Burmese variety.

Tests are difficult. The age-old method of testing amber by its property of developing static electricity when rubbed, and thereby attracting small particles, is no longer useful since many plastics behave in a similar manner. The lack of exhibition of such a property, however, can rule out some fakes. Amber is also thermoplastic at relatively low temperatures, enabling small pieces to be moulded together to form larger more useful examples; during this process dead insects may be introduced to add to the confusion. The insects in natural amber generally display themselves with wings open rather in the fashion of those trapped on a flypaper. Air bubbles in natural amber are generally spherical whereas those in moulded amber are often of extended oval form. Swirls of colour are also often present in moulded examples.

The natural resin, copal, is often used as an imitation, but the most striking characteristic of this substance is its crazed surface which is uncommon in amber. A popular test involving the use of ether (copal resin becomes tacky on contact) is impractical for most people and probably dangerous.

By far the most common materials used in imitation are plastics, and very effective they are too. Many books refer to the 'sectile' (here meant as the ability to peel with a knife) properties of plastics: amber splinters when cut. This test is neither easy nor practical.

In 1983 Sotheby's London sold a spectacular collection of amber bead necklaces; many of the beads were carved in elaborate forms and were of

Chinese workmanship (see plate 26). All known varieties and colours of amber were represented. The sale created new price levels for the material, with several of the necklaces selling for many thousands of pounds. Today, they may be worth double or treble the price.

Coral

Like pearl, coral has its genesis in the sea and is an organic product; also like pearl it is formed of calcium carbonate. In the nineteenth century, coral from the Bay of Naples was carved in Italy and used as cameos or, in naturalistic forms, incorporated into necklaces and brooches. Typically coral is an orange-red; pink varieties known appropriately as 'angel's skin' (or 'peau d'ange') are also popular. Pollution of our seas has destroyed many of the tiny coral producing polyps, and as a result the material is rapidly becoming scarce with prices rising steadily. Coral is commonly imitated by glass and porcelain. A simple and useful test is the judicious application of a small drop of hydrochloric acid: coral, being a carbonate, will effervesce quite strongly.

Jet

Jet shares with amber a fossil origin, in this case wood, being closely allied to coal. It is no surprise to discover therefore that England was a major producer. The town most commonly associated with jet in the nineteenth century was Whitby, on the coast of Yorkshire. The Victorian obsession with mourning jewellery ensured that jet was used for all forms of jewellery, with cameos and necklaces as the most common. Today the material as such has virtually no value outside the sphere of the collector. Such was the popularity of jet during the latter half of the nineteenth century, however, that other materials were used to imitate it. Vulcanite, an early form of rubber, is the most popular and could easily be cast in elaborate forms. A mild heating over a flame will quickly release a rubbery smell absent in jet. Black glass was also used as an imitation. Perhaps uniquely in the world of jewellery, the imitators of jet may well be of equal interest to the collector as the original material they emulate.

Opal

Most people are familiar with the varied and occasionally brilliant colours displayed as flashes within the body of opal. In general, the more rich and pronounced the colours the more valuable the stone, especially if displayed against a dark grey or black background as is the case in 'black' opal (see plate 34). All opals are individual, and have been compared to paintings in terms of valuation, where each should be considered on its own terms. In black opal, blue and green are normally predominant, and where this is the case to the exclusion of other colours, the value of the stone will be restricted. Other hues are more highly prized, especially red and gold in combination with the more common colours, and ideally the colour 'zones' or 'patches' will be evenly spaced throughout the surface of the stone. Black opal has been mined in

Australia since the end of the nineteenth century, before then it was unknown (an important thing to remember when buying antique jewellery). Opals where the body of colour is white or greenish are less valuable, probably because the display of colour is less spectacular. Limpid, translucent varieties are known as water opals. Mexico produces some extraordinary translucent orange gems known as 'fire' opals (see plate 33); in this case the stones are valued for the startling tangerine colour of the stone rather than for the flashes of colour.

Opal is usually cut as a cabochon, or as flat ovals. Rarely is an RI reading (1.45) appropriate, except perhaps in the case of fire opals which might be imitated by pastes, etc. Sadly, the surface of opal is seldom completely flat and this further complicates the matter, since the shadow line on the refractometer is difficult to see. Buyers should be particularly careful of opal doublets which occur with alarming frequency, especially in Far Eastern jewellery (see pastes and composite stones) and commonly exhibit very flat surfaces. Opal is also extremely susceptible to changes in temperature (notoriously under photographic lights). The surface of the stone is easily crazed and cracked, and it is common practice in certain areas for opals to be sold immersed in oil to disguise the imperfections.

For some years, synthetic opal has been produced, notably by Pierre Gilson in France. Fine black opal is so rare, and these new synthetics are so good, that buyers should be extremely careful how and where they purchase such stones. In general Gilson synthetic opals appear 'too good to be true' with very evenly spaced colour splashes which under magnification have clearly defined edges, a phenomenon which has been described as 'lizard skin'.

Opal can also be 'treated' or enhanced, involving heating and soaking the stone in an oil or sugar solution and then burning it off or applying acid. This has the effect of darkening the body colour so that the flashes of colour stand out better (see plate 21). With practice these 'treated' stones are easily spotted, since the play of colour is actually very unlike that in natural opal. Other imitations of opal are in glass (especially those produced by John Slocum in the USA), and synthetic materials such as latex.

Appendix A — The refraction of light and the refractometer

The refractometer is an important instrument for testing gemstones which can be used by the amateur with some practice. The principle upon which the refractometer operates is explained so succinctly by Robert Webster in his exhaustive book *Gems* that it would be difficult to improve upon: '. . . when a ray of light passes obliquely from a transparent medium to one of the lower optical density the ray is refracted away from the normal, and, as the angle of the incident ray is increased there is reached an angle where the refracted ray grazes the surface of the two media in contact. The particular angle, where the refracted ray makes an angle of 90 degrees with the normal, is known as the critical angle. Any further increase in the angle of incidence will cause the ray to be reflected into the medium, that is it is totally internally reflected.'

In the refractometer the 'transparent medium' is a prism of optically dense glass. The stone to be tested is placed on the prism (using the table or other flat facet) with a contact fluid forming a good bond. Light is then shone into the instrument (usually monochromatic light such as sodium) and thereby through the glass prism. Following the principle set out above, some of the light will pass out into the stone, the rest will be reflected back inside the instrument; the reflected light then illuminates a scale viewed through the eyepiece of the refractometer, the 'shadow edge' between the dark and light areas on the scale being the refractive index of the stone (RI). In gemstones which crystallise in the cubic system (e.g. diamonds, spinel, garnet), and all non-crystalline substances such as glass, light passes through as a single ray. In all other gemstones, the ray is split into two which travel at different speeds and have different refractive indices (this phenomenon is called double refraction): In the refractometer this is translated as two separate 'shadow edges'. The difference between the two is known as the DR or birefringence (e.g. sapphire has an RI of 1.76-1.77 and a DR of .008).

In coloured doubly-refractive gemstones each of the rays will be differently absorbed and will thus appear differently coloured to the eye; this phenomenon can sometimes be seen as the stone is rotated (e.g. a red tourmaline will often show two shades of red as it is rotated) and is known as a dichroism, or more generally pleochroism. It is sometimes a useful help in identifying a stone.

Appendix B — Mohs scale of hardness

It is well known that diamond is the hardest substance known in nature. Over 100 years ago, Frederic Mohs set out a table of relative hardness of minerals that is of interest to the gemmologist. Indeed there exist somewhat clumsy aids to testing gems known as 'hardness points', whereby one is encouraged to 'test' a gem by its ability to scratch, or be scratched, by another.

The minerals Mohs used in his scale are set out on the left below, on the right a few extra stones have been added. It should be remembered that the scale is merely an indication of relative hardness and not one of degree; it is said, as an illustration, that the difference between sapphire and diamond (9 and 10) is greater than that between sapphire and talc (9 and 1), even though the latter can be scratched with the fingernail.

1	talc		
2	gypsum		
		2 ½	amber
3	calcite	3	pearl
4	Fluorspar	4	coral
5	apatite		
		5 ½	strontium titanite

6	feldspar	6	opal
		6½	peridot
7	quartz	7	jadeite
		7½	beryl
8	topaz	8	chrysoberyl
		8½	CSZ (cubic stabilised zirconia)
9	sapphire		
10	diamond		

Appendix C — Pastes and composite stones

Pastes are glass imitations of precious stones. What they do very well is match the colour of the gem, but they fail in one important respect — durability; in the majority of cases, pastes are considerably softer than precious stones, and one of the old-fashioned methods of detecting them was to apply a file. This method, however, has little to recommend it, and in fact may lead to the damage of genuine stones.

A surer and safer method of detection is miscroscopic examination:

a) Nearly all glasses contain bubbles, which are generally larger than those detected in verneuil synthetic rubies and sapphires. Sometimes swathes of bubbles are induced within the glass to imitate the complex flaws of such stones as emerald and tourmaline.

b) The colour in glass is often distributed in curved, swirling bands giving a treacly aspect to the interior of the stone.

c) Glass is an amorphous, non-crystalline substance and thus singly refractive, showing only a single shadow edge on the refractometer.

d) Glass feels warmer to the touch than most gemstones.

e) Glass exhibits large shell-like (conchoidal) fractures when chipped.

f) The refractive index of glass can vary widely but is seldom close enough to the stone imitated to pose a problem.

The above are considered to be the most useful tests. Paste is very often encountered in antique jewellery, but in this case it is rare for them not to exhibit scratches and abrasions on their surfaces.

Composite stones pose far greater problems, and take many forms. In order to avoid the problems posed by the relative softness of glass, and the susceptibility of the upper surfaces of pastes to wear and abrasion, workshops started to make 'stones' where the 'table' or top of the stone was of a hard stone, usually garnet, cemented to a coloured glass bottom. These 'garnet topped doublets' were particularly popular between about 1850 and the First World War, especially in 9 carat gold rings in combination with rose diamonds. Examination under a lens will reveal the junction between the two materials and, if viewed from the side, the top of the stone can be seen to be a different colour if light is transmitted through it. Moreover, the almandine garnet top very often exhibits rutile needles. Sometimes the junction between the two materials is at the girdle of the 'stone', and where this is set in a collet it may not be visible. An RI reading of these stones will of course be that of almandine garnet, around 1.83, perhaps sufficiently close to sapphire and ruby to pose problems for the unwary amateur.

Other common types of composite stones are 'soudé emeralds', where two pieces of pale beryl or rock crystal are connected by green stained adhesive (in the former case, of course, having an RI very similar to emerald); opal doublets, which have backs of onyx, black glass or opal matrix; opal triplets, where a further layer on top of the opal is added of plastic or glass; combinations of natural and synthetic minerals to form a doublet, e.g. natural ruby crown, or top, synthetic ruby bottom; and diamond doublets, typically with diamond tops and synthetic corundum bottoms.

CHAPTER ONE
From the late 18th Century to 1820

Few pieces of jewellery dating from the eighteenth century reach us in their original form: precious metal and stones, diamonds in particular, are rare and durable, and ornaments could be dismantled, the metal melted down and the gemstones reset in new mounts to keep up with the changes in taste and fashion.

A small number of diamond jewels in their original closed settings — where the backs of the stones are not visible — (see plate 40) survive in the shape of girandole earrings (see plate 46), the favourite eighteenth century motif consisting of a larger stone, cluster, or ribbon bow motif supporting three pear-shaped drops; necklaces designed as simple rivières; cluster buttons (see plate 65); starbursts, crescents or flowerhead brooches (see plates 56 and 57).

Until the gold discoveries of the 1840s in the United States of America, and later in South Africa, and the first appearance on the market of Cape diamonds in the 1870s, almost all precious jewellery sooner or later had to be remounted.

The regular flow of diamonds from South Africa, and the abundance of precious metal on the market, together with a new and widely spread wealth, changed the situation dramatically, and in the second half of the century the woman who could afford a new piece of jewellery did not have to unmount an old piece in order to have it made. In addition, more pieces of jewellery were handed down from mother to daughter in their original form and have thus survived.

The French Revolution is also partly responsible for the destruction of so much early jewellery. The republican ideals of the Revolutionaires profoundly influenced society, changing habits, life style, government, religion, and even the calendar. Jewels, considered at the time a reminder of the Ancien Régime, seemed to conflict with the new ideals and to be somehow out of fashion. An enormous quantity of jewellery left France, and was remounted abroad or was sold for survival; even the crown jewels were seized by the Revolutionaires and the Parisian jewellers, leaders of fashion in Europe, faced great hardship.

Very little jewellery was produced during the Revolution; such jewels as were made lack in imagination and are of rather poor quality. Somehow the ideals of the Revolution were not suited to jewellery; the rings, bracelets, and brooches in debased metal which have survived are decorated with the profiles of the heroes of the Revolution, Phrygian caps, guillotines and lictorian fasces.

A slow return to normality followed the establishment of the Directorate in France; the supplies of luxury goods accelerated and the jewellery trade started to recover. The feminine ideal was to emulate the classical purity of Greek statues; dresses were of very flimsy material, often dampened to cling more revealingly to the body, high waisted, and free from any unnecessary ornaments that might detract attention from the female figure. These tunics inspired by Greek and Roman antiquity favoured colours such as yellow, white, lilac and pistachio green.

The ideal jewel to complement these dresses and enhance the figure, without drawing too much attention to itself, had to be simple, geometric, and flat (see plate 48).

Wrists, forearms and upper arms were encircled by bracelets designed as simple gold bands. Longchains of flat geometrical linking, decorated with stylised heart motifs or a Greek key pattern, were worn in a variety of ways: around the neck, across the shoulder, crossed on the bosom. Rings were in great demand and worn on every finger.

The favoured hairstyle required hair to be gathered at the top of the head in coiffures that borrowed their names from the classical world: 'à la Titus', 'à la Grecque', and 'à la Cérès' thus encouraging the use of long pendant earrings made of two or three gold links of flat geometrical shape decorated with lozenges, shields, and acanthus leaves. These large but light ornaments, cut out of thin sheets of gold, are known as 'poissardes'.

By the 1800s, jewellery was firmly back in fashion and the jewellery trade started once more to work for a new aristocracy which no longer considered the wearing of jewels to be in bad taste or against a republican ideal.

The coming to power of Napoleon dramatically changed not only the political and social scene, but also the world of fashion and jewellery. His interest in jewellery was well known, but the simplicity and linearity of contemporary jewels did not suit his ideal of power and glory. Josephine Beauharnais' love for dresses and jewels is well known too, and her influence on fashion very pronounced.

By 1803 Napoleon had recovered most of the crown jewels, and, during his official visit to Belgium as first Consul, they were worn again for the first time since the Revolution, on this occasion by Josephine. Soon after, on Napoleon's coronation as Emperor, they were remounted by Foncier and Nitot. It was Josephine's taste that was to guide the Parisian jewellers in this *tour de force*, and the Bourbon jewels were remounted in the shape of laurel leaf tiaras, combs, hair ornaments and bracelets.

At court and on state occasions, precious parures became popular once more. Inspired by Napoleonic classicism and set with rubies, emeralds, sapphires, pearls and diamonds, they favoured decorative motifs such as Greek keys, acanthus leaves, palmettes, formal volutes, laurel leaves, arches and eagles. Although exhibiting fine workmanship and set with very good quality gemstones, these jewels never lost their two-dimensional quality and always showed a certain lack of originality in design.

The Napoleonic classicism brought with it a renewed interest in cameos.

The fashion for cameos and intaglios began soon after the Italian campaign of 1796, when cameos were brought back to France from Italy. Many of these were of Greek or Roman origin, but some were of later periods. Napoleon, fascinated by their beauty and perfection, had some mounted for himself. At the same time he promoted the foundation of a school of gem engraving in Paris, where fine workmanship was established, occasionally in precious stones like emerald, more often in hard and semiprecious stones such as agate, cornelian, jasper and, to satisfy the lowest part of the market, also in the modestly priced shell.

Intaglios and cameos were immediately set in all sorts of jewels such as tiaras, necklaces, bracelets and earrings, usually mounted in simple gold collets, sometimes decorated with seed pearl borders and joined together by means of light and delicate gold chains, and preferably worn with a 'demi toilette' (see plates 54, 73, 79-80 and 82).

The Italians excelled in the art of cutting cameos and intaglios, which at the time was considered in the same rank as the major arts. Among the most famous names was that of Benedetto Pistrucci (1784-1855), whose work, originally patronised in Italy by Elisa Bacciocchi, Napoleon's sister, became extremely sought after in England. Eventually Pistrucci moved to London where he soon became chief engraver to the Royal Mint, designing such famous coins as the sovereign. The carving of gems, and the engraving of dies for coins and medals, are strictly connected, sharing the same technical problems. It is not unusual, therefore, to find gem engravers working in state mints at some stage in their career.

Pistrucci, like most contemporary engravers, often signed his work, but soon realised that even this precaution was not enough to protect it since unscrupulous dealers were selling his carvings and engravings as antiques, after removing his signature. He therefore hid within the carving the tiny Greek letter lambda, that testified the true origin of the work and identified its author (*see* Forrer, *Biographical Dictionary of Medallists,* London, 1904, page 587), but even this was perhaps easily forged. Other famous gem engravers of the first years of the century are: Giuseppe Girometti (1780-1851) who worked for the Pontifical Mint in Rome (see plate 73), Luigi Pichler (1773-1854), Nicolo Amastini (1780-1851), Nicola Berini (b.1770), Filippo Rega (1761-1833), and Marchant (1755-1812), English by birth but trained in Rome. Beware of these names on intaglios as they may have been added to works of a much later date. Pichler, in particular, used to sign his name using Greek letters.

Hand in hand with the craze for classical cameos, the forgery industry flourished, and the doctoring of contemporary pieces became almost an art in itself. Age and discolouration were quickly imparted by means of abrasive solutions, and the final touch was given by breaking the stone and replacing the chipped surface with a gold plate.

Apart from deliberate forgeries, cheap imitations of cameos were soon moulded in glass and porcelain, easily detectable by the absence of tool marks and by small air bubbles trapped into the glass paste. Many glass imitations were simply cast from an original and so bear a signature as well. Doublets were a more sophisticated type of imitation consisting of an opaque white glass relief cemented to a dark background, usually a plaque of onyx or cornelian (see plate 81). Close examination of the contact points, the very flat and uniform background and the absence of tool marks on the relief, are usually enough to give away a doublet.

Roman mosaics made of tiny tesserae of polychrome opaque glass, held within either mother-of-pearl, dark blue, or black glass frames, became the fashion together with cameos and intaglios. Favourite subjects were views of ancient Roman architecture, landscapes, animals, especially birds, and fêtes champêtres (see plate 53). Set in similar ways to cameos and intaglios, within elaborate chainwork, in the first twenty years of the century, they remained in favour throughout the 1800s, flexibly adapting themselves to the different styles of the mounts.

As the Italian campaign brought cameos back into fashion, other landmarks of Napoleonic history had a strong influence on the arts and jewellery. The Egyptian campaign in 1798 introduced motifs inspired by pharaonic Egypt: sphinxes, pyramids, palmettes and papyrus leaves were liberally introduced as elements of design in all sorts of objects, including jewels.

When Prussia rebelled against the Napoleonic occupation, 'Berlin iron' jewels, produced in Berlin from 1804, became the vogue. Between 1813 and 1814 when money was badly needed to equip the Prussian troops, patriotic women were persuaded to give their gold and precious ornaments to the State: in exchange they received iron jewels, often bearing the inscription: 'Gold gab ich für Eisen, 1813' (I gave gold for iron, 1813). Jewels cast in this unusual material assumed very delicate floral or neoclassical openwork forms, lacquered in shiny black (see plate 53). The fashion and the technique of cast iron was not to remain a German monopoly. Soon after the war, jewels in this material were produced in France in fashionable designs of neoclassical inspiration. Gold mesh bracelets with cameo clasps, and necklaces of cameos linked by skeins of chains, were skilfully reproduced in cast iron. Curiously, Berlin iron jewellery remained in favour until the mid-century, adapting its designs to the prevailing taste.

Another sought after but unusual material for jewellery in these first years of the nineteenth century was steel, cut and polished as a precious stone, and widely used to decorate the cheapest range of jewels on the market. The fashion for, and the technique of, cut steel originated in eighteenth century England as a substitute for more expensive diamond jewellery but very quickly spread all over Europe (see plate 43).

Marcasite, a form of iron pyrites, most of which came from Switzerland, was often used as a substitute for diamonds, due to its high metallic lustre.

Sentimental jewellery made its appearance in France as a reaction to the solemn rigidity of neoclassicism, and small circular lockets, pavé-set with pearls or diamonds and with a compartment, mounted asymmetrically, for a lock of the beloved's hair, were quite common (see plate 69). Also popular were jewels made of stones, whose initial letters spelt out names or composed intimate mottoes (see plate 72).

Sentimental and memorial jewellery were particularly favoured in England throughout the nineteenth century, where the rituals of mourning were an important part of social and family life. Very often sentiment and mourning overlapped as, for example, in the case of jewels decorated with a lock of hair, worn either in memory of a deceased relative or as a sentimental reminder of a lover. In the first twenty years of the century, memorial and sentimental jewels very often took the form of rings decorated with a lock of plaited hair protected by a rock crystal cabochon. Brooches to be worn on velvet ribbons round the neck or at the wrists, were also set with locks of hair within pearl, garnet or jet borders. In the strictest period of mourning, only black jewellery, made of jet or Berlin iron was permitted, with some exceptions made for diamonds and pearls.

Diamond jewellery was fashionable in the first two decades, and abundant in England where a wealthy landowning aristocracy was eager to buy precious gemstones. Jewellery design was usually in typical French taste, firstly because London jewellers were always aware of any change in taste dictated by Parisian jewellers, and secondly because large amounts of jewels were brought over from France by the French aristocracy, who had to sell their precious ornaments to survive.

Until the beginning of the nineteenth century gemstones were always mounted in closed settings which did not allow light to pass through the stones from the back. This type of setting had the great advantage of enabling the jewellers to enhance, match and modify the colour of the stones by means of coloured foils placed between the mount and the back of the gems (see plates 40 and 44). On the other hand this technique greatly reduced the brilliancy and the fire of the stones. The jewellers of the turn of the century, realising the importance of light to the brilliancy of diamonds, started to set them in open collets or claws. From then onwards brilliant-cut diamonds were invariably set in open mounts; smaller stones or rose diamonds, and many coloured stones continued to be set in closed mounts for some time. Transitional pieces often have the largest stones in open settings surrounded by smaller stones in closed settings (see plate 51).

Throughout the century, and with very few exceptions, diamond jewels were mounted in a laminate of gold and silver; silver at the front to enhance the whiteness of the stones, and gold at the back to make the jewel more solid and to prevent the staining of skin or clothing.

Tiaras

A typical jewel of the Napoleonic period was the tiara made of diamond-set laurel leaves decorated with ruby berries. Other shapes of tiaras are wreaths of diamond-set leaves; loose openwork designs (see plate 41) — often suspended with pear-shaped pearls and briolettes; pear-shaped drops faceted all over; and those of Hellenistic design, rising in a gabled point above the centre of the brow and sloping towards the sides (see plate 39).

As an alternative to the proper tiara a bandeau of gem-set clusters or cameos could be worn on the forehead, alone or with a matching comb. In addition, diamond rivières (chains of collet-set stones) were worn, skilfully arranged in the coiffure.

Combs

Combs were always present in a parure: worn at the top or at the back of the head, their rectangular surmounts were usually decorated with ribbon, zigzag or arched motifs, often encrusted with pearls and gemstones.

Spanish combs, with metal or tortoiseshell prongs and surmounts set with gemstones or cameos within borders of gold scrollwork, were very common (see plate 42). Another type of comb consisted of a gold filigree gallery surmounted by a row of plain or carved coral or amber beads.

Plate 39. A diadem in gold, enamel, seed pearls and diamonds, c.1800. This is an example of what we would call today a 'Hellenistic' design. The chased oak leaves and trophy at the centre are typical of the 'Empire' style.

Plate 40. A group of three late 18th century diamond jewels. Note the setting viewed from the back, and the fact that the entire mount is in silver. Great care must be taken when dating such pieces; traditional designs like these continued to be manufactured throughout the 19th century in areas of Europe outside the mainsteam of fashion. This is particularly true of the Iberian peninsula.

Parures

Both precious and semiprecious stones were used for parures and demi-parures. Thus complete parures were made in aquamarines, pink and yellow topazes (see plate 45), amethysts, peridots, cornelians, garnets (see plate 44), and even moss or banded agate, for the less well off.

Parisian jewellers often mounted the stones within a very fine cannetille work, imitating a form of lace, enriched with leaves, rosettes and burr motifs. This fashion soon spread to England, where topaz and amethyst became the

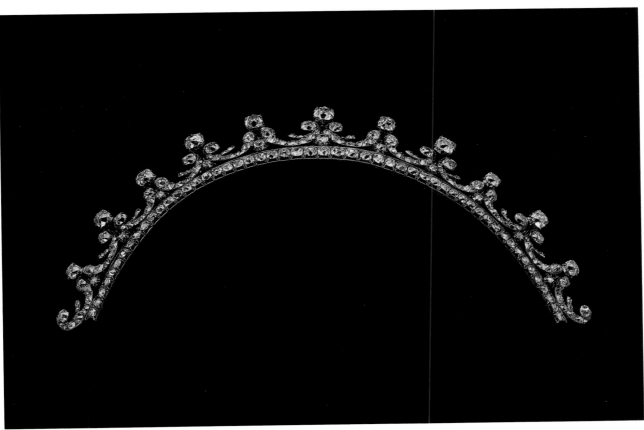

Plate 41. A diamond tiara, probably 1820. Note the very bulky cushion-shaped stones. The mount is gold back, silver front.

Plate 42. A gilt metal and coral diadem, c.1810-20. Originally this may well have been attached to a comb. The milled wire scrolls, the chased rosettes in the frieze, and the punched decoration at the base, are all typical of the date.

Plate 43. A collection of late 18th century/early 19th century cut steel jewellery. Note, on the back of the brooch, how the faceted studs were riveted to the base plate. (see page 57).

Plate 44. A gold and garnet demi-parure, late 18th century. The stones are all in closed settings, with foil enhancing the colour. Suites of this date are extremely rare. Note the archaic rose cutting of the stones.

Plate 45. A topaz and diamond demi-parure, first quarter of the 19th century. Note the flat foliage, the small diamonds surrounding the setting of the topaz and the almost 18th century earring design.

favourite stones, and in both countries the style remained popular until the 1840s.

Between 1805 and 1810 fashion required jewellery to be worn in abundance, and if not the gem-set parures of court and formal occasions, it was a plethora of gold ornaments: several rings worn on each hand, many rows of gold chains around the neck or across the shoulder 'en sautoir', large and long pendant earrings, combs, and many bracelets on each arm.

Plate 46. A pair of garnet earrings, in silver, late 18th century, Spanish or Portuguese. This 'girandole' or chandelier design is typical of the second half of the 18th century, and was revived several times in the 19th century. Closed settings with reflective foil.

Plate 48. A pair of gold, paste and seed pearl pendant earrings, c.1800. The wafer thin gold, tiny seed pearls, and two-dimensional design are typical of the turn of the century. This motif probably originated in France.

Plate 47. A pair of diamond earrings, late 18th century. Typically, the settings are silver. The rose diamonds would seldom have been found in English or French fashionable jewellery after about 1820, though were used, in very small sizes, to highlight mounts and settings throughout the century.

Earrings

Earrings at the time were worn very long, and were usually made of one, two or three flat geometrical elements placed one above the other, often set with cameos. 'Poissarde' earrings were similarly designed and characterised by a loop fitting stretching from top to bottom (see plate 48).

For important occasions the preferred shape was the pear drop that could assume the form of a very elegant and simple pair of pear-shaped pearl drops, or that of a pair of pear-shaped diamonds, simply mounted as drop pendants (see plates 47 and 51).

Plate 49. Silver and paste earrings, 18th century, rare but characteristic. Note the popular opalescent glass.

Plate 50. A pair of gold and hessonite garnet earrings, Catalan, probably early 19th century. This unusual design is only found in north-east Spain, particularly Barcelona. Dating can prove difficult since their production spanned three centuries. Many examples are startlingly long and heavy, requiring unusual mounts to support their weight; these often encircled the ear.

Plate 51. A pair of diamond pendant earrings, c.1800-20. Examples can be found, dating from this transitional period, where the diamonds are either set à jour (with open backs to the mount), or in the older style of closed setting. The latter would be set entirely in silver, the former with gold backs and silver fronts. Sometimes a mixture of both closed and à jour settings is found, as in this case.

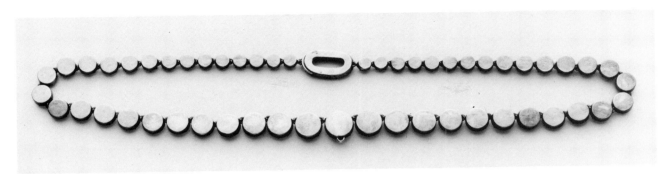

Necklaces

Necklaces took the form of chains of cameos (see plate 54), intaglios, Roman mosaics or gemstones set in light gold mounts within a course of milled gold wire, or tiny seed pearls linked by a skein of delicate gold chains in simple or intricate arrangements.

As already mentioned, long gold chains of small or large links, sometimes set with cameos and often worn en sautoir, were in fashion throughout the century.

On formal occasions diamond rivières (see plates 52 and 55) were often worn in pairs. Diamond set necklaces assumed the form of chains of oval or oblong links, very plain, set with both rose and brilliant-cut stones. Necklaces 'en esclavage' formed of several rows of diamonds of different lengths also made their appearance.

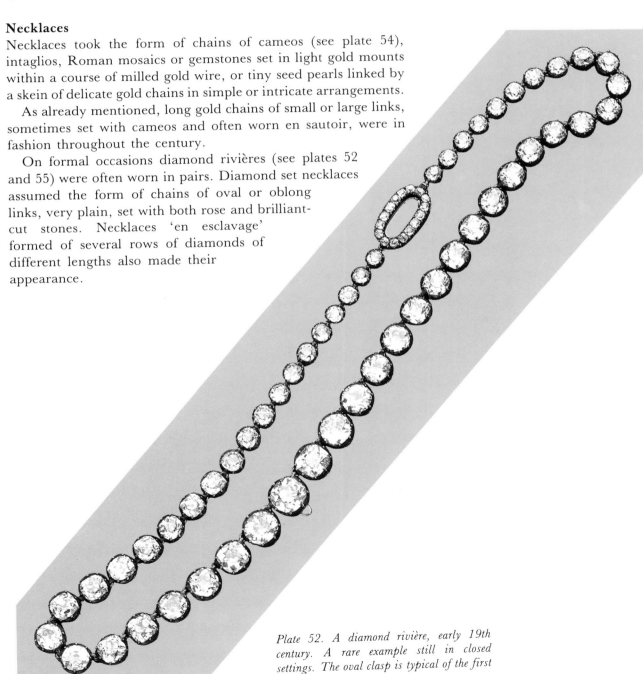

Plate 52. A diamond rivière, early 19th century. A rare example still in closed settings. The oval clasp is typical of the first quarter of the century.

67

Plate 53. Top: A gold and Roman mosaic necklace, early 19th century. Note the small dimensions of the glass tesserae, typical of this early date. Bottom: A Berlin iron necklace. A particularly good example. Note the shiny black lacquer and the fine workmanship of the chain. The cross is decorated at the centre with a heart, a cross and an anchor, symbols of love, faith and hope. Berlin cast iron jewellery, produced in Berlin from 1804, remained popular until the 1840s.(see page 57).

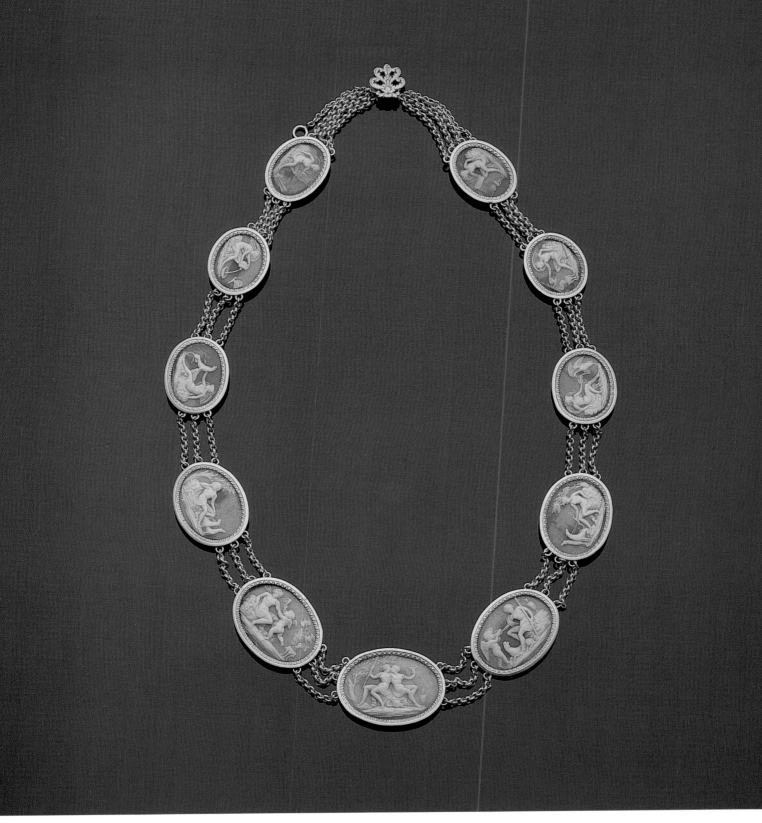

Plate 54. A gold, shell and banded agate cameo necklace, c.1800. Note the chiselled decoration around the edges of the setting, and the slender chain connecting the cameos. The choice of subject matter is typically neoclassical.

Plate 55. An impressive diamond rivière, c.1820, given by George IV to his mistress Elizabeth, Lady Conyngham, who is reputed to have received jewels valued at the time in the region of £80,000. Set à jour in gold and silver.

Plate 56. A diamond star brooch, late 18th century. Mounted entirely in silver in closed settings. Sunbursts, stars and crescents are typical of the late 18th century, and early 19th century, but were revived again in the 1860s and 1890s.

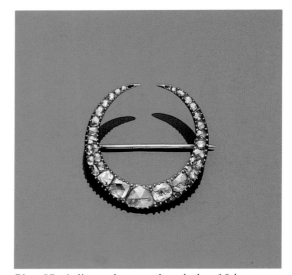

Plate 57. A diamond crescent brooch, late 18th century. Crescent moons are associated with Diana, the goddess of hunting. Note the rudimentary cutting of the stones. Set entirely in silver.

Brooches

Sunbursts, stars and crescents were the most typical shapes of late eighteenth century brooches, and remained in favour throughout the first two decades of the nineteenth century. Frequently mounted with diamonds in closed settings, they are always characterised by a two-dimensional quality (see plates 56 and 57).

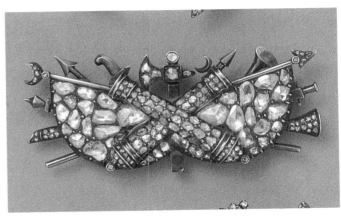

Plate 59. A spectacular diamond trophy-of-arms brooch, c.1800. Probably connected with the Napoleonic war. A rare example.

Plate 58. A citrine and diamond brooch, designed as a trophy, c.1800. Note the slender course of rose diamonds setting the citrine, of unusual colour, possibly a heat-treated amethyst.

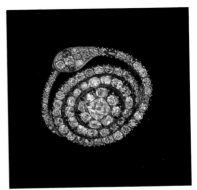

Plate 60. A gold and guilloché enamel brooch, c.1800. Such brooches were often of mourning significance.

Plate 61. A diamond spray brooch, c.1800. Bay or laurel leaves were a popular motif during the Napoleonic period. Note the rudimentary brilliant cutting of the stones.

Plate 62. A diamond snake brooch, first quarter of the 19th century. Snakes re-emerged as a design motif in the 1840s, though they are often used in sentimental jewellery throughout the century.

Sevigné or ribbon bow brooches, a fashionable form of ornament throughout the eighteenth century, continued to be produced in the first quarter of the nineteenth century, mainly set with diamonds and occasionally embellished with coloured stones (see plate 63).

Royal blue enamel plaques of marquise or polygonal shape, set at the centre with a diamond decorative motif — such as an urn, a monogram, or a sprig of flowers — were frequently mounted as brooches within a border of rose or cushion-shaped diamonds (see plate 60).

Possibly connected with the Napoleonic war, were brooches designed as trophies-of-arms, frequently set with rose and cushion-shaped diamonds, and occasionally mounted with coloured stones (see plates 58 and 59).

Simple flowerhead and spiky spray brooches held sway in the late eighteenth century and retained their appeal in the first decades of the 1800s (see plate 66).

The Napoleonic classicism inspired the design of many brooches in the shape of formal sprays of laurel or bay leaves, which lacked the naturalism of the following decades (see plate 61).

Plate 63. A diamond bow or sévigné brooch, late 18th century. The flattened form of this brooch, and the quantity of metal visible on the mount, are characteristic. This is a typical, rather than fine, example.

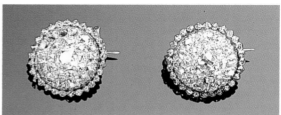

Plate 64. A pair of diamond clusters, c.1800. The brooch fittings are later. Their original purpose may well have been as buttons, either for male or female use.

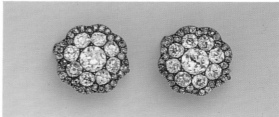

Plate 65. A pair of diamond flowerhead clusters, late 18th century. It is not unusual to see such clusters, which may originally have been buttons, subsequently adapted not only as brooches, but also as rings. This design was also popular in paste.

Plate 66. Two diamond brooches, both late 18th century. The quatrefoil is probably composed of elements from a flowerhead brooch, similar to the accompanying example, or links from a necklace. The backs show clearly the closed silver setting. In both cases, the pin is a later addition; in the case of the quatrefoil, the later gold mount has been used to incorporate the elements. Originally such brooches would have been sewn to the dress.

Plate 67. A diamond Maltese cross pendant, c.1800. The spiky form is reminiscent of 18th century star brooches. The small beads in silver at the ends of the arms are typical of this period, and a useful way of dating.

Plate 68. A diamond Latin cross pendant, c.1800. Typical of the date is the mounting of larger stones within borders of small diamonds.

Plate 70. A diamond lyre pendant, c.1810-20. The lyre is closely associated with neoclassicism. This is a fine example.

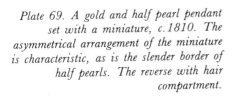

Plate 69. A gold and half pearl pendant set with a miniature, c.1810. The asymmetrical arrangement of the miniature is characteristic, as is the slender border of half pearls. The reverse with hair compartment.

Pendants

Pendants were seldom worn apart from those of cruciform design set with semiprecious stones which very often complemented similarly set necklaces (see plate 68).

Maltese crosses mounted as brooches and pendants were a typically English fashion. The earliest examples, mainly set with diamonds, date from the turn of the century but only in the 1830s and 1840s did the design become widely approved. The late Victorian and Edwardian periods saw another revival of this motif (see plate 67).

Memorial pendants (see plate 69) were often set with a miniature at the front and a lock of hair at the back in a glazed compartment.

Bracelets

In the first years of the century the typical design for bracelets consisted of a wide ribbon of gold mesh with a filigree clasp. Also admired were bracelets made of a line of gemstones, cameos, intaglios or Roman mosaics, linked by a skein of very fine and delicate gold chains, or made of several rows of gold chains of different patterns with a single stone, cameo or intaglio as both centre and clasp (see plate 72).

Diamond and coloured precious stone link bracelets generally assumed very simple geometric designs (see plate 71).

Bracelets were worn in great numbers and not always in pairs following a fashion which remained until 1860.

Plate 71. A diamond bracelet, first quarter of the 19th century. Note the simple geometric design. Most of the diamonds are still in closed settings, which suggests a date before 1820.

Plate 72. A suite of three acrostic bracelets, gold and gem-set, commemorating events in the lives of Marie Louise and Napoleon, one forming the word Napoleon, 15 Aout, 1769 (Napoleon's birthday), another forming the words Marie Louise, 12 Decembre, 1791 (Marie Louise's birthday), and another forming the words 27 Mars 1810 — 2 Avril 1810 (days of their meeting in Compiègne and wedding in Paris). The initial letters of the stones in the bracelets compose the words. These bracelets are extremely rare and are mentioned in H. Vever, La Bijouterie Française au XIXe Siècle, Paris, 1906, page 56, vol.1. as being one of the few jewels commissioned by the Empress.

| Plate 73 | Plate 74 | Plate 75 | Plate 76 |

Plate 77

Rings

The most fashionable ring of the first twenty years of the century was the half-hoop, set with a single or double row of gemstones, the shank made of two or more gold wires soldered side by side and splayed out to form the shoulders, often decorated with a leaf motif. Other rings took the form of flowerhead clusters set with a larger gemstone at the centre (see plate 74) or that of a gem-set navette motif. Small cameos and Roman mosaics were simply collet-set in linear gold mounts (see plates 73, 77, 78 and 79).

Also in fashion were rings mounted with plaques of royal blue enamel, oval or elipse-shaped, decorated at the centre with diamond decorative motifs (see plate 76). Limited by their own shape and function, rings hardly changed their main features throughout the nineteenth century.

Plate 78

Plate 73. A gold and onyx cameo ring, c.1820, signed by Girometti, after the antique. Giuseppe Girometti (1780-1851) was an accomplished gem engraver, medallist and sculptor.

Plate 74. A ruby and diamond ring, and a diamond ring, both c.1800, though the latter could possibly be as late as 1820. The ruby is in the characteristic closed setting of the date, with coloured foil enhancing the colour. Note the rather irregular cut of the diamond and the large culet. The trefoil shoulders are typical.

Plate 75. An enamel and diamond ring, c.1800. Blue guilloché enamel was very popular at this time and was often decorated, like this example, with a diamond monogram. Beware of late 19th/early 20th century jewels which revived this technique.

Plate 76. An enamel and diamond memorial ring, 1790-1820. Many examples are dated and inscribed. Funerary urns were very popular symbols, revived by the 18th century neoclassicists, not only for monumental masonry but also for mourning jewellery. This is a particularly fine example.

Plate 77. A late Roman banded agate cameo of a grotesque mask, mounted as a ring, first quarter of the 19th century. This is a typical example of an ancient gem revived for a neoclassical design.

Plate 79

Plate 78. A banded agate cameo of a gryllus in a simple gold ring mount, c.1800-20. This was a popular subject, no doubt copying an ancient gem. Grylli are grotesque figures of ancient Rome, formed out of portions of several heads united into one. These composite heads, human and bestial in one, often had a mystic or an astrological character, and were believed to exhibit the protective virtues of a talisman (see C.W. King, The Book of Engraved Gems, *London 1866).*

Plate 79. An agate cameo, after the antique, set in a gold ring, c.1800-20. The dished setting, known as 'Roman', was very popular for cameos, particularly in rings.

Plate 80. An important Roman sardonyx cameo, mounted as a pendant, c.1800. The loop is probably later.

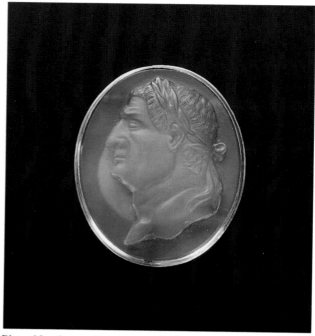

Plate 82. A cornelian cameo of Vespasian, set in gold as a brooch, c.1800. The carving is probably contemporary with the mount.

Plate 81. A paste cameo doublet, c.1810, mounted in gold as a brooch. The side view shows the composition and glue quite clearly. The fashion for cameos made such doublets commercially viable. This example, with its striking colours, could scarcely have been mistaken as a hardstone. However, other doublets are much more difficult to spot.

Plate 83. An unusual hardstone seal, set with diamonds, c.1800. This seal anticipates the 'cameos habillés' of the second half of the 19th century. The seal possibly represents Toussaint L'Ouverture who led the negro revolt against the French in Haiti on 23 August 1791.

Buckles

Buckles were worn at the centre of belts and ribbons that marked the high waistline but sometimes they were used as simple decorative motifs, with no effective practical function. They were usually small in size and oblong, round or oval in shape, often set with pearls, topazes, and amethysts, or simply in gold.

Plate 84. '*Susanna Archer, Countess of Oxford*', *by Sir Thomas Lawrence, c.1790.*
The National Trust for Scotland, Fyvie Castle.

CHAPTER TWO
1820~1840

The year 1820 brought profound changes in fashion and jewellery design. The waistline dropped at last to a more realistic and natural position and it is this year, rather than 1815, which seems to mark the end of the Napoleonic classicism.

The naturalistic style flourished on both sides of the Channel. Leaves and flowers, stylised and subordinated to the general, formal design during the Napoleonic era, began to be more representational. After 1830 it was a triumph of roses, morning glories, fuchsias, cornflowers, ears of wheat and leaves of all varieties (see plates 108, 111 and 112).

The revival of the Marie Antoinette style continued for a few years, supported by the less innovative jewellers who skilfully repeated and reinterpreted, in open settings, typical motifs of the eighteenth century such as elaborate scrollworks and girandoles (see plate 105), and formal clusters within rich foliate scrolls. Very often a transitional compromise between naturalism and formalism is detectable in jewels where stylised flowerheads are associated with rich scroll motifs (see plates 104 and 106).

After the long years of war in Europe, precious metals and stones were relatively rare and highly expensive. In France, the scarcity of diamonds led to the use of large silver collet settings which made the stones look more substantial and reduced the number of diamonds necessary to produce a piece.

All in all, jewels were designed to produce the greatest effect at the least cost and by choice or by force, a large number of semiprecious stones were employed. Amethysts, topazes, aquamarines, chrysoberyls, all mainly of Brazilian origin, were favoured, particularly when mounted in the delicate, and often very elaborate, cannetille work. The gemstones, generally grouped in clusters, were often mounted in closed settings and foiled to enhance and match their colours. The elaborate goldwork, in the form of gold wire, granulation, tendrils, scroll and burr motifs, was sometimes complemented with small leaves and shells, stamped out in differently coloured gold (see plates 89 and 95).

The fashion for cannetille jewellery appeared simultaneously in France and England and enjoyed the peak of its popularity in the 1830s. Filigree work had been known in Europe for centuries, and it is possible that London and Paris jewellers took their inspiration from Portugal, which had a tradition of delicate gold and silver filigree 'peasant' jewellery. In addition gold filigree had been a common goldsmith technique throughout North Africa and along the coast of the Mediterranean, and it may be the case that the newly developed interest and curiosity for popular traditions, and the relative ease of travel, favoured a sophisticated interpretation of the style. By 1840 the delicate and time-consuming processes involved in cannetille had been completely supplanted by gold repoussé work, which since the early 1830s had provided a suitable and relatively inexpensive way of mounting semiprecious stones, aided by the mechanical presses that were developed in England during the Industrial Revolution (see plate 121).

Another characteristic feature of the 1830s was the widespread use of coloured gold in small objects of naturalistic inspiration. A higher percentage of copper in the alloy results in a reddish tone, silver lends a greenish tint. Red, green and yellow gold were combined in a pleasant contrast of matt and shiny surfaces in small brooches, rings and buckles chased with leaf and flower motifs, highlighted with chisel-cut decoration and set with tiny gemstones, commonly turquoises and garnets.

Soon after 1835 a talented Parisian jeweller, Edouard Marchant (circa 1791-1867) started to produce gold ornaments known under the name of 'cuirs' that were to gain great favour. These ornaments, mainly brooches, cameo or enamel frames, or bracelet centres, were made out of a very thin gold leaf, skilfully rolled and cut to resemble leather scrolls and then chased and engraved with various decorative motifs (see plates 113 and 124). By 1840 both Parisian jewellers and their English counterparts were producing cuir roulé jewels in great abundance, especially gold scrolled mounts for shell cameos. At the same time the technique was applied to elaborate ribbon bow motifs employed as brooches or pendant hangers.

During the second quarter of the century enamelling was revived and extensively used in jewellery. Geneva rapidly became the centre of painted enamels. Small copper plaques depicting local landscapes, or young girls in local costumes counter enamelled with the names of the relevant cantons, were produced in great numbers and mounted in bracelets of gold cannetille embellished with tiny coloured gemstones, or mounts stamped out in gold leaves or scrolls, shell or floral openwork design (see plates 107, 119 and 123). Famous works of art were skilfully reproduced in enamel: Renaissance paintings offered a large source of inspiration, and the reproduction of Raphael's 'La Madonna della Seggiola' was a favourite.

At the same time, the technique of champlevé enamel was being revived all over Europe, and the production of beautiful buckles, necklaces and bracelets decorated with polychrome scroll and floral motifs, preferably against black backgrounds, flourished (see plate 88).

Translucent enamelling on guilloché, or engine-turned, backgrounds was another fashionable form of decoration. The favoured colour for the enamel was royal blue, followed by bright leaf green; the geometric patterns, engine-turned on the gold backgrounds, took the forms of spirals or radiating and concentric motifs.

From 1830 onwards, Romanticism and its enthusiasm for anything that could recall the Middle Ages and the Renaissance spread through literature and the plastic and figurative arts, to fashion and decoration. In jewellery it brought with it decorative motifs such as ogives, arches, shields, heraldic figures, saints, angels and putti. By 1840 bracelets and pendants were decorated with gothic architectural motifs or fantastic creatures; longchains and brooches assumed the appearance of miniature medieval sculptures. Froment-Meurice, in Paris, created truly original jewels in the late 1830s and early 1840s, inspired by the Italian and French Renaissance, that were to become models for other jewellers over the next decade. Matt gold and oxidised silver, coral and lapis lazuli were among his favourite materials; his jewels blended architectural and figurative elements and must have created a sensation in their day.

Together with Romanticism, sentiment and symbolism flourished. The Napoleonic taste for the symbolism of gemstones, and for names and mottoes spelt out with the initial letter of appropriate gemstones, quickly spread. In Europe, and especially in England, 'Regard' and 'Dearest' rings and brooches, set with diamonds, rubies, emeralds, garnets, amethysts and sapphires in the correct order were the current fashion (see illustration on page 93). Locks of hair were still concealed in small compartments at the back of jewels. Veiled and unveiled messages of love, rebuses and mottoes, were inscribed at the back of brooches and pendants or inside ring shanks.

The language of flowers was used as a secret code and the flowers that most often appeared in romantic jewels were those able to convey sentiments of love, friendship and affection, such as ivy leaves and forget-me-nots (see plate 98). Combinations of heart, cross and anchor (symbols of love, faith and hope), birds defending their nests from the attack of snakes, or carrying a heart, a branch of olive or a spray of forget-me-nots in their beaks were also common in the early 1830s, and did not lose favour for the next twenty years.

In the early 1820s memorial jewellery added to its repertoire a ring made of a plain band of black enamel within gold borders richly chased with floral motifs. Ten years later forget-me-nots were introduced as a novelty in mourning jewellery, either carved in onyx plaques or set with half pearls against black enamel or onyx backgrounds. Locks of hair set at the centre of circular diamond or pearl pendants, or at the back of gold and gem-set lockets, were a characteristic feature of memorial jewellery of this time (see plates 96 and 98).

Cut steel jewellery remained in favour, and between 1819 and 1830, both in France and in England, complete parures and a variety of accessories and ornaments, were decorated with minute highly polished steel studs.

In 1819 the Duchess of Angoulême may well have been responsible for the revival of coral. Parures of coral, either as beads, in coral branches, or carved, could not be missing from the jewellery casket of the fashion conscious lady for the next three decades.

Plate 85. A.J.B. Hesse. A portrait of a mother and child. Signed and dated 1828. 100cm. x 80cm.

Following the innovations of the early 1820s, when the waistline dropped to just above the hips, Parisian dressmakers in 1829 introduced a further innovation that was to change dramatically the female silhouette: the 'gigot', or leg-of-mutton sleeve, often inflated to enormous dimensions and tapered towards the wrist, gave the upper part of the silhouette a marked triangular shape. The head became the focal point for jewellers, hairdressers and milliners: the hairstyles of the time became an elaborate composition of false locks, real feathers and gem-set aigrettes. Evening gowns were worn very decolleté, leaving ample space for necklaces. Bracelets continued to be worn in great numbers on wrists and forearms, often in pairs, and on the tapered part of the sleeves.

Plate 86. A magnificent diamond tiara or couronne, c.1830. Note the plump proto-naturalistic foliate scrolls and the exceptional size of the piece. The cushion shape of the brilliant-cut stones is clearly visible. Few tiaras of this size and importance have survived.

Hair Ornaments

The elaborate hairstyles of the early 1830s were adorned with a variety of diamond jewels which took the shape of aigrettes, ears of grain or wheat, birds and combs, often combining feathers and false locks of hair (see plate 108). This elaborate and often tasteless style did not last long, and when, between 1835 and 1836, the coiffures became simpler and hair was worn brushed away from the forehead, a new type of hair ornament was introduced: the 'ferronnière'. (This was modelled on the jewel worn by the young lady portrayed in the painting, then attributed to Leonardo, known as 'La belle ferronnière', hence its name.) It was a jewel popular in Italy in the late fifteenth century, consisting of a thin chain worn on the forehead and decorated with a small pendant at the centre. Nineteenth century ferronnières took the shape of delicate chains of small diamond set linking with, at the centre, a small pendant. Few have survived in their original form, and they are now known mostly from paintings and engravings; most ferronnières were altered and transformed into bracelets or necklaces after their short-lived popularity.

Towards the end of the 1830s a new hairstyle was introduced with the hair

Plate 87. A gold and garnet parure, c.1820. The stones are all in closed settings. The flowerhead and leaf motif are typical of this early period. It is not unusual to find an example in its original fitted case. Later garnet jewellery, particularly from Bohemia, intended mainly for tourists, is usually in debased low carat gold, and of lesser workmanship than this early example.

parted at the centre and pulled back in two flat waves framing the face. A new ornament was required to suit this hairstyle: the result was a sort of tiara that encircled the face rather than the crown of the head. Often made of three pieces, it consisted of two lateral, elaborate floral motifs connected by a similar, but lighter, hairband sitting just above the hairline. When not worn as a tiara the three elements could be worn separately as brooches. Extremely successful in design and flattering to the features, this type of tiara remained in vogue for well over a decade.

Parures

Jewellery design between 1820 and 1840 closely followed the evolution of fashion and technical innovations. Gold cannetille parures of the 1820s, set with semiprecious stones and occasionally, especially in England, with rubies

Plate 88. A demi-parure in gold and enamel set with various coloured stones, c.1830, probably North Italian. The stones, which are of poor quality, are mounted in foil-backed settings enhancing their colours. The black champlevé enamel with foliate decoration, often enhanced with white, is typical of Northern Italy.

Plate 89. A gold, ruby and diamond demi-parure, c.1830. The filigree cannetille decoration is absolutely characteristic of the 1830s. Note the chain decoration and the girandole design of the earrings and brooch. The screw-fittings are later, originally simple gold hooks would have been employed. The flat gold leaves are a hangover from the first quarter of the century.

and emeralds, but never sapphires, were garnished with leaves, flowers and scrolls stamped out of variously coloured gold leaf (see plate 89). Almost invariably they include, together with necklace, bracelet and pendant earrings, a cruciform pendant, often adapted as a brooch at a later date. Towards the year 1840 parures of semiprecious stones set in elaborate scrollwork stamped out of gold sheet began to appear. Although manufactured out of thin gauge metal, they have the appearance of great substance.

Roman mosaic parures continued to be fashionable as in the previous decade, but the simple gold mounts were substituted by more elaborate gold cannetille settings (see plate 90).

Plate 90. *A fine gold, Roman mosaic and turquoise parure, c.1820. The gold scrolled tendril motifs anticipate cannetille decoration of the 1830s. These mosaics are unusual in their subject matter which is drawn from the* commedia dell'arte *and peasant costume.*

Earrings

The most popular earrings in the 1820s and '30s were designed as pear-shaped, elongated drops, suspended from a smaller circular surmount set with a single stone or with numerous gems in a cluster arrangement.

Bare shoulders and the hair piled at the top of the head in an elaborate arrangement, favoured earrings of fairly large size.

Necklaces

Rivières were extremely common in the 1820s, set either with diamonds, or semiprecious stones such as topazes, amethysts and citrines, and were often accompanied by a cross pendant and a pair of pear-shaped earrings (see plate 91). The collets were usually very large and chunky, especially in diamond rivières, thereby creating the illusion of bigger stones. Long strings of pearls and gold longchains of flat linking, often of shield shape and engraved, enamelled or gem-set, were also in style.

Plate 91. A gold filigree, turquoise and half-pearl necklace, c.1830. Note how one of the turquoises has decayed and turned green through absorption of oil from the skin. An amethyst rivière, second quarter of the 19th century. This simple design remained popular throughout the century.

Between 1820 and 1830 a large number of garnet necklaces were produced, which took the shape of chains of flowerhead clusters, or garlands of leaves, close-set with circular, pear or marquise-shaped stones, foiled in bright pink to enhance the rather dull brownish red of the garnets. It is not unusual to find these necklaces still in their original boxes, accompanied by matching bracelets, brooches and earrings, often with fittings altered at a later date (see plate 87).

The generous décolletages of 1830s ball and evening gowns encouraged the fashion for large collars worn about the shoulders rather than around the neck, consisting of rich and elaborate arrangements of diamonds and precious coloured stones, or gemstone clusters, connected by chains or festoons of diamonds, often decorated with pearl drops (see plate 92).

Plate 92. A diamond necklace, formed of a pair of bracelets, c.1820-30. Note the cut of the diamonds: the four stones flanking the largest diamond appear to have been recut or replaced, as can be seen from the outline and the larger tables.

In the 1830s longchains were worn in large numbers and in a variety of ways: around the neck, across the shoulders, tucked into the belt or pinned on the corsage to hang in two symmetrical or asymmetrical festoons. The chunky look of many of them should not mislead as they are always very light, being stamped out of thin gold sheet decorated with various minute geometrical patterns on a matt background. The clasps were small masterpieces of goldsmiths' work: generally barrel, or bobbin-shaped and set with minute gemstones.

Elaborate clasps in the shape of a woman's hand are not uncommon and are particularly detailed in the rendering of gloves, cuffs and gem-set rings (see plate 174).

Towards the end of the period snake necklaces appeared for the first time in France, but the craze for serpent jewellery did not spread until the 1840s.

Pendants

Plate 93. A garnet and diamond cross fleury pendant, c.1840.

Pendants were frequently worn at the time on chain necklets, velvet ribbons, or as a compliment to the very popular rivière. The most fashionable shape was that of the cross — Latin, Greek, or Maltese — carved in hardstone and set with gemstones, carved in carbuncle (see plate 93) or set with precious stones, or simply made of gold. The Maltese cross was particularly favoured in England and was very popular set with diamonds (see plate 97) or carved in hardstones such as chalcedony and agate (see plate 94). Gold cannetille and gem-set pendants of Latin cross design (see plate 95) often came *en suite* with similarly set necklaces, pendant earrings and bracelets.

Other favoured types of pendants were variations of the eighteenth century *girandole* or *pendeloque* designs, usually set with precious and semiprecious coloured stones within diamond foliate borders (see plate 99); these pendants often doubled as brooches.

Sentimental and memorial pendants were widely worn in England in the shape of round lockets of gold, enamel and gemstone, often decorated with symbolic motifs such as forget-me-nots and fitted with hair compartments at the back (see plate 98).

Plate 97. A diamond Maltese cross pendant, c.1825. Note the collet-setting of the larger stones. The mount is gold backed, silver front.

Plate 94. A gold cannetille and gem-set brooch/pendant, c.1830. The arms are in carved chalcedony, the centre set with a foiled pink topaz and emeralds. Some of these crosses are still found with their accompanying drop-shaped pendant earrings.

Plate 95. A gold filigree and pink topaz pendant, c.1830. A very good example of cannetille decoration. The heat-treated pink topazes are mounted in foil-backed settings.

Plate 96. A diamond memorial pendant, c.1820-30. The stones are set à jour in open settings, and show rudimentary brilliant-cutting. The colour of the diamonds was not matched due to scarcity of material, which also contributed to the bulky proportions of the stones which were cut for maximum weight retention.

Plate 98. A gold, amethyst, chrysoberyl, and turquoise pendant, c.1825. The forget-me-not at the centre means that the jewel could have been used for sentimental purposes (the reverse has a hair compartment). The filigree burr motifs around the edge give away the date.

Plate 99. A pink topaz and diamond pendant, c.1830. The sprigged foliage around the edges is already beginning to show a lightness that anticipates the mid-century. Note how the drop-shaped topaz shows signs of incipient cleavage. Both topazes have been heat treated to produce the colour.

Brooches

In the 1830s the most acceptable type of brooch was a spray of flowers and leaves, either pavé-set with diamonds or, more economically but equally effectively, with various semiprecious stones in coloured chased gold (see plates 110-112). Around 1835 chased gold was substituted with repoussé work of leaves and flowers surrounding coloured stones.

The naturalism and romanticism of the period produced attractive bird brooches, in coloured gold set with precious and semiprecious stones, and with hearts, olive branches or forget-me-nots suspended from the birds' beaks.

Plate 101. A diamond feather brooch, c.1820. The plump volutes forming the feathers are a characteristic feature of many jewels of the period. The larger diamonds were probably from India (at the time Brazil was the only other source).

Plate 102. A diamond brooch, c.1820. Possibly originally a belt clasp. These designs are often called 'Brandebourg'. Comparison with plate 101 will prove useful for dating such brooches.

The penchant for enamel brought in the fashion for oval plaques enamelled after famous Renaissance paintings, mounted within gold 'cuir roulé' frames. Maltese cross pendants, often provided with brooch fittings, were very popular either set with diamonds or carved in chalcedony or cornelian and decorated at the centre with gold filigree and gem-set floral motifs. Frequently the cheaper hardstone versions came *en suite* with pendant earrings of elongated pear-shaped design (see plates 94 and 97).

Cartouche-shaped 'Regard' brooches set with a row of coloured gemstones at the centre were a favourite gift of the mid-1830s.

Parures de corsage comprising three brooches of similar floral design set with diamonds, and worn one above the other in a vertical arrangement, were also fashionable.

Very fashionable in the 1830s were fairly large brooches designed as

Plate 100. Sir William
Beechey, c.1830-7. Adelaide,
Queen Consort of William IV
(1792-1849). The fashion
for longchains, made from
plaited or woven gold wire as
well as linked chain, dates
from the early 1820s.

elaborate cartouches of foliate scrolls set with diamonds and occasionally enhanced with coloured stones. In addition they often supported three pear-shaped drops *en girandole*, in the eighteenth century tradition (see plates 104-106). Less expensive examples were made of repoussé gold and semiprecious gemstones (see plate 114).

Simpler but equally successful brooches of the 1830s were set at the centre with a large coloured stone within an oblong or rectangular diamond border (see plates 109 and 115).

Plate 103. A magnificent emerald and diamond brooch, c.1825, formerly the property of the Duke of Northumberland. The round emerald shows fine Mughal carving of the early 1600s, and may well have been brought back from India by Robert Clive (1725-1774). The present setting is by Rundell, Bridge and Rundell, Crown Jewellers extensively employed by the 3rd Duke of Northumberland in 1824-6 and 1828-9. It may well be the one described in an account rendered by the firm on 17th March 1829: 'Setting a large engraved emerald with Her Grace's brilliants in a sévigné brooch and furnishing two brilliants — £80'. It is interesting to note that though the emerald came from India, its origins are almost certainly Colombian.

Plate 104. A diamond stomacher brooch, c.1830-40. Note the interlacing of the foliate scrolls. This example had been rhodium plated in the 1930s to imitate platinum. This was popular at the time and detracts from the value of the piece.

Plate 105. A diamond stomacher brooch, c.1830. The use here of large rose diamonds is archaic. The three drops 'en girandole' are typical of the 1830s but rarely seen, since they have often subsequently been adapted as earrings.

Plate 106. An odontolite, turquoise and diamond brooch, c.1840. This is the only example we have seen using odontolite, a form of mammoth ivory. It could easily be confused with turquoise, and the jeweller may well have done so when mounting the brooch. Spotting the difference may well enhance the value of the jewel.

Plate 107. A Geneva enamel brooch set with turquoises, c.1830. The florid plump scrolls are typical. The enlargement shows clearly the damage to the enamel, a damage which is extremely difficult if not impossible to repair. In any case the value of the brooch would not justify the expense. Beware of any enamel damage in jewellery. Lacquer repairs should be spotted under a magnifying glass and tested with the point of a pin (lacquer is softer than enamel). The back of the brooch shows scratch marks where the gold has been tested. Note that the pin has been replaced. The overall condition of this brooch would render it difficult to sell.

A gold and gem-set regard brooch, c.1825. 'Regard' is spelled out by a Ruby, an Emerald, a Garnet, an Amethyst, a Ruby and a Diamond.

Plate 108. A collection of diamond brooches and hair ornaments dating from the late Georgian period.

Plate 109. A pink spinel and diamond brooch, c.1825-30. The delicate 'rinceau' scrolls surrounding the spinel impart lightness to the design and balance the bulk of the diamonds. Note the spinel is set in yellow gold, the diamonds in silver, to enhance the colour.

Plate 110. An enamel and diamond bow brooch, c.1840. Note the guilloché enamel. The working of the gold beneath the enamel is clearly seen in the area of the damage.

Plate 111. A diamond spray brooch, c.1830-40. The leaves and formal design of the flowerhead suggest a somewhat earlier date, even though the bloom is mounted 'en tremblant'. Note how the stones are pavé-set in the leaves in random sizes; at the end of the century, when diamonds were more plentiful, the stones were graded to fit the mount.

Plate 112. A diamond brooch designed as a spray of oak leaves, c.1830. Note the naturalistic approach to the treatment of the leaves which date it to the second quarter of the century. Earlier sprays would have been more rigid and formal.

Plate 113. An unusual brooch commemorating the abolition of slavery in Great Britain and the colonies in 1833-4. The three-dimensional treatment of the subject, enhanced by the applied gold chains, is found in memorial rings and brooches from the latter part of the 18th century. In these latter, often the entire subject is formed from minute pieces of hair. Note the cuir roulé mount.

Plate 114. A gold and amethyst brooch, c.1840. Perhaps transitional from cannetille to repoussé scrolls. The festooned chains are typical.

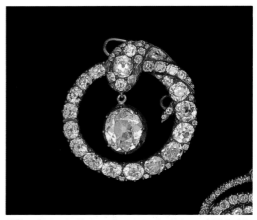

Plate 115. A sapphire and diamond brooch/bracelet centre, c.1840. The slender course of rose diamonds, enclosing the stone, which is cut en cabochon, is often found in jewellery from Russia at this time.

Plate 116. A diamond serpent brooch, c.1820-40. The small diamond points in between the larger stones are typical. Note the cabochon ruby eyes.

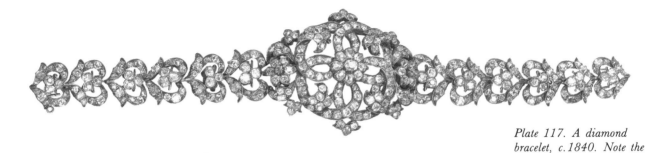

Plate 117. A diamond bracelet, c.1840. Note the repetition of the heart-shaped links and the bulky cartouche-shaped centre.

Bracelets

Bracelets were commonly worn on each arm, even two or three pairs at the same time, throughout the period.

In the early 1820s, bracelets 'à la Jeannette' appeared, consisting of a silk ribbon with a gold clasp.

In the late 1820s and 1830s bracelets made of wide bands of woven linking, decorated with gold cannetille clasps of oval or rectangular shape and set with coloured gemstones, were in vogue.

The 1830s saw the fashion for enamel bracelets; Geneva enamel plaques depicting girls in regional costumes were set in wide articulated bands of gold scroll, foliate and floral design encrusted with small gemstones (see plates 119 and 123). Gold bracelets of large, foliate scroll links, often decorated with

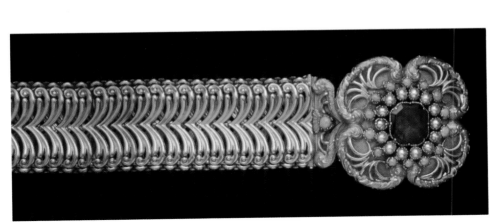

Plate 118. A gold and gem-set bracelet, c.1825. The chromatic combination of turquoise, pearl and garnet was popular in the 1820s and '30s. The contrast in matt and shiny gold places this bracelet in the '20s rather than in the '30s. Note the repetitive scrolled links in the chain.

Plate 119. A gold, enamel and gem-set bracelet, Swiss, c.1830. A rather elaborate example of cantonal bracelets of the 1830s. The arms of each canton are displayed beneath.

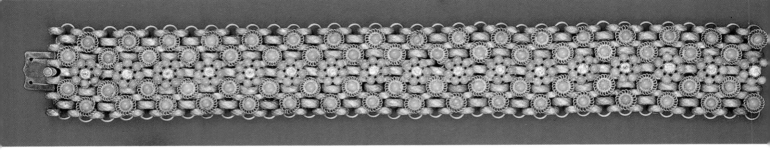

Plate 120. A gold, turquoise and diamond bracelet, c.1830. The turquoise and diamond clusters may well represent forget-me-nots and hence have sentimental or mourning significance.

Plate 122. A gold cannetille, ruby, emerald and half-pearl bracelet. Note the woven chain back which is typical of the 1830s. Seldom now found as one of a pair.

Plate 124. A gold, half pearl and emerald bangle, c.1840, probably French. Inscribed and dated 1841. Note the cuir roulé decoration on the shoulders.

Plate 121. A gold and peridot bracelet, c.1835-40. Peridots were much favoured at this time, and the finest examples came from the Island of St. John in the Red Sea. The elements of the repoussé scrolls were probably stamped out by machine and then assembled.

polychrome champlevé enamels were equally favoured (see plate 121).

Towards the end of the period bracelets designed as wide flat ribbons decorated with blue guilloché enamel, fastened by pearl or garnet clasps, were in demand.

Diamond and coloured precious stone bracelets of the 1830s were frequently set with a central — often detachable — cartouche-shaped motif of foliate scroll design, on a band of scrolled S, or heart-shaped linking (see plates 117 and 126).

Plate 123. A gold, enamel and gem-set bracelet, Swiss, c.1830. These bracelets are uncommon after around 1840. The Geneva enamels of young ladies in regional costume bear the name of the relevant canton on the back in counter enamel, usually in speckled greyish blue.

Plate 125. A gold and Roman mosaic bracelet, c.1830. Glass micro mosaics were being produced in large quantities in Rome after around 1820 to satisfy the demands of the rapidly expanding tourist market. Most examples, like these, were of 'Vedute di Roma'. By the end of the century, the quality had deteriorated and coarser filaments of glass were employed. Note the brown spangled aventurine glass frames.

Plate 126. A rare hessonite garnet and diamond bracelet, c.1840. The luscious orange-brown of hessonite garnet was much admired at this time and enhances the voluptuous diamond-set scrolls.

Plate 127. A gold and hessonite garnet bracelet, c.1830. Note the beaded decoration to the mounts.

Plate 128. A gold cannetille, enamel and diamond ring, c.1830. The stones are in closed settings.

Plate 129. A sapphire and diamond cluster ring, c.1820-30. The sapphire, unusually for this date, is in an open setting, probably because of the high quality of the stone. Note the chased shoulders.

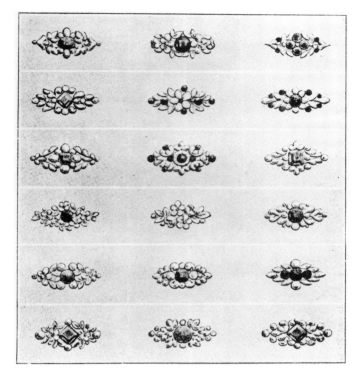

Designs for cluster rings, c.1820. From H. Vever, La Bijouterie Française au XIX Siècle, Paris, 1906.

Rings

Rings continued to be designed as flowerhead clusters set with coloured gemstones within gold cannetille and granulation, or as five stone half hoops (see plates 128 and 129).

In the 1830s the half-hoop 'Regard' ring was the prevailing fashion.

Buckles

The 1830s required narrow waistlines, squeezed into wide material belts. Large buckles of upright oval or oblong design were widely produced in base metal and cut steel, or in gold, often decorated with champlevé enamel.

Designs for buckles, c.1830. From H. Vever, La Bijouterie Française au XIX Siècle, Paris, 1908.

Tiepins

Another jewel particularly favoured by gentlemen of the period was the tie, or stickpin, which often assumed curious and eccentric forms. Among the most stylish motifs were animals' heads, snakes and birds. Almost all materials were employed: enamel, onyx, turquoise, cornelian, diamond and many other gemstomes variously combined with chased gold in naturalistic designs.

Design for a tiepin, the head decorated with a snake poised above a nest, c.1830. From H. Vever, La Bijouterie Française au XIX Siècle, *Paris, 1908. Snakes were to become one of the favourite motifs for jewellery design of the next two decades.*

Plate 130. A three-coloured gold and gem-set vinaigrette/ seal, c.1825-30. The charming and unusual subject makes this a very collectable object. The base of the basket is set with a seal stone which is hinged to reveal a vinaigrette.

Seals

Seals were highly regarded by fashionable gentlemen of the 1820s and '30s. The earliest examples are rather linear in design, with a domed setting and a simple surmount: a lyre, a stirrup, a scroll, or a baluster. Seals of the 1830s are more elaborate, the surmounts usually chased with floral motifs often in variously coloured gold, or carved with fanciful designs such as dogs, birds, stags' heads, etc. (see plate 130).

Generally the family crest or coat of arms was engraved in bloodstone, cornelian, citrine quartz, amethyst, smoky quartz or chalcedony; occasionally examples engraved in more precious stones such as sapphire are seen.

The best seals were worked in 22ct. gold and set with precious stones; the cheapest were worked in base metal, slightly gilded, and set with variously coloured pastes where the crest or coat of arms was substituted by a motto. The middle and most diffuse range was set with quartzes, cornelians or bloodstones in chased gold mounts.

Swivel seals were also popular in the 1830s; commonly they consist of a three-sided prism, carved in semiprecious stones and engraved with different motifs on each side, pinned horizontally and free to swivel in a chased stirrup-shaped surmount.

'Mme. Moitessier', by Ingres, 1856. National Gallery, London.

CHAPTER THREE
1840~1860

The new wealth acquired by the middle classes around the middle of the century and the easier supply of precious metal guaranteed by the discovery of gold in California and Australia, had a positive influence on the jewellery industry, which flourished in the second half of the century.

In England Queen Victoria became an important influence on fashion. Her jewels in particular were carefully copied by the Court and the rest of society. Jewels were worn in great abundance, and intimate jewels of sentiment were in great favour.

In France, Louis Napoleon gave to social life a new interest in luxury after the moderate reign of Louis Philippe. In 1851, in an attempt to galvanise French commerce and industry, he sponsored the participation of French firms in the great Exhibition at the Crystal Palace in London. Jewellery was well represented, the French exhibitors triumphed and were compensated for their efforts by receiving numerous commissions. Lemonnier, Louis Philippe's favourite jeweller, excelled with two parures made for the Queen of Spain in which the naturalistic inspiration was combined with a well balanced structural design. Lemonnier was praised for his fine taste and in particular his conception of the 'ensemble'. He shared his London success with Dafrique, Rouvenat, Marrel, Rudolphi and Froment-Meurice.

In the 1840s, the world of nature, the Renaissance and the Middle Ages continued to provide sources of inspiration. The influence of the medieval designs by Froment-Meurice (1802-1855), spread to England where Robert Phillips (1810-1881) was among the first to produce jewels which shared the same inspiration. Fantasy and originality were the characteristics of these ornaments in which human figures, angels, and heraldic and architectural motifs, were freely incorporated within elaborate foliage and strapwork frames (see plate 166).

Naturalism flourished in jewellery, assuming the forms of very realistic bouquets of flowers, branches, leaves, tendrils, bunches of grapes and clusters of berries. This interest in naturalism, stimulated by the romantic movement, spread to plant collecting and led to the introduction to Europe of new exotic species. Flower symbolism, very strong in the early nineteenth century, was still popular and only diminished in the second half of the century.

In the 1840s diamond-set bouquets of flowers, worn as brooches or hair ornaments, were decorated with cascades of diamond drops suggesting rainfall or seeds falling from the flowerheads. This decoration, known as 'en pampille', remained in fashion until the mid-1850s (see plate 144). Around the middle of the century, royal blue guilloché enamel and bright green enamel on engine turned and chisel-cut backgrounds were closely associated with diamond jewellery of naturalistic inspiration (see plate 151). Very often diamond spray brooches of this period were mounted 'en tremblant', with flowerheads set on watch springs, free to quiver when the piece moved.

At the Paris Exhibition of 1855 Mellerio, Rouvenat and other Parisian jewellers offered splendid garlands and bouquets of flowers set with diamonds and embellished with blue and green enamel.

Among all decorative motifs, snakes seem to have been the most favoured in early Victorian England. Although serpents had been used for rings and bracelets since antiquity, and continued to be in fashion throughout the nineteenth century, it was in the 1840s that they reached the peak of their popularity. The serpent as a decorative motif has a profound mythological significance: in its symbolism connected with wisdom and eternity, in its ancestral power, and simply in its mysterious fascination, which was given an extra frisson by the revulsion for reptiles (see plates 140, 141, 167-171).

Another characteristic jewel of the time was the 'croix-à-la Jeanette'; in its simplest form it assumed the shape of a Latin cross pendant suspended from a heart-shaped motif. Its origins are to be found in French peasant jewellery. Paris and London jewellers adapted this design to the taste of their sophisticated clientele without altering its basic form, and produced a great number of such pendants carved in carbuncle or enamelled in turquoise or royal blue, often decorated with small diamond flowerheads or foliate motifs. It seems that the name of this jewel derives from the tradition in the French provinces to buy and give such pendants on St. John's Day.

The French occupation of Algeria (1830-1847) and the consequent importation to Europe of kaftans, burnouses and all sorts of accessories of Moorish origin, was to set a new trend in fashion. European jewels never copied those of the Middle East, but the knots, ribbons, and twisted cords, the festoons and tassels of North African costumes, were skilfully reproduced in gold and successfully translated into brooches, earrings, and bracelet centres. In the 1850s intricate interlacements of gold ribbons set with coloured gemstones, or enamelled in royal blue and decorated with diamond sprays, were the current motifs for London and Paris jewellers alike (see plates 145 and 146). Cheaper examples were produced in gilt metal set with coloured glass pastes.

In Paris, Edouard Marchand (c.1809-c.1876) introduced the Algerian knot motif in the early 1840s; the fashion lasted at least a decade and was revived in the late 1850s, when the final campaign in Algeria renewed the interest in Middle Eastern motifs.

Another source of inspiration for jewellery and all the applied arts came from Assyria. The publication in 1848 of Sir Austen Henry Layard's *Nineveh and its*

Remains may have been responsible for promoting interest in the design of the treasures found during the excavations of the city, and soon jewels based on Assyrian patterns were produced. Among all Assyrian motifs the Victorians preferred the lotus flower and it was to remain in jewellery design for a long time. This passion for Assyrian jewels foreshadowed that for archaeological jewellery in the early 1860s.

Apart from diamonds, the favourite stones of this period were carbuncles and turquoises. Carbuncles were set among diamond foliage or gold scrollwork to suggest, with their deep, rich colour, a fruit or a berry (see plates 147, 157 and 173). Turquoises, frequently associated with snake jewellery (see plate 140), were also pavé-set on floral brooches, heart-shaped pendants and lockets.

Towards the mid-century cameos were back in fashion; larger and bolder than Napoleonic examples, they were usually carved in very high relief in stones such as onyx, stained chalcedony and amethyst, displaying a strong contrast of two colours with dramatic effect. The Italians were still mastering the art and the works of the Saulinis of Rome best exemplify this new trend.

Shell cameos, too, were larger in size, now carved out of shells imported from the tropical seas of Africa and the West Indies. Greek mythology provided the subjects: Ares, Minerva, Diana, Dionysus, Zeus, Medusa, Heracles, Demeter. From the mid-nineteenth century onwards, female subjects were preferred to male portraits, perhaps as a consequence of the more important role acquired by women in society (see plate 155).

From the 1840s Italy excelled in the production of cameos 'habillés', which consisted of shell carvings where the subject, usually a female figure, was adorned with gem-set jewels and clad in dresses of inlaid hardstone. This technique was pioneered in France by Dafrique who became famous for his 'cameés animés', in particular for his hardstone cameos of negro girls clad in ruby and rose diamond jewels; these were to become popular in the second half of the century (see plate 238).

Coral was particularly in favour between 1845 and 1865, and worn in all possible forms: either carved as beads or naturalistic sprays of leaves and flowers, or left simply in its natural branch form. Coral cameos were also popular. Most coral on the market was carved in Italy, especially in Genoa and Naples (see plate 134 and 137), and the most popular colours were dark red and pale pink.

Seed pearl jewellery was greatly admired in the 1840s and early 1850s. The base or framework of these jewels was carved out of sheets of mother-of-pearl, pierced in open scrolls, flowers and foliate motifs. The tiny seed pearls, chiefly from Madras and China, were sewn to this base with horsehair. Very fragile and delicate, these jewels are seldom found in perfect condition and their repair is difficult, time consuming and usually quite expensive (see plate 135).

Unusual materials were introduced in jewellery by the Victorian interest in novelty and nature. Bog oak, horn, fossile ammonite, petrified wood, granite, opercula (see plate 153), marble and 'Blue John', suitably carved and polished, were mounted as bracelets and brooches. Scottish jewellery of silver set with citrines and agates was highly fashionable, encouraged by Queen Victoria's love for Scotland.

Travelling was becoming much easier and many families began to spend their holidays abroad. Italy was one of the favourite destinations, and Italian jewellers began to produce large quantities of reasonably priced jewels which could be bought as souvenirs. Roman and Florentine mosaics (see plate 175), the former in glass, the latter inlaid with hardstones, left Italy in large quantities together with cameos carved in hardstone, shell, and the lava of Vesuvius. Lava cameos, carved with female profiles, were usually mounted in simple gold or gilt frames and chained together to make bracelets and necklaces. Despite the dullness of the colours (grey, brown, white, green), lava jewels do not lack charm and fascination. Northern Italian or Swiss enamel plaques were frequently mounted as brooches, bracelet centres, or necklace links (see plates 136 and 148).

Around 1840 the practice of 'colouring' gold became fashionable in England. The technique consisted of steeping the piece of jewellery in an acid solution which dissolved the superficial layer of the alloying metal, left on the surface a very thin layer of warm coloured yellow gold and imparted to the piece a soft and pleasing matt aspect.

By the 1840s the manufacture of medium and low priced gold jewellery was essentially mechanical. Birmingham became the major centre, not only of machine-made gold ornaments, set with semiprecious stones, but also gilt metal costume jewellery set with coloured pastes (see plate 149). The invention of electroplating speeded up the gilding process and greatly reduced the cost. Most jewels were produced on the hand press, stamped out of a gold sheet using a vertical screw. Smaller numbers of ornaments were made by the 'deadweight kick stamp' method, that employed a falling weight to punch the metal sheet into the outline of the die. It is important to remember that these machines were entirely man operated. Steam and gas engines were not widely introduced into goldsmiths' workshops until the early 1860s.

In 1854 the use of 9, 12 and 15 carat gold was made legal. A great deal of low carat gold jewellery was then produced at prices often low enough to compete with similar examples in gilt metal.

Jewellery of mourning and sentiment flourished: the finest hair brooches ever produced were made in the 1840s and 1850s in England, by professionals as well as by Victorian ladies, who turned hair-working into a pastime. Apart from basket weave patterns, the favourite subjects were Prince of Wales feathers and landscapes with mourning ladies, weeping willows, and departing ships. The Crimean war and the Indian Mutiny were to be responsible for many women wearing such jewels of remembrance.

Jet jewellery continued to be the most popular form of ornament during the strictest period of mourning, either in the shape of highly polished faceted bead necklaces, or in the form of chains of variously carved links. A black glass

Plate 131. Ferdinand Georg Waldmüller (Austrian 1793-1865). A Portrait of a Young Girl in a Pink Dress, c.1830. 66cm. x 53.5cm.

imitation of jet jewellery was traded under the deceptive name of 'French jet'. Black glass is easily distinguishable from jet, the former being much heavier and colder to the touch than the latter. Vulcanite, an early form of rubber, was later employed.

The fashion of the late 1840s and early 1850s demanded very narrow waists, ample skirts, tight bodices and very generous décolletages in the evenings. The bust became the focal point for jewellery: large brooches and imposing corsage ornaments were produced in abundance and were often worn in combination with fresh flowers. The hair was worn parted at the centre and divided into two bandeaux which completely covered the ears, therefore, for about a decade, earrings were seldom worn. At the Great Exhibition at the Crystal Palace in 1851, where jewellery was very well represented, earrings had no prominent position.

Plate 132. A diamond tiara, mid-19th century, of leaf and berry design.

Tiaras and Hair Ornaments

The tiara, which appeared in the late 1830s, made of three sprays of flowers encircling the face rather than the head, continued in favour (see plate 133). Towards the middle of the century, the two lateral sprays began to be decorated 'en pampille' with cascades of diamonds imitating falling rain, dew drops, or seeds falling from flowerheads. Other tiaras took the form of wreaths of roses, berries, or ears of wheat (see plate 132).

In the 1840s, when the Middle Ages and the Renaissance were the main sources of inspiration, tiaras of architectural gothic design were produced in gold and gemstones. In the 1850s tiaras made entirely of branch coral were extremely fashionable. Towards the end of the period circlets of diamond-set stars appeared for the first time. Women decorated their coiffures, either with purpose-made ornaments such as pins and aigrettes, or other jewels they could find in their jewel boxes, such as brooches, necklaces or rows of pearls. Aigrettes and hairpins were decorated with flowers, leaves, berries and grapes; stars and arrows, set with pearls, diamonds and coloured stones, were also esteemed.

Plate 133. A diamond hair ornament. The naturalistic design is typical of the mid-19th century. The ornament can form three brooches (tiaras that can only function as tiaras were extremely rare at this time). Note the lumpy cut of the stones, which may well have been reused from an earlier jewel.

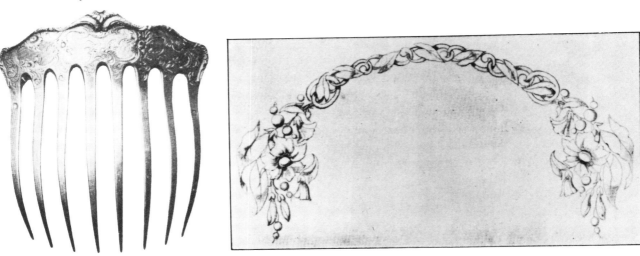

A comb of upright design, c.1840, and a design for a hair ornament, c.1845. From H. Vever,
La Bijouterie Française au XIX Siècle, *Paris, 1908.*

Combs

Combs, fashionable in the 1840s when the hair was worn gathered in chignons at the back of the head, were rather narrow but high, preferably decorated with coral beads or cameos, pearls and diamonds.

Plate 134. A suite of carved coral, mid-19th century, probably Neapolitan. This colour of coral was much favoured and plentiful at the time in the Bay of Naples and surrounding seas. Nowadays coral is very rare in the Mediterranean due to pollution and over exploitation.

Parures

The most characteristic parures of the middle of the century were: of coral carved in naturalistic shapes (see plate 134); set with branch coral; formed of coral cameos; in seed pearls set in floral designs (see plate 135); in gold scrollwork set with semiprecious stones and often embellished with enamel plaques (see plate 136), diamonds and coloured stones, especially rubies; embellished with lava cameos; set with mosaics, both Roman and Florentine; or simply in carved ivory.

Less formal demi-parures were also in demand in the 1840s and 1850s. Generally made of gold repoussé work set with semiprecious gemstones, they combined two or three of the different ornaments of a parure: necklace and earrings, brooch and earrings, necklace and brooch, etc.

Plate 135. A seed pearl parure, c.1850, in its
original case (shown reduced). This example
is in generally good condition, which is
important since repairs are expensive. Note
the pair of bracelets, the long pendant
earrings and the floral design. These suites
are seldom if ever faked. The bottom illustration
shows clearly the complicated manufacture
incorporating horsehair and mother-of-pearl.

Plate 136. A gold, enamel and gem-set parure, Swiss or North Italian, c.1840. Note the stamped-out scrolls, the florid enamel and the use of turquoises. The small, enamelled plaques are also typical with their sweetly sentimental subjects.

Plate 137. A collection of coral jewellery dating from the mid-1800s, showing the various ways in which coral was used.

Earrings

Almost no earrings were worn in the 1840s as the hair completely covered the ears, those few which were worn were usually long (see plate 135). They gradually regained favour in the 1850s when the hair started to be brushed away from the ears, but their size remained comparatively small.

Creole earrings, designed as crescentic hoops, were typical of the early 1850s, but flattened hoops, small spheres, or elongated beads were the most usual forms together with small clusters of leaves chased in gold and set with a gemstone as a bud or berry (see plate 138). Coral hoops and carved coral flowers were frequently worn as pendant earrings (see plate 134). More expensive diamond earrings were usually of conventional floral design.

Necklaces

Necklaces were usually short and worn around the neck rather than around the shoulders, and of floral design (see plate 143). The typical necklace of the 1840s was designed as a snake with the body of gold scale-like linking, the head enamelled in royal blue and decorated with diamond flame motifs and the eyes set with cabochon rubies. Less expensive examples had the body of gold scale linking, studded with turquoises, and the head entirely pavé-set with turquoises and with ruby and diamond eyes. Other examples had the body of gold scale-like linking, and the head set with various coloured gemstones. Often very naturalistic in design, these serpents were usually decorated with a heart-shaped pendant or locket suspended from the jaw (see plates 140 and 141).

Other necklaces assumed the form of gem-set clusters connected by pearl or gold chains, or chains supporting several drop-shaped pendants set with coloured stones within rich foliate borders.

One design consisted of a chain of gold linking joined at the centre by a cartouche-shaped gem-set motif with the two loose ends of the chain hanging beneath it or festooned around it (see plate 139).

Chains of coral and lava cameos were in fashion as were coral bead necklaces and strings of pearls. Rivières of coloured gemstones in simple gold collets with a cross pendant at the front continued to be produced as in the earlier period,

Plate 139. A gold and carbuncle necklace, c.1850-5. Almandine garnets cut en cabochon (carbuncles) were extremely fashionable in the mid-century. This necklace is composed of cuir roulé scrolls. The tassels show the contemporary influence of North African decorative motifs.

with amethyst as a particular favourite.

Velvet or silk ribbons were worn around the neck, crossed on the throat and fastened with a jewelled slide or button. Gold chains were worn throughout the period, either to support a watch, or alone, often decorated with gold and gem-set clasps designed as gloved hands (see plate 174).

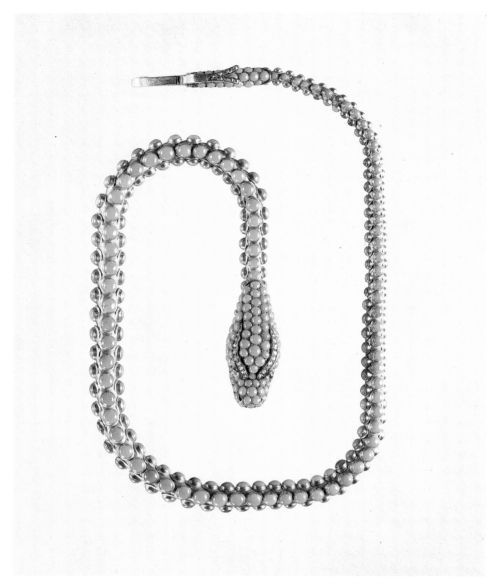

Plate 140. A gold, turquoise, ruby and diamond necklace, c.1845. A good example of a popular design. Towards the bottom of the illustration some of the turquoises have turned green due to oil from the skin. These necklaces have increased rapidly in value in the last few years.

Plate 141 (opposite). Two examples of snake necklaces of the 1840s where the body is scale-like linking, the heads gem-set. Snake necklaces of this quality are widely available although repairs to the linking can be expensive.

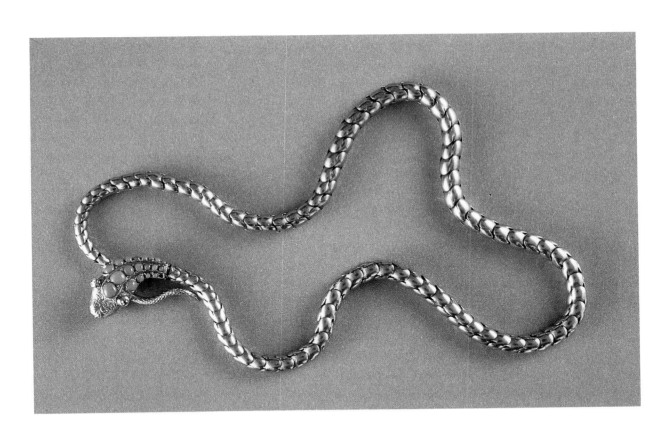

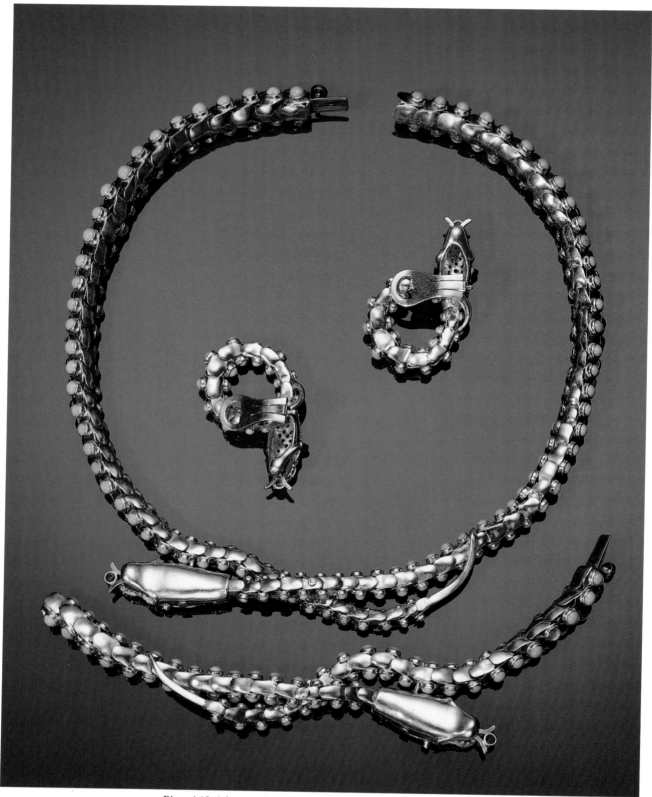

Plate 142 (above and facing page, top). Modern copies of snake jewellery, similar to the necklace of plate 140. Comparison of the illustrations will show the roughness of the collets in the later example. The earlier example would have been set all over with turquoises. The earring fittings are obviously post-war.

Plate 143. A necklace of cinquefoil flowerheads, mid-19th century. The rose diamonds at intervals are unusual.

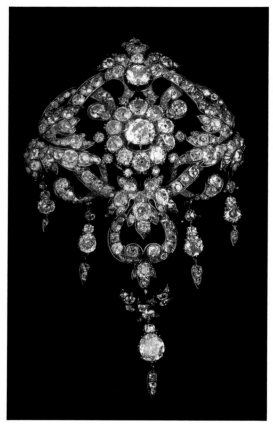

Plate 145. An enamel and diamond brooch, c.1850. The design incorporating a scrolled ribbon and ring motif has been embellished with the typical blue enamel and sprigged diamond foliage. A fine example.

Plate 144. A diamond corsage ornament, c.1850-5. The design is a mixture of North African knot motifs and naturalistic leaves and flowers with drops 'en pampille'.

Plate 146. A gold, enamel, pearl and diamond brooch, c.1850. A similar but cheaper design than plate 145. Here the ribbons have been engraved rather than enamelled.

Brooches

Brooches tended to be large and of oval, oblong or lozenge shape. The design was usually developed along the horizontal axis and often included one, two or three pendants or tassels (see plates 144 and 154). In many cases brooches were fitted with a loop so that they could be worn as pendants as well. In the late 1850s brooches became smaller.

Diamond spray brooches and large corsage ornaments designed as bouquets of flowers, were in vogue in the 1840s and 1850s. They were often embellished with green enamel leaves (see plates 147 and 151), the flowerhead mounted en tremblant, or with cascades of diamonds or pearls 'en pampille'. Cheaper brooches of naturalistic inspiration were made of gold leaves and branches entwined about a gemstone.

Plate 147. A carbuncle (almandine garnet), enamel and diamond corsage ornament, c.1850. The green enamel, more often associated with French jewellery, is unusual in English jewellery at this time. This lush, rich and almost exotic combination of stones and enamel must have suited mid-Victorian taste very well.

Typical of the 1840s and early 1850s were brooches of Algerian design, made of knots, straps, scrolled ribbons, tassels, and cords of gold encircling semiprecious stones such as amethysts, aquamarines and garnets (see plate 149).

Among the fashionable decorative motifs for brooches produced around the middle of the century were enamelled, coiled serpents (see plate 149), leaves and flowers (see plate 150), and bows or knots set with turquoises and diamonds (see plate 146). Royal blue enamel rings or ribbon bows, applied or entwined with diamond foliage (see plate 145), and gold loops or ribbons applied with filigree work and set with garnets, were the most prized designs for brooches of the 1850s.

Brooches in less expensive materials took the forms of shields, garters and crosses set with Scotch pebbles, or carved in ivory, coral or bog oak. Cameos, mosaics and Geneva enamel plaques were frequently mounted as brooches within scrolled leaf frames (see plates 148 and 152).

Plate 148. Two Geneva enamel brooches, by Mercier, of the same subject 'Les violettes', c.1850. The black and white illustration shows that they are both signed on the back in the counter enamel. Both frames are typical in their naturalistic decoration; ivy leaves were particularly popular at this time. These frames were also mass produced in gilt metal.

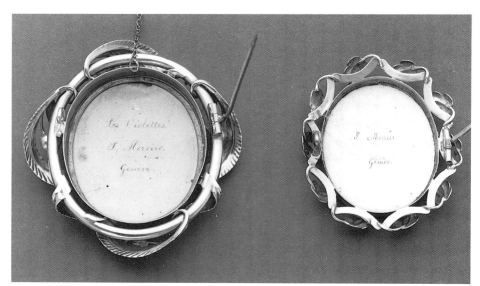

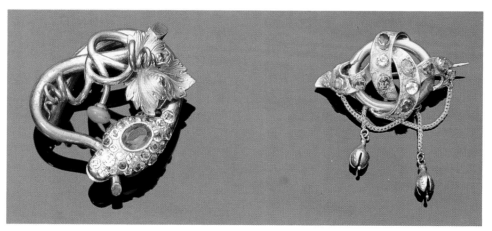

Plate 149. Two gilt metal and paste brooches, typical of the mid-19th century. Both examples show how cleverly such brooches masquerade as the real thing.

Plate 150. A pink pearl and diamond brooch designed as a spray of rose buds, c.1850. Pink conch pearls are rare and can easily be mistaken for coral, although they are more valuable. They seem to have been something of a novelty in the mid-19th century, and are often seen mounted as tiepins.

Plate 151. An enamel and diamond brooch designed as a spray of convolvulus, c.1850, probably French. Spray brooches are seldom more life-like than at this time.

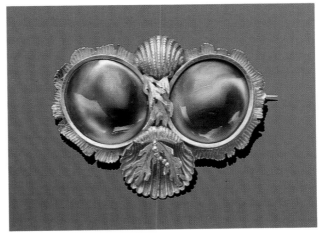

Plate 152. A gold brooch set with a painted Geneva enamel plaque, c.1850. Note the ivy leaves embellishing the frame, and the typical sentimental subject matter.

Plate 153. An unusual gold and operculum brooch, mid-19th century. Opercula (or shell cat's eye) are the 'doors' to the shells of certain molluscs, notably the sea snail Turbo Petholatus. These snails occur in large numbers in the seas of the Far East and were used locally in jewellery. Victorians considered them as a novelty, yet they are rare in jewellery. The design of this brooch cleverly alludes to the origin of the material with its seaweed and shell decoration.

Plate 155. A gold and shell cameo brooch, c.1850-60. The subject matter is typical of the period, and the high quality of the carving is similar to the work of the Saulini family.

Plate 154. A gold, emerald and diamond brooch, c.1845. Note the lozenge-shaped scrolled surmount and pear-shaped drop.

Plate 158. A blue enamel, pearl and diamond locket and chain, mid-19th century. Note the guilloché decoration beneath the enamel, the baton-shaped links and the applied diamond flower, possibly a forget-me-not, for sentiment.

Plate 156. An enamel and diamond pendant, mid-19th century. The sweetly sentimental subject is echoed in the greeting cards of the date.

Plate 157. A carbuncle (almandine garnet) and diamond pendant, designed as a cluster of berries, c.1850.

Pendants

In the 1840s the favourite pendant was the croix-à-la-Jeannette, designed as a cross, sometimes entwined with a serpent, suspended from a heart, simply made of gold, or enamelled and set with pearls, turquoises, rubies or other gems. Particularly attractive are those carved in garnet and decorated with diamonds.

Maltese crosses decorated with blue enamel or set with diamonds were also worn in the 1840s.

Lockets, round and rather small in the 1840s and oval and larger in the 1850s were frequently worn either on chain necklaces or velvet ribbons; they usually opened to reveal a lock of hair and an inscription. The front was chased in gold or enamelled and gemset with insects or floral motifs.

Carbuncle and diamond pendants of naturalistic inspiration were also in favour. Lockets and pendants of sentimental inspiration often took the shape of enamelled and gem-set hearts (see plate 158).

Bracelets

Bracelets were the most acceptable ornament of the Romantic period and were worn in large numbers on each arm, often, but not necessarily, in pairs. During the day they were worn on the wrist and at night on the short white evening gloves or on the bare skin between the glove and the elbow. In the 1840s they were sometimes the only form of ornament.

The typical bracelet of the 1840s was designed as a serpent coiled around the wrist. Cheaper versions were made of gold scale-like linking, sometimes set with turquoises, the clasp, in the shape of the snake's head, enamelled or gem-set. The most expensive examples were made of hinged segments enamelled in royal blue and sprung so that they could be worn without a clasp. The head and the joints were usually set with diamonds, occasionally with Hungarian opals, and the eyes were invariably set with cabochon rubies or garnets. Other hinged examples were entirely pavé-set with turquoises (see plates 167-171).

Between 1840 and 1860 bracelets of velvet, silk ribbon, embroidery, bead work, plaited hair or woven gold were usually adorned with an ornamental clasp. These clasps assumed the form of miniatures or cameos in gold, pearl or diamond frames, of large stones within ornamental borders of foliage, strapwork or scrollwork, or simply of square gold buckles.

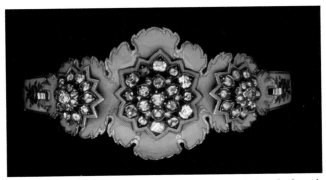

Plate 159. A gold, blue enamel and diamond bangle bracelet, c.1855. The central motif can be detached and worn as a brooch. The star-like flowerhead motif anticipates the 1860s.

Bracelets of sentimental inspiration, consisting of a row of portrait miniatures were not uncommon (see plate 162).

In the early 1840s the expanding bracelet made its appearance. In its simplest form it consisted of a row of gold links connected by strands of elastic, suitably threaded through pierced holes; more sophisticated examples consisted of a chain of gold and gem-set hinged and sprung links (see plate 170). Expanding bracelets were warmly welcomed as they could be worn on

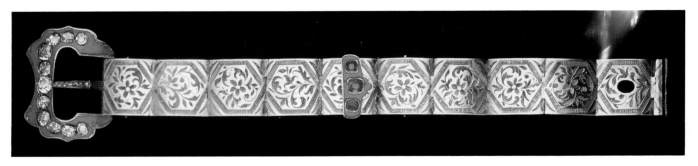

Plate 160. A gold, blue enamel, ruby and diamond jarretière (garter) bracelet, c.1855. The naturalistic decoration is somehow reminiscent of traditional enamelled jewellery from Jaipur, India, and may well have been copied from jewels brought back during the time of the British Raj.

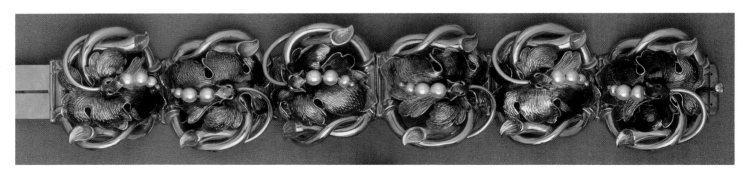

Plate 161. A gold, pearl, and polychrome enamel bracelet, designed as a fruiting vine, c.1850-5. Although this is an English example, enamelled bracelets of naturalistic design originated in France in the mid-century. This is a particularly rich example, still in good condition; the enamel on bracelets is very susceptible to damage during wear.

any size of wrist and anywhere on the arm.

Another arm ornament typical of the 1840s, destined to maintain its appeal for some time, was the 'jarretière' bracelet. This bracelet, or garter, consisted of a gold ribbon or band fastened with a large buckle or slide, gem-set or enamelled (see plate 160). The loose end of the strap was often decorated with a gold and gem-set fringe motif.

A novelty of the 1850s was the manchette bracelet, designed as a wide stylised gold cuff, decorated with gemstones and enamel.

Around 1850 gold bracelets of flexible linking were often adorned with a detachable gem-set pendant of scrollwork or floral design which hung from the centre. Other bracelets of the mid-nineteenth century were made of gold scrollwork linking with a central gem-set cartouche (see plate 165), or as wide gold ribbons with Algerian knot motifs at the centre.

The mid-nineteenth century liking for carbuncles (almandine garnets), inspired the design of attractive bracelets set with large segments of carved garnet, often decorated with gold or diamond scrollwork (see plate 172).

Bangles assumed the form of wide or narrow bands decorated at the centre

Plate 162. A gold bracelet, set with portrait miniatures, the reverse with locks of hair in glazed compartments, c.1850. Before photography (which was still in its infancy at this time) enabled people to record individuals and places at little cost, miniatures like this were the only alternative.

Plate 163. A gold, enamel, pearl and diamond bracelet, c.1850. Articulated bracelets were composed of hinged sections, in this example decorated with enamel and then applied with diamond foliage. The suggestion of a ribbon bow transfixed by a ring and pin is particularly successful (see also a companion brooch in plate 145).

Plate 164. A gold, enamel, emerald and diamond bracelet, c.1850. The front is designed as a trophy of love, comprising Cupid's bow and quiver, and a delicately enamelled heart. The complex design of the scrolled ribbon is typical of the period (see also plate 163).

Plate 165. A gold, ruby and peridot bracelet, the flat engraving of the links is typical. The chromatic combination of ruby, peridot and gold is courageous, and ultimately successful.

Plate 166. A gold, silver, enamel, seed pearl and carbuncle (almandine garnet) bangle, French, by Froment-Meurice, c.1850-5. The two carved silver figures represent Painting and Sculpture. This is an absolutely typical example of the high quality of workmanship associated with this maker.

Plate 167. A gold, enamel and diamond serpent bracelet, c.1845, a typical example hinged in four places and decorated with royal blue guilloché enamel. It is rare for these bracelets to have survived undamaged. Usually the enamel is chipped and the springs are worn. Repairs, where possible, can be extremely costly, and unless carried out by a craftsman will greatly reduce the value. Note the ubiquitous ruby eye.

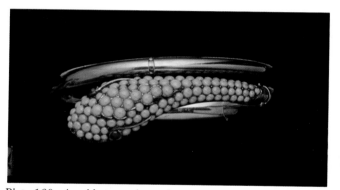

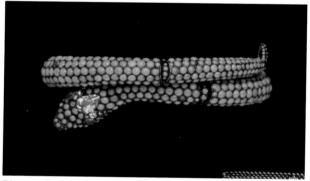

Plate 168. A gold, turquoise and garnet serpent bracelet, c.1845, the body hinged and sprung. This is a less important example than that in plate 167, but shows that the design was so popular that models were produced to suit all pockets; even the eyes were set with garnets rather than rubies.

Plate 169. A gold, turquoise and diamond serpent bracelet, c.1845. This is a good quality example; note how the inner sleeve of the hinge is also set with turquoise, as is the entire body of the reptile.

Plate 170. An unusual gold and turquoise expanding bracelet, dated 1841, the sides and back are hinged and sprung as shown in the detail; this is a variation of the popular snake motif (see plate 169). Expanding bracelets appeared around 1840.

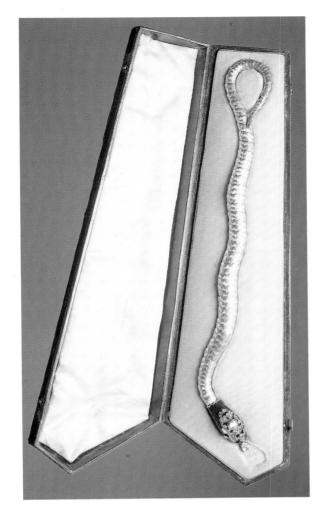

Plate 171 (left and above). A gold, enamel and diamond snake bracelet, c.1840. This example has an ingenious concealed clasp. It is rare to find examples still with their characteristic coffin-shaped case. The pear-shaped diamond suspended from its jaws is obviously a later replacement as a larger enamelled and gem-set drop is more common.

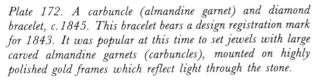

Plate 172. A carbuncle (almandine garnet) and diamond bracelet, c.1845. This bracelet bears a design registration mark for 1843. It was popular at this time to set jewels with large carved almandine garnets (carbuncles), mounted on highly polished gold frames which reflect light through the stone.

with gem-set clusters, especially garnets, turquoise and pearls, or ribbons and knots of Algerian inspiration (see plates 163 and 164).

In the 1840s the Froment-Meurice gothic style influenced the design of numerous bracelets which assumed the shape of bands of ogive-shaped links decorated with knights, angels, and heraldic motifs (see plate 166).

Diamond bracelets decorated with pearls and enamel were simpler and more conventional in design with bands of circular, scroll or S-shaped linking, perhaps set at the centre with a more elaborate motif.

Enamel and gem-set bracelets of naturalistic inspiration, designed as rows of flowerhead clusters, berries or fruiting vines, or set at the centre with a larger floral motif, were also in demand around the middle of the century (see plates 159 and 161).

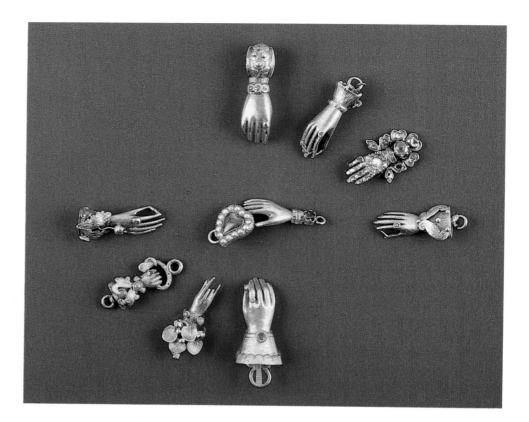

Plate 174. A collection of gold and gem-set necklace clasps designed as gloved hands, c.1840. The details of jewelled rings and bracelets are charming. These clasps are often associated with gold longchains and seem to have been popular between 1830 and 1840.

Plate 175. A collection of Roman mosaic plaques, mostly mid-19th century. The illustration shows the range of subject matter commonly encountered in jewellery. Often the only way of dating these plaques is by the piece of jewellery in which they are set since mosaics with similar subject matter are still produced in Rome today.

Plate 176. *A diverse collection of gold, enamel and gem-set heart-shaped padlock clasp/pendants. This was an enduring motif throughout the 19th century, and this collection dates from between 1835 and 1855.*

Rings

The fashion for snake jewellery also influenced ring design in the form of gold serpents coiled around the finger, and decorated with gem-set eyes. The Middle Ages and the Renaissance inspired gold rings chiselled in high relief with figurative motifs. Half hoop rings continued to be widely produced, set with rubies, sapphires, emeralds, coral and diamonds. The favourite engagement ring of the 1850s was a half-pearl half-hoop ring. Cluster rings often assumed very naturalistic forms (see plate 173), particularly flowerheads. In the 1850s rings of romantic inspiration appeared, carved in coral in the shape of hands or flowers. Towards 1860 the ring designed as a gold strap and buckle made its appearance. Mourning rings were made of gold bands encircled by a plait of hair or decorated with black enamel.

Plate 173. *A carbuncle (almandine garnet) and diamond ring, designed as a berry, mid-19th century.*

Plate 177. 'Leonora di Mantua', by V.C. Prinsep. National Museums and Galleries on
Merseyside.

CHAPTER FOUR
1860~1880

The decades between 1860 and 1880 saw the peak of eccentricity in fashion. Skirts, supported by enormous crinolines, expanded to impractical dimensions, but the bust, in contrast, was tightly laced into uncomfortable corsets; the décolletages of ball dresses were generous. The hair was worn brushed away from the ears, gathered at the back of the head in cascades of curls or in elaborate chignons. Jewels were worn in abundance and earrings were particularly favoured. The jewellery trade flourished in both France and England.

France was once more ruled by an emperor. Eugènie, the wife of the new Napoleon, influenced tastes both in fashion and jewellery; in particular she admired the eighteenth century fashions and made Marie Antoinette her model. She supported the revival of eighteenth century crinolines and had part of the crown jewels remounted in Louis XVI style by Bapst. Her favourite stones were emeralds, which were soon to became the most sought after gemstone in France after diamonds.

The Second Empire in France brought a revival of Napoleonic designs and motifs. Tiaras of elaborate scrollwork suspended with diamond, pearl and emerald drops, and cameo jewellery, returned on a large scale. Cameo carving and gem engraving continued to be an Italian speciality in spite of the competition of German lapidaries from Idar Oberstein. The favoured material was agate, in most cases artificially stained by a process known for centuries: the stone was placed in a sugar solution which was absorbed by its porous layers, then subsequently fired so as to burn the sugar, staining black or dark brown the impregnated layers. The decorative motif was then carved in the white unporous part of the stone, against a dark background. Metallic salts were used to impart artificially the colours of cornelian, chrysoprase and the like (see plates 237, 239, 240 and 241).

The eighteenth century was not the only revival of the time. The jewellers of the 1850s had already revived interest in the Middle Ages and the Renaissance, and continued to work in these styles for two decades or more. In the early 1860s, this eclecticism was further complicated by a new wave of Greek and Etruscan classicism. The pioneer of the classical revival, in Greek and Etruscan style, was Fortunato Pio Castellani (1794-1865). It is known that the early production of his Rome workshop was in the contemporary English and French taste, but there is no means of identifying it, since it was conventional and unmarked.

Castellani, fascinated by the jewels of the antique, produced jewels in Greek and Etruscan style in collaboration with two of his sons, Alessandro (1823-1883) and Augusto (1829-1914). By the end of the 1850s the Castellani workshop in Rome had become an attraction for English visitors, producing splendid gold jewellery, making use of decorative motifs drawn from the classical repertoire such as shells, rosettes, urns, amphorae, rams' heads and the like. The Castellanis approached antiquity with a new open-mindedness; until then, jewellers seemed to believe that there was nothing to be learned from the techniques of antiquity, and only looked to the past for a source of inspiration for design. The Castellanis, however, studied the goldsmith techniques of the past, and concentrated on the difficult task of rediscovering the secret of Etruscan granulation. They achieved remarkable results, perhaps with a method similar, but not entirely identical, to that used by the ancients. Etruscan granulation consisted of covering a gold surface with minute gold spheres, so small that they gave the impression that the slightest blow would dissipate them. The difficulty arose not in the manufacture of such spherules but in soldering them to the gold surface without deforming their shape. In 1870 Alfredo Castellani claimed to have unveiled the Etruscan secret by studying the technique used by the goldsmiths of a remote village in the Appennines. If ever Castellani actually discovered the secret of Etruscan granulation, for obvious reasons he never revealed the processes involved. It is more likely that he worked with a technique very similar but not identical to that used by the Etruscans, which allowed him to achieve good results, but not the delicate and light effect of the original. It is now generally believed that the technique used by the Etruscans is one called 'colloidal hard soldering', described by H.A.P. Littledale in the early 1930s. This technique consists of applying the gold spherules to a gold surface by means of an organic glue in which a salt of copper has been dissolved. The piece is then placed in a reducing heat that melts away the glue and releases the copper which amalgamates with the surface of the gold thus effecting the soldering.

Castellani's replicas and creations were based on original pieces such as those that came to light when the Regolini Galassi tomb was opened in Cerveteri in 1836, and those found in the excavations of Vulci, Chiusi, Orvieto and Tarquinia. The contemporary discoveries of Melos, Rhodes and Knossos also played a fundamental role. In addition, the Castellanis always had free access to the famous Campana collection which included, among other works of art, hundreds of Greek, Etruscan and Roman jewels of very high quality: necklaces, diadems, fibulae, pendant earrings, rings and bracelets often decorated with fine granulation and filigree (see plates 179, 218, 263, 277, 278, 280 and 288).

The Castellanis, linked to the Cavalier Campana by close bonds of friendship, helped and directed him in the formation of his collection. They also restored and reproduced every piece of goldsmith work in the collection for documentary purposes. Therefore, there was no better placed firm than the Castellani's to produce commercial reworkings of the Campana jewels.

The bulla, a lentil-shaped ornament, worn by young Etruscans as an amulet, was transformed into a pendant for women (see plate 220). Fibulae, bracelets and fringed necklaces in Greek style, were admired by fashionable women and encouraged interest in the accurate and skilful works of the Castellanis. Their repertoire included Roman mosaic brooches of Byzantine inspiration with religious Greek and Latin inscriptions (see plates 219 and 221), mounted scarabs (see plate 288), and diadems of oak and laurel leaves (see plate 179).

The Castellanis almost invariably marked their pieces with a monogram of two entwined C's soldered to the jewel. Three types of Castellani marks are known: in the first, the monogram is set at the centre of a cartouche-shaped motif; the second mark consists of the simple monogram; the third and rarest mark consists of the monogram ACC and is possibly associated uniquely with the work of Alessandro Castellani (see plates 219 and 223).

The enthusiasm for antiquarian jewels characterised Italian, French, and English production for two decades. It was only in the 1880s that their appeal began to decline.

Among the other Italians who worked in the archaeological style, Melillo is worthy of mention. Giacinto Melillo (1846-1915) managed the Castellani workshop in Naples until 1870 when Alessandro Castellani returned to Rome, from which city he had been exiled for political reasons since 1859. His jewels had much in common with those produced by Castellani, being inspired by the same Campana collection examples and by jewels discovered during excavations at Pompeii and Herculaneum. Melillo signed some of his pieces with the monogram GM, but the greater part of his work is not signed at all. His production in the archaeological style continued well into the twentieth century (see plates 324 and 418).

Ernesto Pierret (1824-1870), of French origin, settled in Rome in 1857 and worked in the Castellani style, though in a less derivative manner. He frequently used mosaics, intaglios and ancient coins in his creations (see plate 279), and also signed his pieces, either with his name in full or, less frequently, with an elaborate monogram EP within a shield.

Two other names to be remembered are Antonio Carli (1830-1870) who produced jewels of Castellani taste from 1857 in Rome, and Antonio Civilotti (1798-1870) who also was active in Rome in the 1860s.

For some very intricate political reasons, the Cavalier Campana, accused of maladministration, was imprisoned in 1859 and his entire possessions confiscated. The collection, which was put on the market and bought, in 1860, by Napoleon III, immediately aroused great enthusiasm. Well before its official exhibition opened in 1862 at the Louvre, jewels of neo-Greek influence began to appear on the market.

Eugène Fontenay (1823-1887), fascinated by this collection and anxious to

A Carlo Giuliano mark on a piece retailed by Hunt and Roskell.(see page 138).

Carlo Giuliano marks on bracelet clasps.

Carlo Giuliano marks on the backs of pendants.

emulate Castellani, carefully studied the Campana originals and those of other private collections. He avoided simple imitation and soon became the creator of new and ingenious compositions of excellent style and taste, with jewels that were fine, delicate and original.

In London, where Castellani exhibited his archaeological style jewels in 1862, the prominent jewellers working in the classical taste were Robert Phillips (1810-1881) (see plate 208), and John Brogden (active between 1842 and 1885).

Greek and Etruscan art influenced jewellery production not only in shape and design, but also in goldsmith techniques. Engraving and chasing disappeared in favour of contrasts between shiny and matt surfaces, encrusted with filigree and granulation.

The fashion for setting coins in jewels was revived by the interest in ornaments of archaeological style. Between 1860 and 1870 Castellani and Pierret in Rome and Naples, and Jules Wièse in Paris, produced brooches, necklaces and bracelets set with Greek and Roman coins, usually of very common types and of small numismatic value, in simple gold mounts (see plates 223 and 224).

In Paris, from as early as the 1840s, Renaissance and gothic styles had inspired famous jewellers such as Frédéric Philippi and Froment-Meurice (see plate 262), but only with Carlo Giuliano, in the early 1860s, did the style reach its zenith.

It seems probable that the Neapolitan Carlo Giuliano (c.1831-1895) was trained in Rome, possibly in the Castellani workshop where he produced jewels in archaeological style. In about 1860 he came to London and opened a workshop in Frith Street, where he produced jewels for firms such as Hunt and Roskell, Robert Phillips and C.F. Hancock who retailed jewels bearing Giuliano marks in their own stamped cases. Sometimes such jewels bear the retailer's mark in addition to the maker's mark C.G. (see plate above left). His jewels proved to be a success, and in 1874 Giuliano was able to open his own shop at 115 Piccadilly where, after his death, his two sons Carlo Joseph and Arthur, continued to trade until 1912 when the shop moved to Knightsbridge, and closed at the outbreak of the First World War.

Often sensitive to the revival of classical antiquity, Carlo Guiliano excelled in the production of jewels designed in neo-Renaissance style (see plates 248 and 283). He studied the style of the 'Cinquecento' and adapted it to suit the fashions of his day with sure and unfailing taste. Only occasionally did he produce copies of Renaissance jewels. He soon became famous for his lozenge-shaped pendants, pierced in foliate and scroll designs, delicately enamelled and set with pearls and gemstones (see plates 244, 245 and 247), for his line bracelets (see plate 284), and for his necklaces of several rows of seed pearls supporting delicate pendants (see plate 245).

Giuliano eliminated colour almost completely from his compositions, covering the surface of his jewels with white and blue or black piqué enamel

A gold, pearl, enamel and diamond brooch, c.1880, designed as a caduceus, bearing a fake Carlo Giuliano mark. The mark has been placed in a characteristic Giuliano position, by the hinge. The quality of the brooch is high but compare the mark with the originals above.

A gold, enamel and emerald brooch, c.1870, bearing a fake Carlo Giuliano mark. The quality of the enamel is very poor as is the setting of the stones.

(see plate 281). He always preferred the softness of cabochon stones to the brightness of faceted gems (see plate 282). As time progressed, and the fashion for Renaissance jewels diminished, his work relied less on that period, but never lost altogether its overall Renaissance inspiration. His jewels were held in high esteem well into the earliest years of the twentieth century (see plate 321).

Carlo Joseph and Arthur Giuliano worked very much in the style of their father, possibly with a more delicate touch and with a new interest in pastel colours and naturalism (see plates 319, 322, 325, 411 and 425). Giuliano was also sensitive to the fascination for Egypt and from the mid-1860s to the mid-1880s he produced enamelled brooches set with faience scarabs and parures of pharaonic inspiration (see plate 187). A few of the later pieces by Carlo and Arthur Giuliano were influenced by art nouveau in the choice of the colour for gemstones and enamels (see plate 322), but the new artistic movement was never really embraced by the Giulianos.

Like Castellani, the Giulianos usually signed their pieces. The earliest pieces

*Carlo and Arthur Giuliano
mark on a bracelet clasp.*

*Carlo and Arthur Giuliano
mark on a pendant loop.*

by Carlo Giuliano, in archaeological style, were often marked with a monogram C.G. very similar to the entwined C's of Castellani. From 1863, Giuliano jewels were almost always signed with a C.G. monogram in an oval (see page 136). After the death of their father in 1896, Carlo Joseph and Arthur entered a new mark consisting of the monogram C. & A.G. in an oval; this mark remained in use until the closure of the business (see left).

Both Castellani and Giuliano are the subject of an excellent work by Geoffrey C. Munn, *Castellani and Giuliano, Revivalist Jewellers of the Nineteenth Century,* 1983.

Among London jewellers who between 1860 and 1880 worked in neo-Renaissance style, were John Brogden (working 1842-1885), Robert Phillips, Ernesto Rinzi (1836-1909) and the firm of Child & Child.

One of the most acceptable neo-Renaissance jewels of the 1870s in England was the Holbeinesque pendant set with an oval gemstone at the centre, preferably a carbuncle, within a polychrome champlevé enamel border, often decorated with diamonds or chrysoberyls, and with a lozenge-shaped drop (see plate 250).

In France, Renaissance revival took the form of griffins and fabulous animals, chased in gold and silver, often decorated with polychrome enamels (see plate 251). Lucien Falize (1838-1897), the Fannières brothers (Auguste, 1819-1901 and Joseph, 1820-1997), and Jules Wièse (1818-1890), worked in this style.

The cheapest range of Renaissance style jewellery was produced in Austria. Viennese jewels, in enamelled gilt metal set with semiprecious gemstones or glass pastes, are very common, of rough design and rudimentary technique. Usually cast rather than chased, they were only retouched with the chisel, and the enamel was often substituted, in the cheapest examples, with a coloured varnish (see plate 209). Among the favourite subjects were St. George and the Dragon.

In Ireland, revivalism took the form of penannular brooches inspired by Iron Age prototypes. In Scotland, jewels were made of inlaid local 'pebbles', usually jasper. In Scandinavia the ancient Viking jewels were revived and massive gold brooches and bracelets of Nordic inspiration produced, decorated with fabulous animals and runic inscriptions.

At the 1867 Universal Exhibition in Paris, jewels were very well represented. Together with ornaments in archaeological, Renaissance, and Louis XVI revival style, a large number of jewels of naturalistic inspiration were exhibited. The novelty, however, consisted of jewels of Egyptian taste. The revival of the Egyptian style was partly due to the interest aroused by the work on the Suez Canal which was quickly approaching completion. The other element which played an important role in the promotion of Egyptian art and of the Egyptian revival, was the publication of Auguste Mariette's papers on his excavations in the Nile Valley, which provided a rich source of new ideas for decorative motifs. Froment-Meurice, Mellerio and Boucheron in Paris, who were particularly sensitive to the influence of pharaonic Egypt, produced a wide range of jewels where the favourite decorative motifs were falcons, winged scarabs and papyri in opaque green, red and blue enamels. Faience and hardstone scarabs, sometimes antique but more often replicas, were used in bracelets or as brooch centres. Giuliano, himself a collector of scarabs, particularly liked to set them at the centre of gold brooches (see plates 187, 188, 217 and 268).

John Brogden and Robert Phillips also worked in this style. Occasionally, Egyptian revival jewels were made from Roman mosaics of coarse but brightly coloured tessarae, that gave the surface a rather rough appearance. The dramatic effect was achieved through the chromatic contrast between dense and opaque white backgrounds, and bright and brilliant blue, red and turquoise decorative motifs, such as sphinxes, papyri, scarabs and geometric patterns (see plate 264).

Naturalism reached its peak under the influence of Oscar Massin (b.1829, retired 1892), who refined the techniques of 'tremblant' and 'pampille' decoration to such a degree that they were to become models for jewellers throughout Europe (see plate 229). His compositions of rounded flowers and spiky leaves and vice versa, of the 1850s, developed into more naturalistic and botanically accurate arrangements, where the shape and structure of leaves and flowers was successfully combined with ribbon bows, feathers, ears of wheat and rainfalls of diamonds. He introduced lightness and movement into his works, and reduced to the minimum any intrusion of the setting metal, thus becoming a pioneer of the 'monture illusion'. Leon Rouvenat (1809-1874), sensitive to the same naturalistic inspiration, excelled at the Paris Exhibition of 1867 with a much admired life-size branch of lilac, wearable as a brooch or as a hair ornament, which was purchased by the Empress Eugénie.

The 1870s ushered in the fashion for colourless stones, and diamonds became the gemstones *par excellence*. This trend was consolidated in the following two decades and by the 1890s coloured stones seem to have been totally out of fashion. The increased popularity of diamonds was a consequence of the discovery of diamonds in South Africa in 1867 which made the gem far more plentiful and less expensive from the early 1870s onwards.

Military expeditions and political events influenced fashion and jewellery design in the 1860s and 1870s. As a consequence of the French expedition in China and the conquest of Peking and the Summer Palace in 1860, a large number of imperial jades came to France, and were successfully mounted by Fontenay.

The French campaign in Mexico introduced a certain fashion for the exotic which, in jewellery, meant the appearance of gem-set humming birds as brooches and hair ornaments; but Mexican and South American art in general, with its abstract, linear forms, never appealed to the Victorians and their Continental contemporaries.

As a consequence of the opening up of Japan to western trade in the 1850s, and the revolution of 1866, many examples of Japanese art, until then very little known, came to Europe and were to exert a considerable influence on the evolution of ornament and decoration.

Alexis Falize (1811-1898) was among the first jewellers to be fascinated by the elegant stylisation of the natural world characteristic of Japanese art. Having revived Limoges enamels, between 1860 and 1865 he dedicated himself to the study of Eastern cloisonné enamels; in collaboration with Tard, a talented enameller, he produced, in matt gold and opaque enamels, fascinating jewels that had the cachet of novelty, and were inspired by Persian, Indian and, above all, Japanese art (see plates 190 and 242). His son Lucien (1839-1897) continued to work in this tradition and became famous for his jewels made of rectangular or circular cloissoné enamel plaques, inspired by the colours, the stylisation, the balance and the decorative motifs of Japanese art (see plate 260).

In the mid-1870s it became the fashion in Europe to mount small decorative pieces of Japanese metalwork as jewellery. Shibuichi and shakudo, the techniques developed by samurai sword-makers for the decoration of kagamibutanetsuke (sword mounts and guards), entered the world of the jeweller. They consisted of inlaying gold, silver and copper into a dark base, either a silver alloy (shibuichi) or a copper alloy (shakudo). Shibuichi and shakudo plaques, and miniature fans decorated with butterflies, bamboo, flowers and birds, were frequently mounted in gold as brooches, bracelets and earrings (see plate 285).

The Italian Risorgimento set off an interest in anything Italian all over Europe. In jewellery, this trend is characterised, in the early 1860s, by the increased interest in coral, which was, at the time, still abundant in the Mediterranean, where the chief centre for carving was in Italy, notably in Torre del Greco near Naples. Skilled carvers produced beautiful parures of archaeological or naturalistic inspiration, and very fine and attractive cameos (see plates 181 and 182). The subjects of these cameos were mainly borrowed from classical antiquity, but cameos carved with the portraits of men who unified Italy — Mazzini, Cavour and Garibaldi — are also common. More frequently their features appear on lava cameos, together with the profiles of the great Italian poets: Dante, Petrarch and Boccaccio (see plate 180).

A characteristic feature of 1860s and 1870s jewellery was a new, imaginative and varied approach to gemstones and metals, whereby both precious and semiprecious stones began to be treated as materials that had to adapt, in shape and cut, to a design, and not the other way round. Coral and turquoises were calibré-cut to fit into target-shaped mounts (see plate 269); Bohemian garnets were rose-cut and clustered around a carbuncle (cabochon garnet) in star-shaped motifs; carbuncles were carved in the shape of petals and assembled together to form a flowerhead motif, or cut in the shape of bracelet links (see plate 274).

Optical effects were often cleverly exploited by geometric patterns formed of concentric bands of stones and enamels of contrasting colours and textures, or in chequered patterns of gold and enamel, or diamond and coloured gemstones (see plates 210, 211, 270 and 272).

Roman, Florentine mosaics and Scotch pebble inlays gained favour (see plates 232 and 233).

Cabochon stones, especially garnets and amethysts, were frequently inlaid at the centre with a pearl or diamond star, or with a tiny gem-set flower or insect (see plates 212 and 289). The general fashion for setting small stones in larger ones increased the appeal of cameos 'habillés' (see plate 238). The 'bloom' of coloured gold was successfully combined with the brilliancy of diamonds and with the shine of highly polished gold surfaces. Pendants and brooches were frequently decorated with characteristic articulated fringes or tagged drops (see plates 213, 259 and 265).

Tortoiseshell jewels inlaid with gold and silver piqué work were worn in the first half of the century, but it was the 1860s that was to prove their heyday. The technique of piqué work on tortoiseshell, introduced into seventeenth century England by French Huguenots, consisted of moulding the tortoiseshell to the required shape and, when still warm, inscribing the decorative motif on its surface and inlaying it with tiny dots, stripes and lines of gold and silver. The shrinkage of the tortoiseshell during the cooling process secured the metal to its surface. Until the 1860s the process was entirely manual and the favourite decorative motifs tended to be of naturalistic inspiration. When mass, machine-aided production of tortoiseshell piqué jewels began in Birmingham in the early 1870s, geometrical patterns were preferred to naturalistic decoration. The quality became coarser, but the price dropped.

Also characteristic of the 1860s and 1870s was the taste for novelty jewellery. In the mid-1860s naïveté and frivolousness invaded jewellery design: earrings assumed the shape of windmills, scales, baskets of flowers, animals, hammers, lanterns, watering cans and many other objects in everyday use. Made to amuse and to suit an ephemeral whim of fashion, novelty jewels enjoyed esteem but were quickly discarded as soon as the fashion diminished.

The taste for novelty spread to sporting jewellery, a peculiarly English fashion which nevertheless quickly became current in France and the Continent. The earliest examples of sporting jewellery consisted of horseshoe brooches, but soon the repertoire widened to include whips, riding caps, bridles, stirrups, fox masks, hunting dogs, saddles and golf clubs. Sporting jewellery remained in fashion until the end of the century (see plates 376-378, 388, 405 and 445).

The long years of trade and close ties with India created a market for jewellery produced in India or in Indian taste in the 1870s (see plate 184). Souvenirs of Indian sporting expeditions included necklaces and pendants set with tiger claws in gold mounts (see plate 185). Large numbers of miniatures painted in Delhi, representing celebrated Indian palaces and rulers, were incorporated into jewellery. Brilliant green Pertabghar enamel plaques with etched gold mythological, or hunting scenes, and flowers, scrolls, birds, elephants, tigers and other animals, were common as bracelets and necklaces (see plate 186).

The tinted or reverse intaglio was another novelty of the early 1860s that was to maintain its appeal until the First World War. The intaglio was produced by carving deeply into a cabochon of rock crystal from the back, painting the carving with oil colours and then sealing the aperture with a mother-of-pearl sheet. Acceptable subjects were horses, dogs (see plate 406), hunting scenes for gentlemen's buttons, tiepins and cufflinks, and delicate bouquets of flowers and monograms for ladies' brooches and pendants (see plate 261). Ernest Willian Pradier (b.1855) and his son Ernest Marius (b.1881) are perhaps the best known exponents of this attractive craft (see plate 405). Cheap imitations of tinted intaglios soon appeared on the market, consisting of rough cast glass intaglios summarily painted, or of coloured prints mounted beneath a glass dome.

In the 1860s stars were the most common decorative motif in jewellery. Almost every locket, brooch and bracelet had a pearl, diamond or enamel star at the centre. Stars were even carved into carbuncles and cabochon amethysts, and set with diamonds; stars set with half pearls and diamonds were worn as brooches and hair ornaments (see plates 189, 200, 201, 213, 243 and 265). The design of 1860s stars is simple and flat and thus it is usually relatively easy to recognise these early examples from the more elaborate three-dimensional forms of the late nineteenth century.

The fashion for insect jewellery began in the early 1860s, when delicate naturalistic butterflies, bees and dragonflies, as well as less appealing stag beetles, spiders, flies and wasps, were made of gold or set with multicoloured gemstones. Insects were mounted as brooches and worn extensively on the bodice, sleeves and shoulders, in the hair and on veils and bonnets. Their popularity grew in the last two decades of the century (see plates 338 and 340-353).

By the 1860s gas and steam engines were common in jewellery workshops, for mechanisation enabled increasingly larger quantities of very cheap but repetitive jewels to be produced. Inevitably the quality started to decline as low carat gold and 'or doublé' (rolled gold) almost completely replaced gilt metal in the manufacture of cheap jewellery. 'Or doublé' consisted of a thin sheet of gold cemented to a sheet of brass, which was then rolled out to an almost paper-thin thickness. Jewels stamped out in rolled gold were subsequently filled with base metal which imparted weight. Mechanisation was introduced into jewellery workshops almost simultaneously in Europe and the United States. In Europe the major centres of mass produced jewellery were England — especially Birmingham — and Germany. In Amsterdam the wheels used to cut diamonds and coloured gemstones were by now often driven by steam engines, whereas in Idar Oberstein, in Germany, agates were cut by means of hydraulic power.

Plate 178. A ruby and diamond tiara, c.1870-80.

Tiaras and Hair Ornaments

Tiaras of gold leaves in archaeological style or 'à la Greque', with a gabled point at the centre and sloping to the sides, were common in the 1860s as well as more elaborate diamond scrollworks, often of Louis XVI taste, supporting pearl, diamond or emerald drops (see plates 178 and 179).

At the end of the 1870s, the Russian tiara, made of small diamond spikes, made an appearance; this design subsequently developed to more elaborate, radiating motifs, and remained in favour throughout the last two decades of the century (see plate 305).

Pins were frequently worn in the chignons. The most elaborate took the form of diamond stars, birds, flowerheads, sunbursts, crescents, butterflies and humming-birds and the simplest consisted of large beads of jet, gold filigree, or tortoiseshell piqué.

Plate 179. A gold diadem, by Castellani, c.1870, signed with two Cs.

Plate 180. A suite of lava cameo jewellery, around 1860. The lava of Vesuvius was popular as a material for carving cameos from about 1850. The subject matter was usually portrait busts of classical deities, famous literary figures, or heroes of the Italian Risorgimento.

Combs

The conventional head ornament of the period was the comb, worn either on the forehead, as a diadem, or at the back, just above the chignon. The surmounts, mainly of gold or coral beads, set with gemstones or enamelled with geometrical patterns of classical Greek inspiration were hinged to tortoiseshell teeth.

Spanish combs, entirely carved in tortoiseshell were also popular. In the 1870s some combs assumed the form of gold bandeaux, variously decorated, stretching all the way across the forehead.

Parures

Parures of diamonds and coloured precious stones were not very common and were outnumbered by suites of brooch and earrings, or pendant and earrings (see plates 183 and 189).

Gold parures, however, were favoured, either in the archaeological revival taste, or in coloured gold, embellished with small gemstones, or enamelled, typically in turquoise blue (see plates 187 and 188).

One design of the 1860s consisted of a flexible tubular chain necklet supporting variously decorated tagged oval pendants, combined with matching earrings and a bangle, of which many examples still survive in their original fitted cases.

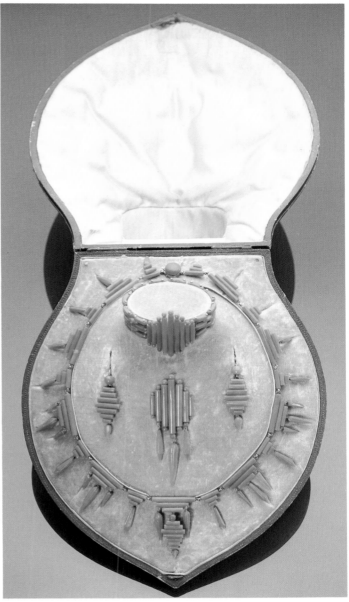

Plate 181. A coral parure, c.1865-70, probably Neapolitan, with a contemporary case (shown reduced). It is extremely rare for coral parures to have survived intact.

Parures of shell or coral cameos, or pavé-set with small calibré-cut turquoises, were also worn (see plates 181 and 182).

More elaborate parures, set with tiger claws decorated with gold floral motifs or mounted in engraved gold, were very fashionable in the 1870s, and many examples were made in India, especially Calcutta (see plate 185).

Versatile suites or demi-parures comprising brooch and earrings or locket and earrings in 'coloured' gold set with turquoises and pink corals retained their popularity throughout the period. Brooches often doubled as pendants.

Occasionally, a brooch and a pair of earrings were pinned on a velvet ribbon and worn around the neck as a choker.

Plate 182. A shell cameo parure, c.1860. This material is commonly mistaken for coral. The lamellar construction of the cameos gives away its shell origin. This is a typical mass-produced example, made for the tourist market.

*Plate 183. A diamond parure, c.1860, the lozenge-shaped pendant is some 20 to 30 years earlier.
This charming suite of jewellery shows an early use of the butterfly as decorative motif. All leaves
and flowerheads in the necklace are detachable, as is the large butterfly.*

Plate 184. A gold necklace with pendant and locket, Indian, probably Madras, around 1880. Tourist jewellery from the Raj.

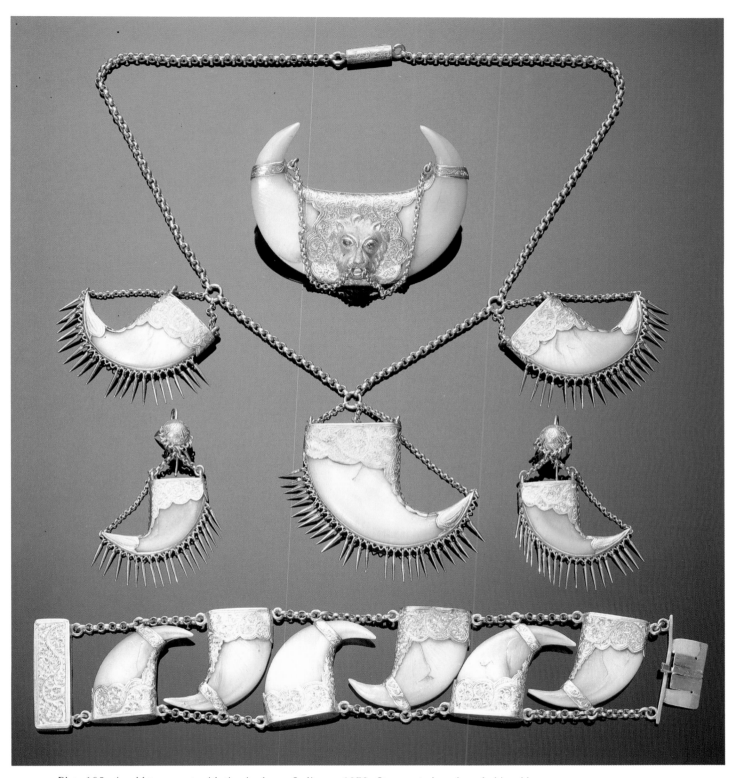

Plate 185. A gold parure set with tiger's claws, Indian, c.1870. It seems to have been fashionable at this time for tiger's claws to be set in jewellery to commemorate hunting trips; much of the goldsmith work was carried out in Calcutta.

150

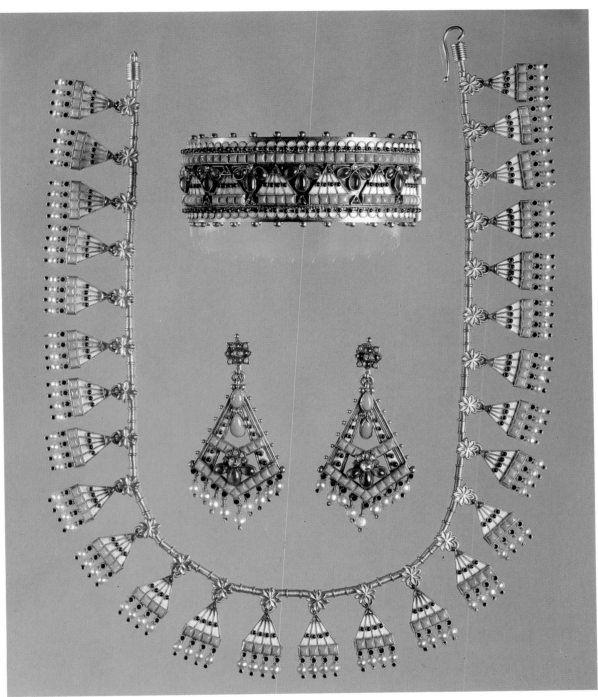

Plate 187. A gold, enamel, ruby, turquoise, seed pearl and diamond demi-parure, by Carlo Giuliano, c.1865, signed C.G. This design is a mixture of Assyrian and Egyptian inspiration.

Plate 186. A gold and Pertabghar enamel parure, Indian, c.1865. Pertabghar (Rajputana) enamels were apparently produced by melting a thick layer of green enamel on a plate of burnished gold and, while still hot, covering it with thin gold cut into mythological, hunting or other pleasure scenes, populated with animals and decorated with scrolls, leaves and flowers. After the enamel had hardened, the gold was worked with a tool to bring out ornamental details. In some cases, it would seem as if the surface of the enamel was first engraved and the gold rubbed into the pattern so produced in the form of an amalgam, and fixed by fire. See G.C.M. Birdwood, Indian Art, part II, South Kensington Museum Art Handbook, *1880, pages 167-168.*

Plate 188. A gold parure, c.1880. Again a combination of archaeological influences, in this case from classical Greece and Egypt.

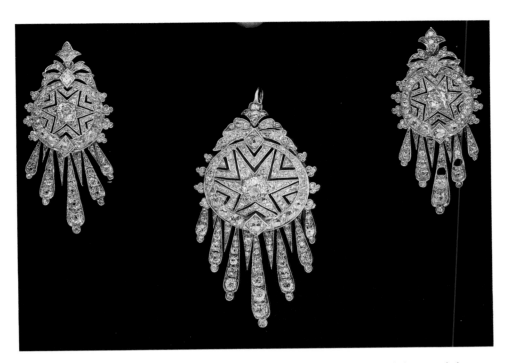

Plate 189. A diamond demi-parure, c.1870. The openwork star motif and the tagged drops are typical. Two stones are missing from the earrings on the right; it is important, when replacing them, to find stones of contemporary cutting rather than modern brilliants.

Plate 190. A gold and enamel demi-parure, by Falize, c.1875. An example of the characteristic enamel designs of this maker.

Plate 191. A pair of gold and lapis-lazuli pendant earrings, c.1870, of popular amphora design.

Earrings

Earrings, worn throughout the 1860s and 1870s, for day and evening wear, favoured hairstyles that required hair to be brushed to the back of the head, the low décolletages of ball dresses, and the simple necklines of daywear. Their size fluctuated throughout the period, but grew to enormous proportions in the late 1860s and early 1870s, when they almost rested on the shoulders. Favourite materials were gold and enamel for day wear and pearls and precious stones for evening wear (see plates 190, 194, 195, 196 and 199).

The designs included spheres, drops, hoops, fringed ovals, crosses, lozenges, flowerheads and stars (see plate 197). The archaeological revival supplied endless sources of inspiration in the form of amphorae, inverted drops decorated with granulation, rosettes, openwork plaques of trellis design, tridents, Greek keys and many others (see plates 191-194).

In the 1870s novelty earrings took the form of insects, fish, flowers, lizards, baskets of flowers, birdcages, windmills, bells, carpenters' tools, fans, keys, plates, and other objects used in everyday life. Although the craze for earrings was widespread, the fashion for extremely large and long pendant earrings was typically English.

Plate 192. A pair of gold and enamel earrings in Etruscan 'a baule' style. The detail of the reverse shows the typical fitting of the period.

Plate 193. A pair of gold and pearl pendant earrings, c.1870, by Carlo Giuliano, signed C.G., in Hellenistic style. A late 4th century BC earring of similar design from Kyme in Acolis is in the British Museum Collection.

Plate 194. A pair of gold, pearl and enamel pendant earrings, by Carlo Giuliano, c.1870, signed C.G. In this case, Giuliano brings his enamelling techniques to an Etruscan inspired design.

Plate 195. A pair of gold and enamel pendant earrings, probably New York or Boston, c.1880.

Plate 196. A pair of gold enamel and gem-set pendant earrings, c.1870, in Holbeinesque style. This popular design is more often found as pendants rather than earrings, see plate 250. Less important examples, like this, are often set with chrysoberyls in place of diamonds.

Plate 197. A collection of typical gold earrings of the 1865-75 period.

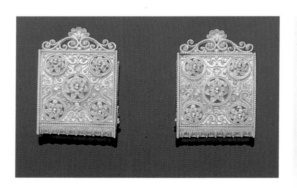

Plate 198. A pair of gold earrings in archaeological revival style, c.1986. These reproductions of reproductions are of alarmingly good quality, good enough to fool us had it not been for the modern screw fittings which raised our suspicions. Now that archaeological revival jewellery fetches high prices, fakes are bound to become common despite the obvious difficulty in manufacture.

Plate 199. A pair of pearl and diamond earrings, c.1860.

Plate 200. A gold, turquoise, enamel and diamond necklace, c.1865. This is a curious combination of an 1840 gold and turquoise chain that may well have formerly been the body of a snake necklace (see plates 141 and 171), and an 1865 heart and star locket.

Necklaces

Necklaces tended to be rather short, often made of 'Brazilian' or flexible tubular linking, and were almost invariably decorated with one, three, five or more pendants of various imaginative shapes (see plates 200 and 201). Greek and Etruscan antiquity offered an inexhaustible source of ideas for such pendants: urns, acorns, amphorae, masks, medallions, inverted drops and the like. Also in fashion were circular domed medallions in blue enamel, star-set with pearls and diamonds (see plate 265), carbuncles decorated with a tasselled fringe, and amethysts inlaid with floral or star motifs. Egyptian, Etruscan and Classical archaeology supplied inspiration for necklaces decorated with

Plate 201. A gold, enamel, pearl and diamond necklace, c.1865-70. Another version of a popular design, see plate 200. In this case the Brazilian chain is original.

enamels, mosaics, cameos and intaglios (see plates 203-208).

Long gold chains continued to be worn freely, draped on the bodice, at the waist, or around the neck. Their primary function, if one were needed, was to support a watch, although they were often worn just for their own sake.

The new model of watchchain, the Léontine, named after a famous actress of the time, consisted of a woven gold ribbon decorated with a tassel at one end and supporting a watch at the other, the two chains conjoined by a rectangular or oval slide, chased and gem-set.

In Paris the chains designed and manufactured by Auguste Lion (1830-1895), were reasonably priced and varied in design.

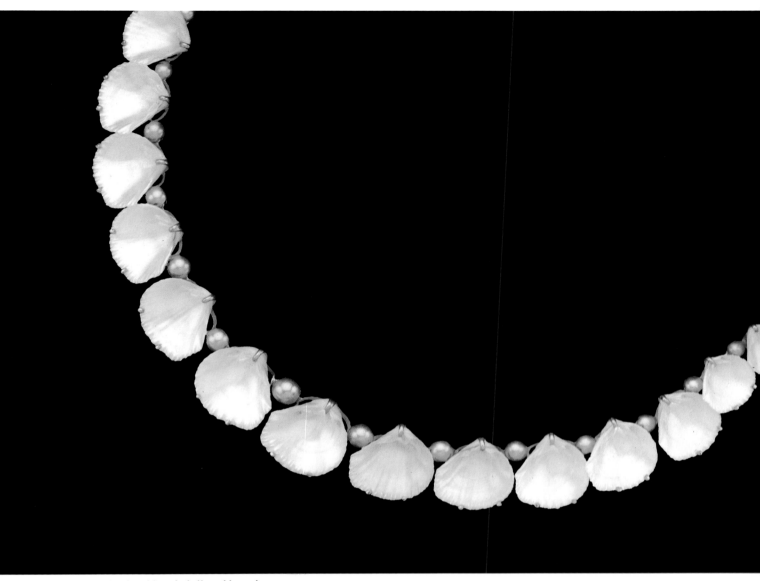

Plate 202. A gold and shell necklace, last quarter of the 19th century, possibly by John Brogden.

Plate 203. A gold and cloisonné enamel necklace, c.1870. This high quality necklace combines Oriental and Etruscan motifs to form an unusual yet successful design.

Plate 204. A gold and Roman micromosaic necklace, and earrings, c.1880. It would be difficult to find a more typically Roman necklace both in iconography and manufacture. Roman mosaic jewels of this size are rare.

Plate 205. A gold and hardstone intaglio necklace, probably Italian, c.1865. The intaglios are mostly ancient, probably 1st and 2nd century AD. The interest in classical cameos and intaglios was revived after a lapse of some fifty years. The inspiration here is scientific-archaeological rather than reflecting the sentimental attitude of the Napoleonic era to antiquity.

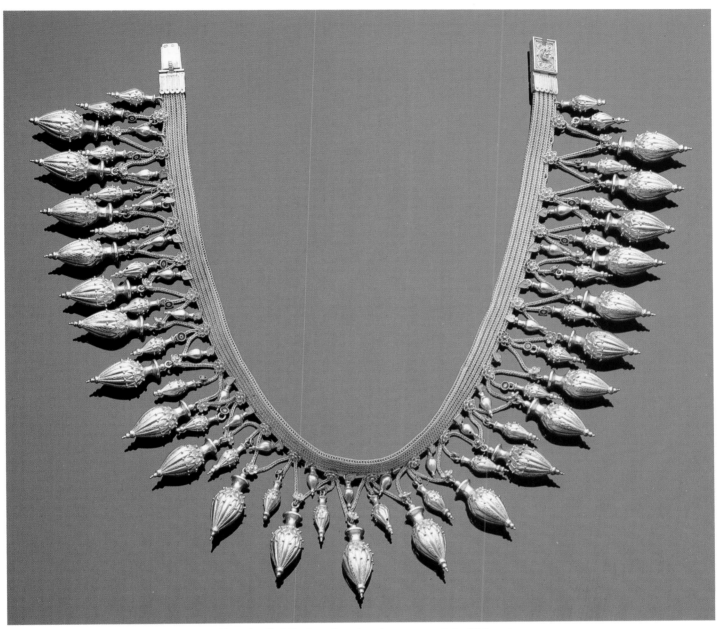

Plate 206. A gold and enamel necklace, by Carl Bacher, Austrian, last quarter of the 19th century, signed C.B. on the clasp. A necklace in Hellenistic style, which closely copies 3rd century BC originals.

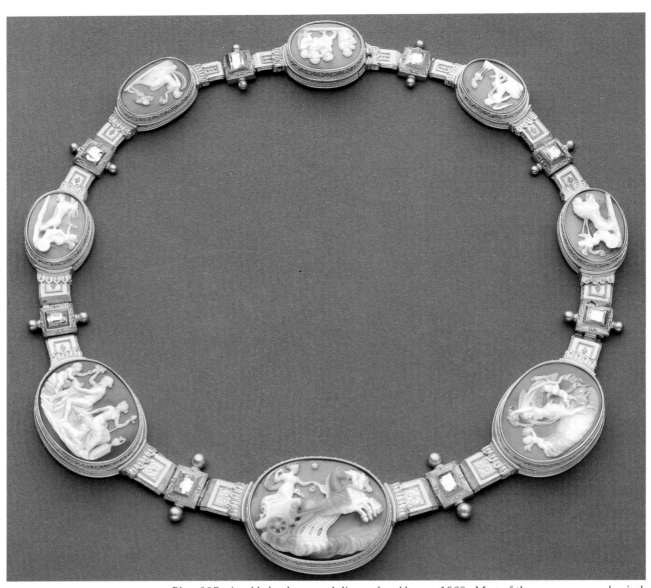

Plate 207. *A gold, hardstone and diamond necklace, c.1860. Most of the cameos are neoclassical, dating from the turn of the 19th century. Perhaps originally they would have been in Empire mounts and were reset like this when the fashion for archaeological jewellery revived interest in cameos. Nevertheless, the necklace combines Etruscan corded wire and granulation with table-cut diamonds in settings commonly associated with the 16th century.*

Plate 208. *A gold necklace of laurel leaves, after the antique, by Phillips of Cockspur Street, c.1870. This necklace must have been a close copy of an Hellenistic (possibly 3rd century BC) original. Note the fine detailing on the leaves.*

Plate 209. A Viennese silver-gilt and gem-set necklace, c.1880, in Renaissance taste (shown reduced). These necklaces were produced in large numbers and nearly always bear the Austro-Hungarian coffin-shaped silver mark on the clasp. Both the garnets and the Habachtal emeralds are of local origin. The quality of the enamel is often very poor.

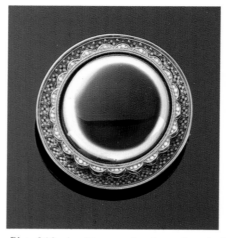

Plate 210. A gold, enamel and onyx brooch, by Phillips of Cockspur Street, a circular brooch, typical of the 1860s. Note the Phillips mark composed of two Ps and the Prince of Wales' feathers.

Brooches

Around 1860 the design of many brooches changed from the horizontal to the vertical axis, assuming an upright rather than a horizontal shape. The new vertical design suited better the alternative function of this ornament as a pendant or bracelet centre (see plates 222, 227, 235, 237 and 274). The rather delicate and elaborate scrolled designs of the early 1860s were replaced, in the 1870s, by a simple gem-set oval border surrounding a central decorative motif, embellished at the compass points by four gems and supporting a similar pendant (see plates 226, 228 and 235). This design prevailed until the end of the century.

A few examples continued to be produced in the typical eighteenth century girandole design (see plate 227).

Circular gold brooches, associated with the 1860s, were frequently set at the centre with a turquoise, coral or enamel dome, or often with an agate, carbuncle, or cabochon amethyst inlaid with pearls or diamonds (see plates 210-212). Tinted intaglios were also in fashion. Circular tortoiseshell brooches with piqué decoration are also characteristic of the period.

Plate 211. A gold, enamel and carbuncle (almandine garnet) brooch, c.1865. Circular brooches with bosses at the centre either in gemstone or enamel were very popular in the 1860s.

Plate 212. A gold, half-pearl and carbuncle (almandine garnet) brooch, c.1860. The carbuncle has been set with a diamond: this practice of setting one stone into another, particularly carbuncles and amethysts, became very popular during the next ten or fifteen years.

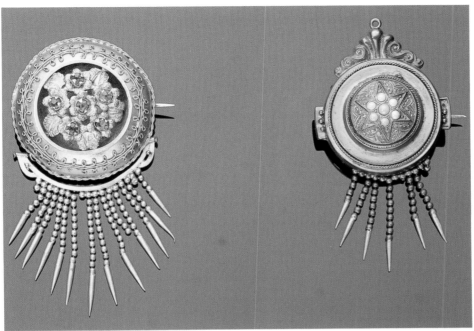

Plate 213. Two gilt metal and paste brooches, c.1870. Clever and effective imitations of the real thing.

Greek, Etruscan and Egyptian designs exerted a strong influence on brooch design (see plates 214, 216, 217 and 218). Corded wire and granulation were used to decorate the oval or circular borders of Roman mosaics, cameos and miniatures mounted as brooches (see plates 219, 220, 221, 225, 232 and 233).

Penannular brooches of Celtic influence, often copying Iron Age originals, and Scottish pebble plaid brooches, were in demand.

Naturalistic brooches, either in gold and semiprecious stones, or set with diamonds and precious coloured stones often mounted en tremblant, assumed the forms of spray flowers, humming birds and peacock feathers (see plates 229 and 230).

Plate 214. A gold brooch in classical taste, c.1865.

Plate 215. A gilt metal brooch, set with a porcelain miniature, probably c.1870. Porcelain miniatures were used in poor quality jewellery instead of enamel.

165

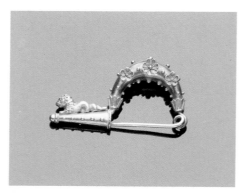

Plate 216. A gold brooch designed as a fibula of Etruscan inspiration, c.1875, almost an academic piece.

Plate 217. A gold brooch in Egyptian style, c.1870-80.

Star and insect brooches gained favour towards the end of the 1860s, and reached their peak in the last twenty years of the century (see plates 338 and 340-353). Diamond star brooches were usually flat and rather simple in design. Insect brooches gave the jewellers yet another chance to exploit their naturalistic interest: set entirely with diamonds, or with diamonds and coloured stones to reproduce the colours of the wings, they are sometimes so realistic that they resemble the work of an entomologist rather than that of a jeweller. Butterflies, bees, dragonflies and spiders were pinned at random all over the corsage, or on veils and bonnets.

In the 1870s sporting brooches became an indispensable part of the day wear of fashionable women. The wide appeal of hunting brooches of saddles and stirrups, riding brooches of caps and horseshoes, golfing brooches of clubs and balls, lasted until the first decade of the 1900s (see plates 376-8 and 388).

Memorial brooches decorated with glazed hairwork miniatures continued to be made in the same style and with the same decorative motifs as in the previous decades.

Plate 218. Two gold brooches by Castellani, both c.1860, and remarkably similar in design. This motif was also employed to form the links of a bracelet, see plates 277 and 278.

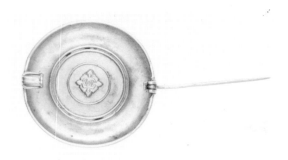

Plate 219. *A gold and Roman mosaic brooch, by Castellani, c.1860. The illustration of the back of the brooch shows clearly the Castellani mark. The dove of the Holy Spirit was a popular motif with Castellani, see plate 220.*

Plate 220. *A gold and Roman mosaic brooch designed as a bulla, after the antique, by Castellani, c.1860, the reverse inscribed 'vivas in Deo', the interior signed with two entwined Cs. Castellani was keen on Roman mosaics in jewellery, often employing Christian iconography as in this example.*

Plate 221. *A gold and Roman miocromosaic brooch, by Castellani, c.1865. The reverse of the brooch is inscribed and dated 1866, such inscriptions are of immense use in dating jewellery. Most Castellani mosaics, as in this case, have the outlines of the design picked out in gold wire.*

Plate 222. *A gold, pearl and diamond brooch, set with a ruby cameo of Cupid, by Castellani, c.1860, the reverse of the pendant signed with two entwined Cs.*

Plate 223. *A gold brooch set with a Roman Republican denarius of L. Plautius Plancus (c.47 BC). The detail of the reverse shows that the coin was mounted by Castellani, c.1865. This small discovery of the signature will augment the value of the brooch considerably.*

Plate 224. *A gold and enamel brooch, c.1860, set with a gold coin (a contemporary reproduction of a late Roman solidus). Classical coins were popular elements of revivalist brooches and necklaces.*

Plate 225. *A gold brooch, set with a Wedgwood plaque, c.1860. The Wedgwood plaque with its cool classical scene is used here instead of a cameo for the same purpose.*

Plate 226. *A carbuncle (almandine garnet), and diamond pendant/brooch, c.1870. This rich combination of stones was greatly favoured at the time.*

Plate 227. *A ruby and diamond brooch, c.1870, of girandole (chandelier) design. The rubies, originating from Burma, are virtually in a natural state as rolled pebbles found in alluvial deposits and may well have been brought back during the Raj.*

Plate 228. *A gold, enamel, aquamarine and diamond brooch, c.1870. The aquamarines are of unusual size and quality, originating from Brazil. One feels that the brooch has been designed as a vehicle for the specimen stones.*

Plate 229. An emerald, sapphire, ruby and diamond articulated brooch designed as a butterfly poised on a wild rose spray, French, c.1880. A superb example naturalistically inspired. The brooch divides into two spray pendants and a butterfly brooch.

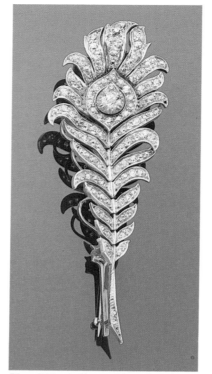

Plate 230. A diamond brooch designed as a peacock feather, c.1870. Boucheron may have been the first to employ peacock feathers as brooches. Usually the spine of the feather is hinged and sprung. The motif remained popular until the end of the century.

Plate 231. A sapphire and diamond brooch pendant, c.1870-80: The Sri Lankan sapphire is held in characteristic diamond-set claws.

Plate 232. A gold and Roman micromosaic brooch of a spaniel retrieving a wild fowl, c.1870. The mount is of high quality and its design and workmanship give clues to its date.

Plate 233. A gold and Florentine mosaic brooch, c.1870. Dating is only possible from the mount.

Plate 235. A pearl and diamond brooch/pendant, c.1860. The colour and lustre of the pearls would undoubtedly have deteriorated with the passage of time. The drop is detachable, making the resulting cluster more suitable as a brooch.

Plate 236. A cameo brooch in shell, carved in high relief, c.1870.

Plate 237. A gold, half-pearl and diamond brooch/pendant, c.1880, set with an onyx cameo of Medusa. Without the mount this cameo would prove difficult to date.

Plate 238. An onyx and diamond cameo habillé, c.1860, mounted as a brooch within a border of rose diamonds. This is a relatively plain example, where only the diadem and earrings are embellished; in some cases many materials are superimposed on the cameo to suggest jewellery and clothing.

Plate 239. A gold, half-pearl and diamond brooch, c.1870, set with a banded agate cameo of a maenad. The quality of the carving is good and this was a very common subject at this time.

Plate 240. A gold and enamel brooch, c.1860, set with a banded agate cameo. Another example of high-relief carving, so typical of the period, which, with its classical subject matter, blends perfectly with the archaeological revival mount.

Plate 241. A gold, onyx and half-pearl pendant, c.1870, set with a banded agate cameo of Flora. Note the high-relief of the carving which passes through several colour layers in the stone. This three-dimensional quality characterises many cameos of the second half of the century.

Pendants

Pendants, the neck ornament in vogue in the 1860s and 1870s, were worn on gold chains, on strings of pearls, or on velvet ribbons. The most favoured was the Holbeinesque pendant, deriving its shape and decoration from the Renaissance but, despite its name, not directly based on designs by Holbein. Typically it consisted of a central gemstone, usually a carbuncle, surrounded by a polychrome champlevé enamel border of floral and foliate motifs, set with diamonds or chrysoberyls, and supported a similarly set and decorated lozenge-shaped drop. The best examples were engraved at the back with scroll

Plate 243. A gold, onyx, half-pearl and diamond pendant, c.1870, used during mourning.

Plate 242. A gold, diamond and enamel pendant mirror case by Falize, c.1880. An excellent example of the cloisonné enamelling technique asociated with Tard and Falize.

Plate 244. A gold, enamel pearl and diamond pendant, by Carlo Giuliano, c.1870, signed C.G. The lozenge design and the black and white piqué enamel were favourite elements in Giuliano jewellery.

Plate 245. A gold, enamel and gem-set pendant, by Carlo Giuliano, c.1870, signed C.G. Again an overall lozenge design, here incorporating delicately enamelled scrolls and fleur-de-lis motifs. The brown zircon at the centre is a typical Giuliano touch.

and floral motifs (see plates 250-255). Holbeinesque pendants often came *en suite* with a pair of similarly designed pendant earrings (see plate 196).

Crosses and lozenge-shaped pendants of Renaissance inspiration, enamelled and gem-set, were also in demand and were usually supported by similarly enamelled chains. Giuliano excelled in the production of such pendants (see plates 244, 245, 246 and 247). Cheaper crosses were made of tortoiseshell piqué, silver and jet.

Classical archaeology supplied themes and shapes for some of the most beautiful gold pendants of the time. Bullae, scarabs, urns and amphorae in matt gold, often decorated with corded wire and granulation, were in fashion from the mid-1860s to the late 1870s (see plates 263, 266 and 268). Large oval gold lockets, particularly popular in the 1870s, were often gem-set, or enamelled and chased with monograms, stars, insects, straps and buckles and serpents (see plates 257 and 258). Towards the end of the 1870s, silver lockets with chased patterns appeared.

Mourning lockets were usually carved in jet and pendants were often decorated with onyx and pearls (see plate 243).

Plate 247. A gold, pearl, enamel and diamond pendant, by Carlo Giuliano, c.1880, signed C.G. By this date Giuliano designs were tending to become more attenuated.

Plate 248. A gold, enamel, pearl and diamond pendant, c.1875-80, by Carlo Giuliano, the back with a glazed miniature or hair compartment, signed C.G. This is an untypical example where Giuliano has employed enamel on a sculptured surface (en ronde bosse).

Plate 246. A gold, enamel and gem-set pendant, by Carlo Giuliano, c.1870, signed C.G. This magnificent pendant is set with sapphire cameos in an elaborate Renaissance style mount.

Plate 249. A gold, enamel, pearl and diamond pendant, c.1875. This example shows the clear influence of Giuliano and may well be by his hand although unsigned.

Plate 250. A Holbeinesque pendant, c.1870, a typical example of a popular design, set with a carbuncle and chrysoberyls. The chromatic combination in the enamels is very characteristic.

Plate 251. A gold, enamel, ruby and diamond Holbeinesque pendant, c.1870. Here the enamel has been sacrificed for precious stones, making a richer and more expensive example. Also a gold, pearl, rose diamond and enamel demi-parure, French, c.1870. A good example of French inventiveness in design. The red gold is a useful clue to the country of origin. Unusual and exotic suites like this can fetch very high prices.

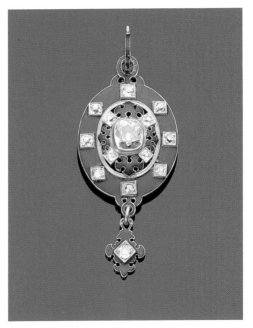

Plate 252. A gold, blue enamel and diamond Holbeinesque pendant, c.1870. The colour of the enamel is unusual.

Plate 253. A gold, enamel, ruby, pearl and diamond Holbeinesque pendant, c.1870. This example is unusual in that it is circular and has retained its original chain and enamelled coulant.

Plate 254. An emerald and diamond pendant, c.1870. Although unenamelled, this pendant is still clearly Holbeinesque in inspiration.

Plate 255. Another gold, enamel, pearl and diamond Holbeinesque pendant, c.1870. Note the floral decoration engraved on the back.

Plate 256. A modern copy of an 1880s gold and diamond pendant, illustrated front and back.

Plate 257. A three-coloured gold and pearl locket, last quarter of the 19th century.

Plate 258. A gold, turquoise and half-pearl locket, c.1880. Note the matt gold, so popular at the time.

Plate 259. An unusual gold and turquoise enamel pendant, c.1870, converted from an earring. It is quite common for pairs of earrings to have been converted into pendants, probably as a result of family division.

177

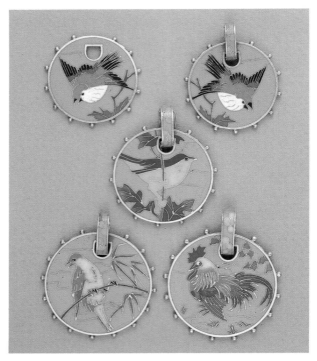

Plate 260. A suite of enamelled medallions, French, c.1870, by Alexis Falize, designed by Lucien Falize and enamelled by Tard. This group of enamels is typical of Falize workmanship showing the clear influence of Japanese art.

Plate 261. A gold, coral, demantoid garnet and enamel pendant, c.1870, set with a tinted crystal intaglio. The size, combination of stones and quality of this pendant make it a truly exceptional example of mid-Victorian taste in jewellery.

Plate 262. A gold, pearl and enamel pendant, set with a Limoges enamel miniature, French, c.1865. This pendant is very similar to one designed by Emile Froment-Meurice which was exhibited in Paris in 1867, (see Vever, La bijouterie Française au XIX Siècle, *page 278).*

Plate 263. A gold and pearl pendant, c.1860, set with a turquoise cameo of Terpsichore, the Muse of dance, by Castellani, signed on the reverse with two entwined Cs.

Plate 264. A gold and Roman mosaic pendant, probably c.1865. Many Egyptian inspired jewels were exhibited in Paris in 1867 as a consequence of the interest aroused by the excavation for the Suez Canal.

Plate 265. A gold, blue enamel, pearl and diamond pendant and chain, c.1865-70. Note the way the star motif has been set into the enamel boss, the half-pearl crescent and the Brazilian chain.

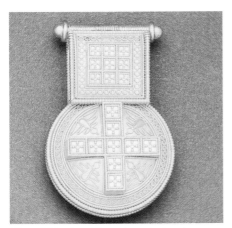

Plate 266. A gold pendant designed as a bulla, c.1860. The archaeological revival style at its most academic. This is a very fine example, showing great precision and craftsmanship.

Plate 267. A gold, onyx and seed pearl pendant, c.1865. This is a very eclectic and unusual jewel. The onyx here is used as an alternative to cat's-eye.

Plate 268. A gold and enamel pendant set with an onyx scarab, c.1865. The scarab is also an Egyptian inspired device, although this example, which is mounted on a swivel, is carved with a female profile on the reverse unlike ancient examples. To complicate the matter further, the mount looks to Etruscan jewellery rather than the Middle East.

Plate 269. A gold, turquoise
and diamond bracelet,
c.1860-70, cased by Hunt
and Roskell. It was not
unusual at this time, for
bracelets to support pendants
in this fashion, although it is
rare for the pendant to have
remained attached. Note the
calibré-cut turquoises.

Bracelets

The fashion for wearing two or three bracelets on each arm continued. Gold bracelets of curb or ship's cable linking — substantial in appearance but often very light — were common, as were flexible gold bands with jewelled centres or clasps (see plates 270, 271, 273, 275 and 276).

The Renaissance revival inspired bracelets of enamelled rectangular linking, often of openwork design, set with coloured gemstones, and gold and enamel bangles of sculptural form (see plate 283).

Greek and Etruscan archaeology inspired bracelets of rectangular gold plaques decorated with fine granulation, corded wire and enamels, ancient coins and cameos mounted in simple gold frames, and rows of round bosses decorated with rosette motifs (see plates 277, 278, 279, 280 and 288).

Diamond bracelets were usually designed as flexible bands of openwork scrolled links (see plate 291).

Bangles became the most fashionable arm ornament of the 1870s. They were usually designed as wide gold bands set at the centre with a circular gem-set or enamelled decorative motif, often detachable, or entirely studded with cabochon or faceted stones (see plates 286, 287 and 289). Wide gold bangles were engraved with Assyrian or Greek motifs in the 1860s; the Hellenistic

Plate 270. A gold, ruby
and diamond bracelet,
c.1860. A fine quality
jewel. The chequerboard
design was a popular
decorative device at this
time.

Plate 271. A gold and
diamond bracelet,
c.1860. The central
diamond motif may be
detached and worn as a
brooch, the articulated
gold back reminiscent of
ruched silk, is often seen
at this time, see Plate
273. Oval diamond
brooches decorated with
quatrefoil and palmette
motifs were very popular
and often have evidence
that they could have been
worn as bracelet centres.

Plate 272. A gold, ruby, black pearl and diamond bracelet, c.1860. A most unusual and rare example not only in the combination of stones, but also in the exclusive use of gold as a setting metal.

Plate 273. A gold, turquoise and diamond bracelet, c.1860-70. Another example with ruched or goffered linking where the centre motif is detachable. Close examination of the illustration will reveal a reeded thumb-piece either side of the centre cluster, by which the two sides can be removed.

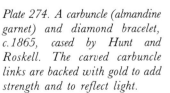

Plate 274. A carbuncle (almandine garnet) and diamond bracelet, c.1865, cased by Hunt and Roskell. The carved carbuncle links are backed with gold to add strength and to reflect light.

design of the gold bangle terminating with a ram's head was successfully revived. Roman mosaics were often set at the front of archaeologically inspired bangles (see plate 290).

Hoops and half-hoops of diamonds and pearls combined with semiprecious stones were usually wider than similarly designed bangles of the last two decades of the century, often set with several rows of pearls and gemstones.

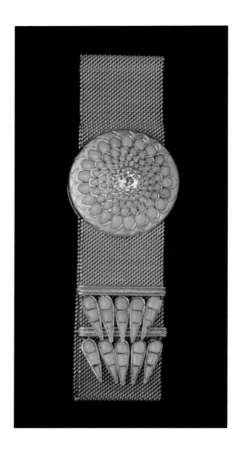

Plate 275. A gold, enamel and gemset bracelet, c.1865-70, set with an amethyst reverse intaglio of a lion. A reverse intaglio is best understood as a negative cameo; the subject is carved out of the back of the stone so that when viewed from the front it appears solid. The enamel frame shows Holbeinesque influences. The ribbon-like gold back is often associated with jarretière (garter) bracelets.

Plate 276. A gold, turquoise and diamond jarretière (garter) bracelet, c.1865.

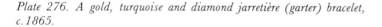

Plate 277. A gold bracelet by Castellani, c.1860. Each link in this bracelet is of a popular Castellani design, that also occurs as brooches (see plate 218). The detail of the back shows that each link is signed and the way they have been mounted on fetter-shaped loops suggest that these elements may have been made for use either as brooches or, as here, bracelet links. The detail of the front shows extensive damage (compare plate 278), this greatly reduces the value, since repairs would be difficult and expensive.

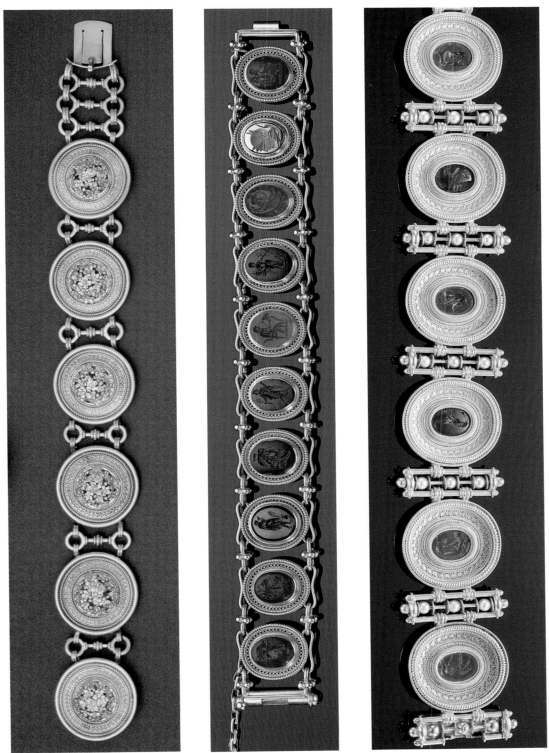

Plate 278. A gold bracelet, by Castellani, c.1860, of similar design to plate 277 but in good condition.

Plate 279. A gold bracelet set with hardstone intaglios, c.1860, by Pierret of Rome, in archaeological revival style. The intaglios here are almost certainly neoclassical (early 19th century), though the head carved in haematite (second from the top) is a modern replacement.

Plate 280. A gold, seed pearl and cornelian bracelet by Castellani, c.1860-5. Here Castellani has used ancient gems. Note the corded wire and granulation borders.

Plate 281. *A gold, enamel, ruby, agate and diamond bracelet, by Carlo Giuliano, c.1865, signed C.G. This superb bracelet shows how cleverly Giuliano echoed the black and white enamel in the carved banded agates. As is usual in Giuliano at this date, colour is kept to a minimum with the economical use of small rubies.*

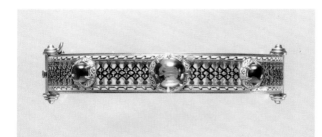

Plate 282. *A gold, enamel and gem-set hinged bangle, by Carlo Giuliano, c.1865, signed C.G. This bracelet illustrates the extraordinary detail of Giuliano enamelling that has seldom been matched. The green cabochon zircon was almost certainly chosen for its unusual colour rather than its value as is the case with the two carbuncle (almandine garnets). Had he employed emeralds and rubies, the effect would have been far less subdued.*

Plate 283. *A gold, enamel and gem-set bracelet, by Carlo Giuliano, c.1870, signed C.G. This is a typical Holbeinesque design, which could scarcely be by any other hand. The cusped collets are reminiscent of the 16th century, as is the florid enamel, though the Renaissance original would not have been of such high quality.*

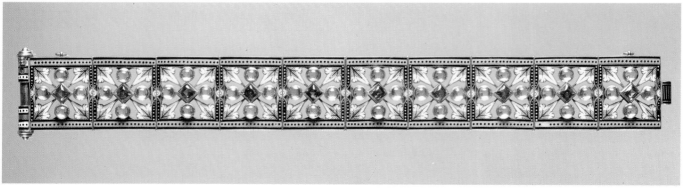

Plate 284. *A gold, enamel, brown zircon and green beryl bracelet, by Carlo Giuliano, c.1870, signed C.G. Again Giuliano has employed semiprecious stones for their colours, where other makers might have been tempted to enhance the intrinsic value of the jewel with emeralds and diamonds. Note the faintly Gothic design, perhaps echoing the work of William Morris.*

Plate 285. A gold bracelet, c.1875, mounted with six shakudo plaques. In the mid-70s it became popular in Europe to mount such decorative pieces of Japanese metalwork as jewellery.

Plate 286. A gold, emerald and diamond bangle, c.1870-5. Note the domed central motif superimposed by a star and crescent. The use of emerald in combination with diamonds is rare in jewels of this type.

Plate 287. A gold, turquoise and diamond hinged bracelet, c.1870. This simple design, bombé at the front, remained popular for some time.

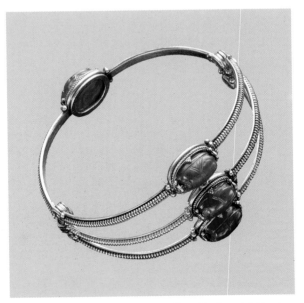

Plate 288. A gold bracelet by Castellani, c.1860, in Etruscan style, set with cornelian scarabs based on Egyptian originals and decorated with corded wire and granulation.

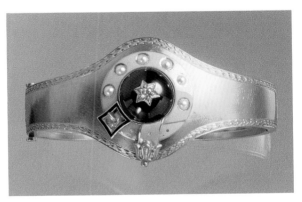

Plate 289. A gold, carbuncle (almandine garnet), and diamond hinged bangle, c.1865. Typical of the date is the garter motif and the garnet inset with a diamond star.

185

Plate 290. A gold and Roman micromosaic hinged bangle, c.1880. The damage to the mosaic would be expensive to repair and would probably be progressive.

Plate 291. A diamond bracelet, probably c.1870-80. The large centre stone shows evidence of new cutting techniques in comparison with the bulky stones on either side.

Rings

Rings continued to be set with a simple flowerhead cluster of stones, or designed as half-hoops. Variations of the latter design included gold bands with a graduated row of gemstones set in a boat-shaped 'marquise' motif, or star-set with three diamonds or coloured stones (see plate 292). Single-stone rings were usually designed as a wide gold band which splayed at the centre in a rosette of claws securing the stone in place.

In 1875 the gypsy ring was introduced as a novelty: it consisted of a gold band into which the gemstone was so deeply set that the table of the stone was level with the surface of the metal (see plate 292). Apart from being attractive and fashionable, this type of setting had the advantage of protecting the gem and disguised 'doublets' or composite stones. Plain gold rings designed as snakes coiled three or four times around the finger occasionally had gem-set eyes (see plates 293 and 294).

Memorial rings were usually designed as plain gold bands encircled by a braid of hair, or decorated with half pearls and black enamel (see plate 295).

Plate 292. A collection of gold and gem-set rings, of half-hoop, rosette, band, strap-and-buckle and boat-shaped designs, c.1870-80. Many stones are in gypsy settings, decorated with star-shaped motifs.

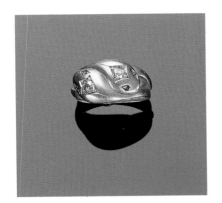

Plate 293. A gold, sapphire and diamond ring, inscribed 1876, designed as a coiled serpent.

Plate 294. A gold, ruby and diamond ring, c.1870, of crossover serpent design. Snake rings remained popular until the end of the century.

Plate 295. A gold, black enamel, pearl and diamond memorial ring, c.1870-80.

Plate 296. Jules Louis Machard, 1891, 'Before the Ball'. Sotheby's.

CHAPTER FIVE
1880~1900

The end of the century was characterised by a reaction against mechanically-produced jewellery. Technical progress and mechanisation made jewellery affordable by the masses but lowered rather than improved the quality of the pieces. The lockets and bracelets that were produced in the last decades of the century in very low carat gold, repetitive in design, roughly made and badly finished, could hardly be called 'jewels'. The public started to reject the fashion of wearing a multitude of pendants, always similar in design, and sets of jewels in debased gold.

The situation was similar all over Europe. At the beginning of the 1880s fashionable women, seemingly wearied of a succession of revivals in jewellery design, of 'second hand' styles and of jewels in which technical skill and erudite research of decorative motifs substituted art, creativity and spontaneity, temporarily abandoned jewellery almost completely.

In England the situation was complicated by a rebellion against Victorian excess in decoration, its ostentation and taboos. The young women of the Aesthetic movement abandoned all ornaments and enjoyed wearing on their simple dresses a plain string of amber beads; they also enjoyed the jewels from India, with their irregularly-shaped or uncut stones, or with the features of Ganesha or other Hindu gods in repoussé gold and silver (see plate 184).

The ornaments of the day were small, delicate and unostentatious, and diamonds disappeared for a time from day wear. At night, for court and formal occasions and at balls, jewels were still worn but in moderation; the preference was given to one beautifully made ornament, set with good quality stones, rather than several mediocre pieces.

Between 1887 and 1890, so little jewellery was worn in England, that many jewellers were concerned for their survival, but jewels did not disappear, and the 1890s saw a revival of their popularity, but with less exuberance.

The desire to break with tradition, to return to artistic jewels, where materials were functional to design, and where spontaneity of inspiration was more important than intrinsic value, is best exemplified by French art nouveau jewellery. The highly decorative, rich, poignant and often opulent nature of the art nouveau style, was particularly well suited to the purpose of jewellery — to enhance feminine beauty — and the era has been covered exhaustively in Vivienne Becker's excellent book *Art Nouveau Jewellery* (1985).

Art nouveau was short lived in jewellery, lasting only from about 1895 to 1910, but although its influence was very strong in the first decade of the twentieth century, its roots, development and full maturity are to be found in the nineteenth century. Nature, and its association with femininity, was the leitmotif of art nouveau as it had been one of the most powerful trends of the nineteenth century, but it took on a totally different aspect, abandoning rhetorical and imitative realism, to embrace imagination, creativity and vividness of interpretation. The aim of art nouveau was to evoke rather than to portray or copy nature.

In jewellery, art nouveau would not have been possible without the botanical obsession of Oscar Massin, and without the discovery of Japanese art which opened the way to stylisations of the natural world, characterised by a strict economy of asymmetrical yet fluid lines. The favourite subjects of art nouveau jewels were those of the nineteenth century naturalistic tradition: flowers, insects, snakes and animals. The great innovation was the imaginative and free approach to such subjects, for the insects of the 1860s became, in the 1890s, fantastic creatures. Butterflies, dragonflies, cicadas and spiders acquired a shocking and sensual quality (see plate 323). Snakes became sinuous and iridescent symbols of life, eternity and sexuality. Unusual and exotic flowers were favoured: orchids, lilies, mimosa, chrysanthemums, dandelions, sunflowers, poppies and mistletoe. Plants and flowers, seaweeds and marine creatures, with their fluid shapes and lines, alluded to life and movement, to the vital circle of birth and death (see plates 309, 328, 438 and 441). Seeds, buds and decaying flowers were used as much as, and were sometimes preferred to, blossoms in their full glory, to symbolise life in its youth, full bloom and decline. Peacocks and peacocks' feathers, swans and swallows became recurrent motifs, offering their symbolism and their elegant shapes to the flowing art nouveau line and to the sensual gleam of iridescent enamels (see plates 306 and 326).

The greatest innovation was the introduction into jewellery of the female form. For centuries, the depiction of the female figure had been excluded from jewels, as if women hated, or considered bad taste, the idea of adorning themselves with the features of another. Art nouveau made the woman's profile, and the naked, sensuous female body, its emblems, and the *fin de siècle* woman, now conscious of her new position in society and of her femininity, wore such jewels with enthusiasm (see plates 416 and 439).

Art nouveau jewellery aimed to subordinate materials as well as motifs to the rule of nature. Materials were selected for their artistic merit and not for their intrinsic value. Horn, opal, enamel, moonstone, moulded pâte de verre, chalcedony, chrysoprase, agate and pearl were preferred to diamonds and coloured precious stones (see plates 307, 309, 314 and 426).

The preferred medium of art nouveau jewellers was enamel, for which they revived antique techniques and introduced new ones. Plique-à-jour enamel, although mentioned by Benvenuto Cellini in 1568 and possibly known to the

Byzantines, was rescued from oblivion by the art nouveau enamellers. The difficult but very effective technique was similar to that of cloisonné enamel, but the cells were left open at the back so that light could pass through and produce an effect similar to that of a stained glass window (see plates 401, 403 and 426).

The genius of art nouveau was René Lalique (1860-1945), a true innovator whose work soon became an example for jewellers both in Europe and America. Lalique's early production, retailed by famous jewellery houses such as Boucheron, Cartier and Vever, was in the conventional naturalistic style. Lalique soon began to introduce fantasy and originality to his work; in the 1880s and early 1890s he dedicated himself to the study of enamelling techniques and started to develop a truly personal and completely original style where artistic design and technical skill were perfectly combined. His efforts culminated in the collection of jewels he presented at the 1895 Exhibition of the Societé des Artistes Français. The soft and flowing lines of his female figures, of his insects and butterflies, had a strong impact on the public. His fame grew and spread, and soon he was considered the rescuer of French jewellery from a drying and decaying process. His participation at the International Exhibition in Paris in 1900 was a triumph, and his jewels were sought after internationally, copied and imitated (see plates 302, 307, 309, 314, 328, 396, 416, 426, 438, 439 and 441).

Many well-established jewellery firms in Paris turned to art nouveau design towards the end of the century, such as Vever, Fouquet, Gaillard, and Gautrait (see plates 306, 311 and 326). Simultaneously, a whole industry devoted to copies and poor imitations developed and cheaply commercialised the new ideas, thus destroying the true spirit of art nouveau, putting an early end to a movement based on creativity, originality and imagination.

Henry Vever's (1854-1942) production in art nouveau style was admired for the perfection of the enamels and goldsmith work. His jewels were new and original and fully embraced the newly rediscovered idea of introducing the female figure into jewellery.

Georges Fouquet (1862-1957), son of Alphonse Fouquet (1828-1911), developed his father's interest in art nouveau and, towards the end of the century, started to produce plique-à-jour enamel jewels of striking design. His short-lived collaboration with Alphonse Mucha (1860-1939), the famous Czech graphic artist and designer, produced extraordinary ornaments of theatrical aspect, decorated with enamel plaques, oriental and exotic in taste, which were dramatic but often difficult to wear. Fouquet's jewels remained much the same until 1908 when, abandoning the naturalistic excess and theatrical inspiration, he fully embraced the moderate and formal ideals of the Edwardian, or garland, style (see plate 466).

In France, a renewed interest in the art of the medallist was also seen at this time. In the late 1880s, among the jewellers who first introduced medals into their creations was Louis Desbazailles. He successfully mounted bracelets and brooches with cast gold plaques depicting allegorical figures as the personifications of the Arts and Seasons, strong in classical inspiration, but rendered with the flowing lines of art nouveau (see plate 424). As time passed, the influence of the new art became stronger in this particular type of ornament, and circular pendants, decorated with female figures emerging from flowers or water, wrapped in their long flowing hair, and decorated with diamond jewels, became the elegant form of art nouveau jewellery, retaining their charm well into the twentieth century (see plate 397).

In Germany this new style was known by the name 'Jugendstil' and in the world of jewellery it flourished from the late 1890s, at first assuming the forms and lines of contemporary French art nouveau jewels. The distinctive characteristics were opulence and a strong symbolism. Flowers were fresher and healthier than their decaying French counterparts. Later, between 1900 and 1905, a reaction to symbolism and naturalistic excess encouraged jewellery design to develop in more geometric and abstract forms, which were to foreshadow the geometricality of art deco. The flowing lines of nature were constricted within ogival and arched outlines or within softened rectangular or triangular forms. The production of Fahrner (1868-1929) and Hirzel (b.1864), were somehow closer to the solid design of the 1930s than to the delicate fluidity of the jewels of the late 1890s.

In Austria the reaction to tradition took the form of a breakaway from the established Vienna Academy, by a group of artists who set up, in 1897, a new organisation called the 'Wiener Sezession'. The aim of the Secessionists was to achieve functionality in the design of buildings and objects by simplifying their forms, and banishing any superfluous ornament. Jewels were composed of squares and rectangles enclosing strong stylisations of leaf and flower motifs, where petals were curled with geometric regularity, and roses reduced to strong, stylised forms. All this shows a connection between the Scottish architect and designer Charles Rennie Mackintosh (1866-1928) and the Wiener Sezession.

Art nouveau influenced the design of most European countries in varying degrees. In Belgium the influence was particularly strong in the linear works of Henry van de Velde (1863-1957). In Scandinavia Georg Jensen (1866-1935) worked silver in fluid and rich stylisations of the natural world. In Italy the movement did not have strong influences on jewellery, although Musy of Turin worked in simplified French taste. In Spain Luis Masriera (1872-1958) worked in a style close to that of Lalique (see plate 403).

In England, the phenomenon of reaction against the past and its stale traditions was embraced by the Arts and Crafts movement, and developed somewhat differently, although aiming at the same results: jewels of artistic rather than intrinsic value and a ban on mechanisation. (The movement has been well covered by P. Hinks' exhaustive book, *Twentieth Century British Jewellery*, 1983.) The origins of the movement can be traced back to the mid-nineteenth century, when the first reactions to mechanisation and to mass production made their appearance. John Ruskin (1819-1900) set the tone of the movement, and William Morris (1834-1896) soon became its leader. Morris's hatred for the use of machines in the production process was soon to limit the movement and prevent its success.

The aim of the movement was to resuscitate the dead tradition of producing jewels designed and manufactured by the same person or, better, by the same artist. Specialisation was rejected, and the dichotomy between designer and manufacturer was rejected with it. Unfortunately, what was missing was the training of the artist in goldsmith, setting and enamelling techniques, and even the best examples of Arts and Crafts jewellery betray an amateurish approach to the handling of the materials. The banning of machinery from Arts and Crafts workshops certainly did not help in this respect, but the great strength of these jewels is in the fresh, new and fundamental approach to design.

Guilds and art schools were created in the 1880s with the Renaissance workshop in mind, to establish workshops where artists could be trained together in various activities. The ideal was to create attractive and artistic jewels from inexpensive materials, to exploit their own properties rather than to create precious jewels where the brilliancy of the faceted and expensive gemstones detracted from the overall design. Silver was preferred to gold, cabochon semiprecious stones to faceted and expensive gems. Mother-of-pearl, enamel and turquoise with its matrix were esteemed. The cherished jewel was the necklace, often of Renaissance inspiration, made of looped chains and frequently set with polished pebbles or irregular freshwater pearls, encaged in fine metal reticulation.

Robert Ashbee (1863-1942) designed beautiful jewels of naturalistic inspiration, often close to French art nouveau design (see plate 440). His name is immediately associated with impressive elaborations of peacocks and peacock feather motifs in silver, enamel, turquoise and opals. Arthur Gaskin (1862-1928) and his wife Georgie (1868-1934) produced attractive compositions of stylised leaves and flowers in silver, enamel, turquoise and opals (see plate 326). Henry Wilson (1862-1934) designed jewels redolent of the Middle Ages, where symbolism and allegory were combined with repoussé work and careful enamelling. Sensitive to the influence of Japanese art, he also produced beautiful stylisations of the natural world. His success has to be ascribed to the fact that, breaking the rule of the movement, he entrusted the task of manufacturing his jewels to professional craftsmen.

The firm of Liberty & Co. had the merit of bringing 'art jewels' to the public at large, combining the design ideal of the Arts and Crafts movement with high quality mass production, thus producing beautiful and fashionable jewels which were at the same time affordable. Liberty retailed jewels designed by various artists under the name of 'Cymric' (see plates 323, 327 and 442). Among the designers were Archibald Knox (1864-1933), whose work, characterised by knots and interlaced ribbons in the Celtic taste, comprised a large part of the 'Cymric' range. Liberty's main competitors were Murrle

Bennet & Co., who produced jewels of almost identical design to those of 'Cymric', and were responsible for the introduction to England of German jewels in Jugendstil taste; the German born member of the firm, Ernst Mürrle, had part of his jewel production manufactured in Pforzheim, Germany.

The Glasgow School of Design, led by Charles Rennie Mackintosh, exerted a strong influence on German and Austrian Jugendstil jewels, but produced very little jewellery itself. The strong, vertical stylisation, and the combination of rectangular motifs constricting fluid lines, typical of the Scottish school of design, appealed to the Middle European taste more than to the English ideals of the Arts and Crafts movement.

The new art movement was not limited to Europe; in the United States firms of jewellers such as Tiffany & Co. and Marcus & Co. often worked very much in the style of Lalique, specialising in 'art jewels' characterised by the use of champlevé, plique-à-jour enamel and semiprecious stones (see plates 349, 401 and 402).

Parallel with the development of these innovative styles, the stream of traditional jewellery continued to flow smoothly, sometimes marginally touched by the influence of art nouveau, imparting to jewels a new lightness and fluid appearance, though more often repeating and reworking old patterns (see plates 398-400).

Naturalism went to the extreme and beautiful, perfectly executed botanical creations were produced in the 1880s: sumptuous and richly set with diamonds, these ornaments could scarcely be worn even on the cuirassed bodices of formal evening dresses. Jewellers, temporarily, seemed to forget that jewels had to be practical and wearable, not simply perfect and three-dimensional (see plates 359, 361 and 366).

In the 1890s, the intensely feminine dress fashion which enhanced rather than altered the natural curves of the figure, brought with it yards of flimsy materials, such as laces and tulle, draped and ruched on the bodice. The jewels had to adapt to the new fashion and consequently became lighter and smaller.

At the end of the 1880s, crescent brooches appeared and became one of the most common ornaments of the 1890s, either pinned on the tulle and lace draped around the neckline, or worn in the coiffure, with the special hair fitting almost invariably provided and cased with the jewel itself (see plates 334-337 and 339).

Almost simultaneously, stars appeared in large numbers in the hair and on the bodices of fashionable women. More elaborate in design, and more three-dimensional than their 1860s counterparts, they remained in great favour until the end of the century (see plates 331-333).

Insects, which first appeared in jewellery in the 1860s, reached the height of favour during the *fin de siècle*, and swarms of flies, bees and butterflies were crowded on to necklines and hairstyles in combination with stars and crescents (see plates 338 and 340-353).

The colourless and brilliant diamond became the stone *par excellence* in the

1870s, and reached its peak in the 1890s. Diamonds were now relatively abundant on the market and affordable; as a consequence, a new interest developed in the quality of the gemstone and many fashionable women preferred a large, good quality specimen to several mediocre diamonds. The emphasis moved from the setting to the stone itself: heavy and large mounts disappeared completely, substituted by delicate openwork collets and unobtrusive claws, that allowed plenty of light to pass into the stone. Thin yet strong knife wires replaced heavy chains in necklaces and pendants (see plate 320). Millegrain settings became popular in all kind of jewels at the end of the century; in this simple form of diamond setting the stone is held in a collet, the setting edge of which is decorated with small beads or grains of metal, usually produced by a knurling or millegraining tool (see plate 303). The rarity of the material had forced diamond cutters to conserve as much weight as possible. Cushion-shaped diamonds were the result of such economy but their shape, fat and bulgy, did not exploit the exceptional optical characteristic of the diamond, its high refractive index and dispersion. To allow light to enter the stone, be reflected out by the back facets and split into the prismatic colours, the cut was modified. The stone became thinner and circular in shape, and the culet was reduced to the size of a pin-point. The new brilliant cut involved a waste of up to 50% of the rough crystal, made possible by the abundance of diamonds on the market.

Although diamonds were the vogue in the last decades of the century, the trend in *fin de siècle* jewellery was to use a larger variety of gemstones.

Kashmir sapphires appeared on the market at the beginning of the 1880s; American sapphires from Montana, pale and metallic, followed ten years later. The bright apple green demantoid garnet, discovered in the Ural mountains in 1860, was often used in naturalistic jewels of the 1880s and 1890s (see plates 353-355).

Opals became the modish companion of diamonds in many delicate *fin de siècle* jewels. The rare black opal from Queensland — which despite its name displays a vibrancy of rich colour — came on the market in the 1880s (see plate 327). Moonstones were used by art nouveau designers (see plates 323 and 372) and in less expensive jewellery: cut 'en cabochon' or carved in the shape of a smiling full moon, they were set at the centre of a bar brooch or at the top of a tiepin. Peridots, combined with diamonds or tiny seed pearls, were mounted in delicate pendants and necklaces of scroll design (see plate 317).

In the 1890s pearls and half-pearls were the preferred alternative to expensive diamonds, for their delicate sheen perfectly suited the pale colours and the soft silks of the dresses of the last decade of the century. The craze for pearls hit all Europe, and women wore them in several rows around the neck or in the hair, combined with sprays of diamonds and feathers.

Opal, chrysoberyl cat's eye, crocidolite (or tiger's eye) and labradorite were successfully carved, or cut en cabochon, to exploit their characteristics and were daringly introduced in jewellery (see plates 340, 381 and 394). Gold nuggets and freshwater pearls, from Scotland and the Mississippi, fascinated jewellers with their irregular shapes.

In the 1880s, silver gained favour for less expensive everyday jewellery. Chains and necklaces, heavily engraved lockets, and brooches stamped out by machinery and bearing names, dates and mottoes such as 'Mizpah' (I will watch over thee), were produced in large quantities (see plate 388).

Novelty and sporting jewellery consolidated the approval they had enjoyed in the previous decade. Anything in the animal or vegetable kingdom and any object related to hunting, riding, fishing and golfing, became suitable motifs for jewellery (see plates 368-379 and 423). Pansies and trefoils, baskets of flowers, dogs and horses, spurs and stirrups, horseshoes and foxes, bicycles, yachts, swords, golfing clubs and fishing rods, were the subjects of many *fin de siècle* brooches, and often decorated the tiepins and cufflinks worn by fashionable gentlemen at the turn of the century (see plates 445 and 448).

Good luck charms and dates and names spelt in diamonds came into vogue as a commemoration of a special occasion (see plates 370 and 387).

Hearts, and pairs of hearts, surmounted by a coronet or a ribbon bow, entirely set with diamonds or with coloured stones surrounded by diamonds, were an approved motif for brooches and rings (see plates 407-409, 413, 432 and 433).

Memorial jewellery was extremely severe in the 1880s, characterised by large surfaces of black enamel simply decorated with a cross or symbolic forget-me-not in half-pearls or diamonds. Towards the end of the century, mourning traditions became less severe and, during mourning periods, instead of purpose made jewellery, women preferred to wear very few jewels or none at all, perhaps a single string of pearls or a small diamond ring.

This analysis of *fin de siècle* jewellery would be incomplete without reference to Carl Fabergé, the famous Russian crown jeweller. Better known for his 'objects of vertu' — animals and vases of flowers carved in hardstone, enamelled and gem-set Easter eggs, frames, boxes and clocks — he also produced a relatively small number of jewels. His creations were often in a sumptuous and elaborate revived French rococo style, embellished with guilloché enamels and garlands of laurel leaves chased in red, yellow and green gold. Sometimes he indulged in pieces of art nouveau inspiration, but often worked in a very plain and sober style, simply setting cabochon stones — amethysts and sapphires in particular — within diamond borders. His jewels, from miniature Easter egg pendants to important gem-set pieces, are always characterised by skilful and precise workmanship (see plate 417).

Plate 297. Sir Luke Fildes, 1894, 'Alexandra, Queen of Edward VII, when Princess of Wales'.
National Portrait Gallery.

Plate 298. A pearl and diamond tiara, last quarter of the 19th century. All the elements may be worn separately as brooches.

Plate 299. A diamond tiara, c.1890, the design is becoming much lighter aided by the use of knife-wires. This example also forms a necklace which is a very useful consideration when purchasing: tiaras that only function as hair ornaments have limited appeal these days.

Tiaras and Hair Ornaments

Tiaras were very much in fashion in the last two decades of the century, and necklaces were often provided with a special rigid metal frame to enable them to be worn as a tiara. This simple device allowed women to have a formal tiara when a special occasion required it. Typically, tiaras assumed the form of a graduated row of spikes alternating with trefoil motifs or, that of a graduated row of scrolled lyre design (see plates 299 and 304). In the same way diamond flowerhead, star and crescent tiaras of the 1890s were provided with brooch

Plate 300. A diamond tiara, last quarter of the 19th century; each of the flowerheads may be removed from the frame and worn as a brooch. The illustrations show the typical brooch fittings which accompany these jewels and the distinctive fitted morocco leather case by Hunt and Roskell.

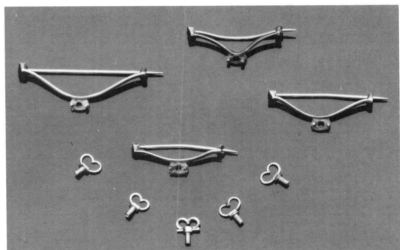

Plate 301. A diamond tiara, c.1890.

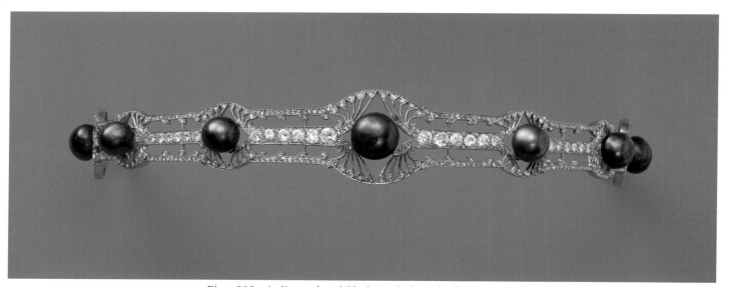

Plate 302. A diamond and black pearl tiara, by René Lalique, c.1900.

200

Plate 303. A diamond diadem, c.1890-1900. This design is reminiscent of Empire jewels. Notice the millegrain setting to the edges of the mount and around the larger stones, which is very typical of the turn of the century.

and hairpin fittings so that the single elements could be worn on the bodice, or in the hair when the full tiara was not required (see plate 300).

Similarly, floral tiaras of the late nineteenth century often divided into three or more sprays, wearable as brooches or corsage ornaments (see plate 298). Other tiaras assumed the shape of elaborate diamond scrollworks or festoons, often rising from diamond clusters and surmounted by pear-shaped diamonds or drop-shaped pearls (see plate 301).

Tiaras of formal design were decorated with garlands and wreaths of laurel leaves towards the turn of the century (see plate 303).

In the 1890s Imperial Russian tiaras became the rage all over Europe. The design, probably based on the Russian headdress, the kokoshnik, consisted of

Plate 304. A pearl and diamond tiara/necklace, c.1890. This is a common design of the period with its slender attenuated drops and knife-wire scrolls.

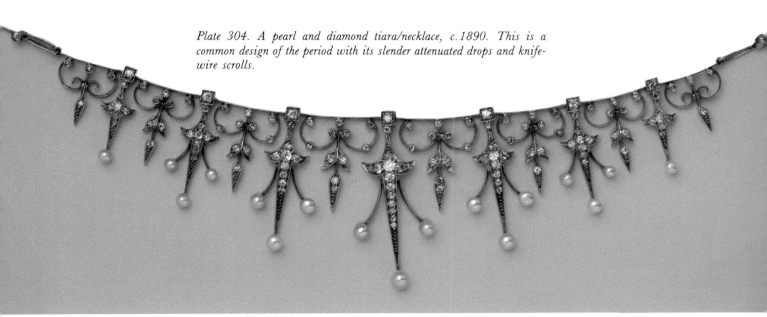

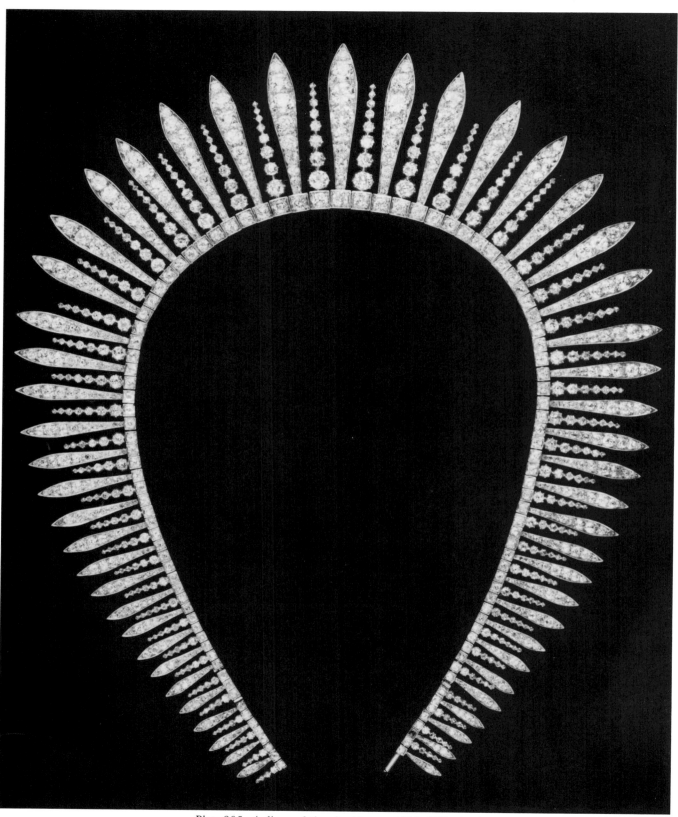

Plate 305. A diamond tiara/necklace, c.1890. This classic design after the Russian kokoshnik is often called 'Tiara Russe'.

Plate 306. A polychrome enamel and diamond head ornament, by Lucien Gaillard, c.1900.

a graduated row of upright and radiating lanceolated leaf motifs (see plate 305).

Pins and brooches in the 1880s and 1890s became hair ornaments; usually pinned in the hair above the forehead, or at the top of the chignon, they were often used to transfix a feather aigrette or a rosette of tulle or gauze. Diamond butterflies, beetles, stars, crescents, trefoils, swallows, paired hearts, horseshoes, knots and the like, were desirable hair ornaments for evening wear.

Art nouveau tiaras and hair ornaments, often made of unusual materials such as horn and enamel, offered their shapes to the imaginative naturalism typical of the style (see plates 302, 306 and 307).

Plate 307. An enamel and horn tiara, by René Lalique, c.1900. Horn is a very unusual material to find in jewellery but Lalique used it to great effect often in combination with enamel and precious stones.

Plate 308. A pearl and diamond comb, c.1890. The jewelled surmount may also be worn as a brooch.

Combs

Combs, either of traditional design or of art nouveau inspiration, which were carved in an unusual material such as horn, or delicately enamelled (see plate 309), all had a vertical tendency, being generally taller and slimmer than those of the previous decade.

In the 1890s, small combs to be worn at the centre of the head, just above the hairline, became the vogue, set with pearls and diamonds, in the form of coronets or miniature tiaras of scroll design (see plate 308).

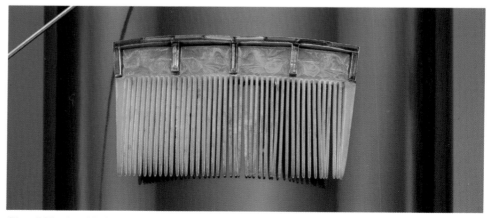

Plate 309. A gold, horn and amethyst comb, by René Lalique, c.1900. Notice the marine creature motifs carved in horn.

Plate 310. A gold, pearl, enamel and diamond demi-parure, c.1890. The combination of pastel opalescent enamel on a guilloché ground is typical of fin de siècle jewellery.

Parures

Altogether, the production of large parures, complete with necklace, brooches, bracelets and earrings, disappeared, since large sets of matching jewels were no longer in fashion. Women preferred to combine brooches and pendants, necklaces and bracelets, according to their own taste and to the shape of their dresses.

Demi-parures were still worn (see plates 310 and 311), and the novelty consisted of large brooches or corsage ornaments of naturalistic inspiration which could be disassembled into smaller sections and worn separately as brooches or hair ornaments.

Plate 311. A demi-parure in pearl, enamel and diamond, by L. Gautrait for L. Gariod, c.1890, and a brooch by the same maker, c.1890. All show the influence of French ormolu furniture mounts of the second half of the 18th century.

Plate 312. A pair of diamond earrings, c.1880-1900.

Plate 313. A pair of opal and diamond earrings, c.1880. The delicate ribbon bow and the way the opal is mounted as a swing centre are typical of the day.

Earrings

The earrings of the 1880s and 1890s were generally very small. The fashionable design for day wear in the 1890s consisted of a single pearl embellished with small diamonds. At night, plain diamond studs of varying sizes were preferred. In 1890 pendant earrings reappeared in the shape of pearl and diamond drops designed to move in order to catch and reflect the light.

Plate 314. A pair of opal and enamel earrings, by René Lalique, c.1900-5, in their original case.

One of the most successful designs consisted of a cascade of bell-shaped flowerheads, graduating in size and chained one to another, free to move and sparkle with each movement of the head (see plates 312 and 313).

The great innovation of the early 1890s was the screw fitting, which enabled women to wear earrings without having their ears pierced.

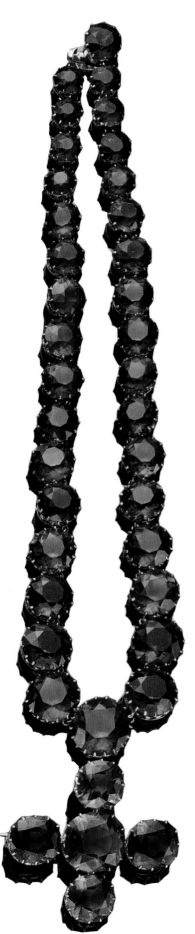

Plate 316. A gold, amethyst and diamond necklace, French, c.1880. Note the flat gold scrolls surrounding the stones.

Necklaces

Among the most acceptable neck ornaments of the 1880s and 1890s was the fringed necklace, designed as a graduated row of collet-set stones or trefoil motifs suspended by means of very thin knife wires from a simple chain necklet. Of more or less elaborate design, this necklace was often set with diamonds, topazes or peridots, and pearls or half-pearls.

The diamond and half-pearl necklace is also typical of the period, designed as a delicate row of flowerheads connected by festooned chains of foliate motifs (see plate 320).

Very delicate and light gold necklets of thin gold wire scrolled in the flowing lines of the art nouveau and set with peridots, amethysts, tourmalines and tiny diamonds featured among the preferred neckwear of the 1890s (see plate 317).

Rivières were also in fashion, especially if set with diamonds cut in the new style and set in openwork galleries (see plate 315).

Many necklaces were designed to also be worn as tiaras. The front of many diamond fringed and scrolled necklaces could be mounted on a rigid tiara fitting provided by the jeweller, and beautifully cased with the necklace in a fitted box (see plates 299, 304 and 305).

The choker, or dog collar ('collier de chien' in France), was perhaps the most characteristic neckwear of this period. Evening dog collars were made of as many as eleven or twelve rows of small pearls, set at intervals with diamond bars, diamond plaques of delicate scrollwork design, or enamel and gem-set plaques of art nouveau inspiration (see plate 328). Other necklaces were often worn together with the dog collar, preferably rows of pearls of graduated length combined with diamond rivières.

Plate 315. An amethyst rivière with detachable cruciform pendant, last quarter of the 19th century. The rivière remained popular throughout the century. Note how these Siberian stones are claw-set.

Plate 317. A gold, peridot and half-pearl necklace, c.1890. Seed pearl necklaces like this were produced in large numbers in England during the closing years of the century. Peridot became a popular stone at this time.

The fashion for dog collars and strings of pearls, worn severally, was led by Alexandra, Princess of Wales, who very often wore a pearl choker combined with strings of pearls on her décolletage. For day wear, dog collars were more comfortable, formed of soft lace or velvet ribbons, set at the centre with openwork diamond plaques or slides of stylised floral design. Another novelty of the 1890s was the sautoir, or longchain, of gold links set with pearls, diamonds or other gemstones, and often terminated with a tassel. Long pearl sautoirs, tucked at the waist or pinned with a brooch to the corsage were a favourite of Princess Alexandra. Both sautoirs and chokers continued to be in vogue into the first years of the new century.

Coral, turquoise and gold bead necklaces were frequently worn in the last two decades of the century, as well as necklaces of small gold and gem-set or enamelled linking (see plates 316 and 318). In the early 1880s amber bead necklaces were the chosen and only ornament of the women who embraced the ideals of the Aesthetic movement.

Plate 318. Three necklaces of the period 1875-1900.

Plate 319. A gold, enamel and gem-set necklace by Carlo and Arthur Giuliano, c.1895. This is a particularly elaborate example for their workshop. If compared with necklaces by their father in Chapter 4 this example shows how they abandoned Renaissance inspiration in favour of a more delicate, feminine design.

Plate 320. A diamond necklace, c.1890-1900. Note the new delicacy and lightness of design and the use of knife-wire to give the impression that the single stones are suspended in mid-air.

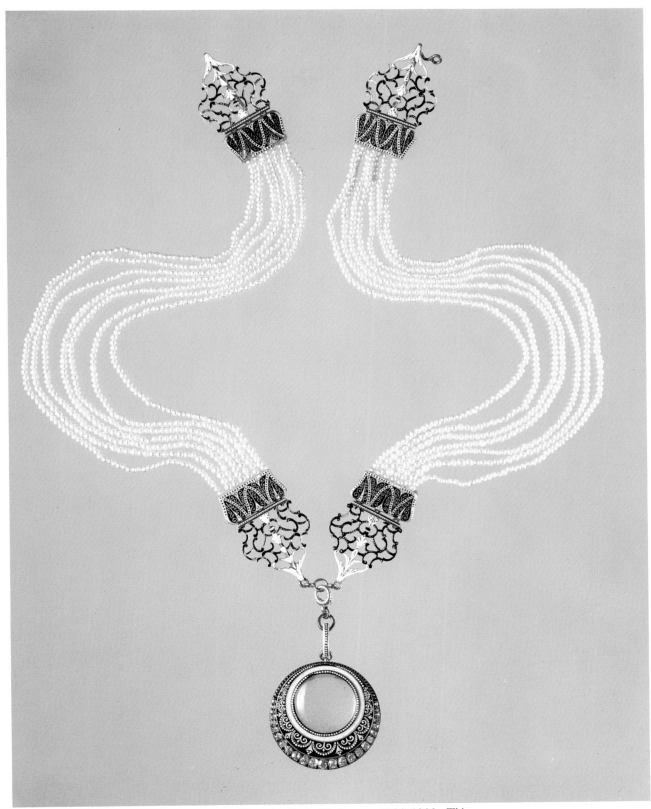

Plate 321. A gold, seed pearl and enamel necklace, by Carlo Giuliano, c.1890-1900. This was a popular design. Note the monochrome enamel and the slender chains of seed pearls.

Plate 322. A gold, enamel and gem-set necklace by Carlo and Arthur Giuliano, c.1900, showing a free approach to foliate motifs, perhaps acknowledging contemporary art nouveau designs.

Plate 323. A gold, enamel, plique-à-jour enamel and moonstone necklace, designed by Fred Partridge and retailed by Liberty & Co., c.1900.

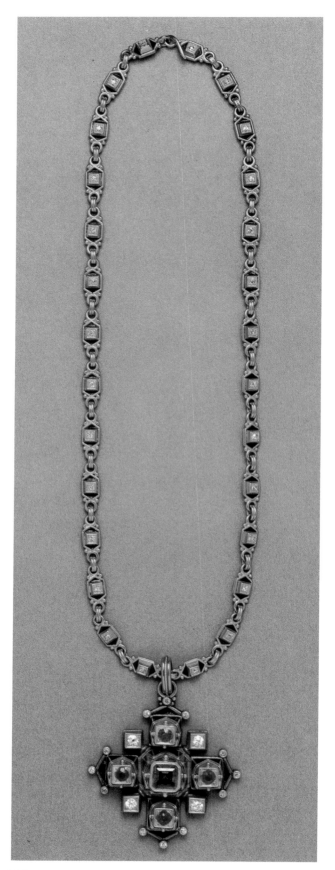

Plate 325. A gold, enamel, pearl and diamond necklace, by Carlo and Arthur Giuliano, c.1890-1900. The crescent scrolls flecked with black enamel are a characteristic feature of their work at this time.

Plate 324. A gold, enamel and gem-set necklace, by Giacinto Melillo, c.1900. The design of this necklace is rather archaic but shows that Renaissance/archaeological jewellery was still popular in Italy. The red stones are synthetic rubies and this is a very early example to employ such stones.

Plate 326. A necklace in gold, opal, plique-à-jour enamel and diamond, by L. Gautrait, c.1900, which compared with the demi-parure of plate 311 shows a far more typical art nouveau design. A brooch and pendant by Arthur and Georgie Gaskin, c.1900-5, characteristic of British Arts and Crafts design.

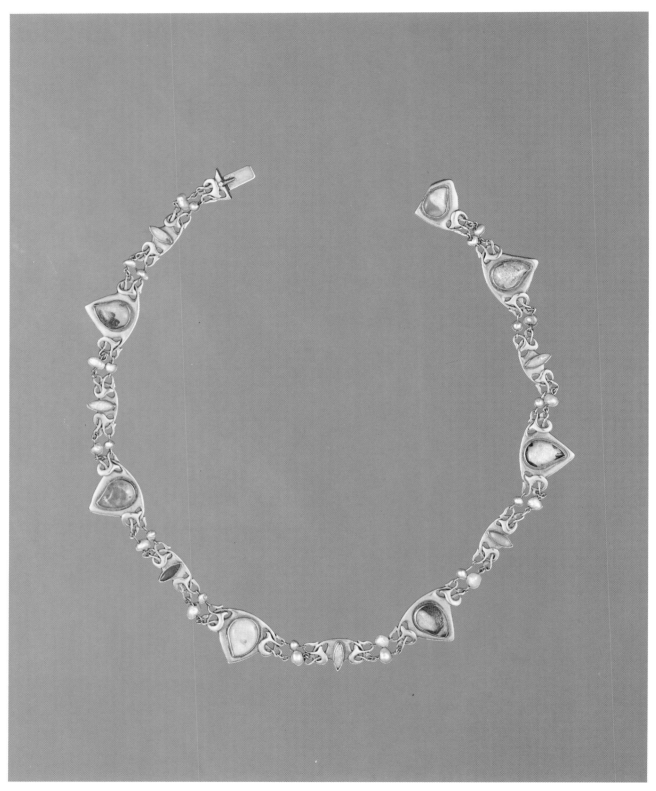

Plate 327. A gold, opal and seed pearl necklace, by Liberty & Co. Notice how many of the new Australian black opals are used in combination with the matrix; this was very popular with Arts and Crafts jewellers. The design shows a Celtic influence which is perhaps a British characteristic in art nouveau jewellery.

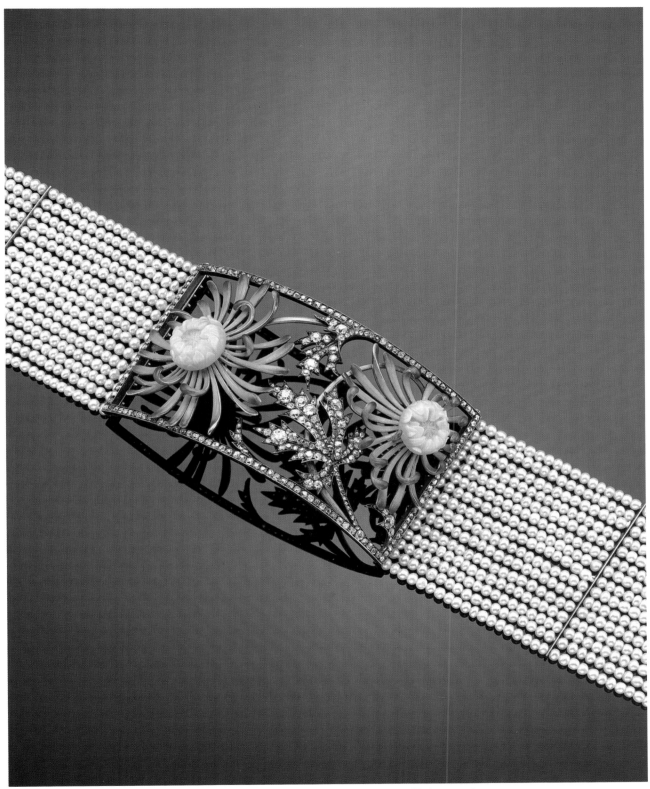

Plate 328. A pearl, enamel, opal and diamond choker, by René Lalique, c.1900. Chokers, or dog collars, which had been brought to popularity by Princess Alexandra, remained in fashion up to the First World War.

Plate 329. A diamond brooch/pendant designed as a sun in splendour, c.1880. Very often the central cluster of such jewels may be unscrewed and worn as the bezel of a ring.

Plate 330. A pearl and diamond brooch designed as a setting sun, c.1880-90. Freshwater pearls from Scottish rivers, particularly the Tay, enjoyed a short-lived popularity at this time.

Plate 331. A half-pearl and diamond star brooch, c.1880.

Brooches

Fin de siècle brooches were usually smaller and more delicate in design than their earlier counterparts, and worn in large numbers along the neckline, or pinned on the lace and tulle draped around the décolletage. It was irrelevant if the design and style did not match: all that was necessary was quantity around the neckline. More elaborate in design than earlier examples, star brooches were made of six, eight, or even twelve or sixteen points, often decorated, between the arms, with a single stone set at the end of a knife wire. Diamond stars were the most acceptable, but cheaper versions set with pearls, opals and moonstones provided successful alternatives (see plates 331-333). Crescent brooches were set with one, two or three rows of gemstones, graduating in size from the centre, usually diamonds in combination with rubies or sapphires. Crescents were also successfully set with opals and pearls or, appropriately, moonstones. Wide crescents of open design were sometimes embellished with a small bird or trefoil or bee (honeymoon brooches). Other crescents of closer and more compact design were occasionally set at the centre with a star motif (see plates 334-337 and 339). Also in favour were sunburst brooches, entirely set with diamonds (see plates 329 and 330), and pansy brooches with coloured gemstones or velvet petals bordered with small diamonds.

Butterflies, dragonflies, spiders, bees and flies set with diamonds and coloured gemstones were the craze of the 1890s (see plates 338 and 340-353). Diamond and enamel swallows, diamond violins, caducei, anchors and arrows, diamond, opal and demantoid garnet frogs and lizards were other fashionable brooch forms (see plates 354, 355, 379, 380, 382 and 390).

Insects were the smart motifs for striking art nouveau brooches with plique-à-jour enamel wings and diamond bodies.

Plate 332. A diamond star brooch, c.1880-90. Note the diamonds collet-set on knife-wires between the arms.

Plate 333. A diamond star or flowerhead brooch, c.1880. Many examples like this have survived.

Plate 334. A diamond crescent brooch, c.1880-90, modified with a wave scroll. An unusual design.

Plate 335. Two diamond crescent brooches, c.1880-90. The more elaborate of the two is of a later date.

Bar brooches appeared in the 1890s and immediately enjoyed a great success. They consisted of a horizontal gold bar set at the centre with a decorative motif and often terminated with two petals or two small gemstones. In its simplest form the bar brooch was plainly set with a single diamond, but its functional shape offered the jewellers a field in which to exploit their fantasy and imagination, thus bar brooches were decorated with crescents and stars, sprays of leaves and flowers, pheasants and chanticleers, swallows and flies, shamrocks and clovers (see plates 336, 377 and 389).

Novelty brooches were adorned with rabbits biting a carrot or holding a turnip, chickens just emerging from diamond or enamel eggshells ('just out' brooches), wingspread bats, or kittens playing with a ball of wool; others assumed the form of gold and diamond wishbones, lyres, winged cherubs,

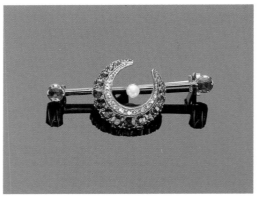

Plate 336. A pearl, sapphire and diamond bar brooch, c.1900. Coloured stones in these relatively cheap brooches are often found to be doublets.

Plate 337. An opal and diamond crescent brooch, c.1890-1900.

Plate 338. A quartz cat's-eye and diamond brooch, designed as a winged beetle, last quarter of the 19th century. The craze for insect brooches even spread to include unattractive members of the entomological world.

Plate 339. Two gem-set crescent brooches, both c.1900. So popular was the crescent motif that it is to be found in jewellery of all price levels. These are lowly examples.

Plate 340. A tiger's eye (crocidolite) and diamond bee brooch and earstuds, c.1890.

Plate 341. A brooch of shells set with opal, quartz cat's-eye, pearl and diamond, last quarter of the 19th century.
Plate 342. A fine ruby and diamond butterfly brooch, c.1880-1900. Here the jeweller has employed high quality stones.

Plate 343. A demantoid garnet and diamond bee brooch, c.1890. Demantoid garnets, which were relatively new to the market at this time, were popular especially in animal jewellery. The detail of the back shows that the brooch fitting is a later addition.

dogs, rabbits, owls, or a carved moonstone 'man in the moon' (see plates 371, 372, 381, 383-389).

Sporting brooches retained the basic designs that first appeared in the 1860s: horseshoes, golf clubs, fishing rods, horns and riding caps, but, towards the end of the century, the repertoire was enlarged to embrace all types of game and pointing dogs, very often realistically decorated with polychrome enamels and set with diamonds (see plates 376-378 and 388). Horseshoes remained the ideal motif, appealing also to less sporting women because of the simple and linear design. In the 1890s horseshoe brooches were often set with two rows of diamonds, one larger than the other, or with a line of diamonds and another of rubies or sapphires. Very occasionally emeralds were used. Plume and feather brooches retained their appeal (see plate 367).

More formal corsage ornaments continued to be produced in the eighteenth century taste, designed as girandoles or elaborate cartouche motifs and entirely set with diamonds (see plates 391 and 392), they were often used with diamond shoulder brooches designed as scrolled knots or ribbon bows.

Plate 344. *An unusual opal, pink sapphire and diamond butterfly brooch, c.1900. This brooch was almost certainly designed as a vehicle for the good quality Australian opals which were beginning to appear on the market.*

Plate 345. *A diamond brooch designed as a swallow-tail butterfly, c.1890. Another fine quality example.*

Rosettes and heart-shaped motifs were also incorporated in brooch designs (see plates 356-358 and 364).

Diamond spray brooches, often mounted en tremblant, continued to be worn by less innovative women (see plates 359-361, 365 and 366).

The versatile nature of brooches often offered their shapes to the fluid naturalistic designs of art nouveau (see plates 396-403).

Plate 346. *A sapphire and diamond bee brooch, c.1880.*

Plate 347. *A gold and gem-set butterfly brooch, c.1900, of a type that was produced in great numbers at relatively low cost.*

Plate 348. *An amethyst and rose diamond dragonfly brooch, c.1900. The wings are mounted on springs 'en tremblant'.*

Plate 349. A fine diamond dragonfly brooch, by Tiffany & Co., c.1900. The body is cleverly articulated. Dragonflies owed their popularity to art nouveau.

Plate 350. A plain gold brooch designed as a winged insect, c.1900.

Plate 351. A gold and rose diamond insect brooch, c.1900. A variation on a popular design.

Plate 352. A modern gold, emerald and diamond bee brooch. The diamonds are eight or Swiss-cut. This would not have been the case in the 19th century.

Plate 353. A demantoid garnet and diamond brooch/pendant/hair ornament, c.1890. We have seen several examples of this brooch, each in its characteristic spider's web case. Demantoid garnets over a carat in weight become quite valuable. This stone in the abdomen weighed approximately 1.5 carats, and was worth perhaps £2,000 on its own.

Plate 354. An opal, demantoid garnet and diamond brooch, c.1900, designed as a lizard. Another popular design which was produced in many materials.

Plate 355. A demantoid garnet and diamond lizard brooch, c.1900. A cheaper version of the example illustrated in plate 354.

223

Plate 356. An opal and diamond pendant, c.1890-1900. Carved opals in jewellery, particularly in the form of hearts, was a popular fin de siècle feature.

Plate 357. A citrine, amethyst and diamond brooch, designed as a pair of hearts surmounted by a ribbon bow, c.1880-90. Although this motif had its origin one hundred years earlier, it became one of the most popular designs of the turn of the century.

Plate 358. A diamond brooch/pendant, c.1880-90. Heart-shaped brooches and pendants were common at this time pavé-set with diamonds. Care should be taken when purchasing such pieces that the cutting of the stone is contemporary with the mount.

Plate 359. An extraordinary ruby and diamond spray brooch, c.1880-1900, Portuguese, designed as an orchid. These flowers were becoming increasingly popular in Europe at this time. All petals and leaves are mounted 'en tremblant' on springs.

Plate 360. A diamond brooch designed as a narcissus, c.1880-90, the flowerhead mounted 'en tremblant'.

Plate 361. A diamond spray brooch, French, c.1880. The informal ribbon bow gathering the posy of flowers and the naturalism of the design are typical French touches.

Plate 363. A modern diamond brooch of rosette design. The pinched collets and relatively modern cut stones are an obvious indication of the date, as is the fact that it is entirely set in white gold, which would not have been employed in the late 19th century.

Plate 362. A modern diamond spray brooch. The baguette diamonds in the stem would not have been found in a 19th century piece of jewellery. The detail of the back of the mount shows the poor quality manufacture; no diamond-set jewel of this size would have been so poorly made a century ago since labour costs were low.

Plate 364. A black pearl and diamond brooch of rosette design, c.1880.

Plate 365. A ruby and diamond brooch designed as a spray of holly, c.1890-1900.

Plate 366. A diamond spray brooch, English, c.1880. The flowerheads are mounted 'en tremblant'.

Plate 367. An emerald, ruby and diamond brooch designed as a peacock's plume, c.1880.

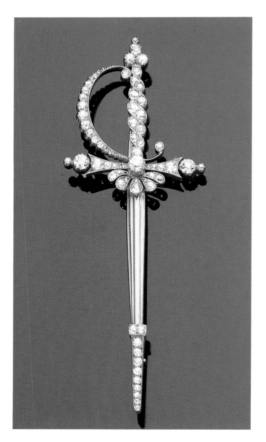

Plate 369. An amethyst and diamond 'giardinetto' brooch, c.1890-1900.

Plate 368. A diamond sword brooch, c.1880-90.

Plate 370. A diamond bar brooch, c.1900. Name brooches were particularly popular around the turn of the century (see also plate 388).

Plate 371. A gold novelty brooch, late 19th century.

Plate 372. A diamond and moon-stone 'man in the moon' brooch, c.1890.

Plate 373. An enamel and diamond yachting brooch, c.1900. Sporting jewels like this were popular from about 1880 onwards.

Plate 374. A gold and diamond bicycle brooch, c.1900.

Plate 375. A gold and seed pearl novelty brooch, late 19th century.

Plate 376. A gold fox mask brooch, c.1890. The popularity of hunting and riding jewels spread quickly from France to England.

Plate 377. A 9 carat gold and seed pearl bar brooch, c.1890.

Plate 378. A gold and gem-set brooch, decorated with horseshoe motifs, c.1890-1900.

Plate 379. A diamond anchor brooch, c.1880-90. The anchor is a common symbol of hope.

Plate 380. A demantoid garnet and diamond frog brooch, c.1890-1900.

Plate 381. A gold and carved labradorite bat brooch, c.1900. Labradorite enjoyed brief popularity at this time, particularly carved as cameos.

Plate 382. A gold and diamond violin brooch, c.1890. Another example of novelty jewellery.

Plate 383. A rose diamond and emerald rabbit brooch, c.1900.

Plate 384. A carbuncle and diamond brooch, designed as an owl, late 19th century.

Plate 385. A carved chalcedony and rose diamond ostrich brooch, c.1890-1900.

Plate 386. A diamond miniature brooch of a terrier, c.1900.

Plate 387. A charming piglet brooch in diamond, c.1900. In many countries in Europe piglets are considered to bring good luck.

Plate 388. A representative collection of silver machine-made brooches from the turn of the century. Many of these bear Birmingham silver hallmarks. Note especially the use of names, the horseshoe and heart motifs and the ever popular 'Mizpah' jewels.

Plate 389. A representative collection of inexpensive gold and gem-set brooches from the turn of the century. Note especially the use of the bird and butterfly motifs, hearts, ribbon bows, star and crescent and elliptical forms.

Plate 390. A typical turn of the century enamel and diamond swallow brooch. Swallows were particularly popular in art nouveau designs.

Plate 391. A diamond brooch/corsage ornament, c.1890. The slender diamond chains and knife-wire are typical of the date for this type of formal and important evening jewel.

Plate 392. A pearl and diamond corsage ornament, c.1900. The design is reminiscent of French ormolu furniture mounts of the late 18th century. Often these jewels were adaptable to form the centre of a dog collar or a belt buckle. This example is still set in gold and silver, though some contemporary jewels were by now set in platinum.

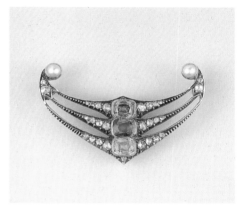

Plate 393. A pearl, diamond, pink sapphire and zircon brooch by Carlo Giuliano, c.1890.

Plate 394. An attractive black opal cameo mounted as a pendant, by Wilhelm Shmidt, c.1890. The first recorded discovery of black opal in Australia (still the only known locality for this gem) was in 1872 in Queensland; it took several years before the first stones appeared in European jewels.

Plate 395. A blister pearl and diamond brooch, c.1900. The ribbon bow surmount and articulated pendant are clues to the date.

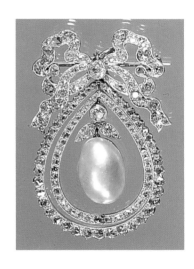

Plate 396. A gold, enamel, pearl and diamond brooch, by René Lalique, c.1895. This is an unusual combination for Lalique of a medieval frieze and art nouveau mount.

Plate 397. A gold and diamond brooch, French, designed as circular plaque cast with the profile of Joan of Arc, c.1900, probably by Edmond Becker. Art nouveau medallions like this example were produced in large numbers and of varying quality up to the First World War.

Plate 398. An opal and diamond brooch, c.1890-1900. The assymmetrical naturalistic design of the mount shows that the jeweller was aware of art nouveau designs and wished to bring an innovative touch to an otherwise formal brooch.

Plate 399. A gold, pearl and diamond brooch, c.1890.

Plate 400. A turquoise and diamond brooch/pendant, c.1900.

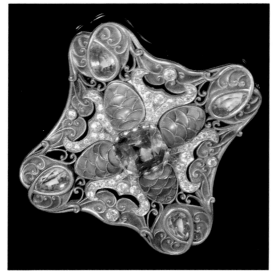

Plate 401. A peridot, diamond and enamel brooch, by Marcus & Co., c.1900. This New York firm operated from a shop at 857 Broadway which specialised in rich plique-à-jour enamel and art nouveau inspired designs.

Plate 402. A gold, opal and enamel brooch by Tiffany, c.1900. Art nouveau influence was not restricted to Europe. Firms such as Tiffany & Co. and Marcus & Co. quickly adopted the new style in the United States.

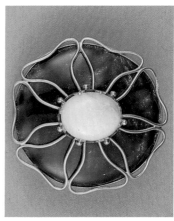

Plate 403. A plique-à-jour enamel, sapphire and diamond brooch/pendant, by Luis Masriera. Based in Barcelona this family firm of jewellers, run by Luis Masriera (1872-1958) and his brother, specialised in art nouveau jewels often incorporating female features in the design.

Plate 404. A modern sapphire and diamond butterfly brooch, with the wings mounted 'en tremblant'. Although the design is typical of the late 19th century, the calibré-cut sapphires, the brilliant-cut diamonds and the white and yellow gold mount clearly indicate that the piece is a modern reproduction.

Plate 405. A collection of tinted crystal intaglios by Ernest and Marius Pradier, dating from around the turn of the century.

Plate 406. A gold and tinted intaglio locket, late 19th century. A typically sentimental turn of the century jewel.

Pendants

Many of the above mentioned brooches were fitted with a loop and worn as pendants (see plates 329, 353, 395, etc.), but the most sought after shape for *fin de siècle* jewelled pendants was the cross and the heart. Latin cross pendants were often set with diamonds, but also with many other less expensive gemstones, or pearls, or simply decorated with enamels.

Heart-shaped pendants and lockets, often surmounted by a ribbon bow, were entirely pavé-set with diamonds or with half-pearls and diamonds. Hearts in green, blue or red guilloché enamels, decorated at the centre with a small pearl or diamond motif, and mounted within a similarly set border, were the prevailing fashion (see plates 356, 358 and 407-409).

Pendants often offered their shape to the fervent naturalistic imaginations of art nouveau and Arts and Crafts jeweller-artists, who produced splendid examples in gemstones and enamels in almost any form suggested by the vegetable and animal kingdom (see plates 403 and 416).

Plate 407. A half-pearl and diamond pendant, c.1880-90, designed as a pair of hearts.

Plate 408. A gold and ruby heart-shaped locket, c.1890, entirely pavé-set with cabochon stones. It is rare in 19th century jewellery for coloured stones to be used without diamonds or pearls.

Plate 411. A ruby, pearl, peridot and diamond lozenge-shaped pendant, by Carlo and Arthur Giuliano, c.1895. This jewel perhaps looks back to their father's work of the 1870s or is possibly old stock.

Plate 409. A ruby and half-pearl heart-shaped locket, c.1900.

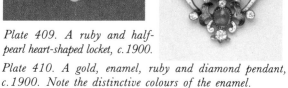

Plate 410. A gold, enamel, ruby and diamond pendant, c.1900. Note the distinctive colours of the enamel.

234

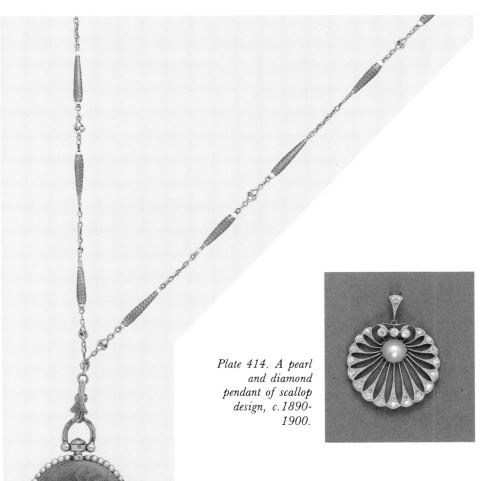

Plate 414. A pearl
and diamond
pendant of scallop
design, c.1890-
1900.

Plate 413. A pearl
and enamel
brooch/pendant
applied at the centre
with a pearl and
diamond pair of
hearts,
c.1890-1900. The
white enamel border
is characteristic,
punctuated at
intervals by gold
dots.

Plate 412. A gold, enamel, seed
pearl and diamond watch and longchain, by Tiffany & Co., c.1900.
These pendant watches which were
made both in the U.S.A. and in
Europe (notably by Cartier) are very
often decorated with pale blue,
mauve or grey enamel. The fine
engine-turning beneath the enamel is
reminiscent of jewels dating from one
hundred years earlier.

The flowing lines of art nouveau also influenced the design of less innovative jewels which took the form of very delicate foliate and scrolled pendants, set with half-pearls, peridots, amethysts and turquoises (see plate 400).

Gold lockets were worn with the same enthusiasm as in the previous decade but became smaller and circular in shape, decorated at the centre with a monogram or a small jewelled motif.

Towards the end of the century it became fashionable to wear, attached to an enamelled longchain, a small watch/pendant, similarly enamelled and often gem-set (see plates 412 and 415), or a lorgnette (see plates 443 and 444).

Plate 415. A gold, enamel and diamond spherical pendant watch, c.1900. Ball watches seem to have first appeared around this time.

Plate 416. A gold and enamel pendant by René Lalique, c.1900.

Plate 417. A collection of jewels by Carl Fabergé, dating from the turn of the century, and including four examples of his famous miniature eggs which were fashionable Easter gifts in Russia.

Bracelets

Bracelets continued to be worn in numbers, as many as four on each arm. Bangles were the modish form of arm ornament, both wide and narrow. Wide gold bangles decorated with pearls, diamonds or other gemstones continued to be produced as in the previous decade, and were in fashion in the 1880s (see plates 427, 428 and 430). In the 1890s narrower bangles were preferred, either designed as half hoops of diamonds, sapphires, emeralds, pearls, or opals, or as thin gold hoops set at the centre with gem-set flowerhead clusters, scrolled or marquise-shaped motifs (see plates 429 and 431). Typical of the 1890s were multi-hoop bangles, the backs composed of two or three fine gold wires, the

Plate 418. A gold and enamel bracelet in Etruscan style by Giacinto Melillo, c.1900. The quality of the workmanship in this and plate 421 is exemplary and probably exceeds that of the ancient originals.

Plate 419. A ruby and diamond bracelet, c.1900. The rope-like diamond chain is characteristic of this date.

Plate 420. A gold, seed pearl, sapphire and rose diamond bracelet, late 19th century.

Plate 421. A gold bracelet in Etruscan style, by Fasoli, c.1900.

front set with a gem-set flowerhead cluster, often detachable and wearable as a brooch, or with a horseshoe or a heart-shaped motif (see plate 422).

Another innovation of the 1890s was the crossover bangle, designed as a gold wire crossed and overlapped at the front and decorated at the ends with floral motifs or other decorative devices. Open-ended hinged bangles which sprung to clasp the arm, were often made of twisted or fluted gold and decorated at the two ends with gold or gemstone beads.

Towards the end of the century, curb link bracelets were in vogue, produced both in heavy 18 carat gold and in hollowed 9 carat gold, thus suiting every pocket, and often sported a padlock clasp or supported a collection of charms, coins and medallions. Sometimes, at the centre of the links, they were set with small turquoises or opals. Other daywear bracelets assumed the form of gold links of various patterns, set at intervals with small gemstone clusters (see plate 420).

Towards the end of the century, bracelets of rope-like diamond chains, often decorated at the front with a cartouche-shaped motif, were fashionable (see plate 419).

Bracelets made of several rows of pearls on a diamond plaque clasp, or designed as velvet ribbons decorated with diamond openwork slides, were often worn to match the pearl or velvet chokers.

Plate 424. A gold bracelet by G. Desbazailles (the son of Louis), in art nouveau style, c.1890. The four plaques, struck by the medallist Vernier, represent the Arts of Music, Sculpture, Painting and Architecture.

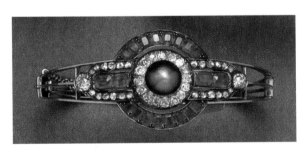

Plate 422. A black pearl, ruby and diamond hinged bangle, c.1880-90.

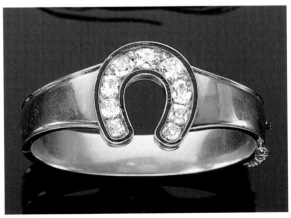

Plate 423. A gold, enamel and diamond hinged bangle, c.1880-90.

Plate 425. A gold, enamel and gem-set bracelet by Carlo and Arthur Giuliano, c.1900 (shown enlarged to illustrate the details of the workmanship and the impressed makers' mark on the clasp). The twelve stones are those mentioned in the Book of Revelation *as the foundation and gates of the heavenly Jerusalem. The detail of the back shows the sculptural treatment of the mount.*

Plate 427. *Two gold bangles of typical design, set with sapphires and diamonds, c.1880-90. Care should be taken when purchasing these bracelets that the sapphires are not doublets. A gold triple bangle, c.1890, another popular design of the date.*

Plate 428. *A diamond bangle, c.1880; note the flattened wire construction to the back and the pierced 'gallery' to the sides of the front.*

Plate 429. *A turquoise and diamond bangle, c.1890, of typical knife-wire construction.*

Plate 426. *A gold, pâte de verre and enamel bracelet by René Lalique, c.1900-5. Note the pâte de verre intaglios of Ceres and the green plique-à-jour enamel flecked with gold.*

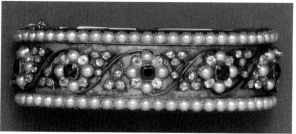

Plate 430. *A gold, sapphire, half-pearl and diamond bangle, c.1880.*

Plate 431. A collection of gold and gem-set bangles, c.1890-1900.

Rings

Although the function of the ring limited its shape, constricting the jeweller's imagination to elaborations of old designs, towards the end of the century some new patterns appeared. The most successful innovation of the 1890s was the crossover ring, set with two diamonds, or with a diamond and a pearl or perhaps a coloured precious stone between scrolled shoulders. With minor alterations to the basic design, the crossover ring has survived the whims of fashion until the present day.

Another new design was the two, three, four or more, part ring (see plate 435), consisting of two or three gold wires joined at the back and set at the front with gemstones or gemstone clusters.

Hearts and paired hearts, surmounted by a crown or by a ribbon bow, set with coloured gemstones within a diamond border on a thin gold shank, were

Plate 432. A diamond ring designed as a pair of entwined hearts, c.1890.

243

Plate 433. A half-pearl and diamond ring designed as a pair of hearts with a ribbon bow surmount, c.1890-1900.

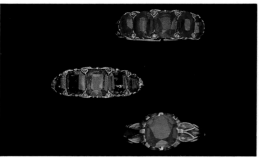

Plate 434. Two half-hoop rings and a single-stone ring with fluted shoulders, typical of the late 19th century.
Plate 435. A five-hoop ring, set with rubies, sapphires, emeralds and diamonds, c.1890. The pinched collets around the coloured stones are typical of the date.

Plate 436. A gold and diamond single stone ring, French, c.1900. The matt rich coloured gold makes this ring typically French.

another novelty of the 1890s, although the design had its origin in the eighteenth century (see plates 432 and 433).

The solitaire ring gained favour towards the end of the century, and the wide gold mounts of the previous decades were replaced by thinner shanks and more delicate settings. Massive gold mounts of sculptural inspiration, often in art nouveau style, were à la mode in France (see plates 436 and 439). Jewellers working in the art nouveau style often adapted foliate and floral designs as well as female figures to the shapes of rings (see plates 438 and 439). Rings of half-hoop, marquise and cluster design, and gypsy-set rings continued in production (see plates 434 and 437), along with gold snake rings with jewelled eyes, and gold rings of strap-and-buckle design.

Plate 437. A gold, royal blue enamel, seed pearl and diamond marquise-shaped ring, late 19th century. Care should be taken that these rings are not confused with the late 18th century prototypes. The seed pearls and the delicate enamel are clues to the date.

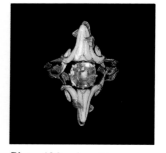

Plate 438. A gold, enamel and peridot ring, by René Lalique, c.1900.

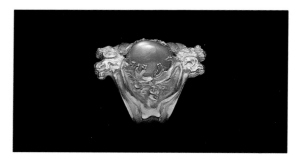

Plate 439. A gold and star sapphire ring, by René Lalique, c.1900. The shoulders are cast in low relief with two nude women, their hair encircling the stone.

Buckles and Clasps

Wide belts were very much in fashion towards the end of the century; their large ornamental clasps very often assumed the form of leaves and flowers of flowing art nouveau design constricted within more formal and geometrical borders. The clasps, often in oxidized silver, or enamelled and set with cabochon semiprecious stones, became one of the cherished ornaments of women sensitive to the ideals of the Arts and Crafts movement (see plates 440 and 441).

Silver, enamel and gem-set belts were also in vogue (see plate 442).

Plate 440. A silver, enamel and amethyst buckle/cloak clasp, designed by C.R. Ashbee, c.1902, for the Guild of Handicraft.

Plate 441. A gold, diamond, opal and enamel buckle, by René Lalique, c.1900.

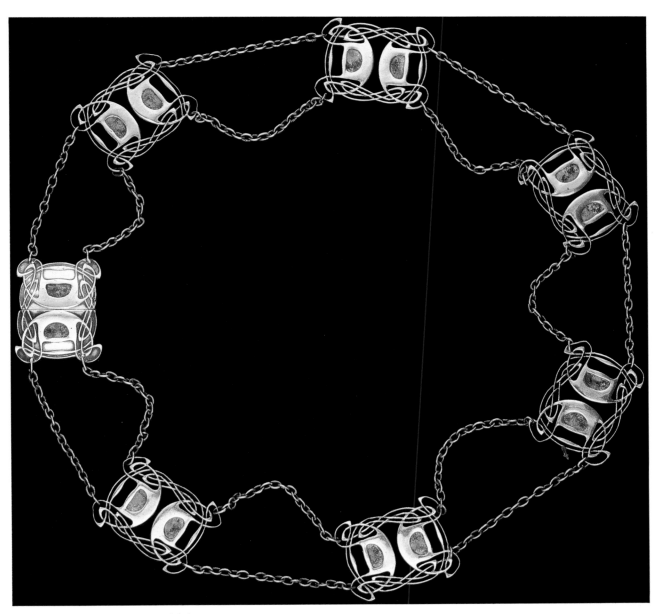

Plate 442. A silver and enamel belt,
by Liberty & Co., c.1905.

245

Plate 443. A gold and baroque pearl lorgnette, c.1890. Lorgnettes were popular ornaments on long-chains. Pockets on dresses were rare.

Plate 444. A diamond lorgnette, c.1900.

Plate 445. A gentleman's dress suite of gold and enamel cufflinks and buttons, c.1900.

Plate 446. A pair of gold and enamel cufflinks, c.1900, depicting the Four Vices.

Plate 447. Two pairs of gold, enamel and gem-set cufflinks, c.1900.

246

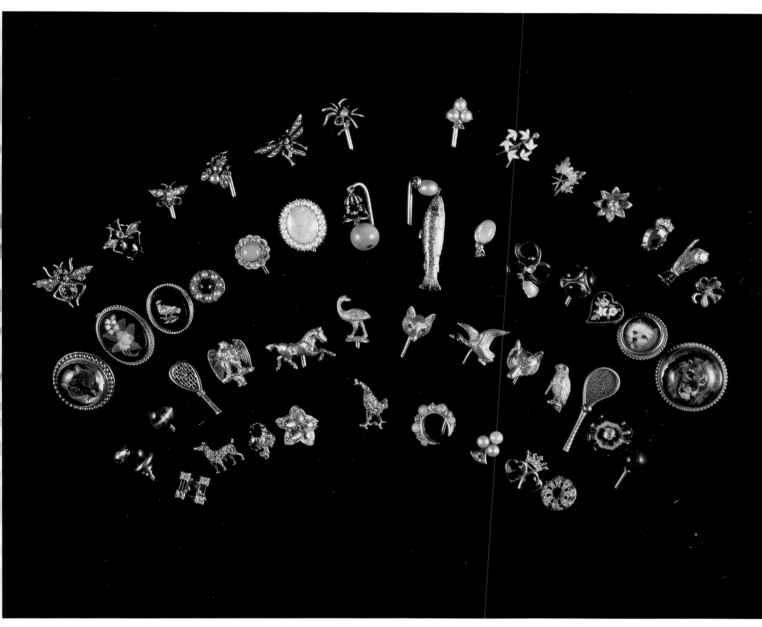

Plate 448. An interesting collection of gold and gem-set tiepins dating from around the turn of the century.

Plate 449. Francois Flameng, 1908, 'Queen Alexandra'. The Royal Collection. Reproduced by Gracious Permission of Her Majesty The Queen.

CHAPTER SIX
1900~1920

The year 1900 did not bring with it the expected changes and innovations in social, political and artistic life that so many people had anticipated. The influence of the nineteenth century stretched into the twentieth century for over a decade, and it was not until the outbreak of the First World War in 1914, and the Russian Revolution some four years later, that Europe and America finally put the old century behind them. Indeed the first decade of the new century was characterised by a sense of Europe holding its breath; certainly England has never been as prosperous before or since and more jewellery was purchased during those years than at any period in history.

When the war finally arrived, galas and formal receptions disappeared overnight and jewels were locked in security vaults or sold for survival. During the war, very little, or no jewellery was produced, and jewellers often turned their skills to the military industry or went to the front. Precious metals became scarce or restricted, and, in many countries, gold jewellery was donated to the state to finance the war. The prophetic words of Lord Grey in 1914 that 'The lights are going out all over Europe...' were also to prove true of the Bunsen burners in the jewellery workshops in Birmingham.

The first decade of the new century saw both the bloom and decline of the trends started in the last years of the nineteenth century, such as art nouveau and the Arts and Crafts movement. Revivalist jewellery was produced by Carlo and Arthur Giuliano until 1914 with much the same spirit as the 1890s. Fabergé continued his refined guilloché enamel production. 1890s crescents and stars remained in vogue throughout the first decade of the new century.

New designs, of course, appeared, but rather than a break with tradition, they were, once more, elaborations of old themes. Edwardian jewellery and the contemporary jewellery of the rest of Europe, which did not fully embrace the revolutionary innovations of the art nouveau, were characterised by a lightness and delicacy which had their roots in eighteenth century jewellery and goldsmith design. The Louis XVI style, with its fluid rococo cartouches and rocaille decorations, supplied an inexhaustible source of inspiration to those jewellers who did not dare the extremes of the art nouveau, but admired the fluidity of its lines. Garlands and ribbon bows, entrelac-de-rubans motifs, hearts and paired hearts were resuscitated and became the leitmotif of early twentieth century jewellery (see plates 451, 453, 488, etc.)

The master of the 'garland style' was Louis Cartier who encouraged his designers to consult original eighteenth century pattern books and to wander through the streets of Paris and take sketches of eighteenth century architectural details. Garlands, laurel wreaths, bow knots, tassels and lace motifs were among his favourite decorative devices. His royal, aristocratic and, above all, rich clientele on both sides of the Atlantic wore his delicate, articulate, light and insubstantial creations with enthusiasm: dog collars, devant de corsages, pendants and tiaras (see plate 450).

The lightness and delicacy of early twentieth century ornaments would not have been possible without the introduction of platinum in jewellery. Platinum had occasionally been used in jewellery in the nineteenth century, but it is not until the beginning of the twentieth century that it was used on a regular basis. The relative softness of silver required a large quantity of metal to form the setting, and it had in any case, to be backed with gold, for extra strength, and to prevent the silver from staining the skin and clothing. The result was inevitably a heavy object, bulky and uncomfortable to wear if large, and due to tarnish at some stage. The strength and rigidity of platinum allowed the jeweller to reduce the quantity of metal needed in a mount to the minimum with the added quality of untarnishable whiteness (see plate 453). The rigid quality of platinum also enabled the jeweller to fret the metal, by means of a piercing saw, into lace-like, or delicate geometrical, patterns. Circular platinum plaques, pierced in this way, became the background for pendants and brooches decorated with floral and garland diamond motifs (see plates 488 and 490). The garland style influenced the production of almost all jewellery houses in the early years of the century. George Fouquet turned to swags and garlands, piercing and millegrain settings after his experiments in the art nouveau style (see plate 466). Henry Vever combined flowing art nouveau lines with informal patterns of eighteenth century inspiration. Lacloche, Boucheron, Chaumet and Mellerio also followed the fashion closely (see plate 459).

Cartier, in 1902 and 1909 respectively, opened his shops in London and New York, where his jewels in the garland style, already famous all over the world, became readily available to his wealthy English and American clients drawn from the royal houses, the aristocracy, trade, commerce, and the world of the theatre. The delicacy and finesse of these jewels, well suited the dress designs of the beginning of the century.

The leaders of *haute couture* in Paris were, at that time, the Worth brothers, who dressed the most fashionable women in their delicate softly coloured silks: lilac, pink, yellow, mauve, straw and hydrangea blue. Pearl and diamond devant-de-corsages of elaborate, openwork lattice design, together with dog collars and long sautoirs, only occasionally highlighted with amethysts or turquoises, perfectly complemented the serpentine lines of these dresses.

When, around 1910, the combination of black and white came into fashion, diamond, onyx and occasionally black enamel jewellery in the garland style became the craze of the moment, together with diamond jewels applied or pinned to black ribbons of silk moiré or velvet (see plate 496).

These black and white enamel jewels soon became an alternative to the gloomy mourning jewels of the nineteenth century. Sober and discreet, but at the same time elegant and fashionable, they could be worn either at smart occasions or during mourning or half-mourning, since the rules of etiquette — after the severity of the Victorian age in England and of the Second Empire in France — were becoming more and more flexible.

A break from the monochrome of platinum and diamond jewellery, and from the formality of the garland style, came with the presentation in Paris and London of Diaghilev's Ballets Russes. In 1910 the first performance of *Schéhérazade* in Paris, was a sensation both for the public and critics alike, with the opulence and brightness of its costumes and scenery, and with the swirling movement of the production. Bakst's costumes, inspired by the colourful and rich dresses of a sultan's harem, and the stage designs in bright orange, carmine, vermilion, royal blue, emerald green and gold, had such a powerful effect that Parisian couturiers immediately turned to the Orient in search of inspiration. Paul Poiret created harem dresses with Turkish trousers decorated with tassels and turbans topped with aigrettes.

In jewellery, the Oriental influence brought with it more discreet forms such as lotus flowers, cusped arches, peacock feathers and stylised minarets (see plates 493 and 501). Tassels and aigrettes became the rage and coloured gemstones began to re-emerge in the creations of the great jewellers. Cartier became the master of bold chromatic experiments which were to become fashionable in the 1920s, successfully combining sapphires and emeralds, jade and sapphires and carved and frosted rock crystal with faceted gemstones. Poiret's influence on jewellery was not limited to inspiration from the Orient; he eliminated the tight bodices of the earlier years and replaced them with soft and comfortable tops of pleated silk, liberated women from corsets, and designed fluid, high-waisted dresses underlined by a cord or ribbon under the bust. The emphasis shifted to straight, vertical lines, and jewellery had to conform to the new silhouettes. Corsage ornaments disappeared, replaced by epaulettes of vertical design fastened to the shoulder. Short necklaces and dog collars gave way to long chains and sautoirs.

Egypt supplied another source of exotic inspiration. The recent archaeological discoveries made by Edward Ayrton in Thebes and by Sir Flinders Petrie in Lahun, brought a new wave of interest in the pharaonic world; many jewels were designed with ancient Egypt in mind, thus reviving a fashion which already had appeared twice in the nineteenth century, and which foreshadowed the 1920s Tutankhamen craze.

Jewellery was worn in abundance in the exuberant and light-hearted first decade of the century. Chokers were worn with sautoirs or strings of pearls, bracelets on each arm and rings on almost every finger. Tiaras, bandeaux and aigrettes were worn in the evening, at the theatre and on formal occasions.

Although clad with pearls and diamonds, Edwardian women never fell into the trap of ostentation like their Victorian forebears, who all too often donned almost the entire contents of their jewellery boxes as a display of wealth. Novelty and sporting jewellery continued as day wear as in the late nineteenth century. Bar brooches and lucky charms were still produced to the nineteenth century patterns. The true novelties of the time were the motorcar and aeroplane brooches; jewels of yachting inspiration also appeared, perhaps as a consequence of the King's enthusiasm for sailing (see plate 373). To commemorate the coronation of King Edward VII in 1902, charming minute brooches were produced, delicately enamelled and gem-set (see plate 470).

Among the favoured stones of the Edwardian era, were amethysts and peridots: their intense yet soft colours were well suited to the delicate creations in the garland style. Also characteristic of the period were turquoises, pale blue sapphires from Montana, orange fire opals from Mexico, black opals from Australia and demantoid garnets from the Urals, frequently combined with tiny pearls or diamonds (see plates 476, 502 and 513).

The traditional nineteenth century styles of cutting — brilliant, rose, pear-shaped and cabochon — somehow limited the design of jewels. Therefore, in the early years of the new century, the lapidaries developed new cuts to suit the needs of the new Oriental and garland styles.

Calibré-cut stones had already been used by the Victorians, but mainly in connection with turquoise, coral and other semiprecious stones. Rubies, emeralds, sapphires and amethysts began to be calibré-cut and set together with baguette, trapeze, triangular and marquise-shaped diamonds (see plates 471, 484 and 485).

Briolettes were used in garland style jewellery; suspended among the swags of a tiara, or at the centre of a pendant, they added a touch of movement to the formality of the design (see plate 508).

Cabochon stones had been fashionable in the nineteenth century with revivalist jewellery and later with Arts and Crafts and art nouveau creations. This cut had usually been confined to semiprecious stones and mediocre quality precious stones of small size. In the new century, a new interest developed, and an increasingly large number of good quality coloured precious stones were cut en cabochon.

The outbreak of the war put a sudden and dramatic end to the light-hearted spirit of the beginning of the century. Life changed overnight and jewellery disappeared, to be sold or safely hidden in security vaults. Precious metals became scarce, and platinum, which was used in the armament industry, disappeared almost completely from the market; in England, the government formally forbade any trade in it. The few jewels produced during the four years of the war were, in most cases, hardly more than trinkets of bellic inspiration: fighter planes, tanks, submarines, good luck charms, talismans and amulets, and regimental badge brooches occasionally made of gold and diamonds, but more frequently of silver or base metal. Cartier produced attractive diamond brooches and pendants, using the symbols of war as decorative motifs, such as miniature replicas of cannons and fighter aeroplanes.

Tiaras

Tiaras are perhaps the most characteristic jewel of the early twentieth century. The preserve of a moneyed élite and *de rigueur* for formal and festive occasions, tiaras were characteristic of their exuberant, stylish and wealthy age. During the very early years of the century, diamond tiaras assumed winged designs, or were composed of five or seven star-shaped or flowerhead cluster motifs, or followed the lanceolated design of the Imperial Russian tiaras of the late nineteenth century (see plates 300 and 305).

Among the new designs, the meander tiara, designed as a band of rigorously geometrical Greek key motifs, was perhaps the favourite. Stylised laurel and acanthus leaves were utilised as decorative motifs for formal tiaras of bandeau design.

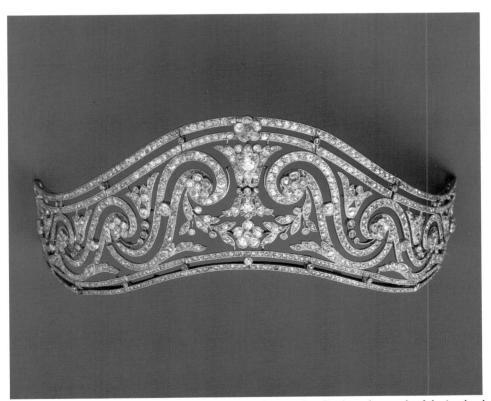

Plate 450. A diamond tiara, by Cartier, c.1900-5 (shown reduced). A good example of the 'garland style'.

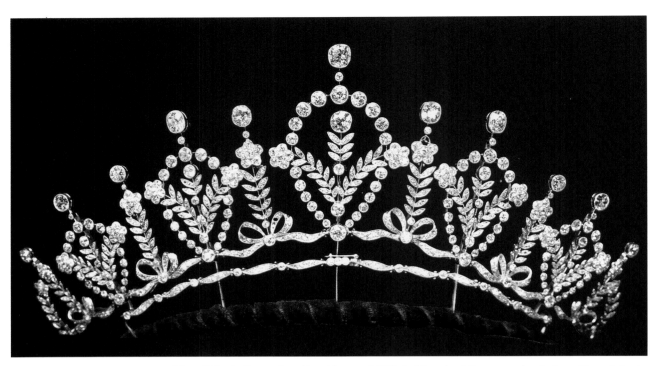

Plate 451. A diamond necklace/tiara, c.1900-5. Note the delicate running leaf motifs and slender ribbon bow.

Floral tiaras of naturalistic inspiration were still produced; the garland style inspired tiaras of looped and festooned design, supporting pearl drops, briolettes and pendeloques, at once delicate and effective (see plates 450-453).

By 1910 tiaras had become unfashionable in Paris. Soon after they were abandoned in New York, but in London, where the strict court etiquette had not changed, tiaras continued to be produced and worn.

The bandeau, designed as a simple ribbon to be worn on the forehead or just above the hairline, soon became fashionable; better suited than the tiara to the straight and simple lines of the new dresses, in addition it was easier to wear, being simply tied with a ribbon at the back of the head (see plate 454). The garland style supplied the decorative motifs. Paul Poiret encouraged women to wear bandeaux with a detachable, vertical motif at the centre, usually a large drop-shaped pearl or a pear-shaped gemstone. Less formal bandeaux took the shape of bands of tulle or lace matching the colour of the dress, with diamond-set slides or buckle motifs.

Aigrettes, already fashionable in the 1890s, became the ever-present companion of the dresses designed by Worth and Poiret. Until 1910, the most acceptable motifs for aigrettes were drawn from the vegetable world: leaves, flowers and ears of wheat. After that date, the Ballets Russes supplied an inexhaustible source of inspiration: Persian leaves, Chinese gongs, lotus flowers, papyrus, and Indian sarpeshs — the traditional turban ornament — of precious stones, decorated with rare and exotic bird feathers.

Diamond winged motifs, worn with an egret plume, which first appeared in the 1890s, reached the peak of their popularity around 1910.

Plate 452. A diamond tiara, c.1900-5.

The late nineteenth century fashion of wearing brooches in the hair slowly disappeared, but crescent brooches, mounted on hairpins, continued to be worn up until the First World War, often in combination with feathers.

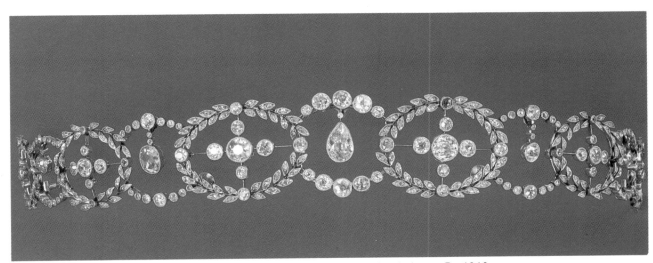

Plate 453. A diamond hair ornament, German, c.1910, mounted entirely in platinum. By 1910 platinum had taken over from gold and silver as the preferred setting metal for diamonds.

Parures

The tendency to abandon sets of matching jewels, which began at the end of the nineteenth century, continued. Combinations of pearl necklaces and diamond bracelets and earrings, not necessarily of the same design but in the same style, were worn instead of parures; these almost completely disappeared from the production of the famous jewellery houses. Sets of matching jewels came back, to a certain extent, in the 1930s, but only on a large scale in the late 1940s.

Earrings

Diamond earstuds were frequently worn in the first decade of the twentieth century, but, until Poiret's revolutionary innovation in feminine fashion, the prevailing design for earrings consisted of delicate pendants of garland style which complemented the feminine, lacy and delicate dresses of the time.

Among the most successful designs were garlands of tiny diamond leaves, with a diamond or coloured stone swing centre, and diamond, aquamarine and emerald briolettes suspended from articulated chains of millegrain-set diamonds (see plates 455 and 456). Other pendant earrings assumed the form of cascades of small, stylised raceme drops (see plate 457).

Plate 454. A diamond bandeau/bracelet of lace design, c.1910. By this date bandeaux had become the fashionable alternative to tiaras as they were easier to wear and doubled as bracelets, choker, plaque brooches, etc.

Plate 455. A pair of diamond and emerald pendant earrings, c.1905-10. Long pendant earrings were firmly back in fashion with the new century.
Plate 456. A pair of diamond pendant earrings, c.1910.

Plate 457. A pair of diamond pendant earrings, c.1910. This design is most unusual in that the drops seems to be tapered in reverse.

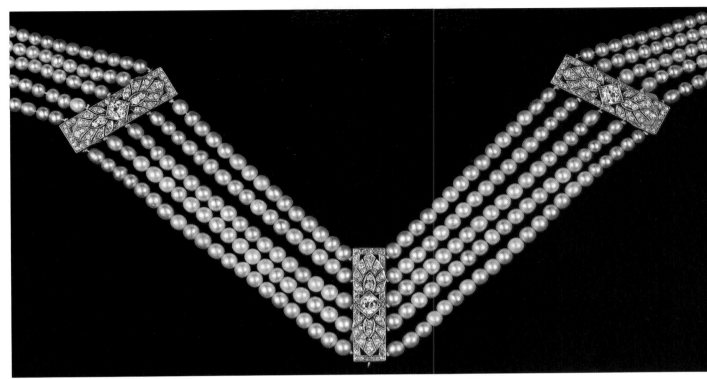

Plate 458. A pearl and diamond choker necklace, c.1910. Necklaces worn high on the neck, like a dog collar, remained fashionable up to the First World War.

Necklaces

Dog collars, which first appeared at the end of the nineteenth century, and were associated with the Princess of Wales, continued to be the most acceptable form of neck ornament until the outbreak of the First World War. Entirely set with diamonds, they assumed the form of pierced bands in the garland style, decorated with swags and festoons of leaf motifs, scrolls, and stylised flowers, and were often worn on a black silk or velvet ribbon, which enhanced the delicate lacy effect of the decorative motifs.

Pearl chokers became even wider than those of the late nineteenth century, sometimes strung with as many as twenty rows of small pearls, held together by diamond plaques (see plate 458). Chokers were often worn with several rows of pearls, which left no space for the large necklaces of the nineteenth century tradition.

Sautoirs were as popular as chokers. The most expensive examples took the form of long ribbons of woven seed pearls or diamonds, terminating with two fringed tassels. The tassels were often substituted by a circular or octagonal pendant, pierced with geometrical or stylised floral patterns in the garland style, and delicately set with diamonds (see plates 466 and 469).

Less expensive examples took the form of long gold chains of varied and complex linking, set at intervals with small pearls, turquoise matrix, Mississippi pearls often encaged in gold wire, or with enamelled baton motifs, alternating with pearls. They were worn doubled or trebled around the neck,

Plate 459. A diamond necklace, by Lacloche, c.1910. This illustrates the perfection of the 'garland style'.

Plate 460. A diamond necklace, c.1910. The yellow or 'canary' diamond at the centre of the pendant, probably emanated from the Cape mines in South Africa, and would have been something of a curiosity at the time.

tucked in the skirt, or festooned on the bosom, much in the same way as nineteenth century longchains.

Sautoirs designed as twisted ropes of tiny seed pearls terminating with diamond capped tassels were simply knotted on the bosom (see plate 465). Another attractive type of sautoir consisted of a long chain of diamonds or variously coloured gemstones, spectacle-set (encircled at the girdle with a fine gold or platinum wire, similar to a spectacle frame, see plate 468).

Sautoirs of onyx and coral beads were currently fashionable. The sautoir particularly well suited the new fashion which required simple dresses of straight vertical line, and was to become the most approved form of neck ornament of the 1920s.

Around 1900 a special form of necklace, the Lavallière, appeared, which consisted of a very simple chain necklet supporting a pear-shaped pendant or a drop pearl. A variation of the Lavallière was the Edna May pendant, named after the famous American actress, which consisted in a simple collet-set stone or cluster, suspended from a smaller stone by a fine simple link, on a slender chain necklet. Similar, but slightly more elaborate in design, was the negligé pendant, consisting of a gem-set surmount supporting two drops hanging side by side on links often of unequal length (see plates 461 and 462).

Fine chain necklets, often set at intervals with diamonds, supporting variously shaped delicate pendants in the garland style were among the neck ornaments in vogue at the time (see plates 460, 463 and 464).

Necklaces of more formal design fully embraced the new style and assumed the form of delicate garlands tied with ribbon bows (see plate 459).

Plate 461. A diamond negligé pendant and chain. This characteristic ornament of its day was always designed as two drops, usually gem-set, and of unequal length.

Plate 462. Two negligé pendants on chain necklets, c.1905-10, one set with a baroque pearl and diamonds, the other with emeralds and diamonds.

Plate 463. A diamond necklace and pendant, c.1905, in the 'garland style', mounted in platinum.

Plate 464. A pearl and diamond pendant on a chain necklet, c.1905-10.

Plate 465. A seed pearl and diamond sautoir, c.1900-10.

Plate 467. A photograph by Laurie Charles, c.1900, of Marie Tempest. Victoria and Albert Theatre Museum.

Plate 466. A seed pearl and diamond sautoir with rosette pendant, by Georges Fouquet, c.1905. Sautoirs, at this time, seem to be either woven chains of seed pearls, as in this example, or rope-like skeins as in plate 465.

Plate 468. A diamond sautoir, spectacle-set with cushion-shaped stones.

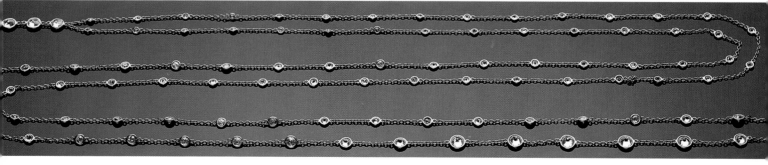

Plate 469. *A magnificent aquamarine, pearl and diamond sautoir and detachable pendant, c.1905. Nowadays, the green colour of the aquamarine would have been 'improved' to a deep blue by artificial means. In our opinion the green hue of this exceptional stone, which weighed over 150 carats, is well suited to the jewel.*

Brooches

Typical of the first ten years of the century were bodice ornaments or devant-de-corsages, which were large brooches often sewed directly to the dress rather than pinned to it by means of brooch fittings. The chosen motifs were those of the garland style: acanthus leaves, laurel wreaths, ribbon bows, abstract pierced lattices (see plate 502). When, around 1910, the bodice disappeared from women's fashion, corsage ornaments became impossible to wear and, in most cases, were broken up and reset as jewels of smaller size.

As in the last years of the nineteenth century, smaller brooches were worn, until 1910, in large numbers. Among the favourites were those designed as enamelled roses, daisies, primroses, waterlilies with diamond centres, and velvet pansies with petals bordered by a fine row of diamonds.

Brooches and brooch/pendants in the garland style assumed the form of wreaths and swags of millegrain-set diamonds surrounding larger coloured stones, often crowned by a ribbon bow motif (see plates 473-476, and 487). Plaques and cartouche-shaped motifs, often pierced in a lattice pattern and set with diamond garlands, were among the most characteristic brooches of the time. Bar brooches continued to be set at the centre with variously designed

Plate 470. *An enamel, demantoid garnet and diamond commemorative brooch, 1902, celebrating the coronation of Edward VII.*

Plate 471. *A magnificent ruby and diamond brooch, designed as a swallowtail butterfly, c.1900-5. Note the way the rubies have been calibré-cut to fit the mount; this would not be found in a 19th century example.*

263

Plate 472. A baroque pearl
and diamond brooch, designed
as a winged insect, c.1910.
The platinum setting is a good
clue to the date.

Plate 473. A moonstone cameo and diamond brooch, c.1905.
Plate 474. A Sri Lankan sapphire and diamond brooch, c.1905.

decorative motifs, or with a single, large brilliant-cut diamond (see plates 488, 492 and 494-496). Piercing, pavé and millegrain setting were the techniques used in most plaque brooches (see plate 497).

Other brooches assumed the simple shape of a line of calibré-cut coloured stones, or that of a row of diamonds millegrain-set and graduated in size from the centre (see plates 503-506).

Bow brooches were either pierced and entirely set with diamonds, or made of black velvet edged with diamonds (see plates 477-482). Sport and novelty

Plate 475. A spinel and
diamond brooch/pendant,
c.1905. Red spinel, although
a beautiful gem, is rare and
seldom found in jewellery; its
value, however, does not reflect
its rarity.

Plate 476. A fire opal and diamond brooch/
pendant, c.1905-10. Although mined since
the 1870s in Mexico, fire opals first
appeared in European jewellery around the
turn of the century.

Plate 477. A diamond brooch, c.1910, designed as a ribbon bow with articulated drops. Note the marquise-shaped diamonds which were beginning to be popular around this time. Although the larger drop appears to have several stones missing, this is in fact intentional as the smaller drop is designed to overlap the edge. Unlike 19th century ribbon bows, early 20th century examples are often articulated.

Plate 478. A modern copy of an Edwardian diamond bow brooch, the detail of the back shows the clumsy piercing and drilling of the mount and the poor quality hinges. The fact that the stones are modern brilliant and eight-cuts gives away the date.

brooches continued to be worn, and besides the late nineteenth century motifs, new forms appeared such as acrobatic monkeys, car steering wheels, aeroplanes, tennis rackets and the like.

Hearts, pairs of hearts, winged motifs and marquise-shaped plaques decorated with red, blue or green guilloché enamel and set at the centre with a diamond decorative motif within a border of pearls, were among the sought after designs for small brooches of late nineteenth century tradition (see plates 413 and 499).

Insect and animal brooches continued to be produced in the first decade of the century as in the 1890s (see plates 471 and 472).

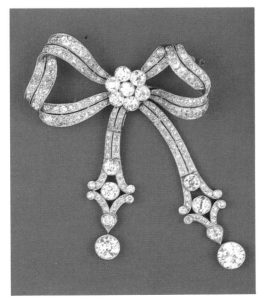

Plate 480. A diamond brooch, designed as a rigid ribbon bow, c.1910.

Plate 479. A diamond ribbon bow, c.1910, with articulated drops. Note that the larger diamonds are millegrain-set.

Plate 481. A modern ribbon bow brooch. It is hard to believe that an early 20th century example would have been set in yellow gold, so this brooch can hardly have been made to deceive but merely as a pastiche.

Plate 482. A diamond brooch, c.1910, designed as a formal ribbon bow, decorated with black velvet.

Plate 483. A diamond brooch, c.1910, of entrelac-de-rubans and garland design, set in platinum.

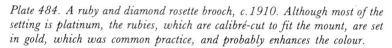

Plate 484. A ruby and diamond rosette brooch, c.1910. Although most of the setting is platinum, the rubies, which are calibré-cut to fit the mount, are set in gold, which was common practice, and probably enhances the colour.

Plate 485. An amethyst and diamond rosette brooch, c.1910, another example of stones being calibré-cut to fit the mount and the design. Notice the millegrain edge to the setting.

Plate 486. A high quality modern sapphire and diamond brooch in Edwardian style, made in Thailand. Note the modern cutting of the diamonds.

Plate 487. An aquamarine and diamond brooch, c.1910.

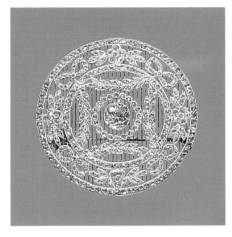

Plate 488. A diamond brooch, c.1910, entirely saw-pierced in a delicate lattice design, perhaps reminiscent of petit point embroidery. Note how all the settings have millegrain decoration, and many of the stones are rose-cut. Platinum, with its rigid characteristics, made such delicate yet strong designs possible. Occasionally brooches and pendants of similar design have detachable guilloché enamel plaques to act as a background.

Plate 489. A pearl, enamel and diamond watch/pendant, c.1910. The black and white illustration shows the reverse.

Plate 490. A diamond oval plaque pendant, c.1905-10. Note the characteristic pierced trellis, and the way the coloured diamonds are millegrain-set.

Plate 491. A diamond plaque pendant and brooch surmount, by Lacloche, c.1910.

Pendants

The most typical pendant of the early twentieth century assumed the form of a circular plaque, saw-pierced in a lattice pattern, and applied with very delicate ribbon bows, garlands of flowers, or geometrical motifs, millegrain-set with diamonds (see plate 491). These pendants very often had a set of interchangeable guilloché enamel backgrounds which matched, with their delicate pink, mauve, green and blue, the soft colours of contemporary dresses, and were worn on long chains of baton-shaped linking, similarly decorated with guilloché enamel.

Plate 492. A pearl and diamond plaque brooch, c.1910. Here the leaves and flowers are applied, and this is therefore a less expensive example.

Plate 493. A diamond plaque brooch, c.1910, by Boucheron, Paris. Although apparently of ancient Greek inspiration, the feeling here is more of Diaghilev and the Ballet Russes.

Plate 494. A diamond circular plaque brooch, c.1910.

Plate 495. A sapphire, pearl and diamond brooch, c.1910. A slightly unusual lozenge design. Readers should be aware that rapidly rising prices have rendered the faking of these plaque brooches economically viable.

Plate 496. A pearl, black enamel and diamond brooch/pendant, c.1910. Although honeycomb piercing was common at this time, it was unusual for it to be enamelled.

Plate 497. A ruby and diamond oval plaque brooch, c.1910-20. This brooch exhibits proto-art deco design with its rigid contours. Note how nearly all the settings are millegrain.

Garlands and bows were utilised as decorative motifs for lozenge, or fancy-shaped pendants (see plates 507 and 508).

The cases of pendant watches were also decorated with guilloché enamel, and applied with a latticework of tiny diamonds (see plate 489).

Another typical pendant of the early twentieth century assumed the shape of a lozenge or modified triangle, entirely pierced with delicate lace motifs and set with diamonds, resembling a folded or ruched pocket handkerchief, and was known as a 'handkerchief' pendant (see plate 498).

Less expensive pendants assumed the form of fine gold scroll-and-leaf motifs, set with seed pearls, amethysts, turquoises and peridots, and art nouveau continued to influence the design of many pendants during the opening years of the century (see plate 500).

Plate 498. A pearl and diamond sûreté pin, c.1910-15. Note the lozenge-shaped 'hankerchief' pendants.

Plate 499. A pearl, moonstone and diamond brooch, c.1910.

Plate 500. A pearl, turquoise and diamond brooch, c.1905, still showing art nouveau influences.

Plate 501. A magnificent pearl and diamond corsage ornament, c.1910, showing Oriental influences in the design.

Plate 502. A large sapphire and diamond corsage ornament, by Chaumet, c.1910. The sapphires are almost certainly from the Montana mines in the U.S.A. ('new mine') and are characteristic of Edwardian jewellery.

Plate 503. Two bar brooches, both early 20th century, one set with rubies and diamonds, the other with pearls, sapphires and diamonds.

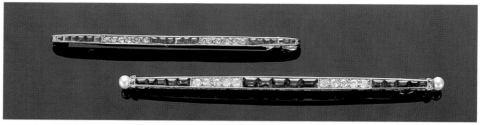

Plate 504. A long pearl and diamond bar brooch, c.1905.

Plate 505. A sapphire and diamond bar brooch, c.1910. Note the calibré-cut sapphires.

Plate 506. A sapphire and diamond bar brooch, c.1910.

Plate 507. A diamond pendant, c.1910.

Plate 508. A fine sapphire and diamond pendant, c.1910. Note the sapphires, calibré-cut to fit the mount, and the diamond drop at the centre cut 'en briolette'.

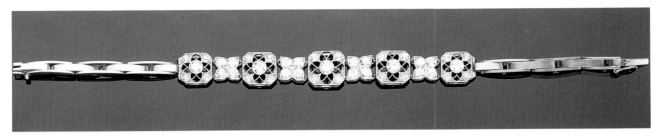

Plate 509. *A diamond bracelet with expanding chain back, c.1910. Many diamond bracelets were made to a similar design at this time.*

Bracelets

The Victorian fashion of wearing three or four bracelets or bangles on each arm died out, but women still enjoyed to wear one, often on each arm. Bracelets were usually thinner than their late nineteenth century counterparts, often set with a single course of calibré-cut stones or with multiple rows of gems of contrasting colours, and these were to remain one of the most favoured forms of arm ornament right up until the present day.

Bracelets set at the front with a row of gem-set decorative links or with a delicate elongated motif, pierced and tapered at the sides, on a chain back of expanding linking, became fashionable (see plates 509 and 510). These bracelets had the double advantage of fitting well most wrist sizes, and being less expensive than bracelets gem-set throughout. Thin, late nineteenth century bangles, continued to be used in the first years of the new century, the most acceptable design being the half-hoop of diamonds, graduating in size from the centre, often combined with coloured stones.

The fashionable garland and bow motifs often encircled the wrist with their delicate forms (see plate 511).

Plate 510. *A diamond bracelet with chain back, c.1910-20. The decoration here anticipates the geometric motifs of the 1920s.*

Plate 511. *A diamond bracelet in the 'garland style', c.1905.*

Wristwatches and Pendant Watches

Ladies' jewelled wristwatches had been produced by firms such as Cartier from the late 1880s, but it was not until around 1910 that they became widely worn. Small rectangular, oblong or octagonal bezels were entirely pavé-set with diamonds and worn on fine black moiré silk straps or black cordettes. Cartier produced very attractive examples, mounted on bracelets of several rows of seed pearls and diamonds (see 626).

At the same time, pendant watches of rectangular or oblong form, often decorated in the Oriental style and set with onyx and diamonds, were worn around the neck on sautoirs, black cordettes or black silk ribbons.

Plate 512. A ruby and diamond ring, c.1910.

Plate 513. A fine black opal and diamond ring, c.1910. The opal displays an exceptional play of colour, and may well be from the White Cliffs opal fields in New South Wales, Australia.

Plate 514. An emerald and diamond ring, c.1910. This unusual ring is exceptionally well pierced, but would be fragile in wear.

Plate 515. A sapphire and diamond ring, c.1910. The heart-shaped bezel set with a Burmese sapphire and crowned by a ribbon bow is typical of the day. Note the chain shank.

Rings

Rings were worn several at a time, often one on each finger. The half-hoop ring continued in favour, either set with diamonds alone or diamonds in combination with coloured stones, due to its unobtrusive and easy-to-wear shape. Single-stone diamond rings and crossover rings continued in production as in the last decade of the nineteenth century.

Larger rings, especially in the shape of circular, rectangular, oblong, oval or marquise bezels, were entirely pavé-set, or pierced and pavé-set, with diamonds, on thin shanks (see plate 514).

Typical of the period were rings set with oval, marquise, or circular-cut diamonds within borders of calibré-cut stones of contrasting colours, or mounted with a coloured precious stone within borders of small millegrain-set diamonds (see plates 512 and 513).

Heart-shaped and bow motifs, which were decorative devices of the garland style, appeared on rings as well (see plate 515). One of the most successful and typical rings of the time consisted of a pear-shaped coloured stone, mounted within a diamond heart-shaped border, and surmounted by a ribbon bow.

Buckles
Until Poiret redesigned the feminine silhouette, fashion dictated narrow waistlines squeezed into wide belts, and as a result buckles became an indispensable accessory.

For daywear, buckles were generally enamelled and reminiscent of art nouveau; for evening wear, they assumed the forms of diamond plaques of openwork design, pierced and millegrain-set with diamonds in the garland style (see plate 516).

Smaller buckles and slides, simply set with a row of diamonds, were also worn in the hair, attached to a bandeau of silk or tulle which encircled the head as a diadem.

Plate 516. A ruby and diamond belt plaque, c.1905, pierced and millegrain set with circular cut stones. The plaque has been subsequently mounted as a brooch.

Plate 517. 'Gertrude Lawrence'. Cecil Beaton photograph. Sotheby's London.

CHAPTER SEVEN
1920~1940

At the end of the First World War, the reaction to four years of suffering and privation took the form of a period of exaltation, creativity and *joie de vivre*. The new motto was 'Live and forget the past'. The traditions, fashions and values of the pre-war society were soon put aside. Etiquette changed, so that conformism was rejected and freedom of expression become the new rule.

The war profoundly changed the role of women in society. During the years of the conflict, many had taken up the activities of men forced to the front: driving ambulances, or working in factories, farms and offices. The delicate creatures of the early years of the century became strong and mature women, conscious of their ability and competence in their new jobs. Constricting bodices, long skirts and elaborate hairstyles were abandoned in favour of the more practical and functional shorter dresses and cropped hairstyles, which enabled women to perform their new duties with greater freedom.

When the war ended, many women, proud of their emancipation, stayed on in their jobs, and favoured the new tendency of fashion towards a masculine look, characterised by a thin and flat silhouette, and a short hair cut, 'à la garçonne'. Trousers understandably became an emblem of the emancipated woman for day wear, yet women demanded clothes which were sexy and dramatic at night. Never before had day wear and evening wear showed such profound differences: geometrical and rigorous short dresses of the day were substituted, at night, by fluid and sleeveless tunics which concealed the natural curves of the feminine body, but were cut low at the back. The waistline dropped to the hips, often underlined by a sash decorated with a brooch, while the skirt was short enough to reveal the knees, often with slits to enable women to enjoy the movements of the new dances such as the Charleston, tango, and foxtrot. The couturier responsible for this dramatic change in female fashion was Paul Poiret.

The androgynous, yet sexy, woman of the 1920s enjoyed heavy make-up in the form of bright red lipstick, white powder, and heavy black pencil strokes around the eyes, which gave their faces an exotic and mysterious appearance, enhanced by soft cloche hats, worn low on the eyebrows.

Coco Chanel, in the late 1920s, launched her sporty, yet elegant and classy fashions, which were to remain in vogue for some time. Her classical two-piece suits (accompanied by yards of strings of pearls, natural or imitation, and gold or gilt chains) became the indispensable garment for all fashionable women.

The 1930s fashions were generally more restrained: the waistline returned to a more natural position and the loose and shapeless tops were substituted by more feminine garments, which once more enhanced the natural lines of the female body. The fashions which suited the years that followed the economic crisis of 1929 eschewed the excesses of the 1920s.

For day wear, Chanel's tailored suits, both practical and comfortable, set new standards; evening wear was best epitomised by the long and feminine dresses of Madame Grès and Madeleine Vionnet, cut diagonally and draped with precious and gleaming silks and satins, which tightly embraced the figure. The typical cloche hat of the 1920s gave way to more inventive forms such as tricorns, turbans, and small rounded boxes.

In order to follow these revolutionary innovations in fashion, jewellery changed accordingly. The large floral spray brooches of the nineteenth century were not suited to these dynamic and flimsy garments, neither were the early twentieth century corsage ornaments, or the constricting and uncomfortable dog collars.

Jewellery assumed more geometrical and linear designs; the garland style, which employed delicate feminine motifs with a predominance of white, black and pale pastel colours, was replaced by dazzling outbursts of vivid, primary colours. Jewels became an accessory, strictly dependent on the shape and colour of the dress on which they were worn, rather than a precious ornament to represent a display of wealth as had been the case in the pre-war years. Many fashionable women, obsessed with perfection, had clothes designed to suit a particularly important piece of jewellery.

Paradoxically, the scantily clothed woman of the 1920s loved to cover herself with jewellery: several bracelets were worn at the same time on arms left bare by evening dresses. The daringly low backs of dresses promoted the fashion for sautoirs and necklaces worn at the back rather than at the front, or, alternatively, decorated with pendants on the clasp. At night, bandeaux became the 'in' thing to wear, either entirely set with precious stones, or made of material and decorated with a gem-set brooch or slide.

For the sporty, active and emancipated woman it was *de rigueur* to wear a wrist-watch — the symbol of the new fast and dynamic life — both by day and at night. Jewelled evening wrist-watches offered jewellers a new field in which to exploit their creative imagination.

The ideal jewel of the 1920s had to complement a particular dress, be an ornament expressly designed for a particular woman, or be chosen to suit her tastes, lifestyle and features. The intrinsic value and the quality of workmanship had to complement the artistic value of the design. Both famous jewellery houses and artist-jewellers rejected mass-produced, repetitive ornaments. The result was an extremely varied and rich production, which found sources of inspiration in the Far East, the Middle East and South American civilisations, but also approached jewellery with a new creative freedom, sensitive to the contemporary styles of painting and sculpture. The new passwords of decorative arts were: geometry, chromatic contrast, linearity and stylisation. These qualities became the emblems of 'modern' and art deco jewellery.

The famous Exposition Internationale des Arts Décoratifs et Industriels Modernes in Paris in 1925, which gave its name to the new style, dedicated a substantial part of the exhibition to jewellery. The main criterion by which jewels were selected was originality, but derivative designs were not penalised if freshly interpreted, reworked and translated. The ambitious aim was to promote a 'social art', or, better, to associate art with modern industry and to establish a close relation between the two.

The new style which stemmed from a rejection of the excesses of art nouveau naturalism, was perhaps foreshadowed by the delicate linearity of the garland style, had its roots in the chromatic contrasts popularised by the Ballets Russes, found sources of inspiration in the exotic forms of Oriental, African, and South American art, and was influenced by the contemporary Cubist and Fauve movements in Art.

The Vienna Secessionists, with their austere style which confined the flowing art nouveau lines to geometric contours, aimed to reduce each object to its utilitarian lines and to abolish every unnecessary decorative ornament, played an important role in the evolution of design towards geometrics, stylisation and essentials.

Similarly in Germany, the Bauhaus, founded in 1919 in Weimar by Walter Gropius, promoted a return in arts and crafts to basic, formal concepts, free from superfluous ornamentation, where aesthetic ideals were combined with functionalism.

The obsession of Dufy, Matisse and the other Fauve painters with colour, led them to abolish perspective, chiaroscuro and detail in favour of chromatic contrasts and essentially simple lines.

Futurism was another movement which greatly influenced the designs of many avant-garde jewellers. Marinetti's Futurist Manifesto praised speed, machines and urban life, suggested that artistic inspiration had to come from the mechanical world, and encouraged the removal of decorative excess in favour of geometrical lines.

Distant and exotic civilisations also inspired many creations of avant-garde and even more conservative jewellers. In November 1922 the joint efforts of Lord Carnarvon and Howard Carter, culminated in the opening of the tomb of Tutankhamen, in the remote Valley of the Kings of Egypt. Their remarkable discovery, perhaps the most important archaeological find of the twentieth century, aroused interest and excitement around the world. The opening of the quartz sarcophagus of the young pharaoh revealed his famous gold mask, his gold pectoral, armlets, diadem and rings. The tomb soon became one of the favourite travel destinations, and Egyptian civilisation an inexhaustible source of inspiration for the figurative arts, literature, fashion, the cinema industry and jewellery design.

Pyramids, sphinxes, obelisks, palmettes, lotus flowers, scarabs, hieroglyphs and imitations of hieroglyphs became current motifs in jewellery, together with the stylisations of Egyptian divinities: Isis, the falcon god Horus, the lion goddess Sekmeth, etc. The flat, two-dimensional quality and the bright chromatic contrasts of Egyptian art, were particularly well suited to the ideals of art deco. Turquoise blue faience, and the lapis lazuli and cornelian inlays of pharaonic art were frequently reproduced in enamels and precious stones.

Cartier, Boucheron, and Van Cleef and Arpels were strongly influenced by the fascination of Egypt and quickly adapted their production (see plates 595, 596 and 649).

The Persian style revived by Paul Poiret around 1910 continued in favour. Persian carpets and miniatures supplied a rich source of inspiration for chromatic combinations and decorative motifs: plants and flowers, leaves and arabesques of Islamic influence invaded brooches, aigrettes and vanity cases. The linear and geometric forms of Islamic art with its stylisation of natural forms was well suited to the ideals of the art deco, as were the bright combinations of primary colours on pottery and mosque tiles.

The primary colours of Jaipur enamel jewellery inspired many of the ruby, emerald and diamond creations of the late 1920s. The sarpesh (the traditional Indian turban ornament) became a motif for pins and brooches, often decorated at the top with a swing drop. Tasselled turban ornaments were transferred from Indian traditional costumes to necklaces and sautoirs, and the typically Indian necklace of ruby, sapphire and emerald beads was introduced to Europe and westernised with diamond plaques pierced in geometrical patterns. Indian beads were also frequently mounted in clusters on bracelets, brooches and clips (see plate 581).

Carved rubies, sapphires and emeralds, typical of Indian jewellery, also found their way to Europe, and in the shape of flowerheads, leaves, fruits and berries, were frequently mounted in jewels of Oriental inspiration and in the 'giardinetto' brooches of western tradition (see plates 566, 578 and 580).

The Far East supplied exotic motifs such as pagodas, dragons, Chinese characters, symbols and stylisations of nature. The favourite stones of the East — coral, pearl, mother-of-pearl, and jade — and the characteristic lacquers, were introduced in Western jewels and vanity cases (see plates 565, 638-640 and 643).

African art became another source of inspiration. The two 'Expositions Coloniales' of Marseilles and Paris (in 1922 and 1931) introduced sophisticated European eyes to the fresh and original forms of tribal art. The *Revue Nègre* of Josephine Baker was to fascinate Paris society in 1925, and to popularise the rhythms and traditions of Black Africa. As a consequence, African masks were reproduced and appeared as elements of jewellery design. Large bangles simply carved in ivory or wood, or made of metal, came into vogue and were worn, several at a time.

Archaeological research in central and South America attracted attention to the Mayan and pre-Columbian civilisations, and the geometrical quality, characteristic of Central and Southern American art, was introduced into jewellery design: concentric square and rectangular motifs and Mayan pyramids and steps were used as motifs in the decorative arts (see plate 645).

At the 1925 Exposition des Arts Décoratifs, jewellery was well represented, grouped with clothing, fashion, accessories and perfumes in the general 'Parure' class. The jewels exhibited shared a tendency towards geometry, linearity, stylisation, and contrast of colour and materials; closer examination reveals a dichotomy between the creations of the 'bijoutiers-artistes', the innovative, radical, artist-jewellers, and the 'bijoutiers-joailliers', the moderate, well established and famous jewellery houses.

The bijoutiers-artistes presented jewels of artistic more than intrinsic value, of extreme freedom and novelty of inspiration; materials were chosen for their decorative character and employed in a pictorial and sculptural way. Influenced by contemporary artistic movements and the machine age, they created jewels of very simple, angular, geometric form, which reduced to the minimum, or completely abolished, unnecessary decoration. Flat and linear as a painting or drawing, or three-dimensional as sculpture, their creations based on circles, triangles, rectangles, trapezes, etc., often resembled works of art rather than ornamental jewels.

The bijoutiers-artistes also favoured large metallic surfaces, often decorated with lacquers and enamels, and carved hardstones such as jade, coral, onyx, rock crystal and lapis lazuli. Among the faceted stones, their main choices were aquamarine, citrine, topaz and amethyst. Diamonds were employed to pick out a decorative motif, and coloured precious stones seldom appeared in their creations.

The best known artist-jewellers of the time were George (1862-1957) and Jean (b.1899) Fouquet, Gérard Sandoz (b.1902), Raymond Templier (1891-1968, see plate 529), Jean Desprès (1889-1980), and Jean Dunand (1877-1942). Their obsession with modernism and their total abolition of any decorative excess, encouraged them to leave the Société des Artistes Décorateurs. In 1929, Fouquet, Templier and Sandoz, soon followed by Després, joined the Union des Artistes Modernes, commonly known as UAM. The aim of this association was to promote and defend modern art, which, they believed, had to originate from contemporary life. They produced monumental pieces of jewellery: imposing bangles, sculptural rings and massive pendants. The manchette of gold or other metal, decorated with lacquer or enamel, came back into fashion. Prismatic designs of Cubist inspiration became the focal point of voluminous pendants, set with large, step-cut semiprecious stones, or enamelled in geometrical patterns of mechanical conception. Metal played an important role in their creations, either polished or matt. White and yellow gold, platinum and its new, cheaper substitute alloys — platinor and osmior — silver, and even steel were used with the skill of the sculptor. Burnished, beaten and reeded effects were introduced. Miniaturised decoration was rejected for ornaments which could be seen, understood and appreciated from a distance. The artist-jewellers played with broken lines, strong angularity and volume in search of a dynamic rather than a static effect. Arrows, fountains, jets of water, gears and comets enhanced this aim.

The bijoutiers-joailliers, the famous Parisian jewellery houses, conformed to the geometric and the chromatic effects of the new style, but with moderation. Never reaching the extremes of Jean Fouquet, Gérard Sandoz or Raymond Templier, they strengthened their lines, abandoned delicacy in favour of bolder effects, introduced into their creations unusual colour contrasts, but seldom strayed away from precious stones. In their more innovative jewels, they daringly combined semiprecious stones such as onyx, coral, jade and rock crystal, with diamonds, rubies, emeralds and sapphires (see plates 552, 585 and 589). If the diamond continued to be the gemstone *par excellence* many other gems, both precious and semiprecious, were equally popular. This became particularly evident after 1925, in contrast with the early 1920s which is strongly characterised by a tendency towards a monochromatic effect; combinations of platinum, diamonds, pearls, onyx and rock crystal, were typical of many creations of the post-war years (see plates 541, 543, 545 and 626).

The bijoutiers-joailliers were fascinated by Persia, Egypt and the Far East, and borrowed from these civilisations decorative themes and chromatic combinations.

To suit the variety of new, exotic motifs, realised with strictly geometrical lines, the gem cutters experimented with new shapes. Along with the baguettes and the calibré stones of the first years of the century, trapezes, semicircles, half-moons, barrels, triangles and prisms made their appearance (see plate 576). Calibré-cut coloured precious stones with curved surfaces were often used in combination with faceted diamonds in jewels of Egyptian inspiration or floral design (see plates 553, 595, 596 and 598). Hardstones were carved into geometrical shapes which became the central motifs of brooches and pendants, or bracelet links (see plates 585 and 589).

The desire to create effective chromatic combinations, encouraged the lapidaries to carve a wide range of hardstones: onyx, crystal, coral, jade, lapis lazuli, malachite, turquoise, stained chalcedony, amber and chrysoprase, all frequently combined with faceted precious stones.

The fascination of the Orient, encouraged many jewellers to use in their creations, rubies, sapphires and emeralds carved in India in the shape of birds, flowers, leaves and berries in the traditional Mogul manner, or copied in Idar Oberstein (see plates 566, 578, 580 and 597).

The popularity of pearls continued to grow during the first years of the century, and their scarcity and high price, encouraged a group of Japanese scientists, led by Mikimoto, to develop the technique of pearl cultivation. The first cultured pearls appeared on the market in 1921 and, notwithstanding the strong opposition from natural pearl merchants, they quickly became a typical feature of the jewels of the 1920s and were worn both by day and by night, alone or combined with precious or hardstones.

Platinum had become the metal *par excellence* in jewellery, but its rarity and high cost had soon encouraged the research for cheaper substitutes. In 1918 an alternative metal was found, consisting of an alloy which took the name of osmior, plator or platinor.

The use of lacquer was a characteristic of the 1920s. The lacquer technique, borrowed from the Far East, soon replaced enamelling in cheaper jewellery and 'objects of virtu', thanks to its elasticity and malleability. Lacquer, however, is considerably softer than enamel and consequently less durable.

The jewels of the 1920s favoured circles, ovals, rectangles and squares and were, essentially, light and simple; only towards the end of the decade did they become heavier and chunkier. Many were designed so that they could be taken apart and worn in different forms: bandeaux and sautoirs were divided into bracelets and clips, brooches into clips, and necklace pendants were occasionally worn as earrings, etc. (see plates 520, 526, 535-537, 593, etc.)

Many of the bijoutiers-joailliers who exhibited at the 1925 Paris Salon influenced, through their designs, the jewellery production of the 1920s and 1930s, thus contributing to the creation, in jewellery, of a definitive art deco style. The following is an outline of the work of the principal houses.

Cartier embraced the new fashion but always maintained the moderation, style and balance typical of the famous maison which had to meet the tastes and the requirements of a privileged élite. Cartier's 1920s production in art deco style was derived from the formal and geometrical composition of the garland style, rather than from the contemporary Cubist experimentations. The Far East, India and Persia were strong influences on Cartier's production in design, subjects, choice of materials and chromatic combinations. Original Indian carved beads and Chinese mother-of-pearl inlaid plaques were often used in their 1920s creations of Oriental inspiration. Chinese pagodas, chimeras and dragons, Egyptian hieroglyphs and carved stones are common motifs in their creations, as are animal and flower stylisations, strongly geometrical annular or penannular brooches, straight band bracelets, and formal sautoirs of more European inspiration (see plates 544, 547, 548, 554, 568, 580, 585 and 589).

Boucheron produced large, striking brooches, oval or scrolled in shape, and inlaid with carved jade, coral and lapis lazuli in geometrical and stylised shell patterns, embellished with courses of small diamonds. The floral motifs were newly interpreted and stylised by Boucheron in simplified sprays and bouquets of diamonds, outlined with black enamel or onyx, occasionally embellished with corals. Alongside these naturalistic stylisations, Boucheron also produced more abstract and geometrical jewels, making use of zigzag, circular and angular patterns (see plate 577).

Chaumet and Mellerio were open to the various sources of inspiration of the period, and produced jewels of Oriental taste, making use of carved precious and semiprecious stones: giardinetto brooches set with carved rubies, emeralds and sapphires; vanity cases set with stylised lapis lazuli and coral flowerheads, etc. Sober and strictly geometric jewels set with pavés of diamonds, embellished with coloured stones, were also present in their collections.

Lacloche's production of the 1920s is characterised by the bright colours and strong geometrics of lacquered and enamelled cigarette and vanity cases, set with diamond and precious stone decorative motifs of mixed inspiration. At the 1925 exhibition, together with jewels of Chinese inspiration, Lacloche presented a series of rectangular pendants in the 'narrative' style, depicting anecdotes of fables of La Fontaine, drawn with simple and geometrical lines, set with precious coloured stones against a background paved with diamonds. Egyptian and naturalistic inspiration were also characteristic of Lacloche's production of the 1920s (see plates 531 and 598).

Mauboussin was particularly attracted to floral stylisations which frequently appeared in bracelets and brooches, where coloured stones and enamels contrasted with the white brilliancy of diamonds. Rather than the angular geometry of prismatic forms, Mauboussin preferred the curved lines of ovals and circles, often enclosing floral stylisations, and jewels of Oriental inspiration (see plate 646).

Van Cleef and Arpels were sensitive to the influence of the Egyptian archaeological discoveries, and brought out a series of jewels, especially flexible band bracelets, decorated with ruby, emerald and sapphire pharaonic motifs (see plate 596). More geometrical jewels in diamond and other precious stones were also produced (see plates 535, 537 and 584).

Other jewellers active in the 1920s, who contributed to create the aesthetic style of the late 1920s, and whose names are perhaps less known, are Aucoc, René Boivin (see plate 552), Herz-Belperron, Ostertag and Worms. Although French jewellers excelled in the production of art deco jewellery, an international contribution to the formation of the new style came from the Italian Ravasco and Janesich (see plates 557 and 566), from Wolfers, the Belgian and from Jensen, the Dane.

By the 1920s it was common practice for the major jewellery houses to sign their pieces in full or with a monogram. In addition, many of their pieces bear stock or design numbers to aid identification. Sadly these numbers are not consecutive and thus it is not possible to date jewels without access to the jewellers' archives.

The Wall Street crash of 1929, and the consequent economic crisis, were to change dramatically the style of life, dresses, and also jewels. The effervescent spirit of the 1920s gave way to a greater sense of moderation and responsibility. The short, straight lines of dresses were substituted by more feminine draped garments in shiny and soft materials. Jewels changed, but not in a predictable way, to more feminine and delicate shapes. On the contrary, they became even larger and bolder, in massive constructions of plaques, ribbons, straps and buckles. Paradoxically, the financial crisis only marginally affected jewellery, and the creations of the 1930s exhibit an opulence of gemstones and designs unknown in the previous decade. Bracelets became wider and chunkier and were worn in large numbers on each arm (see plate 613). Clips, typical of the 1930s, were always worn in pairs (see plate 584). The pendant earrings of the 1920s were replaced by large clips which encircled the whole lobe, and were well suited to the hairstyles of the time, with the hair piled on top of the head, or worn short, but cut and brushed in softer lines than the garçonne style (see plate 531).

The large, massive jewels of the 1930s usually employed diamonds, and, if the 1920s had been the years of supremacy of colours and chromatic contrasts, the early 1930s became the period of 'white' jewellery.

The daring gemstone combinations of the 1920s gave way to large surfaces entirely pavé-set with diamonds of different shapes and cuts, occasionally enhanced by a touch of colour such as a ruby, a sapphire or an emerald. Colour did not disappear completely, but the multicoloured combinations of precious, semiprecious and hard stones, so typical of the previous years, were replaced by sober monochromatic or bichromatic creations, where the dramatic effect was achieved through the use of differently cut stones of various sizes.

Plaque brooches of geometrical outline or designed as stylised buckles, clips and double clips of mitre or triangular design, and bracelets of wide buckle-shaped links, were the typical ornaments of the early 1930s. The multipurpose characteristic of many jewels of the 1920s, became an even stronger feature in the 1930s. Bandeaux separated into bracelets, clips, brooches and chokers. Double clips were often worn as brooches, on purpose-made fittings, or were secured at the front of a wide bangle. Earrings were frequently provided with a detachable drop, and often combined with a brooch, to create another larger example. Necklaces were frequently decorated with detachable pendants or clips.

Together with the fashion for large jewels of bold and stylised design, the 1930s saw a revival of interest in nineteenth century jewellery, but whitened with a wash of white gold, or rhodium plated.

From the mid-1930s, the flat, two-dimensional and geometric character, typical of the jewels of the post-war period, gradually moved towards richer, three-dimensional, and curved forms. Volutes, scrolls, domes, spirals, fans, bows, and stylised leaves and flowers, reappeared in bold sculptural designs (see plates 587, 592, 622-625).

In 1937 the supremacy of white metal finally came to an end; after three decades of platinum, white gold and white metal alloys, yellow gold came back into fashion on a large scale. Wide bangles set at the front with gem-set buckle motifs, chokers of tubular linking decorated with gem-set clips, jarretière bracelets with jewelled clasps made of yellow gold, became the craze of the moment, and offered the great advantage of being suitable for both day and evening occasions. Brooches and bracelets became the current forms of

Plate 518. 'Schiaparelli'. Cecil Beaton photograph. Sotheby's London.

Plate 519. 'Alice, Lady Wimborne'. Cecil Beaton photograph. Sotheby's London.

ornament, briefly eclipsing other jewels and foreshadowing, with their geometric, yet plastic forms, the ornaments of the 1940s.

Around 1934 Van Cleef and Arpels created the famous 'Ludo hexagone' — or honeycomb — bracelet, which was produced and widely copied, throughout the 1940s. Designed as a wide band of small hexagonal gold plaques, often star-set at the centre with a gemstone, preferably a ruby or a diamond, they were usually decorated with massive volute or buckle-shaped clasps, invisibly-set with matching gemstones (see plates 720-723).

The invisible mount or 'serti invisible', a revolutionary gemsetting technique adopted by Van Cleef and Arpels in 1935, consisted of setting the gems in such a way that no metal at all was visible from the front. To achieve this effect, the stones, suitably cut in rectangular or square shape, were slid on to metal rails, which ran into grooves cut at the back of the stones thus rendering the setting invisible. Emeralds were rarely invisibly set because of their brittleness, the harder sapphires and rubies were the favourite stones for this type of setting. Particularly suited to the realisation of jewels of floral inspiration, this effective technique was soon imitated, with varying success, by many contemporary jewellers, and is still as popular today as it was in the 1930s (see plate 586).

A new wave of naturalism appeared in the mid-1930s. Still controlled by the simple lines of geometrism, three-dimensional flowerheads, birds and insects reappeared, especially in Cartier's collection (see plates 571 and 572). Ladybirds, roses and camellias, Indian and blackamoor heads became the most distinctive subjects of Cartier's clips and brooches of 1937 and 1938.

Tiaras, Bandeaux and Hair Ornaments

The most typical head ornament of the 1920s was the bandeau, which, in France, completely replaced tiaras. In England, where strict court etiquette continued to dictate the wearing of elaborate head ornaments on certain occasions, tiaras continued to be produced in traditional designs, sometimes modified by the geometric patterns of the 1920s.

The bandeau, with its simple linear shape, well suited the art deco style, and, worn low on the forehead, below a bobbed style, was the ideal complement to the new hair-cut à la garçonne. It also suited particularly well the vertical, straight lines of the new evening dresses, which required an equally simple head ornament rather than an elaborate tiara. The bandeau of the 1920s abandoned the delicate motifs of the garland style, and adapted the geometrical shapes which characterised art deco: meanders, palmettes, lozenges, honeycomb patterns, and the like. Diamonds, with their white brilliancy, were obviously the favourite gemstone for an ornament to adorn the delicate features of the face, but the chromatic obsession of the 1920s discreetly appears in many examples, which though pavé-set with diamonds, are embellished with larger coloured gemstones: rubies, emeralds and sapphires.

In line with the typical multipurpose characteristics of 1920s jewellery, the bandeaux were often designed to form bracelets, clips, brooches or chokers, which were worn when the head ornament was not required (see plate 520).

Bandeaux continued to be worn in the early 1930s, but in the second half of the decade they lost favour, replaced on formal occasions by tiaras which, having abandoned the garland and swag motifs of the Edwardian period,

Plate 520. A ruby and diamond bandeau, c.1920. The bandeau is the jewel which perhaps more than any other characterises the 1920s; worn around the forehead it must have created a sensation. Sadly very few have survived, most have reverted to their alternative uses as bracelets and brooches and have been divided amongst members of a family. The design of this example with its palmettes and scrolls can be seen as being transitional between the delicate forms of the pre-war years and the bold geometric lines of art deco.

Plate 521. A magnificent diamond tiara by Cartier, London, c.1930-5 (shown reduced). Very few tiaras have survived from between the wars, and the design of this example is unique. Possibly the only reason why it has not been broken up is that it may be disassembled and the elements worn as clips and brooches.

assumed heavy and elaborate fan, scroll and stylised flower shapes (see plate 521). Their return was accompanied by longer hairstyles, elaborately piled at the top of the head.

In the 1920s, when a bandeau was not worn, the hair was often decorated with clips and slides in the shape of arrows, open circles and annuli, either entirely set with diamonds or carved in hardstone and decorated with diamonds. Many of the stylised, polychrome brooches of the 1920s, were often worn in the hair.

Aigrettes were in fashion, often secured by velvet or silk ribbons which encircled the head. The design of the Indian sarpesh (turban ornament) inspired the curved leaf shape of many aigrettes of the 1920s, with the double clip of the 1930s occasionally arranged in the hairstyle.

Parures

Parures were completely absent both from the jewellery boxes of fashionable women, and from the catalogues of famous jewellery houses.

Jewels were often made to match in colour and design (see plate 522), but women combined them to suit their tastes, dresses and moods.

Plate 522. A suite of jewellery in aquamarine and diamond, by Luis Sanz, Madrid, c.1930.

Earrings

Earrings in the 1920s suited the short hairstyles, which left the ears exposed; long pendant earrings compensated for the low cut, short hemmed, low waisted straight dresses. Earrings assumed various geometrical shapes, but invariably consisted of a pendant which varied in length from about two to nine centimetres, and were designed as cascades of stylised blossoms or briolettes suspended from articulated diamond chains, as simple torpedoes carved in hardstone, or as jewelled dart or lance-like drops. Tassel, fringe, girandole and chandelier earrings, of diamond and coloured gemstones, became the indispensable accessories of evening wear (see plates 523, 526-528 and 533).

In the mid-1920s, Cartier launched bell-shaped earrings, inspired by Indian originals, consisting of a diamond-shaped surmount, which supported an articulated grape-like cluster of cabochon stones (see plate 530).

The Afro-American influence on art and fashion inspired Creole earrings, which were either carved in hard or semiprecious stones, set with diamonds and precious stones, or simply made of a metal annulus.

Plate 523. A pair of ruby and diamond pendant earrings, c.1920-5. Long earrings suited the change in hairstyle and dress design which took place in the 1920s.

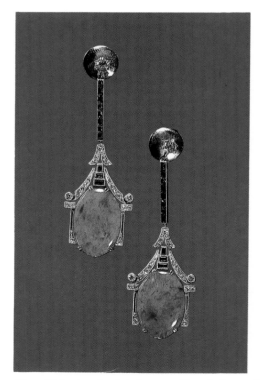

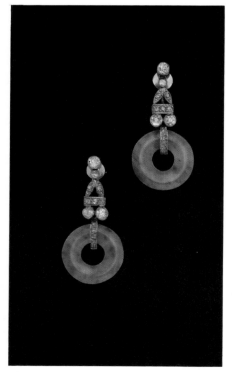

Plate 524. A pair of jade, emerald and diamond earrings, c.1920-5. As an acknowledgment to the jade, the design here shows Chinese influence.

Plate 525. A pair of jade and diamond pendant earrings, c.1920. The annular jades are known as Bi, and were imported in large numbers from China.

Plate 527. *A pair of diamond pendant earrings, late 1920s. In this example we can see how, by this date, diamonds were being cut in a number of adventurous ways.*

Plate 526. *An unusual pair of diamond pendant earrings, c.1925-30, with a diamond set bar (not illustrated), which enables them to be worn as a brooch.*

Plate 528. *A pair of diamond pendant earrings, late 1920s. The arched motif anticipates the 1930s.*

A combination of Eastern and Western influences contributed to the creation of pendant earrings formed of a Chinese jade Bi (ring), suspended from a diamond, onyx or enamelled chain (see plate 525). Chinese jade carvings and jade plaques were often mounted as pendants on gem-set surmounts (see plate 524).

It is perhaps possible to recognise the earlier examples by their simple design and moderate length, as late 1920s earrings tended to be longer and more elaborate.

Earrings continued to be popular during the 1930s. The hair, still worn short or gathered elaborately at the top of the head, promoted earring designs which, having abandoned the excessive length of the late 1920s, assumed the

Plate 529. A pair of aquamarine and diamond pendant earrings, by Raymond Templier, c.1930. Plain areas of metal are characteristic of Templier's designs.

Plate 530. A pair of ruby bead and diamond pendant earrings, late 1920s, retailed by Drayson of Bond Street, London. Emerald, sapphire and ruby beads from the Indian subcontinent were beginning to appear in European jewellery at this time.

Plate 531. A pair of ruby and diamond earclips, French, 1930s, by Lacloche.

Plate 532. A pair of emerald and diamond cornucopia earclips, 1930s. Earclips started to be popular during this era.

shape of scrolls, leaves and stylised shells, often supporting simple pearl drops or more elaborate pendants (see plates 531, 532 and 534). The basic design of the 1920s, which consisted of a small surmount supporting a large pendant, was reversed, and the new earrings were designed as large surmounts, often embracing the whole of the ear lobe with their scrolled volutes, supporting a smaller, occasionally detachable, pendant or tassel (see plate 534).

Earclips, introduced in the 1920s, became very fashionable and assumed the form of elaborate clusters of leaves and flowers, often of large size.

Pendant earrings of the 1920s and 1930s were multipurpose: combined with a plaque brooch or a necklace of matching design, they were often used as larger corsage ornaments (see plate 526).

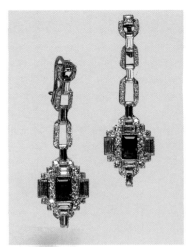

Plate 533. A pair of emerald and diamond pendant earrings, c.1925-30. Note the use of diamonds cut as baguettes.

Plate 534. A pair of diamond earclips, 1930s. Note the typical snail scroll design of the surmount.

Necklaces

The favourite necklace of the 1920s was the sautoir, decorated with a tassel or a pendant, in many materials: diamonds, pearls, coral, semiprecious and hard stones, but also silk and imitation beads. The sautoir was the ideal accessory for the low-waisted dresses of the time and became a symbol of the 'roaring twenties', in the form of long chains of rectangular diamond linking, supporting elongated pendants of geometrical design (see plates 535-537), of long strings of precious stone beads, alternating with pearls and supporting large cabochon pendants, or of strings of pearls supporting seed pearl tassels, capped by a hardstone or an enamel dome-shaped surmount.

Long strings of hardstone beads or pearls, natural or cultured, were often tied in a knot at the front or at the back, to attract attention to the low-cut back décolletages of evening dresses.

Multistrand necklaces of precious stone beads of Indian inspiration were usually long, often decorated with diamond plaques and important clasps, and adorned with pendants and drops which enhanced the back décolletage.

Necklaces continued to be an important element in the jewellery fashions of the 1930s, often in the shape of medium length chains set with precious stones, supporting elaborate pendants of geometrical design. Another contemporary design consisted of a chain of diamond linking supporting a fringe of cabochon or carved emeralds, rubies and sapphires of Oriental inspiration. Stylised ribbons, scrolls and entrelac-de-rubans were also current motifs for short necklaces of sculptural design (see plates 538 and 540).

Multipurpose diamond necklaces of geometrical design were constructed in such a way that the central motif could be detached and worn as a clip, brooch, or pendant, or as a bracelet, attached to a wide gold bangle (see plate 539). In the late 1930s the reintroduction of gold to jewellery brought in a fashion for flexible chains of tubular linking of varied length, decorated with gem-set

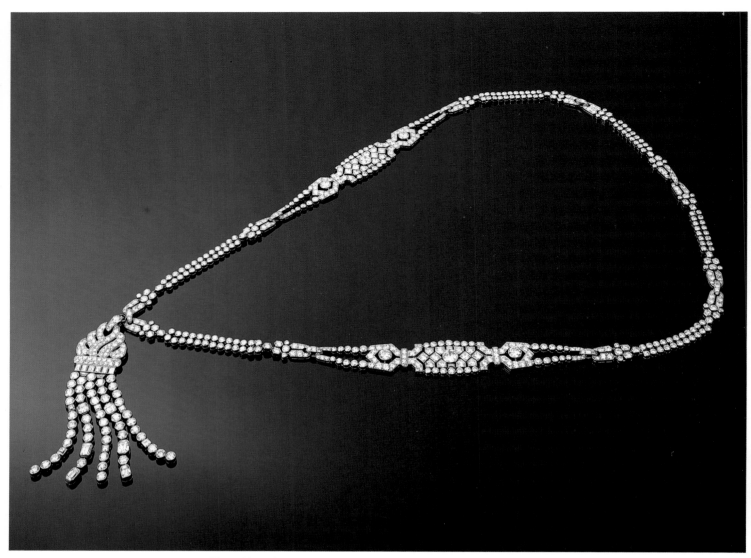

Plate 535. An important diamond sautoir, by Van Cleef and Arpels, Paris, c.1925 (shown reduced), also forming bracelets, a necklace and a pendant.

clips of geometrical or floral design. Easy to wear, suited to afternoon or evening dresses alike, these tubular necklaces were to become one of the favourite ornaments of the 1940s (see plate 661). The clips which fastened the tubular linking were of bold geometrical design: heavy scrolls decorated with diamonds, stylised bows or buckles set with calibré-cut rubies and sapphires. The naturalistic style of the last years of the decade inspired clips designed as stylised flowerheads set with rubies, diamonds and blue and yellow sapphires.

Natural and cultured pearls continued to be used, often in the form of several rows of graduated pearls, set with diamond plaques or clips at each side of the festooned centre.

Plate 536. A diamond sautoir, late 1920s, also forming bracelets, a choker and a pendant.

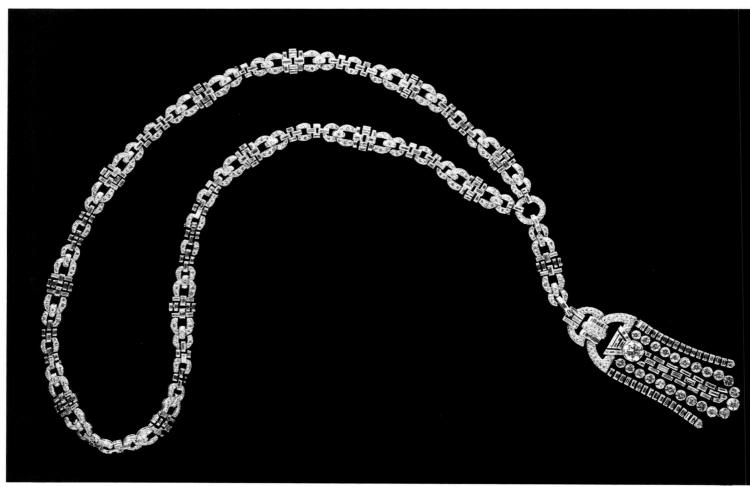

Plate 537. A diamond sautoir, by Van Cleef and Arpels, late 1920s (shown reduced), also forming bracelets, a choker and a pendant.

Plate 538. A diamond necklace, c.1935. The design is typical of the three-dimensional quality characteristic of jewels of the time.

*Plate 539. A ruby and diamond necklace, by Cartier, c.1930. This necklace was also supplied
with a gold bangle to which the two smaller clips can be applied. Shorter necklaces became popular
during the 1930s, in contrast with the sautoirs of the 1920s.*

Plate 540. A magnificent ruby and diamond necklace, by Van Cleef and Arpels, c.1939, formerly the property of the Duchess of Windsor. The clasp bore the puzzling inscription: 'My Wallis from her David, 19 VI, 36'. It transpired that the Duchess had had the necklace redesigned in 1939: the original was a rigid formal design, typical of the mid-1930s, quite unlike the flowing, almost casual lines shown here.

*Plate 541. A fine onyx
and diamond
necklace/pendant, by
Cartier, Paris, 1920,
showing a mixture of
Oriental influences.
The early 1920s at
Cartier are characterised
by jewels in onyx and
diamond.*

Pendants

Long neck ornaments, which moved and swung with the body to the rhythm
of the 1920s dances, brought pendants to the forefront of fashion. Worn on
long silk cords, chains or strings of pearls or beads, their shapes, not restricted
as in the case of bracelets, rings and necklaces to the particular function of
encircling wrists, fingers or necks, offered jewellers complete freedom of
expression. Perhaps more than any other ornament, pendants could be
adapted in their shapes to the strong geometrical lines of art deco. The artist-
jewellers created large ornaments characterised by metal plaques of various
geometrical shapes, decorated with brightly coloured enamels and large
semiprecious stones, where the influence of mechanism was particularly
evident; they also experimented with large prismatic forms in different metals
and hardstone plaques of onyx, coral and rock crystal. Although fascinated by
the geometrical, the bijoutiers-joailliers did not experiment much and
produced attractive pendants of triangular, rectangular, trapeze or elongated
form, set with diamonds and coloured precious stones in geometrical patterns
of various inspiration. Straight lines, zigzags, half circles and steps, but also
Chinese, Indian and Egyptian motifs were used as decoration (see plates 541,
566, 569 and 576).

Lacloche presented, at the 1925 Paris Exposition, his celebrated rectangular pendants depicting particular scenes from the fables of La Fontaine. Cartier often set carved emeralds in mounts of Indian inspiration and Mauboussin enclosed multicoloured stylised flowers within geometrical frames.

Fringes, tassels, and cascades of beads were among the most popular decorative motifs. Open trapezes and rectangles of onyx or rock crystal, decorated with diamond plaques, were suspended on silk ribbons or long strings of pearls, as well as multicoloured baskets of flowers.

Pendants did not disappear in the 1930s but the fashion for shorter neck ornaments tended to incorporate them in the design of necklaces.

Brooches

Brooches in the 1920s were worn on the shoulders, belts and sashes, or pinned on to the fashionable cloche hats. The most typical designs consisted of an open centred circle (or hexagon, square or rectangle), carved in rock crystal and decorated at the sides with diamond-set symmetrical motifs. Variations on this theme included jade, onyx and coral rings flanked by palmette motifs, and diamond open circles or ellipses, decorated at the side with bow or scroll motifs (see plates 552, 556, 561, 585 and 589). The Celtic brooch was revived (see plate 557): Cartier redesigned it as an open ring, with a sliding pin and bayonet clasp, set throughout with a pavé of diamonds, embellished with onyx, coral, or small precious stones.

Typical of the mid-1920s was the 'giardinetto' brooch, designed as a diamond basket or vase containing stylised flowers, leaves and fruits, set with cabochon or carved rubies, emeralds and sapphires (see plates 566, 578 and 580). Tiny trees in their vases, inspired by the Japanese bonsai, became another motif for small brooches set with diamonds and coloured stones. Arches, pagodas, skyscrapers, temples with columns, all offered their geometrical outlines to small brooches, where triangles, baguettes, trapezes, semicircles and hexagons, cut in diamond or other precious stones, skilfully combined to suit the architectural design (see plate 647).

 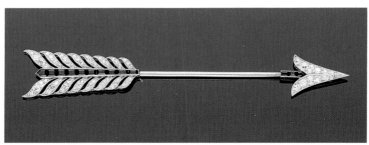

Plate 542. A sapphire and diamond brooch, c.1920, still showing pre-war influence.

Plate 543. An onyx and diamond sûreté pin, c.1920. The shaft of the arrow would have been concealed beneath the material of the dress.

Plate 544. A sensational emerald and diamond epaulette, by Cartier, c.1920. Epaulettes were worn attached to the shoulder of the dress and hanging over the breast or down the back. Few have survived. This example is set with three Indian emerald beads, two of which were carved in the late 19th century. The design is an adaption of a traditional turban ornament, and shows the interest at the time in all things 'Oriental'.

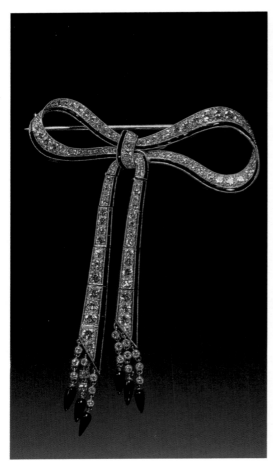

Plate 545. An onyx and diamond bow brooch, c.1920. The combination of the attenuated form, and onyx with diamonds forming a black and white colour scheme, is typical of the early 1920s.

Plate 546. A jade and diamond brooch, c.1920-5, of unusual design.

The sûreté pin was another characteristic feature of the 1920s; in its basic form, it consisted of a metal pin with a decorative device at each end, one fixed, the other made to slide over the pointed end of the pin, and screwed or secured by an interior spring. Its size varied, and the favourite design was that of the arrow, but sûreté pins decorated with palmettes, papyri, or pear-shaped terminals, were also in fashion (see plates 543, 547, and 548).

The Egyptian world inspired numerous brooches decorated with architectural motifs, divinities, scarabs and lotus flowers, borrowed from the culture of the Nile.

Less extravagant brooches assumed the shape of small oval or rectangular plaques, pierced and set with diamonds and coloured stones in light and delicate geometrical designs (see plates 542, 562 and 563).

S-shaped brooches, and brooches designed as open, broken rectangles, similar to door knockers or chest handles, set with diamonds and terminated with cabochon or carved gemstones, came into vogue in the late 1920s (see plate 564).

Ribbon bow brooches continued in favour during the 1920s, but the fluid and natural outlines of the late nineteenth century and early twentieth century

Plate 547. A diamond sûreté pin, by Cartier, c.1925.

Plate 548. A sapphire, onyx and diamond sûreté pin, by Cartier, New York, 1927.

Plate 549. A sapphire and diamond bow brooch, c.1920.

Plate 550. An onyx and diamond bow brooch, in 1920s style but modern. The metal is white gold instead of platinum and the cutting of the diamonds is of a much later date.

Plate 551. A white gold, platinum, rock crystal and diamond brooch, c.1930. The use of large metallic surfaces in combination with rock crystal and diamonds, the contrast between matt and shiny surfaces make this monocromatic piece typical of the day and a compromise between the skills of the 'bijoutier-artiste' and the 'bijoutier-joaillier'.

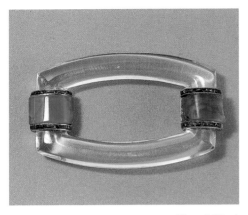

Plate 552. *A carved rock crystal, blue stained chalcedony and sapphire brooch and ring, by Boivin, Paris, c.1925-30.*

Plate 553. *A diamond and gem-set brooch, c.1925. Notice the way the calibré-cut coloured stones have domed surfaces. Due to rising prices these brooches are now being faked in large numbers.*

Plate 554. *A charming onyx, emerald and diamond brooch, by Cartier, Paris, 1926.*

Plate 555. *An enamel, ruby and diamond golfing brooch, c.1925.*

Plate 556. *A rock crystal, ruby and diamond brooch, c.1925-30. The rising sun, or setting sun, became an emblem of the 1930s, particularly in England.*

were replaced by more rigid and stylised shapes (see plates 545, 549 and 560).

Pendant brooches came back into fashion in the form of vases of flowers or geometrical plaques, suspended from simple diamond bars, or that of arched motifs, supporting articulated cascades of gemstones (see plate 564).

The large corsage ornaments of the early twentieth century gave way to small geometrical plaques, pierced and set with diamonds and coloured stones, often decorated with detachable drops wearable as ear pendants, to bar brooches supporting drop panels (see plate 546), or to long 'epaulettes', or shoulder ornaments (see plate 544), which enhanced, with their vertical design, the straight and rigorous lines of the 1920s dresses. Despite their large size, these ornaments were relatively light due to the use of platinum, and therefore

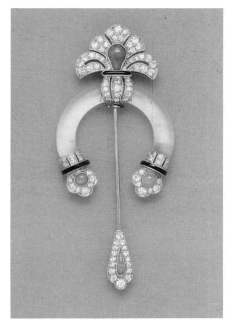

Plate 557. A jade, onyx, rock crystal and diamond sûreté pin by Janesich, c.1925. The design is based on Celtic Iron Age penannular brooches.

Plate 558. An emerald, onyx and diamond skirt pin, c.1925.

Plate 559. An emerald and diamond double clip, c.1925-30. It is unusual for double clip brooches to be asymmetrical, normally both halves of the double clip are identical.

wearable on the flimsy and delicate materials favoured by couturiers for their evening creations.

Novelty brooches of the 1920s featured motor cars, planes, yachts, tennis rackets and golfers of stylised design, all celebrating the newly discovered passion for a sporting, active and fast life (see plate 555).

The most typical ornament of the 1930s was the clip. In its simplest and most characteristic form, it assumed the shape of a mitre or triangular motif, provided, at the back, instead of a pin, with a sprung plaque-shaped fastening, which clasped the edges of the garment.

Clips were usually made in pairs, and worn on each side of the neckline, on the edges of the lapel or, more daringly, clasped on the edge of an evening bag, in the hair or at the centre of a belt. Generally provided with a special fitting, they could also be worn as brooches or as the centre of a bangle.

The earliest clips were of simple geometric design, of moderate size, and if worn in pairs both clips were perfectly identical and symmetrical. Later examples had similar but asymmetrical clips which, when worn together as a brooch, looked as if they had been twisted along the vertical axis.

After 1935, clips and double clips, although maintaining strictly geometrical shapes, exhibited a more sculptural character, obtained by using raised, slightly three-dimensional motifs, such as volutes, spirals, pleated ribbons and the like (see plates 559, 574, 575, 579, 584, 590-594).

Towards 1940 totally asymmetrical double clips came into fashion, designed as informal sprays of leaves or flowers; as design evolved towards less formal

Plate 560. A fine sapphire and diamond bow brooch, late 1920s. Note the way the sapphires have been calibré-cut to fit the mount with no setting metal between them, and the domed surfaces of the stones.

Plate 561. A diamond hat brooch, c.1920-5.

Plate 562. A sapphire and diamond plaque brooch, by Tiffany, New York, c.1925-30.

Plate 563. A sapphire and diamond plaque brooch, c.1925.

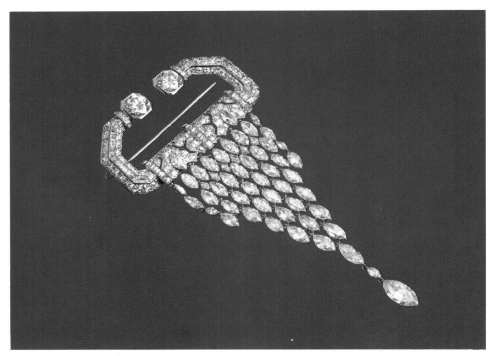

Plate 564. A diamond brooch of drop panel design, c.1925-30. The door-knocker-shaped surmount was a popular motif at this time.

Plate 565. A jade and diamond brooch, c.1925. This design was also popular for earrings.

Plate 566. A coloured stone and diamond 'giardinetto' pendant/brooch, by Janesich, c.1925. Note the carved coloured stones from India, popular with many makers at the time, especially Cartier.

Plate 567. A carved emerald, ruby and diamond lapel watch, c.1925.

Plate 568. An onyx, carved emerald, pearl and diamond lapel watch, by Cartier, Paris, 1923. Designers at Cartier used Indian carved coloured stones in many of their creations during the 1920s.

creations, their size tended to increase. In addition the fastening device changed, and in the late 1930s the sprung plaque was substituted by two sprung prongs, less likely to damage the garments. Clips tended to assume informal, voluminous and sculptural shapes which foreshadowed the 1940s (see plate 588).

Many 1930s brooches were designed as open circles, variously decorated at one side with a bow or with a draped ribbon, but the most typical was the

Plate 569. A jade, onyx and diamond pendant, c.1925. As was typical practice when mounting jades at this time, the surmount is a Chinese inspired design.

Plate 570. A diamond lapel watch, c.1925-30.

Plate 571. A gold, enamel, ruby and diamond ladybird clip, c.1937.

Plate 572. A gold, enamel and gem-set clip, by Cartier, c.1935.

plaque brooch. Often massive in appearance, and mainly set with diamonds, occasionally embellished with a coloured central stone, they assumed the shape of rectangular, oval or elongated octagonal motifs of openwork, geometrical design. Strapworks and strap and buckle motifs were the prevailing types of decoration for these brooches, but geometric compositions of zigzag, semicircles, steps and stylised flowers provided suitable alternatives (see plates 582 and 583).

The sûreté pin of the 1920s continued to be worn throughout the 1930s, as was the safety pin, or 'epingle à nourrice', realised in gold wire, and decorated with a row of gold and hardstone beads, or with the head carved in hardstone.

Towards the end of the 1930s, the stylised naturalism which had made its appearance in jewellery, inspired the design of Cartier's ladybird, rose and camellia brooches, and the creation of his famous Indian and blackamoor head clips, carved in hardstone, enamelled and decorated with diamonds (see plates 571 and 572).

At the same time, Van Cleef and Arpels began the production of their renowned leaf and flower brooches, invisibly set with rubies and sapphires and embellished with diamonds (see plate 586).

306

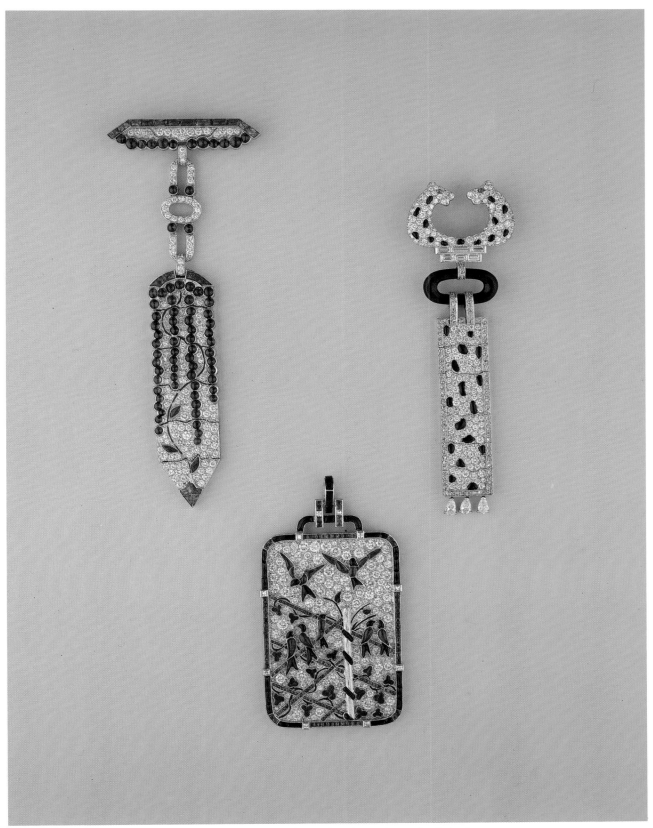

Plate 573. Two modern diamond and gem-set brooches and a pendant in art deco style. Imitations of the 1920s and 1930s pieces are common these days and have been traded as genuine.

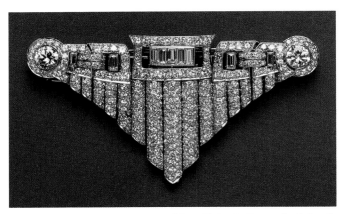

Plate 574. A diamond triple clip brooch, c.1935. The suggestion of organ or Pan pipes here is very successful. Triple clips are uncommon.

Plate 575. A fine sapphire and diamond double clip brooch, c.1930-5.

Plate 576. A diamond brooch/pendant of drop panel design, c.1930. Note the use of diamonds cut in a variety of ways.

Plate 577. A ruby, rock crystal and diamond clip, by Boucheron, Paris, c.1930. Clips and other items of jewellery in carved hardstone and embellished with precious gems are typical of Paris in the late 1920s and early 1930s, pioneered by firms such as Herz Belperron which operated from a shop in the Rue Châteaudun.

Plate 578. A diamond and coloured stone 'giardinetto' brooch, c.1925-30, set with carved rubies, emeralds and sapphires.

Plate 579. A diamond double clip brooch, 1930s, designed as a stylised butterfly.

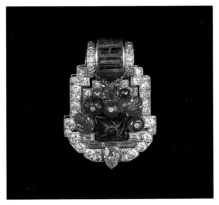

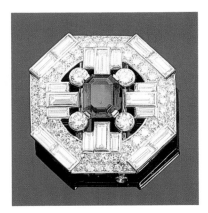

Plate 580. A diamond and coloured stone 'giardinetto' decorating a clip, by Cartier, London, c.1925-30.

Plate 581. A ruby and diamond clip, late 1920s, by Cartier, London. Most of the rubies are Burmese beads held in place by diamond headed pins.

Plate 582. An emerald and diamond brooch, by Boucheron, Paris, c.1930-5. The design offers a typically 1930s textural contrast between the sheer surfaces of the baguette diamonds and the animated display of the pavé-set brilliants.

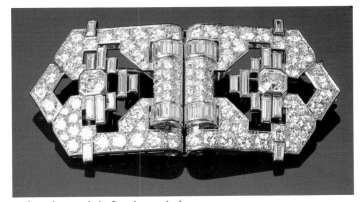

Plate 583. A diamond plaque brooch, c.1935. Typical of many brooches made in London and often set with stones of inferior quality. Ten years ago such brooches appeared in large numbers at auction. Their fate was to be broken up and as a result they have become less common and consequently sought after.

Plate 584. A diamond double clip brooch, by Van Cleef and Arpels, Paris, c.1930.

Plate 585. A fine onyx, emerald and diamond hat brooch, by Cartier, Paris, c.1920-5. This became one of Cartier's most popular designs, often imitated.

Plate 586. *A celebrated invisibly-set ruby and diamond clip, by Van Cleef and Arpels, Paris, 1936, designed as holly leaves, from the collection of the Duchess of Windsor. According to Van Cleef and Arpels, this was perhaps the first invisibly-set brooch made by the firm.*

 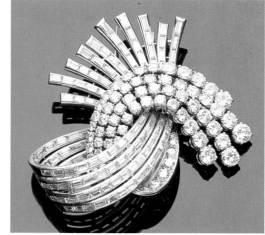

Plate 587. *A citrine and diamond clip, mid-1930s, in an architectural design.*

Plate 588. *A diamond clip, late 1930s, of informal, almost casual design.*

Plate 589. *A sapphire, rock crystal and diamond brooch, by Cartier, c.1925-30.*

Plate 590. A diamond double clip brooch, c.1930, in a design of ammonites or seashell scrolls.

Plate 591. A diamond double clip brooch, 1930s.

Plate 592. A pair of diamond clips, by Boucheron, c.1935.

Plate 593. A ruby and diamond double clip brooch (the clips are separated for illustration), 1930s.
Towards the end of the 1930s the design became more asymmetrical and less formal.

Plate 594. A sapphire and diamond double clip brooch, 1930s.

Bracelets

Band bracelets were the vogue arm ornament of the early 1920s. Usually designed as chains of narrow, articulated, geometrical plaques and links, or set with courses of gemstones of contrasting colours, they became, in the mid-1920s, wider, flexible, gem-set bands.

The geometrical style of the 1920s well suited the linear shape of these bracelets. Zigzags, triangles, concentric squares, stylised buckles, chevrons and chequered patterns, stylised leaves and flowers pierced in platinum and pavé-set with diamond and multicoloured gemstones of all shapes, became the most sought after decorative motifs (see plates 598, 599, 603, 604, 607, 614, 616 and 617).

The fascination for pharaonic Egypt, inspired many bracelets designed as wide bands, pavé-set with diamonds and decorated with Egyptian architectural motifs, sphinxes, scarabs, lotus flowers and the like, skilfully set with cabochon calibré-cut coloured stones, whose curved surfaces strikingly contrasted with the brilliancy of faceted diamonds. Van Cleef and Arpels specialised in the production of such bracelets (see plates 595 and 596). Boucheron preferred stylised floral motifs, set with diamonds within enamel borders, and stylised flowers carved in multicoloured hardstones, inlaid in diamond frames. Cartier excelled in the design of bracelets of Indian inspiration, set throughout with

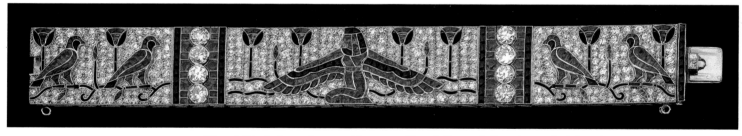

Plate 595. A fine ruby, sapphire, emerald and diamond Egyptian revival bracelet, by Lacloche, Paris, c.1925.

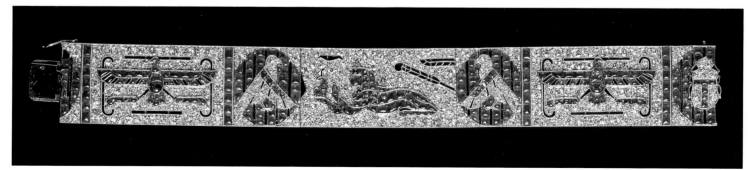

Plate 596. A diamond and coloured stones Egyptian revival bracelet, French, c.1925. Van Cleef and Arpels also made jewellery in Egyptian taste.

312

Plate 597. A collection of jewellery in Indian taste, set with carved coloured stones, c.1930, the bracelet by Cartier, London.

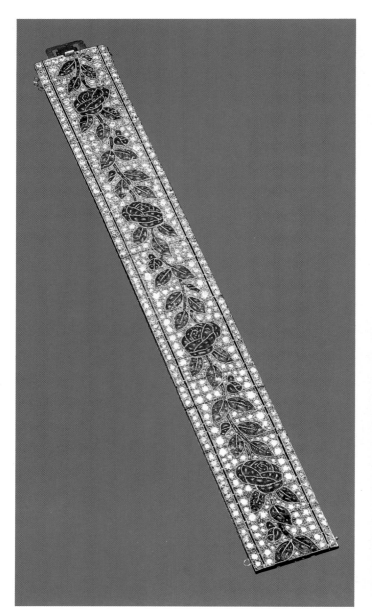

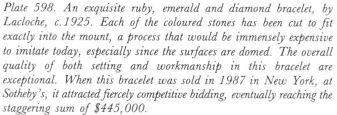

Plate 598. An exquisite ruby, emerald and diamond bracelet, by Lacloche, c.1925. Each of the coloured stones has been cut to fit exactly into the mount, a process that would be immensely expensive to imitate today, especially since the surfaces are domed. The overall quality of both setting and workmanship in this bracelet are exceptional. When this bracelet was sold in 1987 in New York, at Sotheby's, it attracted fiercely competitive bidding, eventually reaching the staggering sum of $445,000.

Plate 599. A sapphire and diamond bracelet, 1920s.

Plate 600. A diamond bracelet, c.1925.

Plate 601. A platinum bracelet, supporting gem-set charms. The fashion for collecting charms and wearing them on a bracelet took root between the wars and was particularly popular during the 1950s and '60s.

Plate 602. A ruby and diamond bangle, by Lacloche, c.1925.

rubies, emeralds and sapphires, carved in the shape of leaves, flowers and berries (see plate 597).

Other bracelets of the period took the form of rows of carved hardstone plaques, alternating with jewelled or enamelled links (see plates 608-610).

The fashion for collecting commemorative or novelty charms and wearing them on a chain bracelet began in the 1920s and became widespread in the 1950s and 1960s. Charm bracelets of the 1920s were usually made of platinum and set with calibré-cut stones (see plate 601).

Thin gem-set bangles were worn in great numbers, at night, on the bare arm, on evening gloves, and even on the upper arm, often to hide a vaccination

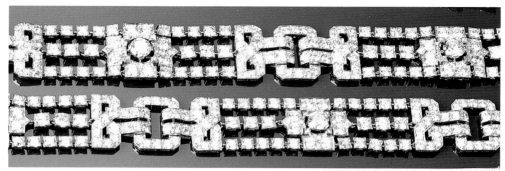

Plate 603. A pair of diamond bracelets, by Hennell, London, c.1925.

Plate 604. A ruby and diamond bracelet, French, c.1920.

Plate 605. A white gold, onyx and diamond cuff bracelet, c.1925-30.

scar (see plate 602). For day wear, larger bangles of plain or enamelled gold, or carved in ivory in African taste, were very fashionable, and worn in great numbers on each arm. Simple hoops carved in jade or other hardstone were popular too. Manchettes and cuff bracelets came back into favour (see plate 605), enamelled or gem-set. Particularly striking are Cartier's bangles of Oriental inspiration, carved in coral or lapis lazuli, hinged with enamelled gold plaques, and decorated with various precious stones.

Wide and massive link bracelets, mainly set with diamonds, became, together with the double clip, the chic ornament of the 1930s. Worn several at a time, often on evening gloves, these heavy ornaments paradoxically became the indispensable companion to the draped evening dresses of the time. Designed as rows of rectangular or elongated octagonal plaques, decorated with strapwork and buckle motifs, they perfectly matched the plaque brooches. The preferred gemstone was the diamond, but many of these bracelets were set with a coloured gemstone at the centre of each plaque, or with courses of smaller calibré-cut coloured gems (see plates 613-615 and 618).

Other bracelets set with diamonds and coloured stones assumed the massive and sculptural forms of wide straps decorated with bulky buckles, large scrolls and ribbons (see plates 620, 623 and 625).

Thinner bracelets in the 1920s tradition continued to be produced in the

Plate 606. An emerald and diamond bracelet of escalier design, by Cartier, Paris, late 1930s.

Plate 607. An emerald and diamond bracelet, c.1925-30, of popular strap-and-buckle design.

Plate 608. An attractive diamond and hardstone bracelet, c.1925. The leaves and flowers are skilfully carved in coral, malachite, cornelian and chalcedony and inlayed in a lapis lazuli background within diamond borders, showing Japanese influence.

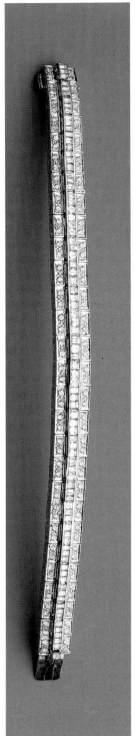

Plate 609. A sapphire and diamond bracelet, c.1930, the white gold links probably replace carved hardstone hoops, which on a bracelet were easily broken.

Plate 610. A gold, enamel and stained chalcedony bracelet, French, c.1925-30. The enamel is imitating jade.

Plate 611. A modern line bracelet: notice the large amount of metal visible and the poor quality of manufacture, which makes the bracelet inflexible.

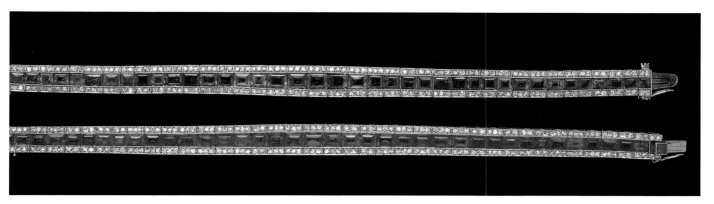

Plate 612. A pair of line bracelets, 1920s, one set with rubies and diamonds, the other with emeralds and diamonds. Such bracelets were often worn in pairs.

Plate 613. A diamond bracelet of exceptional size, c.1930. An expanded ring and buckle design.

1930s (see plates 616 and 617). Also in favour were bracelets made of several rows of pearls or semiprecious and precious beads, alternating with diamond plaques of geometric design.

'Escalier' bracelets, simply made of gold or set with gemstones of contrasting colours, became the vogue around 1935. Designed as articulated bands of rectangular prism links, these bracelets gave the *trompe-l'oeil* effect of a moving staircase by playing on the contrast of white and coloured gemstones, or on the reflection of light from the polished gold surfaces (see plate 606).

From about 1936, it became fashionable to wear a pair of clips secured to the front of a wide metal bangle.

The 'Ludo' — or honeycomb — bracelet, first designed by Van Cleef and Arpels in 1934, soon became popular, foreshadowing its great success in the 1940s. Designed as a wide band of hexagonal links, invisibly articulated, often star-set at the centre with a tiny ruby or diamond, it was usually decorated with a massive clasp of scroll or buckle design, invisibly set with sapphires or rubies, and decorated with small diamonds (see plates 720-723).

Plate 614. A diamond bracelet, 1930s.

Plate 615. A diamond bracelet, c.1930.

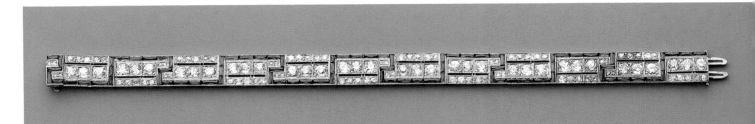

Plate 616. A synthetic sapphire and diamond bracelet, c.1930. It is not uncommon for these long calibré-cut coloured stones to be synthetic at this time.

Plate 617. A sapphire line bracelet, Sri Lanka, 1930s. The poor quality of workmanship and the lack of diamonds make this example typical.

Plate 618. A fine diamond bracelet, 1930s. The three-dimensional quality is typical of the date.

Plate 619. An aquamarine and diamond bracelet, c.1930. Although unsigned, this bracelet is typical of the Cartier, London workshop.

Plate 620. A ruby and diamond bracelet, by Chaumet, Paris, c.1930-5.

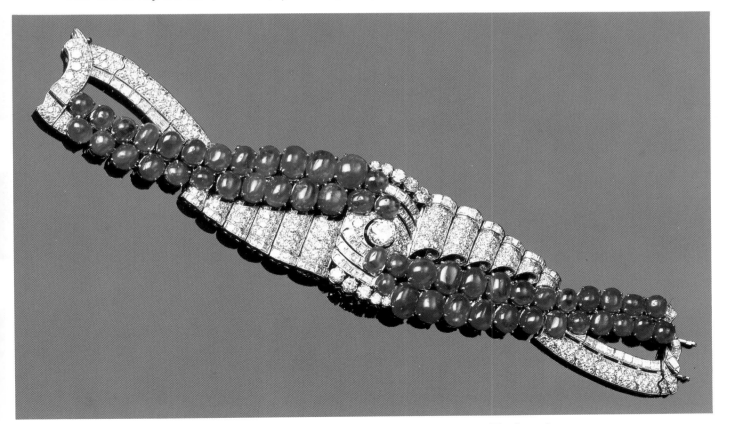

Plate 621. An unusual ruby and diamond bracelet by Drayson, London, c.1935. The firm of Drayson in Bond Street, London, created jewels of strong art deco influence along French lines, usually incorporating coloured stones in the design.

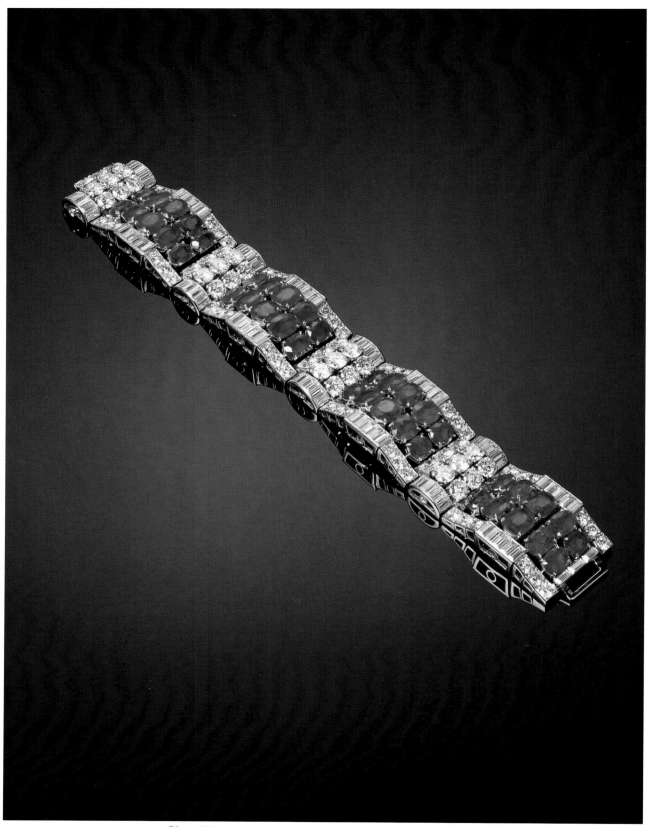

Plate 622. A ruby and diamond bracelet, by Van Cleef and Arpels, Paris, 1936, given by King Edward VIII to Mrs Simpson on the 27th of May, and inscribed: 'Hold tight'.

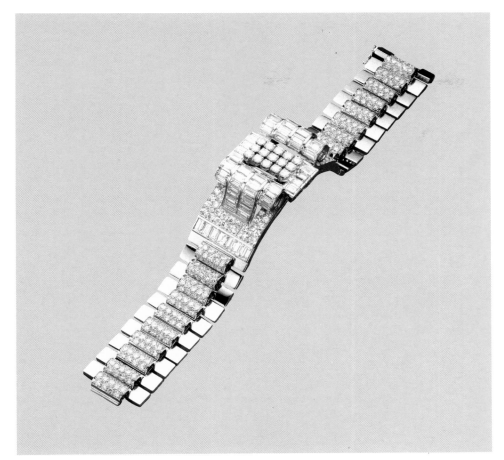

Plate 623. A diamond bracelet by Cartier, Paris, c.1935.

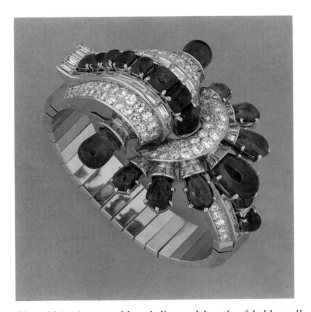

Plate 624. An emerald and diamond bangle of bold scroll and fan design, by Boucheron, Paris, 1935-40.

Plate 625. An exceptional sapphire and diamond bracelet, by Van Cleef and Arpels, Paris, 1937, from the collection of the Duchess of Windsor. Note the way the sapphires have been ingeniously set showing no claws. This bracelet must be considered something of a tour de force.

Wrist-watches

Gem-set evening wrist-watches were worn throughout the 1920s, mainly in white gold and platinum, and set with pavés of diamonds, embellished with calibré-cut onyx, and occasionally with coloured gemstones.

The rectangular, octagonal or circular bezels, were pavé-set with diamonds between shoulders of geometrical design. The straps were generally of black silk moiré, black silk cordette, metal mesh, seed pearls or thin diamond linking (see plates 626-631).

Around 1925, pendant or 'fob' watches of circular or rectangular design, with the back of the case set with precious gemstones, became the last word in fashion, and temporarily, the appeal of evening wrist-watches diminished (see plates 567, 568 and 570), but the phenomenon was short lived, and soon gem-set wrist-watches came back into fashion, where they remained throughout the 1930s.

Plate 626. A pearl, diamond and onyx bracelet watch, by Cartier, Paris, c.1920. This type of wrist-watch was introduced just before the First World War, but influenced designs of the 1920s.

Plate 627. A diamond wrist-watch, by Cartier, c.1920-5. Note the cordette bracelet and the typical enamelled buckle.

Plate 628. A pearl, onyx and diamond watch, by Cartier, c.1920, though probably designed c.1913.

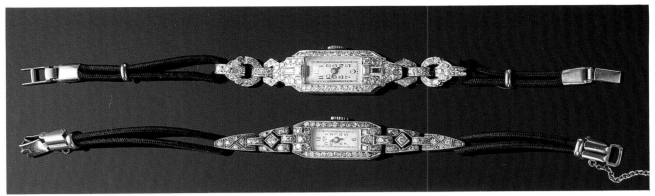

Plate 629. A pair of diamond wrist-watches of popular design, on black silk cordette straps, 1920s.

Plate 630. A diamond wrist-watch, set with baguette and brilliant-cut stones, c.1925. The 'tonneau'-shaped bezel is typical of the inter-war years.

Plate 631. A diamond wrist-watch, c.1925-30.

Rings

Rings of the 1920s, generally mounted in platinum, were often set with a coloured stone, frequently cut en cabochon, within a geometrical border, pavé-set with diamonds (see plates 632 and 633). The same geometrical outline to the bezel was also typical of rings set at the centre with a variously cut large diamond, within a border of calibré-cut stones. Coloured stones, precious or semiprecious, were often claw-set between bombé-shaped shoulders, or pavé-set with baguette or circular-cut diamonds (see plate 634).

Eternity rings, set with diamonds or calibré-cut coloured stones, were worn in various colour combinations on the same finger. Triple-hoop eternity rings, consisting of a central diamond hoop and two lateral half-hoops of contrasting colour, which swivelled to create various colour combinations, were also in fashion (see plate 636).

In 1924 Cartier created the triple ring, consisting of three entwined hoops of differently coloured gold which, together with the matching bracelet, is still produced today in more or less its original form.

Large step-cut diamond solitaire rings first appeared in the mid-1920s, and have remained in vogue.

The creations of the artist-jewellers, who were less interested in the intrinsic value of the gemstones, tended to assume larger sculptural geometric forms,

Plate 632. A ruby and diamond ring, c.1920-5. The rubies have been carefully calibré-cut to fit the mount. This is an expensive and time-consuming process; excellent copies are now being made in Thailand, however; close examination is necessary.

Plate 633. An emerald and diamond ring, c.1925-30.

Plate 634. An emerald and diamond ring, c.1925-30. The poor quality emerald is here helped along by attractive pavé-set shoulders.

Plate 635. A diamond ring, c.1935. The bulkiness of the design is typical of the date.

Plate 636. A diamond eternity ring and a sapphire, ruby and diamond triple-hoop ring, 1920-30. It is very difficult to 'size' eternity rings, and so they can be bought relatively cheaply second-hand. The triple-hoop example shows how the two outer diamond hoops are hinged and may be worn flanking either the rubies or the sapphires.

characterised by sharp, neat lines. Metal and hardstone plaques were the chosen materials and precious gemstones were used sparingly.

In the 1930s the general trend was towards larger rings, often set with a single stone between geometrical shoulders (see plate 635).

Dress rings of flamboyant design made in platinum and pavé-set with diamonds or coloured gemstones became very popular.

Van Cleef and Arpels created, in 1935, the 'boule' ring, consisting of a wide gold shank which enlarged to accommodate a bombé bezel, invisibly set with calibré-set stones.

Towards the end of the 1930s the first yellow gold rings appeared, set with diamonds and coloured gemstones in buckle and strap motifs, which foreshadowed the 1940s 'cocktail' rings.

Vanity Cases, Cigarette Cases and Evening Bags

After the First World War, cosmetics became big business. Powdered pale faces, bright red lips, and eyes underlined with heavy strokes of black pencil, were the vogue of the time.

Vanity cases, containing compartments for compressed powder, rouge, lipstick, mirror and tortoiseshell or ivory comb, became an indispensable accessory for fashionable women. The earliest examples consisted of small circular or rectangular compacts suspended from finger rings by means of variously decorated chains, together with a matching lipstick holder. Later examples assumed the form of larger rectangular boxes, for which Van Cleef and Arpels patented the name 'Minaudière'.

Made of gold, silver, white metal alloy or gilt metal, vanity cases were often simply decorated with guilloché patterns of geometrical inspiration: concentric rectangles, steps, stripes, zigzags, honeycomb motifs, and embellished with a gem-set thumbpiece. The large rectangular surface of the lids offered the ideal ground for the art deco jewellers to exploit their imagination. Brightly coloured enamel and lacquer surfaces were applied with gem-set decorative motifs of

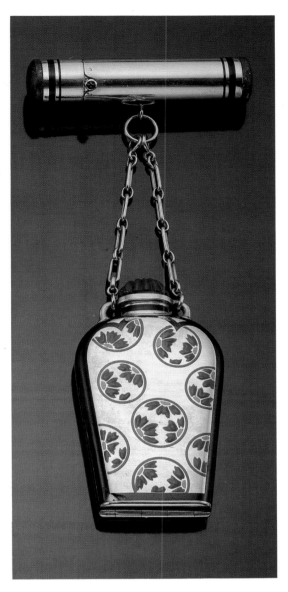

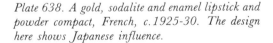

Plate 637. A gold, enamel and diamond lipstick and powder case, c.1925-30.

Plate 638. A gold, sodalite and enamel lipstick and powder compact, French, c.1925-30. The design here shows Japanese influence.

geometric and Oriental inspiration: Persian motifs, Chinese pagodas, clouds or symbols of long life, Japanese dwarf trees, abstract decorations, and Chinese landscapes in polychrome enamels or inlaid with mother-of-pearl and semiprecious gemstones. Cartier often set original nineteenth century Chinese plaques of lacquer, mother-of-pearl and hardstone marquetry on the lid of his vanity cases. Chinese carved jade and coral plaques were also well suited to this purpose (see plates 637-642, 645 and 647).

Smoking was fashionable in the 1920s, and the liberated women of the time smoked in public, using long cigarette holders. They kept their cigarettes in cigarette cases, similar in design and decoration to their vanity cases (see plates 643 and 644), or in larger table boxes (see plate 646).

Jewelled evening bags were typical accessories of the 1920s; made of embroidered silk brocades threaded with gold and mounted in gold, enamel and gem-set frames of geometric, Egyptian, Persian, Chinese or Indian

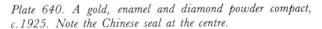

Plate 639. A gold, enamel and diamond powder compact, by Lacloche, Paris, c.1925. Here the influence is clearly Chinese. Note the diamond 'shou'.

Plate 640. A gold, enamel and diamond powder compact, c.1925. Note the Chinese seal at the centre.

design, they were the ideal complement to the evening dresses of the time (see plates 648 and 649).

Black silk and black suede 'pochettes' were more discreetly decorated with gem-set clasps of strictly geometrical design, and continued in use during the 1930s. When a proper jewelled evening bag was not available, a pair of clips clasped to the edge of a silk 'pochette' brilliantly solved the problem.

Plate 641. A silver-gilt, coral and enamel compact, by Cartier, 1933.

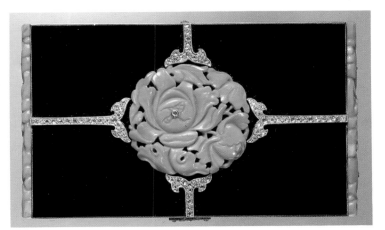

Plate 642. A gold, enamel, nephrite and diamond powder compact, by Cartier, c.1925.

Plate 643. A pair of cases in enamel, coral, jade and diamond, c.1925, one used for cigarettes, the other for make-up. Again the Chinese influence is very strong as the carved jades and coral would have been imported.

Plate 644. A cigarette case by Lacloche Frères, Paris, c.1925. The lid and base are set with black lacquered panels inlayed with mother-of-pearl dyed in various shades of green, pink and blue. Mother-of-pearl inlay plaques were very popular with art deco cases and compacts of Chinese inspiration; though originally imported from the Far East they were soon imitated by western lapidaries.

Plate 645. A gold, enamel powder compact, by Cartier, c.1925. Note the stepped pyramid decoration.

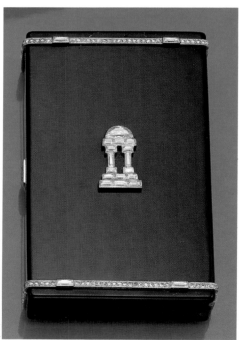

Plate 646. An aventurine quartz, diamond and gem-set table cigarette box, by Mauboussin, c.1925. Floral motifs set with calibré-cut multicoloured stones were particularly favoured by Mauboussin.

Plate 647. A gold, platinum, diamond and black enamel compact, by Cartier, Paris, c.1930. Arches, temples, pagodas and skyscrapers built with fancy-cut stones were popular motifs with Cartier jewellery of the time, especially brooches.

Plate 648. An enamel, citrine and diamond evening purse, c.1925. Note the Japanese influence in the diamond mounts which echoes the design of the original silk brocade pouch.

Plate 649. A gold, enamel and diamond evening purse, c.1925. Although unsigned, this is almost certainly the work of Van Cleef and Arpels, Paris. The enamel intentionally imitates coral and jade. The interest in Egypt and things Egyptian probably stems from the opening of the tomb of Tutankhamen in 1922.

Plate 650. 'Princess Elizabeth'. Photograph by Cecil Beaton, 1948. National Portrait Gallery.

CHAPTER EIGHT
The 1940s~1950s

For the second time in the century, the outbreak of war slowed down the production of the jewellery industry in Europe. Precious metals again became rare, platinum was almost unobtainable, gold was scarce and rationed everywhere.

In France, the Banque de France forbade the sale of precious metal, and those who wished to commission a piece of jewellery in gold had to supply the entire quantity of metal required. If precious metals, gold and platinum, were melted, twenty per cent of the fine content had to go to the State. Precious gemstones were affected as the supply of South African diamonds and Siamese and Burmese rubies and sapphires was very irregular.

Many craftsmen volunteered for, or were conscripted into, the armed forces, or turned their skills to the armament industry. Large scale bombing of the industrial centres, particularly in England and Germany, reduced production still further. In Germany, the jewellery centre of Pforzheim suffered heavy attacks, and production came to an almost total standstill. The very few jewels produced in Germany during the war years were mainly in silver, decorated with enamel, or made of very thin gold wire. In England, the major jewellery houses, such as Cartier, prudently transferred their valuable stocks to places less likely to be affected by the destruction of the war, but Birmingham, the major centre of the jewellery industry, was badly affected by the bombing. Only in France was the situation slightly better; in the German occupied Paris of the early 1940s, the famous jewellery houses continued their business, admirably coping with the scarcity of precious materials and labour. Old jewels were broken up and remounted, and precious stones, stocked in the pre-war years, were used parsimoniously.

The austerity of the war years only marginally affected the fashion for wearing jewellery. In times of economic instability jewellery represents a valuable source of portable capital. The lack of confidence in paper money merely served to encourage people to search for alternatives, and precious metal and gemstones were purchased whenever available, thus the market for antique and second hand jewellery naturally flourished.

Although the jewellery business did not cease completely during the war, the production of those years is characterised by a lack of new ideas in design. The famous jewellery houses continued to produce jewels based on pre-war models: massive, decorated with scrolls, straps and buckles, and bridge motifs, mainly made of gold and set with diamonds combined with rubies and sapphires, often synthetic, to overcome the scarcity of natural stones.

The gold jewels of the late 1930s, with their bold sculptural designs, reached the peak of their popularity in the early 1940s. What differentiates the jewels of the 1930s from those of the 1940s is a different approach towards the use of gemstones. In the 1940s, the opulence of large gems and the richness of surfaces entirely pavé-set with diamonds or invisibly set with rubies and sapphires, was substituted for gems which were limited in size and number to the great advantage of large metallic surfaces.

The scarcity of precious stones turned attention towards semiprecious stones. Citrine quartz in all its colour variations, from lemony yellow to deep brown, and aquamarines, amethysts and topazes enjoyed great favour. The scarcity of gold did not influence the shape of jewels, which remained massive looking and voluminous, but they became lighter, made of thin sheets of metal. At the bottom end of the market, jewels were hollow inside, or made of a very thin sheet of gold cemented to a sheet of base metal. New alternative alloys were produced; the percentage of copper in 9, 14 and 18 carat gold was raised, thus imparting to the metal the characteristic reddish tinge typical of many jewels of the war years. Palladium, the lightest of the six members of the platinum group of metals, was first introduced in jewellery.

Documentation for 1940s jewellery is relatively scarce, as many jewellers' archives, drawings, photographs and descriptions were destroyed during the war. In addition, many jewels of the 1940s were melted down and reset in the following decades when the fashion for lighter and more naturalistic creations led them to be rejected as examples of bad taste. The appreciation of the jewels of the 1940s, and the fashion for their bulky design, is a fairly recent phenomenon, which first appeared in Italy, France and the United States in the early 1980s, and is now widespread in Europe.

During the war, women again took up the jobs left vacant by men called to arms, whether in industry, in commerce and in offices, or took an active part in the assistance of war casualties by driving ambulances and working in hospitals. For economical and practical reasons, their skirts once more became shorter. Feminine attire of the 1930s changed to masculine, well-tailored suits of military inspiration, characterised by straight, knee-length skirts, and long, tight-fitting jackets, with wide padded shoulders. Shoes had to be comfortable, and the new orthopaedic models had cork soles to replace leather which was scarce. A touch of femininity was given by the square neckline of the slim line dresses, and by the small circular or tricorne hats, frivolously decorated with flowers and veils. The bold, massive jewels of the time were well suited to this style of fashion. Voluminous clips worn on the jacket lapels or at the sides of the square necklines, well balanced the large padded shoulders. Massive and chunky bracelets, and large dress rings, combined very well with the sober attires of the time (see plates 664, 681, 688, 720-726).

At the end of the war, fashion reacted to the austerity of the previous six years. In 1945 the new names of French couture, such as Balmain, Givenchy and Balenciaga, presented feminine dresses, characterised by ample, short skirts, and generously décolleté tops, covered up by short bolero-style jackets. In 1947 Christian Dior triumphed with his 'new look', typified by ample, mid-calf skirts, cut in yards of light materials, thin waistlines, and tightly fitting tops with pointed necklines. Colours and precious materials came back into fashion after six years of forced sobriety and privation, and the masculine, broad-shouldered silhouette of the war years gave way to a more feminine and frivolous look.

Jewellery changed accordingly. The massive geometrical jewels of the early 1940s were replaced by large gold jewels of more naturalistic inspiration. Precious stones came back on a large scale, freely set in scrolled and curved gold mounts, pleated, knotted or fretted in tulle, or lace-like patterns. The flat geometric forms of art deco were substituted for voluminous, three-dimensional volutes, scrolled leaves, and bows of elaborately interlaced ribbons. Naturalism made a triumphant return in the shape of opulent, exotic flowers, birds, animals, leaves and snowflakes (see plates 653, 689, 690, 696, 697, 699-701 and 703). In 1948 Cartier produced the first fully three-dimensional panther brooch; commissioned by the Duchess of Windsor, it was designed as a golden panther flecked with black enamel, outstretched on a large cabochon emerald. Many other 'great cats' jewels followed, commissioned throughout the 1950s and 1960s by famous names such as the Windsors, Princess Nina Aga Khan and Barbara Hutton. Panther and tiger jewels, still popular today, are produced at Cartier's with the same vigour, plasticity and sense of movement of the late 1940s (see plates 704, 705 and 732).

Gold continued to be the preferred metal in all its shades of colour: white, grey, yellow, green, pink and red, and worked in all possible ways: tied in ribbons, fretted in lace-like rosettes, twisted as corded wire, etc. The supremacy of platinum was definitely over.

Among the precious stones, diamonds were the favourite, often combined with calibré-cut rubies and sapphires. Semiprecious stones such as amethysts, citrines, topazes and turquoises were frequently combined with precious stones in bold yet successful chromatic effects (see plate 675). The jewels of the late 1940s, shared with the earlier production the tendency towards massive-looking ornaments, and foreshadowed the 1950s interest in naturalism; also, in the use and choice of gemstones they fall between the parsimony of the early 1940s and the opulence of the 1950s.

As frequently happens after a war, the desire to restore the values of the pre-conflict years, encouraged many conservative jewellers and many women less sensitive to the changes of fashion, to go back to the shapes and the models popular in the late 1930s. Many pre-war creations, such as the Van Cleef and Arpels honeycomb bracelets or the invisibly set flowerhead brooches, were already established as 'classics', and therefore perfectly suitable for the 'new look' dresses (see plates 687 and 720-723).

Plate 651. *'Tilly Losch'. Cecil Beaton photograph.* Sotheby's London.

The economic boom which followed the war, the desire to rebuild and restore what had been destroyed, the determination to reconstruct a new wealth out of the rubble, characterised the early 1950s. Both industry and the economy flourished, and consumerism, after the years of privation, made its appearance, with television opening the way to immediate communication of images from all over the world. Travelling and holidaying abroad became popular after years of border restrictions, and owning a car became a reality for many.

The visual arts and as a consequence the decorative arts, opened up a variety of contrasting influences. Abstraction and surrealism, which made their appearance in the 1930s, achieved widespread popularity. Abstract expressionism and action painting were the avant-garde movements. The aesthetic of design tended towards free, light, simple, essential and functional lines. Industrial design was in its infancy, attempting to combine aesthetics and functionality. The straight and angular lines of art deco were abandoned in favour of rounded, aerodynamic surfaces. Curved lines characterised the design of all sorts of objects, from the expensive and exclusive sports car to the humble refrigerator or television set. Furniture assumed rounded, shell-shaped forms supported by thin tapered metallic legs. The simple and essential Scandinavian style became a model for the furniture industry.

The United States led the way in the field of design, but the Italians were developing their unmistakable style, independent from other contemporary experiments, both original and innovative, functional yet elegant.

Jewellery design could not escape this change towards curved, informal and free lines, which were particularly suited to the fashion of the time.

Christian Dior remained the king of Parisian couturiers until his death in 1957. His feminine silhouette, characterised by narrow waists, ample puffed skirts, rounded small shoulders and pointed, heart-shaped necklines, remained in vogue, with small variations, throughout the period. The other names of French fashion: Balmain, Givenchy, Balenciaga, etc., followed Dior's example and created the image of the very feminine woman, who enjoyed dressing up at night in expensive and richly embroidered silks and laces, wore opulent jewels on the generous décolletages, and on special court occasions, balls or débuts, indulged in hairstyles which suited a tiara. Fur coats were all the rage, and diamond jewellery their best companion.

The reopening of Chanel's atelier in 1954, reintroduced the famous and classic two-piece suit, which became the most fashionable garment for day wear, with gold jewels and strings of pearls as the most suitable ornaments.

Although Paris was the undisputed leader in the field of fashion and jewellery, Italy was making great progress. Shubert, Yole Veneziani, Biki, Emilio Pucci and Sorelle Fontana, presented their original collections in the 1950s, which were to foreshadow the success of Italian fashion design of the following decades. In jewellery, names like Bulgari, Cusi, Faraone and Settepassi, were responsible for many outstanding creations, which were in no way inferior to the contemporary French models.

Newly acquired general wealth, and the post-bellic industrial development, stimulated the growth of the mass-produced jewellery industry, and jewels produced in the goldsmith centres of Valenza Po and Arezzo, contributed to publicise abroad the popularity of 'Made in Italy'.

To define the style of the jewels of the 1950s is a difficult task, so disparate were the sources of inspiration and extremely varied the ways in which they were interpreted. Naturalism, exoticism, abstraction and conventionality coexisted to meet the differing tastes of women and the urge to get away from the austerity and uniformity of the war years.

The general tendency was towards lightness and movement; the solid and massive metallic surfaces of the 1940s were substituted for twisted wires, lattice patterns, fretted lace motifs and woven gold mesh (see plates 655, 657, 667, 675, 677, 712 and 731). Closely claw-set gemstones were often preferred to the large geometric surfaces pavé-set with gems of the previous decades.

Another characteristic of the 1950s was a return to a differentiation between jewels for day wear and ornaments for evening wear; the former in the shape of gold necklaces and bracelets of simple design, occasionally and discreetly set with precious or semiprecious stones, the latter in the form of rich and opulent parures of diamonds and coloured precious stones.

Day jewellery was a triumph of gold in the form of tubular chains, corded wire, fringes, pleated motifs, and woven patterns (see plates 654-657, 707 and 718); evening jewellery preferred platinum, white gold and palladium for the setting of cascades and festoons of brilliant-cut, pear-shaped, marquise and baguette diamonds (see plates 671, 678, 679, 729 and 730).

Diamonds were, without question, the gemstone *par excellence*, but emeralds, rubies and sapphires added colour and vitality to many evening creations. Unusual combinations of gemstones such as rubies and turquoises, diamonds and multicoloured citrines, topazes and emeralds were utilised. Coral and turquoise were the favourite semiprecious stones. Cultured pearls regained the popularity they had lost in the previous decade, and double or triple graduated rows became the indispensable ornament of fashionable women. Natural pearls came back into fashion, and their value, which had dropped dramatically in the 1920s at the time of the invention of cultured pearls, started to rise again. In combination with diamonds, they were frequently chosen to decorate necklaces, rings and earrings.

Among the favoured decorative motifs of the 1950s, were flowers and leaves, either naturalistically reproduced, or schematically sketched in outline (see plates 655 and 656). Flowerheads, bouquets, sprays and all sorts of leaves and ferns, characterised many brooches, clasps and earrings (see plates 657, 718 and 719).

The exoticism of tropical flora particularly fascinated jewellery designers. The animal kingdom, both domestic and wild, was another acceptable subject for jewellery, especially for brooches; dogs, cats, horses and snakes all appeared in jewel designs of the time. Birds in particular became the subject of endless interpretations, either simply made of gold or expensively set with precious stones. Humming-birds and birds of paradise, owls and parrots, cockerels and chickens were depicted perched on flowering branches or in flight. Panthers, tigers and lions offered their sensuous forms to clips, brooches and bracelets; even the inhabitants of the underwater world: fish, starfish, shells and seahorses, found favour (see plates 713-717).

Volutes, helixes, spirals and turban motifs characterised creations of more abstract inspiration (see plates 654 and 659). The ribbons and bows of the 1940s continued in the form of lighter and often informally sketched motifs, often combined with leaves and sprays of flowers, simply outlined in gold wire, or fretted in lace-like patterns, embellished with diamond decorative motifs (see plate 707).

The jewels of the 1950s certainly lack the strength of design typical of the jewels of the previous decades, and did not offer radical innovations either in form or the chromatic use of stones, but are always recognisable: gold wires, plain or twisted, and cascades of diamonds, with movement and lightness are their most typical characteristics.

Tiaras and Hair Ornaments

During the 1940s jewelled hair ornaments were not in vogue. The austerity of the war and the different economical situation of the years which followed, were certainly not conducive to the creation of such superfluous forms of ornament, but brooches and clips were occasionally used to adorn a particularly elaborate hairstyle.

Tiaras made a come-back in the 1950s: débuts, court occasions, balls, and the rich and sumptuous evening dresses of the time, once more required the wearing of precious tiaras, but the time for purpose-made hair ornaments was definitely over, and most tiaras of the 1950s simply consisted of necklaces suitably supported by rigid metallic structures. A particular style or design for tiaras therefore did not exist, but all types of draped, swagged, floral or foliate necklaces, turned upside down, became suitable hair ornaments.

Clips and brooches were often used to enhance the elegance of the elaborate piled up hairstyles.

Parures

After decades of obscurity, parures comprising bracelet, brooch, necklace and earrings, came back into fashion in the 1940s. Among the most typical parures are those comprising a necklace and a bracelet of tubular gold linking, decorated with gem-set flowerhead clasps, a matching flowerhead brooch and a pair of earclips. Made popular by Van Cleef and Arpels and Cartier, they were widely copied and imitated (see plate 661).

The fashion for matching sets of jewellery promoted the creations of many demi-parures, comprising brooch and bracelet or brooch and earrings in the

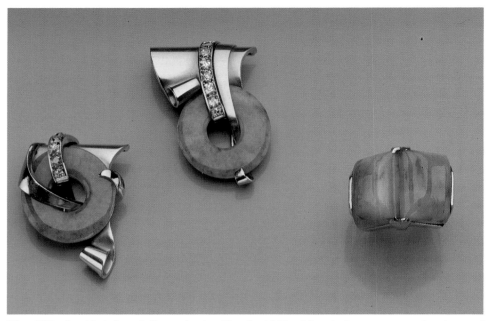

Plate 652. A gold, jade and diamond suite, French, 1940s. Note the large expanses of undecorated metal, and the sculptural scrolls.

typical designs of the time: bows, knots, scrolls and volutes (see plates 652 and 653). This trend continued through the 1950s, when the new wealth, the abundance of gemstones, and the glamour of evening wear promoted the creation of complete sets of jewellery of twisted gold wire and gemstones, or entirely set with diamonds and designed as light and airy foliate, floral, spiral, scroll and ribbon motifs (see plates 655-660).

Plate 653. An aquamarine and ruby suite of brooch and earclips, by Tiffany & Co., c.1945-50. Naturalism has returned to jewellery after the war years. It would have been extremely uncommon before 1940 for coloured stones to be set without diamonds.

Plate 655. *A pair of leaf-shaped earclips and a matching ring, c.1950, in ruby and diamonds.*

Plate 654. *A gold and ruby demi-parure, c.1950. An English interpretation of a Van Cleef Paris design. Note the lack of diamonds.*

Plate 657. *A suite in gold and diamonds, c.1950-5. Note the yellow gold corded wire which Cartier and Van Cleef and Arpels had pioneered in the mid-1940s in combination with diamonds; before this date diamonds were invariably set in white metal.*

Plate 656. *A suite of gold, enamel and diamond, by Jean Fouquet, c.1955. Jean Fouquet (born in Paris, 1899) was a member of the famous family of Parisian jewellers which had been founded by his grandfather Alphonse (1828-1911). The family, which included Jean's father Georges, excelled in nearly every style from the Renaissance revival of the 1870s through art nouveau and art deco, to modernism and the naturalistic revival of the 1950s.*

Plate 658. A gold, jade, ruby, sapphire and diamond suite, by Rudolph Charles von Ripper, c.1955. Von Ripper (1905-1960) born in Klausenberg, Transylvania, and imprisoned in 1933 for his anti-Nazi caricatures, subsequently distinguished himself during the war when he joined the American Army having become a United States citizen in 1943. A colourful man, he enjoyed a varied life after the war, receiving a Guggenheim fellowship for 1946-7, and managed to fit in such pursuits as the Foreign Legion and Circus Harlequin, and was an inmate of the Oranienburg and keeper of the Dali jewels.

Plate 659. A sapphire, turquoise and diamond suite, 1950s. Typical of the post-war years are unusual chromatic combinations of stones. Turquoise was particularly popular.

Plate 660. A gold, diamond and gem-set suite, French, c.1955.

343

Plate 661. A gold, ruby, sapphire and diamond suite, by Cartier, London, 1945. Note the 'gas pipe' linking and the colourful choice of stones.

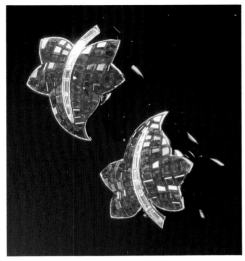

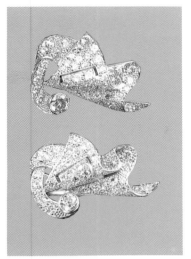

Plate 662. A pair of ruby and diamond invisibly-set earclips, by Van Cleef and Arpels, New York, c.1940, from the collection of the Duchess of Windsor.

Plate 663. A pair of diamond clips, adapted as earrings, c.1945. The black and white illustration shows the added fittings.

Plate 664. A pair of gold, ruby and diamond earclips, c.1940, also wearable as dress clips.

Plate 665. A pair of gold, ruby and diamond scroll earclips, c.1945. Note the two-coloured gold.

Earrings

Earrings were worn throughout the 1940s, mainly in the shape of earclips, designed as large gold fan-shaped motifs, knots, ribbon bows, flowerheads, scrolls, shells and volutes; these were made of multicoloured gold, embellished with rubies, diamonds, or other coloured gemstones, often repeating the design of clips and brooches (see plates 664 and 665). More important examples were similarly designed and entirely pavé-set with diamonds or invisibly set with rubies or sapphires (see plates 662 and 663). Although pendant earrings were not very fashionable in the 1940s, scroll or fan-shaped earclips were occasionally embellished with a gem-set drop (see plate 666).

Larger step-cut stones, mainly citrines and amethysts, were also mounted as earrings, flanked or surmounted by a gold scroll or shell motif.

The fashion of the 1950s, which left complete liberty to wear the hair long,

Plate 666. A pair of gold, onyx, ruby and diamond earclips, c.1945.

Plate 667. A pair of gold and diamond earclips by David Webb, 1950s.

Plate 668. A pair of diamond pendant earrings, 1950s. Often the tassels are detachable.

Plate 669. A pair of diamond flowerhead earclips, c.1950.

piled up at the top of the head, or medium length, swept behind the ears, favoured both long pendant earrings and compact earclips.

Gold was the preferred material for day earrings, which were usually short, in the design of leaves, scrolls, turbans, spirals, clusters, helixes and flowerheads, often set with small diamonds, and occasionally decorated with drops and tassels (see plates 654, 659, 660 and 667). Gold Creole earrings were popular for day wear, but the type of earring which best exemplifies the 1950s is that designed as a boule of gold wire, studded with gemstones, often rubies and turquoises, or rubies and sapphires or diamonds.

Earrings for evening wear tended to be rich and sumptuous in design, and lavishly set with precious gemstones. The designs were the same as those for day wear, except that gold was substituted by diamonds. Gem-set scrolls,

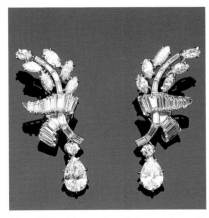

Plate 671. Two pairs of diamond earrings, both late 1950s, although these designs were popular for another ten or fifteen years.

Plate 670. A pair of diamond pendant earrings with detachable drops, by Van Cleef and Arpels, modern, although this design with its yellow gold mount originated in the late 1950s.

curled leaves, flowerheads, rosettes, turbans and cornucopias, often of considerable size, became the surmounts of long, articulated cascades or tassels of baguette diamonds, terminated with marquise or pear-shaped drops, occasionally stretching almost to the shoulders and free to move, glitter and reflect the light (see plates 668-671).

Pearls were either simply set within diamond petalled borders, or in the shape of large drops, suspended from scrolled or foliate diamond surmounts.

Necklaces

Necklaces were usually short in the 1940s, and encircled the base of the neck with chunky gold chains of fancy linking or twisted wire (see plate 676), massive diamond scrolls, or elaborate arrangements of coloured stones (see plates 672 and 673).

Among the most typical necklaces were those designed as chains of Brazilian or flexible tubular linking, knotted at the front or at the side with a gem-set ribbon bow, or decorated with gem-set flowerhead clusters, sprays of leaves and flowers or fan-shaped motifs, often detachable and wearable separately as clips or brooches (see plate 661).

Towards the end of the 1940s, necklaces in the shape of precious 'bibs' of articulated gold plaques of geometrical design, alternating with coloured stones, were used to adorn the generous décolletages of the glamorous 'new look' evening dresses (see plates 674 and 675).

In the 1950s, necklaces were worn both for day and evening wear. Generally short, sometimes in the shape of chokers tightly fastened at the base of the neck, they were the ideal complement to the generous heart-shaped décolletages of evening gowns, and to the simple necklines of day and afternoon dresses.

Gold necklaces in the shape of swags and garlands of plain or corded wire, were designed as flat mesh ribbons, made of bands of plaited wire or twisted in the form of slim 'torsades', and set with small diamonds or coloured stones.

Plate 672. A substantial diamond necklace, c.1940.

Another typical design consisted of a row of slim lanceolated leaves or dart-shaped motifs, graduated in size from the centre.

Particular attention was given to the front of the necklace, which often grew in size assuming the shape of a bib, as in the previous decade. Bib necklaces were made in the form of rounded or pointed ornaments of articulated gold linking or elaborate corded wire networks, encrusted with gems.

Shells, spirals, turbans and bows, realised in gold wire or fretted in gold sheet, and set with small gemstones, often decorated the side or the front of gold chains of tubular linking in the 1940s tradition, and were detachable and wearable as clips or brooches (see plate 677).

Important gem-set necklaces for evening wear, assumed the form of diamond draped motifs, tied at the centre or at the side in informal knots, or were decorated with articulated tassels or cascades of gemstones (see plates 678 and 679).

Clips of shell, turban, leaf, stylised flowerhead or helix design, often decorated

Plate 673. A sapphire and diamond necklace, by Cartier, c.1940, from the collection of the Duchess of Windsor. This is an unusual and dramatic use of sapphire beads.

Plate 674. A gold and gem-set 'bib' necklace, by Cartier, Paris, October 1945. The use of large expanses of yellow gold so randomly set with gemstones would have been unimaginable before the war. When this necklace was first worn by the Duchess of Windsor, it caused a sensation. It is interesting to note that the Windsors were obliged to supply the stones themselves, in this case breaking up two gem-set brooches, two pairs of earrings and an emerald ring (see Susie Menkes, The Royal Jewels, London 1986).

Plate 675. A gold, turquoise and amethyst bib necklace, by Cartier, Paris, 1947. This would have been a totally innovative combination of stones, especially when mounted in a lattice of corded yellow gold wire, and it was to influence taste in jewellery for several years.

Plate 676. A gold and diamond necklace, c.1945. Note the buckle-shaped lateral motifs similar in design to contemporary clips. A gold, ruby and sapphire clip, by Van Cleef and Arpels, c.1947. The lace-like gold motif around the flowerhead cluster is typical of the time.

Plate 677. A gold and diamond necklace and clip, c.1950.

the front of simple baguette or circular-cut diamond bands.

Torsades of gemstones of contrasting colours, entwined ribbons of diamonds, rubies, sapphires and emeralds, and lace-like bands of precious stones were often suspended with elaborate central drops of eighteenth century inspiration, or decorated at the side with tassels, sprays, clusters of berries, cornucopias, and informal cascades of diamonds and coloured stones.

Pearls, both cultured and natural, came back into fashion, in the shape of several graduated rows on gem-set clasps, or draped at the front between two symmetrical diamond motifs, often detachable and wearable as clips.

Long strings of pearls were worn twisted several times around the neck, and torsades of small pearls and gold chains or coloured semiprecious beads, especially coral, were also in fashion.

Plate 678. A diamond necklace, 1950s.

Plate 679. A diamond fringed necklace, 1950s.

Clips and Brooches

Clips and brooches in the 1940s were often inflated to enormous size to compensate for the scarcity of precious gemstones, and took the form of large gold scrolls, buckles, fans and rosettes (see plates 680, 681, 688 and 698).

The ribbon bow was perhaps the favourite motif, of formal or informal design, large or small, made of yellow or red gold, often fretted in lace, or tulle-like patterns, and usually decorated at the centre with a gem-set cluster or knot. Its typical plastic three-dimensionality distinguishes it at first sight from all nineteenth century, early twentieth century and art deco bows (see plates 685, 696, 701 and 702). The most expensive examples were entirely pavé-set with precious gemstones.

Similar in conception to the bow brooches were ornaments designed as drapes of pleated material tied with gem-set ribbons or twisted in a spiral (see plate 695).

Already in favour in the early 1940s, flowerheads, sprays of leaves and ears of wheat made of multicoloured gold sheet and set with diamonds and calibré-cut rubies and sapphires, became particularly popular after the war (see plates 676, 682-684, 687, 689, 697, 699, 708 and 709).

The movement towards naturalism in jewellery design of the late 1940s is well exemplified by the animal brooches, which took the exotic shapes of birds

 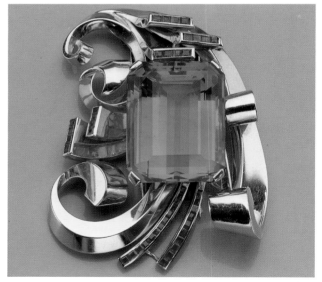

Plate 680. A massive citrine, sapphire, ruby and diamond clip, c.1940-5. Citrines became very popular during the war, largely perhaps because of the restricted supply of precious gemstones.

Plate 681. A gold, ruby and citrine brooch, c.1940-5. Note the liberal use of polished yellow gold in sculptural scrolls and the absence of diamonds.

Plate 682. A gold, ruby and diamond suite, 1945-50. The red gold is very characteristic of the 1940s.

Plate 683. A gold and ruby flower brooch, 1940s.

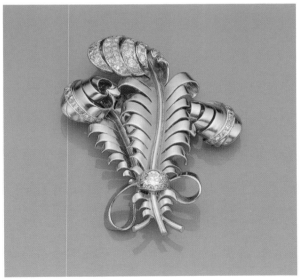

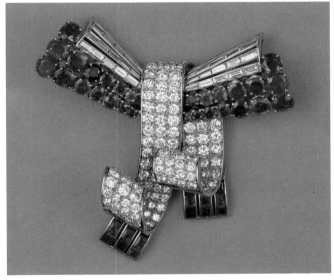

Plate 684. A gold and diamond brooch, probably by Mellerio, 1940-5.

Plate 685. A ruby and diamond bow brooch of bold sculptural design, c.1940, by Drayson of New Bond Street, London.

of paradise as well as the more friendly and domestic cats, dogs and songbirds. Snakes, panthers, tigers, lions, parrots and the like populated the rich and opulent fauna of late 1940s brooches, characterised by plastic, vigorous lines, and a sense of movement (see plates 686, 704 and 710).

Flower brooches assumed the exotic shapes of orchids as well as the more familiar forms of daisies, roses, anemones and the like, often arranged in informal bouquets made of variously coloured gold tied with gem-set ribbons. A favourite gemstone combination for floral brooches consisted of blue and

Plate 686. The celebrated flamingo brooch, by Cartier, Paris, 1940. Purchased by the Duke of Windsor just before the German occupation, it was created by Jeanne Toussaint. The subject and the sheer size of the brooch make it exceptional for the day. This brooch is now available in paste from as little as £10 and may be bought from New York to Hong Kong.

yellow sapphire petals embellished with rubies and diamonds.

Van Cleef and Arpels excelled in the production of flowerhead brooches, invisibly set with calibré-cut rubies and sapphires (see plate 687). The same tendency towards naturalism inspired, in the late 1940s, the production of many figurative brooches. The first Van Cleef and Arpels 'ballerina' brooch was produced in 1945; the design remained in vogue for some two decades and was widely imitated. Many flower girl, clown and golfer brooches followed (see plates 691-694 and 706).

Clips continued to be worn in the early 1950s but the fashion was gradually

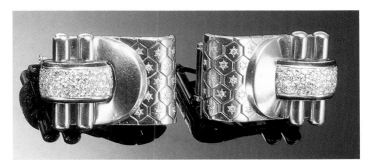

Plate 688. A pair of gold and diamond clips, by Van Cleef and Arpels, c.1937. Although it originated before the war, this honeycomb design (Ludo-hexagone) became immensely popular in the '40s and was widely imitated.

Plate 687. A sapphire and diamond chrysanthemum brooch by Van Cleef and Arpels, Paris, c.1940. Note the invisibly-set leaves.

moving towards a preference for brooches which, in the second part of the decade, became the ideal ornament to pin at the side of the décolletages.

The strengthening of interest in naturalism influenced the design of brooches, which assumed the shape of animals, flowers and especially leaves, which in all their forms, lanceolated, heart-shaped, rounded or elongated, became the leitmotif of 1950s brooches. For day wear they were simply outlined in gold wire and occasionally embellished with gemstones; for evening wear, they were more elaborately designed and set with an abundance of diamonds and coloured precious gemstones, often decorated with cascades or rainfalls of baguette and pear-shaped stones (see plates 655-657).

Flowers, too, which were schematically sketched in corded wire and embellished with diamonds, or more naturalistically designed and lavishly set with precious stones, often assumed the exotic and elaborate shapes of orchids and fuchsias, or the simple forms of five-petalled wild roses (see plates 657 and 719).

Ribbon, bow and rosette brooches of 1940s tradition, continued to be made of fretted gold or gold wire, and often associated with sprays of leaves and flowers (see plate 707). Fan-shaped and draped ribbon motifs often combined with leaves, ferns and stylised feathers were also common in designs of many 1950s brooches (see plate 718).

The association of naturalism and abstraction produced many brooches, typical of the 1950s, designed as spiky and jagged entwined leaves decorated with diamonds and coloured stones. A combination of the two tendencies is also noticeable in brooches where flowerheads and leaves are schematically sketched rather than botanically designed.

Plate 689. *A gold, sapphire and diamond brooch, c.1945. This design is a product of the renewed interest in naturalism after the war.*

Plate 690. *A ruby, moonstone and diamond brooch, c.1945. Another example of the complete freedom of choice in gemstones.*

Plate 691. *A gold, diamond, ruby and sapphire dancer brooch, by John Rubel Co., New York, c.1945. John Rubel Co. was the manufacturing jeweller for Van Cleef and Arpels in Paris and New York. The association was dissolved in 1943 and John Rubel Co. relocated to 777 Fifth Avenue, New York, with branches in Paris and London. The first 'ballerina' brooch was produced by Van Cleef and Arpels in 1945; the design remained popular with the firm for about two decades and was widely imitated.*

Plate 692. *A palladium, sapphire and diamond ballerina brooch, c.1945.*

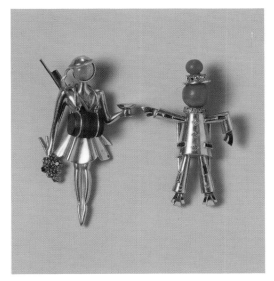

Plate 693. A gold, sapphire and ruby flower girl brooch, by Lacloche, Paris, c.1940-5.

Plate 694. A gold and gem-set clip, by Lacloche, c.1945, designed as a girl in battledress with a bouquet of flowers, a glass of champagne and a gun on her shoulders.
A gold, coral and gem-set clip designed as a clown.

Plate 695. A pair of gold and diamond clips, c.1945-50.

Animals were subjects for amusing and informal and easy to wear gold, enamel and semiprecious stone brooches, designed as winking cats, little dogs, caged birds and the like, were very fashionable. Parrots, tigers, lions and birds of paradise offered their nobler forms to more expensive and important creations lavishly set with multicoloured precious stones (see plates 711-717).

The famous jewellery houses, such as Cartier, Van Cleef and Arpels, Fouquet, Boucheron, and Mauboussin and also the lesser known jewellers, adopted the contemporary naturalistic inspiration, and produced attractive brooches of floral and animal design.

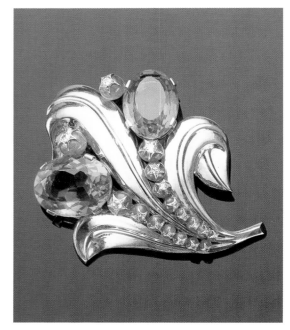

Plate 696. A diamond bow brooch, probably by Leitao of Lisbon, Portuguese, 1945-50.

Plate 697. A citrine, emerald bead and diamond brooch, c.1945. This brooch has the feeling of having been made from whatever gemstones were available or those that the client could supply.

Plate 698. A gold, ruby and diamond brooch, by Tiffany & Co., New York, c.1940-5.

Plate 699. A two-coloured gold, ruby and diamond clip, c.1945.

Plate 700. A two-coloured gold, ruby and diamond brooch, c.1945. Another example of the popular combination of ruby and a large expanse of gold.

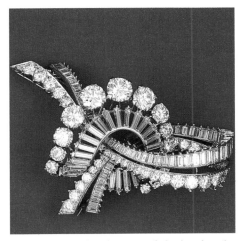

Plate 701. *A diamond clip, c.1945. The sculptural three-dimensional aspect of the jewel makes it 1940s rather than 1930s.*

Plate 702. *A diamond clip of looped ribbon design, c.1945-50.*

Plate 703. *A gold and diamond snowflake brooch, late 1940s. Van Cleef and Arpels first produced brooches to this design in 1947.*

Plate 704. *A sapphire and diamond clip, by Cartier, Paris, 1949, from the collection of the Duchess of Windsor. This was one of the first three-dimensional 'great cat' jewels by Cartier and the result of the collaboration between Jeanne Toussaint and Peter Lemarchand. The Sri Lankan cabochon sapphire weighs 152 carats.*

Plate 705. *A coloured diamond and onyx leopard clip, by Cartier, London, 1965. Although the first three-dimensional articulated 'great cat' jewels were first made in the early 1950s, the style has proved so successful that they are still being produced by Cartier today.*

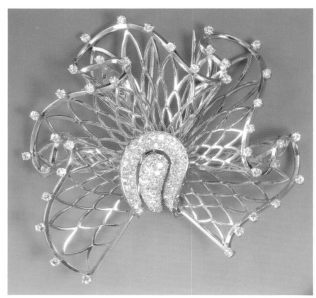

Plate 706. A gold and gem-set brooch, 1940s.

Plate 707. A gold and diamond clip, French, c.1950.

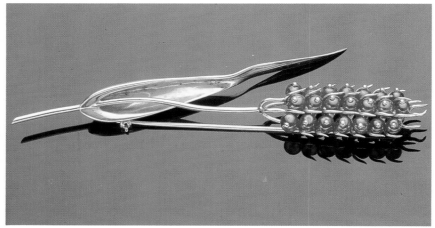

Plate 708. A gold, sapphire and diamond flowerhead brooch, 1940s. Note the substantial yellow gold scrolls/petals. By the 1950s the design would have been less ponderous. Compare with plate 707.

Plate 709. A gold and ruby brooch, by Boucheron, London, c.1945-50.

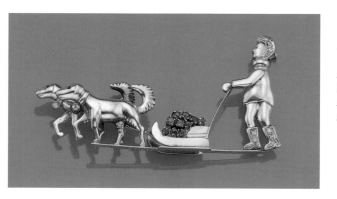

Plate 710. A gold and gem-set brooch, by Lacloche, c.1945-50, designed as an Eskimo with a sledge drawn by huskies.

Plate 711. Three gold, enamel and gem-set brooches, Italian, by Enrico Serafini, 1950s. Enrico Serafini (1913-1968) opened his own workshop in Florence in Piazza Santa Felicita 4, on 15th September, 1947. His jewels of the 1950s are characterised by a strong naturalistic style.

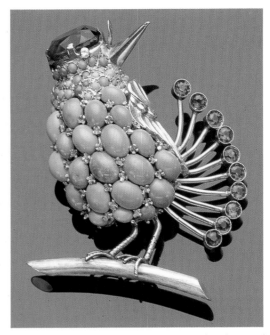

Plate 712. A gold, amethyst and turquoise scarecrow brooch, c.1950. Typical of the frivolous and amusing creations of the early 1950s.

Plate 713. A gold, amethyst and turquoise bird brooch, c.1950.

Plate 714. A pair of gold and gem-set novelty brooches, both mid-1950s. Van Cleef and Arpels first introduced winking cat brooches of similar design in 1954. Many of these animal caricatures seem to have been influenced by the popularity of Walt Disney cartoons.

Plate 715. A gem-set bird clip, French, c.1950-5.

Plate 716. A gold, enamel and diamond brooch designed as an elephant's head, Italian, by Enrico Serafini, 1950s.

366

Plate 717. A gold, enamel and diamond panther brooch, Italian, by Enrico Serafini, c.1960.

Plate 718. A gold and gem-set feather brooch, by Boucheron, 1950s.

Plate 719. A ruby and diamond spray brooch, by Van Cleef and Arpels, New York, 1950s.

Bracelets

Bracelets were among the most popular jewels of the 1940s; mostly made of variously coloured gold, they consisted of articulated bands of more or less elaborate linking, always bulky and voluminous in appearance. Clasps were large and three-dimensional, designed as bombé medallions, stylised buckles or bridge motifs, often set with diamonds, rubies and sapphires.

The Van Cleef and Arpels' 'honeycomb' bracelet, created in the previous decade, continued to be very fashionable and was widely copied and imitated by many other jewellers (see plates 720-723).

Gold 'tank' chains or 'bicycle' chains, as well as other motifs inspired by industry, were often set with semiprecious stones such as amethysts, citrines and peridots (see plates 724-726). Other currently popular bracelets consisted of wide gold bands of basket or chevron linking, and of tubular chains of flexible linking variously decorated and with gem-set clasps. Wide gold cuff-bracelets, set at random with various precious and semiprecious stones were in vogue (see plate 728).

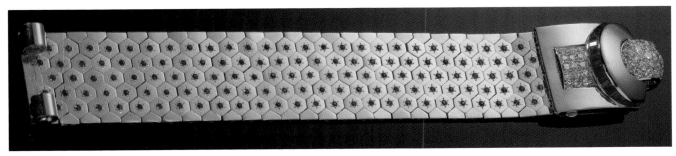

Plate 720. A gold, ruby and diamond 'Ludo-hexagone' bracelet, by Van Cleef and Arpels, c.1940. A design popular from the late 1930s to the 1950s.

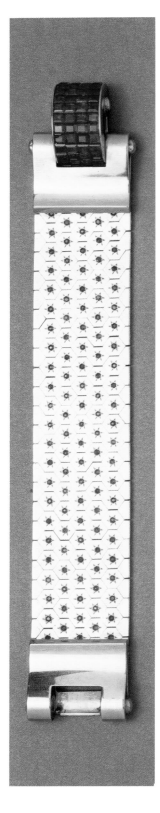

Plate 721. A gold and ruby bracelet, also of 'Ludo-hexagone' design, by Van Cleef and Arpels, c.1940.

Plate 722. A gold and diamond 'Ludo-hexagone' bracelet, by Van Cleef and Arpels, 1940s.

Plate 723. A gold, ruby and diamond bracelet, c.1945. A variation of the popular Van Cleef and Arpels prototype, see plates 720-722.

Plate 724. A two-coloured gold and amethyst bracelet, c.1940. Typical of wartime jewels is the use of 9 carat gold and semiprecious stones. This bracelet would almost certainly have been made in Germany, and bears English import marks.

Plate 725. A gold bracelet, by Cartier, c.1940. 'Tank tracks' and 'bicycle' chains were a popular source of inspiration for bracelet linking of the time.

Plate 726. A stylish gold bracelet, c.1940.

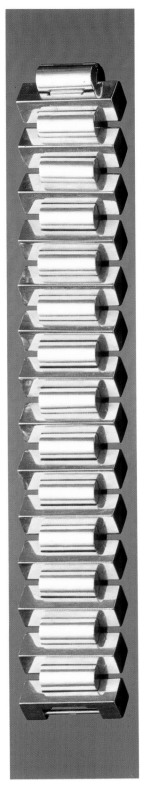

Towards the end of the 1940s, the most fashionable type of wrist ornament consisted of a wide band of woven gold enhanced with floral clasps. More formal bracelets for evening wear set with diamonds and precious coloured gemstones were often decorated at the centre with a bulky, three-dimensional scroll or buckle-shaped motif (see plate 727).

The jarettière bracelet of the Victorian era, was reintroduced in the late 1940s, and was to become the most typical bracelet of the 1950s. Designed as a wide band of gold mesh or flexible linking, it was decorated with a gem-set slide or clasp, the loose end embellished with a variety of fringes, tassels, or pendants.

Wide bands of gold were made of a variety of fancy linking: herringbone, plaited, lozenge-shaped, baton-shaped, etc., often decorated with a gem-set rosette clasp (see plate 731).

Also in demand were bands of gold mesh, twisted or gathered at the centre and decorated with a gem-set motif, or decorated with one or two confronted scrolls, shells or fan-shaped motifs. Other bracelets assumed the form of bands of flowerheads, leaves or rosettes, made of gold and set with diamonds or coloured gemstones.

Bangles were also fashionable in the 1950s; for day wear simple gold hoops supporting charms were worn in large numbers and wider bangles, made of several rows of corded wire, tended to be enlarged at the front in bombé-shaped motifs set with clusters of variously coloured gemstones. Other bangles in gold wire were decorated at the front with gem-set entwined leaves or

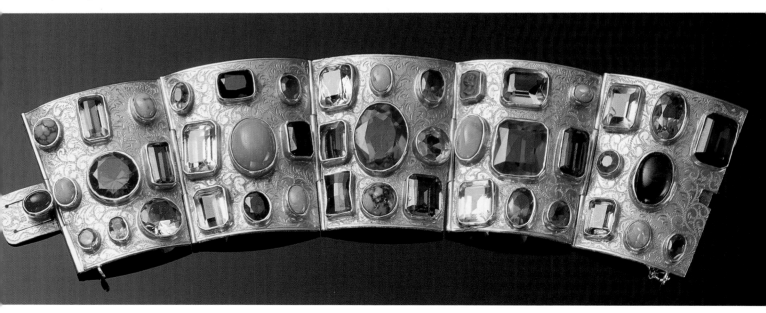

Plate 729. A diamond bracelet, 1950s.

Plate 730. A diamond bracelet, late 1950s.

Plate 731. A gold and gem-set bracelet, 1950s. The use of gold corded wire and the chromatic combination of gemstones is typical of the date.

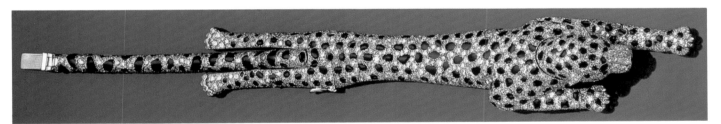

Plate 732. An onyx and diamond panther bracelet, by Cartier, Paris, 1952. Part of the celebrated collection of 'great cats' belonging to the late Duchess of Windsor.

elaborate turban motifs.

With the return to fashion of pearls, bracelets were designed as bands of four, five or more rows of pearls — natural or cultured — on a flowerhead clasp. Torsade bracelets consisting of several twisted rows of small pearls were also in demand. Strings of coral, turquoise or other semiprecious beads, were often used in the same way.

Bracelets for evening wear, which tended to repeat the floral and garland patterns of necklaces, and favoured diamonds, usually consisted of a large, three-dimensional central motif, of swag, scroll, flowerhead, fan, or turban design, often tapering at the sides, and attached to a slim bracelet, set with a simple course of baguette or circular-cut stones (see plates 729 and 730). The naturalism of the late 1940s and 1950s inspired many bracelets decorated with the forms of wild and exotic animals (see plate 732).

Wrist-watches

Jewelled wrist-watches were very stylish in the 1940s; their design repeated the shapes of contemporary bracelets as wide gold bands, set at the centre with small square or more often circular dials, sometimes concealed by a gem-set hinged cover (see plate 737); other designs were chains of Brazilian or tubular flexible linking, set with a small watch between gem-set shoulders of buckle-shaped design (see plates 735, 736 and 738-740). The favourite gemstones were rubies (often synthetic) and diamonds.

One of the most typical and characteristic wrist-watches of this period was the 'Cadenas' wrist-watch, which was created by Van Cleef and Arpels in the mid-1930s, and continued in production until the 1960s. It consisted of a double chain of Brazilian linking, in platinum or yellow gold, with a stirrup-shaped clasp, pavé-set with diamonds, in which the watch was discreetly inserted in a vertical position (see plates 733 and 734).

Jewelled wrist-watches continued in favour in the 1950s, and became an almost indispensable accessory for the woman of fashion who wore them on evening gloves, or on the bare wrist during the day. Their shapes followed closely those of contemporary bracelets and rings, and they often consisted of

Plate 733. A diamond bracelet watch by Van Cleef and Arpels, 1940s. This model known as 'Cadenas', first produced in the late 1930s, remained popular after the war.

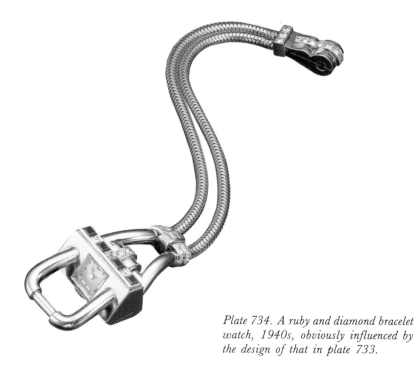

Plate 734. A ruby and diamond bracelet watch, 1940s, obviously influenced by the design of that in plate 733.

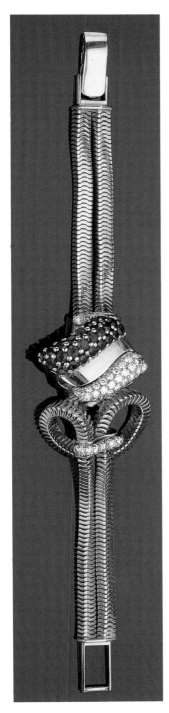

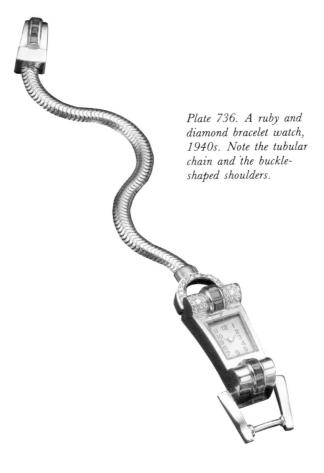

Plate 735. A gold, sapphire and diamond bracelet watch, c.1945.

Plate 736. A ruby and diamond bracelet watch, 1940s. Note the tubular chain and the buckle-shaped shoulders.

Plate 737. A gold and diamond bracelet watch, by Rolex, late 1940s. The jarretière design and the honeycomb linking make it typical of the date. The watch face is concealed under the diamond hinged cover.

a gold mesh or twisted wire bracelet, set at the centre with a small circular dial, sometimes concealed by a jewelled hinged cover in the shape of a dome, a turban, a scroll, a flowerhead, or a rosette (see plate 741).

When the dial was not concealed by a gem-set cover, the shoulders, in the form of fans, scrolls or foliate motifs, were often set with diamonds or other gemstones. More expensive examples, designed specifically for evening wear, consisted of thin line bracelets set at the centre with a small circular dial within a foliate or petalled border, and were entirely set with variously cut diamonds.

Plate 738. A ruby and diamond wrist-watch, 1940s. Note the 'gas pipe' linking so typical of the 1940s. Take care that coloured stones in these bracelet watches are not synthetic.

Plate 739. A gold and diamond bracelet watch, 1940s. Note the sculptural scroll hinged cover concealing the watch face.

Plate 740. A gold and diamond bracelet watch, late 1940s.

Plate 741. A gold and gem-set bracelet watch, early 1950s. Note the mesh bracelet suggesting a ribbon tied at the centre with a ruby and diamond knot.

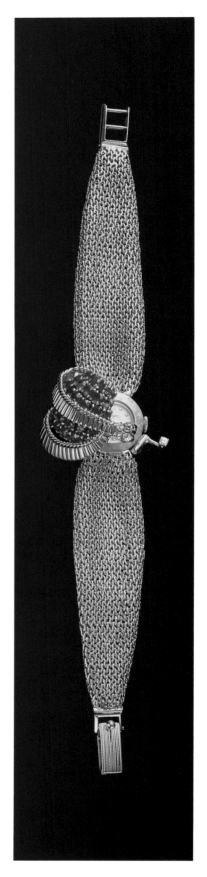

Plate 742. A ruby and diamond ring, by Chaumet, Paris, c.1940.

Plate 743. A gold and diamond dress ring, 1940s.

Plate 744. A citrine and diamond ring, c.1940-5. Note the size of the stone.

Rings

Rings, which tended to be heavy and massive in the 1940s, were usually decorated with geometric motifs such as prisms, cylinders, trapezes, or stylised scrolls, often asymmetrically combined. These rings have been associated with 'the cocktail hour', which had become a fashionable element in society entertaining. The preferred metal was gold, either red or yellow, though platinum was also used, and the favoured precious gemstones, diamonds and rubies, usually of small dimensions, were either star-set in curved metallic surfaces, or closely pavé or invisibly-set in geometrical motifs mounted between voluminous scroll, fan or ribbon-shaped shoulders (see plates 742, 743 and 745).

Large semiprecious stones were often mounted between bulky and three-dimensional fluted or scrolled shoulders, decorated with gems of contrasting colour (see plates 744 and 748).

The bezels of the most typical rings of the 1940s assumed the form of a book, or of a stylised bridge, a ribbon bow, a turban or a buckle. Other rings adopted the rounded and fluted form of a melon, occasionally set with a gemstone at the top, or were designed as a boule (ball), either entirely pavé-set with gemstones, or made of gold and set with variously coloured gems (see plates 746 and 747).

Towards the end of the decade ring designs became lighter, foreshadowing the fashion of the 1950s for delicate reticulation encaging the stones, which replaced the large metallic surfaces of the previous decade.

Rings in the 1950s were often worn several at a time. The fashion for massive rings continued well into the 1950s, with the design moving towards curved and rounded forms, away from the angular geometry of the previous decade.

Large bombé bezels, entirely set with precious stones, or made of elaborate networks of corded gold wire, embellished with precious and semiprecious stones, replaced cylinders and prisms, buckle and bridge-shaped motifs. Among the most popular designs were turbans, scrolls, helixes and volutes, made of corded or twisted gold wire embellished with gems, and set at the centre with a larger stone, often built high off the finger.

Cluster rings were very fashionable, either simply set with a pearl or a coloured stone within a border of diamonds, or more elaborately designed as stylised flowerheads, with the centre and the petals set with stones of various cuts and contrasting colours, often embellished with gold corded wire (see plate 749).

Plate 745. A diamond 'cocktail ring', c.1945.

Plate 746. A gold and ruby 'boule' or dome ring, c.1940.

Plate 747. A ruby, sapphire and diamond 'boule' ring, c.1940.

375

Plate 748. A yellow gold, blue and yellow sapphire and diamond ring, c.1945-50.

Plate 749. A gem-set cluster ring, 1950s.

The crossover ring was no less fashionable during the 1950s, particularly in the shape of elaborate scrolled leaf motifs or volutes in gold and gemstones. Another typical ring of the 1950s consisted of a truncated conical bezel, made of gold wire or fretted in gold sheet, set at the top with a large stone, often cut en cabochon.

The vogue for large rings encouraged the claw-setting of large coloured precious stones between diamond scrolled shoulders; if a coloured precious stone of sufficient size was too expensive, large corals, turquoises and amethysts offered suitable and attractive alternatives.

Plate 750. A gold and gem-set compact, by Van Cleef and Arpels, New York, c.1945, applied with a rose diamond and sapphire ballerina.

Plate 752. An unusual gold, enamel and diamond compact, by Enrico Serafini.

Plate 751. A compact, by Boucheron, Paris, c.1940-5. This was a popular design, often executed in white metal alloy due to the scarcity of precious metal.

CHAPTER NINE
1960~1980

The well-being, comfort and economic stability which everyone had sought in the post-war years, and which was largely re-discovered in the 1950s, was called into question in the 1960s when protest, controversy and dispute developed at all levels of society. Restlessness, agitation and rejection of the establishment by the younger generation characterised the decade socially, and was reflected in the visual arts, fashion and jewellery design.

After the mid-1950s, the transformation of Abstract Expressionism (Action Painting) into the Colour Field Painting of Mark Rothko, Helen Frankenthaler and Morris Louis, in which the canvas is stained with thin, translucent colour washes, brought colour into prime position. The optical illusions achieved in paintings by Vasarely and Richard Anuszkiewicz — the

'Princess Lee Radziwell'.
Photograph by Cecil Beaton,
1961. Sotheby's, London.

chief exponents of 'Op Art' — inspired fashion and jewellery designers as well: this is typified by Courrèges' and Cardin's innovative creations in the fashion field, and by jewels characterised by geometrical, splintered shapes set, seemingly at random, with coloured gemstones.

In jewellery this movement is epitomised by Andrew Grima of London who discovered endless ways of texturing metal, moulding it into bold and daring shapes and setting it with large surfaces of uncut crystals, or gemstones chosen for their chromatic interest more than for their economical value: bi-coloured tourmalines, opals, agates, opal boulders, baroque pearls, sapphires and moonstones cut en cabochon, lapis lazuli, citrines etc., all embellished with sprinkles of small diamonds (see plate 797).

The opulent but measured elegance of Dior's sophisticated 'New Look' was challenged by designers such as Cardin, Paco Rabanne and Courrèges, who had been inspired by Op Art, science fiction and space travel: A-line mini-shifts bisected by zig-zag patterns and brightly coloured. Mary Quant brought the mini-skirt to the high street, Vidal Sassoon cut hair in short, severe bobs. Young people from all over the world made pilgrimages to Carnaby Street to buy their up-to-date garments. By the late 1960s New York boutiques had followed suit and were stocking such items as hot pants and baby doll dresses. White boots, vinyl overcoats, white sun-glasses horizontally slit at the centre, psychedelic colours, black and white chequered patterns, all types of trousers, from hip-hugging leggings to elegant versions for the evening, were 'all the rage' in this decade, when the break with tradition brought into vogue all that was innovative, shocking and daring. Jewels went hand-in-hand with this trend and became amusing and unconventional (see plates 791 and 794).

Patronage and surplus wealth are vital to the jewellery industry and the 1960s provided an abundance of both. New money widened the clientèle and the increase of wealth allowed more substantial purchases. At the same time, however, the increase in crime spread a feeling of unease about displaying jewellery too openly. Two classes of jewels started therefore to emerge: jewels to keep in the bank, usually set with large, important stones in relatively simple mounts, and jewels for fun, to be worn at all times and enjoyed.

Altogether, the traditional distinction between important diamond jewellery for evening wear and less expensive gold ornaments for daywear disappeared in favour of a new dichotomy between unique, one-off creations, and less expensive, informal, but still stylish creations with strong design, for women who were starting to buy their own jewels as well as their clothes and accessories. Van Cleef and Arpels were the first among the famous jewellery houses to understand the new needs of the market and first opened their boutique in 1954. By the 1960s their boutique line was highly successful with designs as famous and popular as their amusing animal brooches and their parure 'Twist' of gold and semi-precious beads twisted into cord motifs (see plates 755, 784, 785).

Vivid use of colour, interplay of different textures, and the use of abstract designs are typical of 1960s creations. Cabochon stones of strong colours were very much in favour (see plates 792 & 826); their smooth, polished surfaces usually combined with textured mounts. The use of uncut gemstones, crystals in their original shapes and other natural objects, unworked by human hand, became widespread among jewellers throughout the world. Original effects were achieved by combining faceted and uncut stones in brooches and rings: aggregates of amethyst, dioptase and emerald crystals, or circular, shell-like chalcedony nodules encrusted with minute quartz crystal growths and highly reflective brilliant-cut diamonds (see plates 797, 804, 831).

Interest in unusual textures, relatively cheap materials and vibrant colour combinations prompted jewellers on both sides of the Atlantic to introduce natural shells in their creations. David Webb in New York, Darde et Fils in Paris, and Andrew Grima in London made use of exotic and colourful sea-shells, especially in earrings; this continued a technique first devised in the 1940s and carried out for decades by Verdura who enjoyed purchasing shells for a few dollars at the New York Natural History Museum and transforming them into beautiful jewels (see plates 765 & 766).

Nature, transformed by abstraction and stylisation into purely decorative forms, became a trademark of 1960s' jewels. In the intricate mounts, often enveloping cabochons of coral and turquoise, it is easy to recognise the shape of roots sprawling in the earth and it is not difficult to discern in the geometry of metal batons surrounding a gemstone the entwined combination of twigs in birds' nests.

Abstract forms and different textures somehow reminiscent of the moon's surface or the bed of the sea were achieved by means of new techniques such as melting gold under controlled temperatures. Plain, smooth, or sand-blasted surfaces of gold suddenly became boring: chiselled, reeded, hammered, corded, plaited and twisted effects were the vogue of the 1960s (see plates 764, 791, 796).

The inspiration seen in many jewel creations of less abstract design came from objects, plants and animals which had been associated with jewellery in the previous decades, but the trademark of their 1960s re-interpretation is usually a light-hearted, amusing, and witty feeling and a general stylisation of their forms. This is particularly true of David Webb's animal jewels such as his frog earrings brightly enamelled in lime green and his black and white enamel panther bangles, certainly inspired by Cartier's 'Great Cats' designed by Jeanne Toussaint, but re-interpreted in a light-hearted Disneyesque way (see plates 767, 812). Van Cleef and Arpels' amusing, witty and easy-to-wear animal jewels which had started life in the previous decade with a winking cat, the 'Chat Malicieux', were augmented in the 1960s with equally successful lions, owls, monkeys, giraffes etc. made of gold and studded with precious and semi-precious gemstones (see plates 784, 785). As the decade progressed, Van Cleef and Arpels created, as an answer to the increasing demand for whimsical ornaments, a line of jewels decorated with gold lion masks set with gemstones, reportedly originally inspired by the door-knockers of the Italian Consulate in New York (see plate 833).

Plate 753. A gold and diamond ring and a pair of earrings by Boucheron of stylised starburst design, 1960s.

In this vogue for animal jewellery, almost every jeweller followed suit and produced his own version. Jean Schlumberger, through his department at Tiffany's in New York, offered extraordinary three-dimensional brooches in the shape of spiky, twisted fish, made of yellow gold and set with unusual combinations of gemstones such as rubies and demantoid garnets.

Jewels of higher intrinsic value, created by the famous 'maisons', such as Cartier, Van Cleef and Arpels, Boucheron, Chaumet and Mauboussin, followed, understandably, more traditional paths. They were often designed or decorated with stylised flowerhead clusters supporting opulent cascades of gemstones, but their broken, jagged contours, achieved by alternating brilliant-cut and marquise-shaped diamonds, differentiated them quite clearly from the production of the previous decade (see plates 787, 789). Contorted lines and brutal, thorn-like outlines characterised the style of the mid- to late 1960s (see plates 756, 801, 802). Diamonds, the gemstones 'par excellence', continued to be as popular as ever, but rubies, emeralds and sapphires were used more abundantly than in the previous decade. Turquoise, with its distinctive colour and waxy lustre, made its re-entrance into expensive jewels, highlighted with diamonds.

No longer concerned with conformism, equilibrium or symmetry, jewellers favoured, for their expensive creations, cascades of large and voluminous gemstones, starbursts, explosions of jagged clusters and stylised, flaming star motifs (see plates 770, 805). Geometrical symmetry was abandoned in favour of a balanced asymmetry and movement. The outlines of jewels were broken and jagged, and to obtain this effect, pointed stones — marquises and pear-shaped — were favoured. In rings and brooches the central, most important stones — a diamond or a coloured gem — were often raised on prongs above the rest of the setting so as to project it outside the mount (see plate 827). Even the most traditional and expensive necklaces, designed as rivières of large size diamonds created by such jewellers as Harry Winston, favoured the jagged effect created by marquise or pear-shaped diamonds, at times supporting important coloured stone drops. Brooches very often assumed the shapes of stylised, asymmetrical garlands of leaves and flowers set with diamonds and coloured stones; perhaps the best examples are the brooches of the line 'Guirlande' designed by Van Cleef and Arpels (see plate 789). The traditional bi-chromatic combinations of diamonds with rubies, emeralds or sapphires remained in vogue, but jewellers did not hesitate to combine all the coloured precious gemstones together, in a fashion reminiscent of Indian traditional jewellery (see plates 778, 779).

By the mid-1960s jewellery was worn with abandon both during the day and night: a ring on each finger, two bracelets on each arm, earrings and necklaces. The full parure of matching jewels, however, was not revived and smaller sets of jewels, such as earrings and ring, brooch and earrings, necklace and bracelet were favoured. Creations of different jewellers were, by now, happily worn together as each lady attempted to create her own personal style.

The economic growth of the 1960s came to an end in the early 1970s, when the Arabs turned off the tap of cheap oil and, as a result, prosperity. The recession that followed sobered and tempered attitudes and spread a feeling of uncertainty and instability. The day of the lady covered in jewels as an obvious display of her status and wealth had passed. Jewels were seen, in the West, to arouse resentment and to inspire thieves. Happily for the jewellers, the economies in the Gulf thrived.

In the field of fashion, the early 1970s is characterised by a trend for a certain ethnic look: caftans, exotic prints, fringed shawls, full skirts, boleros, ruffled blouses, flared trousers, mini tops and crushed velvets. High fashion was struggling to survive. More and more couturiers began to sell their names on scarves, sun-glasses, scents, and began their prêt-à-porter or ready-to-wear departments. The whole conception of fashion was changing, allowing different styles, different lengths, different materials to be in vogue at the same time.

The same was true in the field of jewellery. The style of the 1970s does not submit to any aesthetic rule, and the whole decade shows very little unity. Whilst it is relatively easy to recognise a piece of 1960s jewellery thanks to its asymmetrical geometricism, it is almost impossible to generalise the trends of the following decade. Sometimes jewels tended to return to traditional shapes (see plate 780), others looked to exotic civilisation for sources of inspiration (see plate 798). If in the first years of the decade the spell of geometrical abstraction of the 1960s is still alive (see plate 800), by the mid-1970s the 'modernity' of geometrical jewellery is definitely considered *démodé*.

During the 1970s, the trend started by the most important jewellery houses of differentiating between, on one hand, unique creations set with exceptional gemstones, mostly made on commission, and, on the other hand, more readily available products at affordable prices for a wider but still discriminating and demanding clientele, was consolidated. More women than ever were now buying their own jewels and the most popular jewellery tended to be in the medium price range. The phenomenon was equally evident on both sides of the Atlantic and jewellery houses from Tiffany to Van Cleef and Arpels began seasonal collections that were aware of current style, colour and shapes in fashion.

Perhaps the most typical characteristic of jewels of the 1970s is the re-introduction in their manufacture of non-precious material, such as rock crystal, coral and exotic woods (see plates 776, 777, 782, 783, 799), the almost exclusive use of yellow gold, together with a trend for variously and vividly coloured ornaments, a development of the chromatic effects of the 1960s (see plates 798, 814, 820).

Among the famous names in the jewellery world to experiment with these materials was David Webb, who created a collection of jewels formed of carved rock crystal links or elements mounted in gold and embellished with diamonds, achieving a striking effect through the juxtaposition of colourless, often frosted crystal and highly refractive brilliant-cut diamonds. Van Cleef and Arpels too, in Paris, made great use of rock crystal in their celebrated suites comprising long chains with pendant drop, earrings and often a ring as well, made of oval or lozenge-shaped links mounted in gold and highlighted with diamonds. Coral is another material which came back into fashion and reached the peak of its popularity in the mid-1970s after having almost disappeared from jewellery since the 1920s. The innovation of the decade was the introduction of carved woods, extensively used by Boucheron and Van Cleef and Arpels for their suites of long chains and pendant earrings of carved links or flowered elements (see plate 799). Part of this vogue for strong colours was the use of materials such as malachite, rose quartz, cornelian and ivory. Common to all jewels made of these carved materials was the employment of polished, rounded, rich and opulent shapes, completely different from the dramatic spiky dynamism of 1960s design (see plates 758, 761, 775).

Many jewellery designs of the late 1960s and 1970s were definitely influenced by India. This is particularly true of the many necklaces and pendant earrings set with rubies, emeralds and diamonds in a colour scheme typical of Jaipur enamels, and in the wide use of cabochon stones in stylised flower arrangements that was so typical of Indian eighteenth and nineteenth century traditional jewellery. Amongst the first jewellers to embrace this trend was Van Cleef and Arpels whose creations, inspired by the parures worn by the Maharanis and then translated into Western taste, became the models for many other jewellers (see plates 772, 774, 779, 798). The sautoir, the long pendant earrings 'en pampille' and 'en girandole' abandoned in the late 1930s came back in the 1970s imbued with Indian influences. These were often accompanied by superb medallions worn as clips or suspended from long chains reminiscent, in their design and colours, of the stylised flowers and star motifs of Indian inspiration or of the opulent forms of Byzantine ornaments. It is not surprising that the Middle East and India inspired jewellery design, for many aspects of artistic, cultural and intellectual life looked at these areas of the world and were influenced by the Orient in the 1970s.

It is important to note that throughout this decade the metal favoured for the setting of all gemstones, including diamonds, was yellow gold and not platinum or white gold. Since the eighteenth century diamonds had been set, almost invariably, in white metal to enhance the whiteness of the stones, and only in the 1970s did jewellers switch to yellow gold. This probably had several explanations. Firstly, the influence of Indian jewellery, where diamonds were traditionally set in yellow gold; secondly, the desire to break from tradition; thirdly, the attempt to make diamonds — the gemstone 'par excellence' — a gem more wearable at any time of the day and to give a more casual look to the most glamorous and evening-orientated of all gems; and finally the importance and emergence of Middle Eastern buyers and taste. The sheikhs, who had made their extraordinary fortunes through oil, had become serious and devoted jewellery buyers, and their preference for yellow gold mounted jewellery strongly influenced the market in the 1970s.

Diamonds remained as popular as ever, mounted alone or used to highlight the colour of rubies, sapphires and emeralds or that of semi-precious stones. However, pear-shaped and marquise diamonds which had been favoured in the post-war years and had been used in the 1960s to achieve jagged and broken outlines in the most up-to-date creations, started to give way to baguettes and step-cut diamonds, either mounted alone in solitaire rings or in groups or courses in necklaces, bracelets and brooches — a trend that was to be consolidated in the 1980s.

Bulgari of Rome started to surge to international fame in the late 1970s. Having perceived quite clearly what the market was asking for, the firm produced casual and wearable jewels, which were at the same time sophisticated, and were suitable for both daytime and evening occasions. Bulgari popularised yellow gold in a new and original way, moulding it into clean, polished and bold lines, reinforcing the new vogue for baguette and step-cut diamonds and the fashion for large cabochon coloured gemstones. Bulgari also revived in the last years of the 1970s the late nineteenth century practice of setting ancient coins or engraved gems and mounted them in solid gold chains; these were to become their trademark for the 1980s (see plate 817).

Tiaras and Hair Ornaments

The advent of the 1960s marked the final disappearance of tiaras from the design books of the jewellers. With very few exceptions all tiaras worn after this date were the product of the previous decades or of the nineteenth century, and since the increasingly rare occasions that still required them tended to be formal — weddings or state related — the lack of contemporary, modern and up-to-date designs for this type of ornament did not really matter.

As the 1960s progressed, so the 1950s use of adorning evening hairstyles with gemset clips and brooches disappeared completely, together with the elaborate piled-up coiffures of that decade.

Parures, Demi-Parures and Suites

Matching sets of jewellery were very much in favour in the 1960s and 1970s, and complete parures comprising necklace, bracelet, brooches, ring and earrings were not unusual. Demi-parures comprising brooch and earrings were particularly in vogue in the 1960s, while the most typical set of jewellery of the following decade comprised a sautoir and earrings, or a ring and earrings. General rules anyway did not exist and all sorts of combinations of jewels, matching in design, can be found in this period. Their shapes, their designs and their materials are those described in the following sections dedicated to earrings, necklaces, brooches, bracelets and rings (see plates 753 to 762).

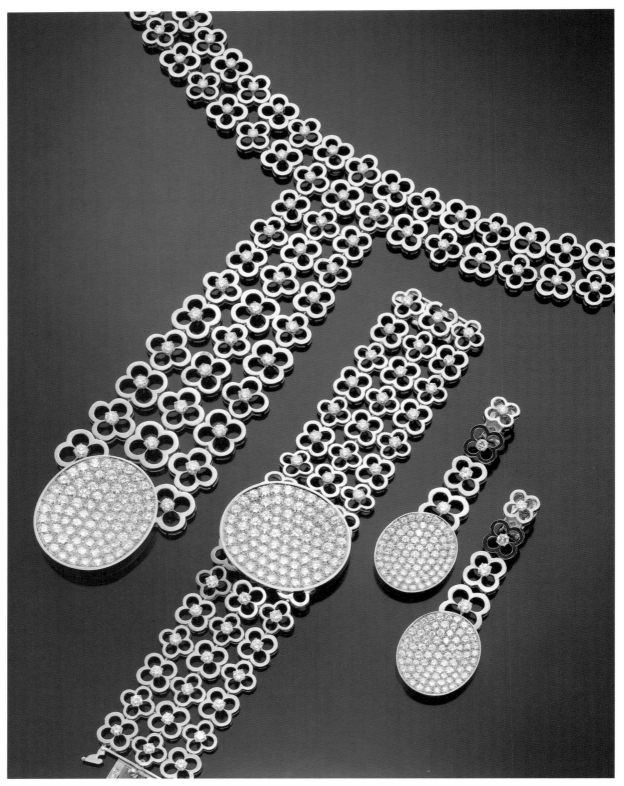

Plate 754. A gold and diamond parure by Mauboussin, late 1960s. It is difficult to imagine a set of jewels more typical of its period and more in tune with contemporary dress fashion. The necklace is in fact a choker with a long pendant. During the same years Mary Quant had popularised mini dresses, often in crochet or chain-mail fabric which enclosed the neck and left the shoulders bare.

Plate 755. A gold, cultured pearl and turquoise bead parure 'Twist' by Van Cleef and Arpels, c.1962. The parure 'Twist', designed as a torsade made of a string of pearls combined with a string of hardstone beads and a chain of gold beads was first designed by Van Cleef and Arpels in 1962 and remained popular throughout the decade.

Plate 756. A sapphire and diamond suite of jewellery comprising: necklace, brooch and pendant earrings, 1960s. Note the V-shaped front of the necklace, the asymmetrical design of the cluster brooch, the marquise- and pear-shaped sapphires and the beaded claws which make this set a typical example of the decade.

Plate 757. A yellow gold, sapphire and diamond ring and brooch, late 1960s. The use of textured gold and the informality of the design make this set a very representative example of the period. It was during the 1960s that marquise-shaped coloured precious stones began to appear.

Plate 758. A cabochon ruby, turquoise and diamond parure by Mauboussin, c.1970, entirely set in yellow gold. The large cabochon rubies have been used purely for their colour rather than their quality as gems. The detachable pendant will become one of the most typical features of the 1970s.

Plate 759. A suite of gold and diamond brooch and earclips by Kutchinsky, London, 1970s. Note the typical angular design and the texture of the gold.

Plate 760. A diamond brooch and a pair of earrings by Van Cleef and Arpels, c.1970. The design of the brooch in particular shows a continuing use of Indian motifs.

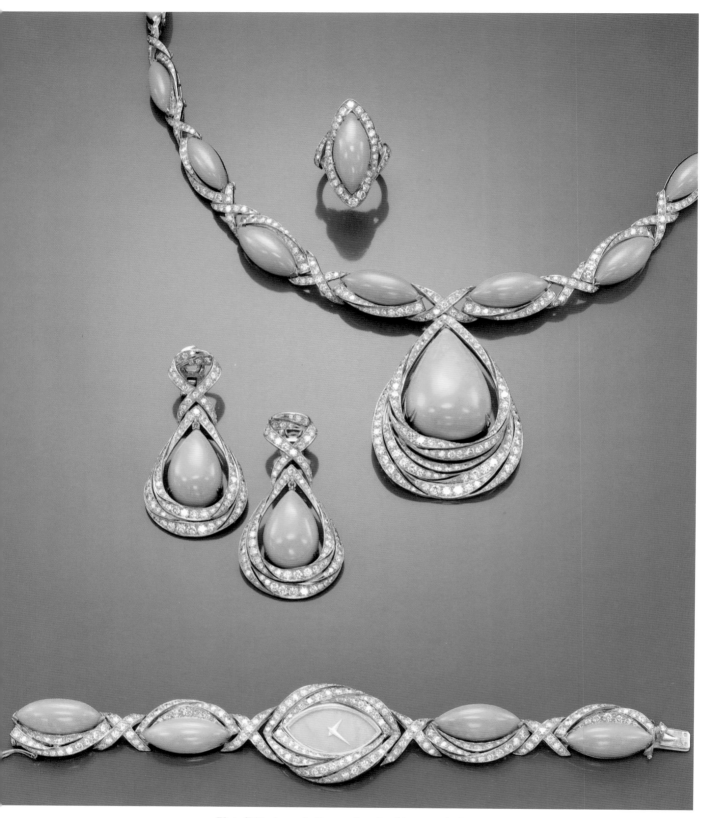

Plate 761. A coral, diamond and gold parure by Piaget, early 1970s. It is at about this time that famous watchmakers such as Piaget, Patek Philippe and Chopard started to produce sets of jewels with the watch brought in as part of the parure.

Plate 762. A set of gold, coral, chalcedony and diamond jewels, and a gold and chalcedony bead sautoir, all by Van Cleef and Arpels, c.1970. These very influential designs sparked off many imitations.

Plate 763. A ruby, emerald and diamond necklace and earrings, c.1993. 1970s designs have recently enjoyed a fashion renaissance. This parure, so reminiscent of Van Cleef and Arpels' style of the 1970s, was made in Bangkok circa 1990. The back of the mount reveals how quickly cast each of the elements has been. The gold at the back is rarely properly polished and finished and there is sharpness to the edges of the mounts which disappears over the years as the jewel is worn.

Earrings

Earrings were popular in the 1960s in a variety of shapes and lengths, provided they were of noticeable size and highly decorative. The final effect was not necessarily achieved by the setting of single, expensive stones, but by exploiting striking contrasts of textures, materials and colours (see plate 753). The severe short hair bobs made fashionable by Vidal Sassoon and the simple necklines of contemporary fashion left ample space for them.

The widely spread interest in unusual materials prompted jewellers such as David Webb and Verdura in New York, and Darde et Fils in Paris, to make use of exotic shells in the design of their ear ornaments (see plates 765, 766). All sorts of different sea shell shapes were adapted to both short and long pendant earrings. Andrew Grima in London encased long, tusk-shaped shells from the South Pacific in gold wire cages and suspended them from the earlobes. Other fashionable, colourful, whimsical and unpretentious earrings were inspired by plants, animals and unusual objects. Good examples of this trend are the green enamel frog earrings, studded with gold beads, created by David Webb and the gemset pineapple earclips designed by Verdura (see plate 767).

The abstraction and asymmetrical geometricism that dominated 1960s jewellery design prompted the creation of a plethora of examples of earclips in all kind of materials, easily recognisable by their jagged contours, textured metal surfaces, and strong colours (see plates 753, 764).

More traditional earrings were created with rounded, button or domed shapes realised in textured, plaited, woven or corded yellow gold set at

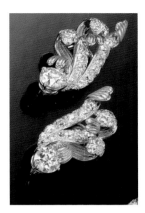

Plate 764. A pair of gold and diamond earclips designed by Schlumberger for Tiffany, c.1960. Schlumberger started to work for Tiffany in 1958 and dominated the 1960s look of the firm.

Plate 765. A pair of gold and shell earrings by Darde et Fils, Paris, c.1965. Shell earclips were made popular during the 1960s, notably by Darde et Fils, Verdura, Seaman Shepps and David Webb and by illustrious owners such as the Duchess of Windsor. They are still popular today and can be seen in such jewellers as Fred Leighton of New York.

random with small diamonds and coloured gemstones (see plate 771). Cabochon turquoises and corals, or large mabé or baroque pearls, were also popular mounted as earrings encaged in sprawling root motifs or set at the centre of asymmetrical compositions of small geometrical shapes cast in gold.

Earrings of high intrinsic value continued of course to be produced in these years, but they followed more restrained and traditional paths. Among the most popular forms were stylised flowerheads or asymmetrical clusters, at times supporting opulent cascades of variously cut gemstones. Their overall design, although reminiscent of the 1950s, can be easily distinguished from the flowing, continuous curved lines of the previous decade by their spiky, broken and jagged contours (see plates 768, 769, 770).

In the 1970s, earring design, as was the case in fashion, clothing and hairstyles, seems to break free from all constraints and becomes extremely varied with a clear preference for large and bold shapes.

Plate 766. Three pairs of gold and shell earclips by David .Webb, New York, 1964/65, from the collection of the Duchess of Windsor. Since the Duchess of Windsor jewellery sale in 1987, shell earrings have enjoyed renewed popularity. See plate 765.

Plate 767. A pair of gold, enamel and cabochon ruby earclips, by David Webb, New York, 1964, from the collection of the Duchess of Windsor.

Plate 768. A pair of diamond pendant earrings, c.1965, typical for their irregular and spiky cluster design.

Perhaps the most typical form of earring of this decade is that designed as a large circular or oval hoop suspended from a similarly shaped smaller surmount (see plate 777). The hoops were mainly carved in hardstones such as rock crystal, onyx, coral, lapis lazuli or materials such as ivory, tortoiseshell or exotic woods. Sometimes they were made of gold sparingly set with diamonds and brightly enamelled in contrasting colours. All major jewellery firms from Van Cleef and Arpels to Boucheron and Mauboussin in Paris, Kutchinsky in London, David Webb in New York, etc., produced their own version of this extremely successful and popular type of earring, which was very often accompanied by a long chain *en suite* supporting a pendant which repeated, in an enlarged form, the motif of the jewel (see plate 783).

The extremely flattering design of the hoop-in-hoop earring was also adapted to more expensive creations, lavishly set with expensive gemstones, the hoops either entirely mounted with diamonds, or with diamonds and rubies, emeralds or sapphires.

The inspiration for many other expensive pendant earrings was Indian: large cascades and girandoles of rubies, emeralds, sapphires and diamonds, often carved en cabochon, reminiscent of the shapes and the colouring of traditional Jaipur jewellery (see plate 774).

Short earrings tended to favour the half-hoop shape, simply attached to the

Plate 771. A pair of gold and chalcedony earclips by Van Cleef and Arpels, late 1960s.

Plate 769. A pair of of diamond earclips by Boucheron, mid-1960s. The design could be 1950s, what makes them 1960s is the use of virtually every possible cut of diamonds and in particular the use of beaded claws to secure the baguette diamonds.

Plate 770. A pair of emerald and diamond earclips, 1960s, of typical informal cluster design. Note the use of pear-shaped emeralds.

earlobe by means of a clip fitting. Variations on this theme ranged from relatively inexpensive examples made of variously textured gold to more important creations carved in hardstone and embellished with diamonds or entirely set with precious gemstones (see plate 776).

In 1971 Van Cleef and Arpels launched the earrings 'Roses de Noel', the petals carved in white or pink coral and the centre set with diamonds. Their success prompted the production of many similar examples designed as flowerheads, the petals carved in hardstone or brightly enamelled (see plate 773).

Plate 772. A pair of ruby, emerald and diamond earclips by Van Cleef and Arpels, c.1970. The stylised leaf design is reminiscent of Indian boteh *motifs and the choice of colours is typical of Jaipur enamels.*

Plate 773. A pair of white coral and diamond earclips by Van Cleef and Arpels, early 1970s, a design that was interpreted in other materials.

Plate 775. A pair of lapis lazuli and diamond earclips by Tiffany, 1970s.

Plate 774. A pair of cabochon emerald, ruby and diamond earrings by Van Cleef and Arpels, c.1970, of typical Indian inspiration.

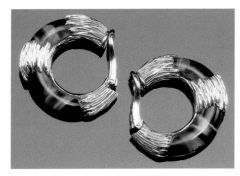

Plate 776. A pair of gold and crocidolite earrings by Kutchinsky, early 1970s, an example of a much favoured earring style.

Plate 777. A pair of onyx, rock crystal and diamond earrings by Boucheron, late 1970s, of typical linked ring design.

Necklaces

In the 1960s the most popular and wearable necklaces tended to be short, sitting just at the base of the neck in bands of differently worked gold, occasionally embellished with diamonds, coloured or precious stones.

Another variation of this was a simple rigid metal band encircling the neck and supporting a large pendant of abstract design set with small diamonds or with a large semi-precious gem within a border of spiky gold work (see plate 754). Slabs of agate, crystal aggregates and baroque pearls were among the favourite materials decorating the front of such collars (see plate 800).

More elaborate and expensive examples often assumed the shape of short collars, pointed or enlarged at the front to form a short bib motif, set with diamonds, preferably marquise or pear-shaped, alone or combined with precious coloured stones in arrangements of stylised leaf and flowerhead motifs (see plate 756). The overall effect was always that of an extremely dynamic jewel, with jagged, irregular outlines and stones set in prongs on different planes to achieve a feeling of depth and volume. The diamond supremacy of the 1950s gave way to a wide use of rubies, sapphires and emeralds in combination with diamonds. Turquoises were introduced in high jewellery in the 1960s and their rich and distinctive colour was exploited in combination with diamonds in many necklaces of this type.

Pearl necklaces remained in favour, appealing to the most traditional part of the market, and were occasionally given gold or diamond clasps of the asymmetrical geometric design so typical of the period.

The necklace 'Twist', created by Van Cleef and Arpels in 1962 *en suite* with a matching bracelet and ring, made of a row of coloured stone beads twisted around a row of gold beads, achieved great popularity and prompted many jewellers to produce their own version of the torsade necklace. Examples set with turquoises and corals were very popular (see plate 755).

Even the most expensive and lavish diamond creations, such as those produced by Harry Winston, seemed to conform to the general 1960s rule that required jagged and broken outlines. His necklaces assumed the shape of rivières of marquise diamonds, mounted vertically next to each other, occasionally supporting a large drop-shaped pendant with an important

Plate 778. A ruby, sapphire, emerald and diamond collar by Mauboussin, 1967. This necklace was exhibited at the Montreal World Fair in that year. It is typical in the highly chromatic use of stones and for the Islamic influence in the design which will be a trend in the early 1970s.

central gem, such as a diamond or a coloured stone, enclosed within a border of pear-shaped or marquise diamonds.

The trend for short necklaces changed dramatically in the 1970s when the ethnic inspiration of fashion urged women to wear long skirts, frilled blouses, boleros, fringed shawls and other similarly fussy garments. Short, geometric necklaces of abstract design became redundant and the trend shifted to the use of long chains and sautoirs which would swing with the rest of the clothing.

Perhaps the most typical ornaments of the 1970s are sautoirs made of elongated links, mostly oval or lozenge-shaped, carved in hardstones such as coral, onyx, rock crystal, lapis lazuli or materials such as exotic woods or ivory, mounted in yellow gold and occasionally highlighted with diamonds. These sautoirs generally supported a large, often detachable, pendant which matched the design of the earrings that were usually produced *en suite.* Jewellers on both sides of the Atlantic produced their own versions of these sautoirs, always characterised by bold, opulent shapes and rich, vivid colours (see plate 783). In lighter to wear examples the hardstone links were substituted with similarly shaped gold elements vividly enamelled with bright colours.

The more expensive versions of these sautoirs took the form of grand chains of yellow gold lavishly set with coloured precious gemstones, often cut en cabochon and highlighted with diamonds. They usually also supported large pendants similarly set and often decorated with pear-shaped drops, reminiscent, in their opulent shapes and chromatic combination, of traditional Indian jewellery (see plate 758).

Gold chains of all sorts of traditional or fancy linking were extremely popular and worn in great abundance, twisted several times around the neck or *en sautoir.* The gold links were often alternated or set at intervals with carved hardstone beads or with small enamelled elements: beads, stylised flowerheads, geometrical shapes decorated with opaque, translucent and

Plate 779. This magnificent emerald, ruby, diamond and cultured pearl necklace and earrings is one of the finest examples of the highly chromatic jewellery produced by Van Cleef and Arpels in the late 1960s. Here a traditional Indian 'Thali' collar has been transformed into a unique and spectacular necklace, the earrings are equally influenced by Eastern designs. The necklace, which was manufactured and reworked in 1965 and 1966, is perhaps the earliest example of the re-emergence of Indian-inspired jewels.

Plate 780. A superb diamond necklace by Van Cleef and Arpels, early 1970s. As was so common with important diamond necklaces of this period, the back could be detached to form a bracelet and the front worn as a choker.

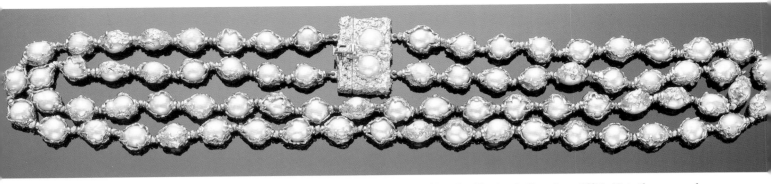

Plate 781. A gold and cultured pearl necklace by Charles de Temple, c.1970. Note the way each pearl is encaged in textured gold work.

Plate 782. Three gold and hardstone sautoirs of the 1970s, all French, one set with jasper, by Chaumet. Note the textured gold and the unusual semi-precious hardstones such as crocidolite, jasper and rock crystal. Sautoirs, long necklaces which were developed before the First World War, enjoyed a renewed popularity in the 1970s.

occasionally *plique-à-jour* enamel (see plates 762, 782).

The traditional string of pearls did not cease to find support amongst the most traditional clientèle, but the most fashionable way of wearing pearls was in long strings encaged in gold textured work in the manner made popular by the London jeweller Charles de Temple (see plate 781).

Under the spell of the Indian influence, necklaces made of beads of coloured precious gemstones or coral came back into fashion, worn in several rows or twisted in *torsades* set at the front with gold decorative motifs in the shape of flowers or animal masks.

Towards the end of the 1970s, short necklaces came back into fashion again designed as rigid bands of yellow gold, entirely pavé-set with diamonds and highlighted with coloured gemstones, or simply set at the front with a gem-set decorative motif.

Plate 783. A gold, coral and diamond sautoir, by Boucheron, c.1974. This necklace is a good example of the 'boutique' jewellery produced by the 'grandes maisons' of Place Vendôme in the mid-1970s with the Middle Eastern market in mind. Note the exclusive use of circular-cut diamonds in yellow gold settings combined with carved corals in the popular 'peau d'ange' (angel's skin) shade.

Brooches

Brooches were very popular in the 1960s and were very often sold *en suite* with earrings of matching design. Among the favourite designs were stylised sun or starburst motifs made of textured metals set at random with small diamonds or with a large semi-precious gemstone at the centre; clusters of geometric metal shapes combined with step-cut aquamarines or citrines; cabochons of hard or semi-precious stones enveloped with gold sprawling root motifs; and splintered, jagged, broken plaques of metal highlighted with gemstones of contrasting colours. They all share in common broken outlines, three-dimensional qualities, and textured surfaces of metal contrasting with polished gemstones (see plates 757, 796).

The interest in natural materials, unworked by hand, prompted the production of many brooches of abstract design set with gemstones, crystals or aggregates of crystals, such as amethyst, dyoptase or emerald, within asymmetrical clusters of geometrical metal forms. Very popular too in this period, and in the first half of the 1970s, were brooches mounted with circular, shell-like nodules of chalcedony encrusted with minute crystalline growths of quartz, embellished with brilliant-cut diamonds or pearls (see plate 797).

Brooches of higher intrinsic value, set with diamonds and precious coloured stones, were often designed as irregular, asymmetrical clusters or starbursts and favoured the use of pear and marquise-shaped gems to obtain the jagged outlines typical of the age (see plate 756). In these three-dimensional creations, the largest, central stone was often claw-set above the rest of the mount as if it were about to spring out of it.

Naturalism, as a source of inspiration, does not disappear from brooches, but realistic interpretation tends to be substituted by stylisations even in the most expensive and elaborate creations. Van Cleef and Arpels freezes the flowing lines of leaves and flowerheads into the geometrism of his 'Guirlande' brooches; Cartier, Mauboussin and Boucheron tended to stylise leaves and flowers into spiky, pointed shapes (see plates 786, 787, 788, 789, 790, 792).

Animal brooches were very much in favour in the 1960s in the form of stylised, often idealised, amusing and whimsical creatures. The 'Chat Malicieux', launched by Van Cleef and Arpels in 1954, was followed in 1962 by the 'Lion Ebouriffé' and two years later by a 'Bebé Lion' who reigned over a collection of charming and easy to wear brooches designed as squirrels, giraffes, elephants, tortoises, etc. (see plates 784, 785). All jewellers produced

Plate 784. A gold, enamel and diamond brooch by Van Cleef and Arpels, designed as a giraffe. One of the many amusing animal designs developed by Van Cleef in the 1950s and early 1960s, widely copied, imitated and reinterpreted by other jewellers.

Plate 785. A gold and gemset lion brooch by Van Cleef and Arpels. The brooch 'Lion Ebouriffé' was created by Van Cleef and Arpels in 1962 as part of their large collection of animal brooches, informal, amusing and easy to wear (see plate 784).

their own version of animal brooches, usually made of gold and set with semi-precious stones highlighted with diamonds and occasionally lavishly mounted with precious coloured stones (see plate 794). Birds, from parrots to birds-of-paradise, were particularly popular in the early years of the decade.

In the 1970s the popularity of brooches started to decline. Partly as a whim of fashion, partly because the widespread vogue for long chains and sautoirs left little or no space at all for an ornament to be pinned next to it, brooches lost their appeal. Among the relatively few new brooch designs of this decade, the most typical were those made to match the long sautoirs carved in hardstone: entwined rings or variously shaped links embellished with diamonds and mounted in gold. Also typical of the period are four or five petalled stylised flowerheads, carved in hardstone or wood, mounted in yellow gold and decorated with brilliant-cut diamond centres (see plates 793, 799).

The influence of Indian traditional jewellery on the production of the 1970s prompted the creation of several cluster brooches entirely set with diamonds

Plate 786. A coral, ruby and diamond flower brooch by Kern, 1960s. Note the stylisation of the natural forms and the jagged outlines.

Plate 788. A diamond bow brooch, c.1965. A rather restrained mainstream brooch of the period, set in platinum.

Plate 789. An emerald and diamond brooch 'Guirlande' by Van Cleef and Arpels, c.1960.

Plate 787. A sapphire and diamond flower brooch by Mauboussin, 1965. The spikiness of the design and the complete abstraction of the natural forms are typical of the 1960s.

Plate 790. A ruby and diamond brooch by Roger King of Roy C. King Ltd., London, c.1960, designed as a cluster of toadstools mounted in articulated settings on a mound of cabochon rubies. This brooch, commissioned by Collingwood Ltd. of London, was the winning entry in the 1962 British 'Jewel of the Year' competition. The international panel of judges remarked that this brooch represented new trends in construction and design.

Plate 791. A pair of gold and cultured pearl brooches, c.1965, by Wagner. Note the geological inspiration of the design, a cross between gold nuggets and sea worn rocks.

Plate 792. An opal, citrine quartz, pearl and diamond brooch by Chaumet, 1960s. Note the stylised floral design set seemingly at random with stones chosen for their curious chromatic combination.

Plate 793. A chalcedony and diamond four leaf clover brooch by Van Cleef and Arpels, c.1970. A design re-worked in different materials such as coral, lapis lazuli and wood.

Plate 794. A gold, coral and diamond puppy brooch, by Mauboussin, late 1960s.

Plate 795. A ruby and diamond brooch by Van Cleef and Arpels, c.1970. A much imitated and copied design, also seen in emeralds and sapphires. The quality of the stones alone normally indicates if the piece is an original work by Van Cleef and Arpels or a copy (see plate 814).

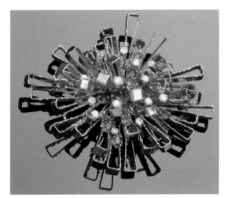

Plate 796. A gold, emerald and diamond brooch, by G.Weil, c.1970. Note the geometric shape and the textured gold, typical features of the 1960s and early 1970s.

Plate 797. A chalcedony nodule encrusted with quartz crystal mounted as a brooch by Andrew Grima in 1974 with gold and diamonds. A typical iconoclastic jewel from the Grima workshop. The prototype of this design dates back to the early 1960s.

Plate 798. A diamond clip, by Van Cleef and Arpels, early 1970s. The design, which shows a clear Mughal influence, was also popular for pendants to be worn on long chains. To set this jewel, which carries important diamonds, entirely in yellow gold before the early 1970s would have been almost inconceivable.

or with diamonds and coloured precious stones of clear Mughal inspiration (see plates 760, 798).

Animal brooches continued to be produced, mainly in yellow gold and set with colourful semi-precious stones, repeating the designs of the previous decades. Brooches set with gemstone crystals in abstract, asymmetrical mounts remained popular well into the 1970s (see plate 794), while brooches of high intrinsic value tended to follow the more traditional paths of floral stylisation (see plate 795).

Plate 799. A bois d'amourette *and diamond brooch/pendant by Van Cleef and Arpels, Paris, c.1972. Pendants of this type used to be produced* en parure *with carved link sautoirs and hoopshaped earrings.*

Plate 800. An amethyst and gold pendant by David Deakin, 1972. A design typical of the 1960s which remained popular in the early 1970s. Note the setting of an aggregate of amethyst crystals which is encased in gold articulation.

Pendants

The 1960s fashion for short necklaces did not seem to favour pendants, especially in the field of precious jewellery. At times the spiky diamond ribbons which encircled the neck were provided with detachable pendants of informal cluster design often set at the centre with a large coloured stone, or a large diamond, within a jagged border of navettes and pear-shaped smaller stones. On the other hand, the most innovative designers of the decade, who were more interested in the final effect rather than the intrinsic value, liked to suspend from plain gold ribbons pendants of various abstract shapes made of textured gold embellished with small diamonds, or set with natural crystals or hardstones encaged in gold work (see plate 800).

The grand re-entrance of the sautoir in the 1970s prompted the production of a large number of pendants of different shapes, but always of grand and bold design. Among the most typical are those carved in hardstones such as rock crystal, onyx, coral, lapis lazuli or wood, which matched in shape the links of the sautoir. They were often detachable and provided with brooch fittings (see plates 758, 783).

The late 1960s and 1970s fashion for jewels inspired by traditional Indian design encouraged the creation of long chains or shorter necklaces made of yellow gold encrusted with emeralds, rubies and diamonds, supporting large pendants in the shape of cascades of gemstones; others were of *girandole* or *chandelier* design, reminiscent of the jewels of the maharanis. Van Cleef and Arpels produced some exceptional examples, entirely set with diamonds in yellow gold mounts or set with multicoloured stones, often cut en cabochon and highlighted with diamonds (see plate 779).

Bracelets

Bracelets were very popular in the 1960s, either in the shape of flexible gemset bands or rigid bangles. The most typical design, consistent with the general trend of the decade, consists of a band of variously cut diamonds — or diamonds and coloured gemstones — mounted seemingly at random so as to create the effect of a saw edge (see plates 801, 802, 811). More traditional designs assumed the form of wavy ribbons of diamonds and coloured gemstones, three-dimensional and with jagged outlines; this differentiates them from their 1950's counterparts (see plate 803).

A particularly successful bracelet design of the 1960s consisted of entwined or plaited ribbons of gemstones of contrasting colours and cuts, such as a

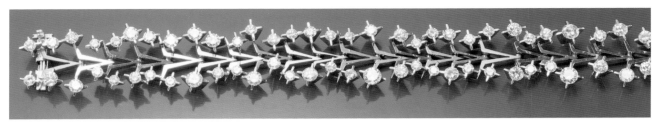

Plate 801. A diamond bracelet, c.1960, clearly influenced by space exploration. Star and rocket motifs are combined into a three-dimensional spiky design.

Plate 802. A diamond bracelet, c.1965. Note the severe, almost brutal spikiness of the design and the platinum mount.

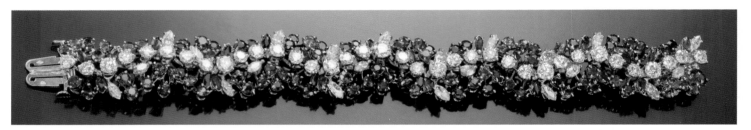

Plate 803. A sapphire and diamond bracelet, French, c.1965. Note the following: a) the innovative use of sapphires cut like diamonds; b) the way each stone is individually set and separated or raised from its neighbour involving a complicated wire mount; c) the wavy and informal design.

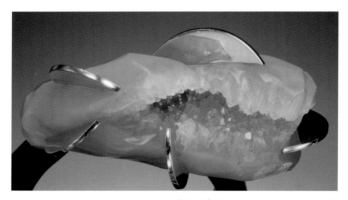

Plate 804. A carved quartz, gold and ruby bangle, by Chaumet, Paris, c.1965. A natural cave of quartz crystals was revealed simply by cutting and polishing away the corner of a geode. The charming addition of the clusters of rubies nesting at the centre completes a typical flight of fancy of the mid-1960s.

Plate 805. A gold, mabé pearl and diamond bangle by Lacloche, c.1965. The designer has here obviously looked at late Victorian star brooches and has added mabé pearls in a typical 1960's encrustation of gold.

Plate 806. A ruby and diamond bracelet by Chaumet, c.1965. Note the different cuts of the diamonds incorporated apparently at random in the design.

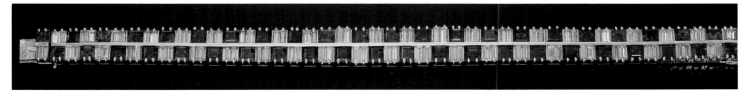

Plate 807. A sapphire and diamond bracelet, French, 1960s. Note especially the beaded claws holding in place the calibré-cut sapphires and baguette diamonds. This type of setting is closely associated with 1960's jewellery.

Plate 808. An emerald and diamond bracelet, French, 1960s. Note that the stones are still entirely set in platinum and white gold. The last flourish of white metal before the dominance of yellow gold in the 1970s.

Plate 809. A gold, turquoise and diamond bracelet by David Webb, 1960s. The torsade design and the corded wire are hangovers from the 1950s but remained popular for twenty years. The fact that the diamonds are set in platinum or white gold rather than yellow gold suggests the 1960s rather than 1970s.

Plate 810. A diamond bangle, 1960s, note the organ pipe arrangement of the baguette diamonds. So typical of the 1960s is the raised beaded claw holding each baguette diamond in place.

course of baguette diamonds entwined with a line of cushion-, pear- or marquise-shaped coloured stones (see plate 808).

Plain diamond and diamond and coloured gemstone line bracelets came back into fashion and quickly became as popular as they had been in the 1920s. They can easily be recognised from their earlier counterparts by their beaded claw settings (see plate 807).

Plate 811. A diamond bracelet by Gubelin, late 1960s. Note the asymmetry of the design and the combination of baguettes and marquises set at random.

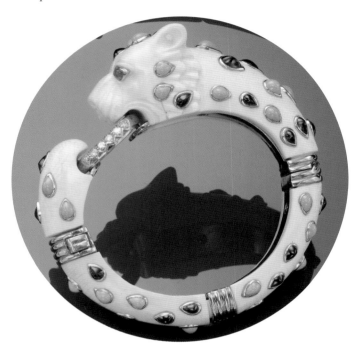

Plate 812. A carved coral, coloured stones and diamond bull's head bangle by David Webb. Animal bangles by David Webb began to be produced in the 1960s and proved so popular that they are still being produced by the same company today. They owe their origin perhaps to the 'Chimera' bangles designed by Cartier in the 1920s and to their 'Great Cats' bangles and bracelets of the 1950s.

Plate 813. A Snow Leopard bangle carved from ivory and set with turquoises, sapphires and diamonds, by Van Cleef and Arpels, New York, 1973.

Plate 814. A coral, emerald and diamond bracelet by Van Cleef and Arpels, c.1970. Another jewel showing Islamic influence in the design widely copied in Bangkok and Hong Kong, so beware of imitations.

Plate 815. A gold, ruby and diamond bracelet by Van Cleef and Arpels, late 1960, much copied as plate 814. The motifs are drawn from Islamic tile decoration.

Plate 816. A diamond bracelet, mid-1970s. Note the exclusive use of brilliant-cut stones and the yellow gold mount.

Flexible *torsades* of pearls, gold chains and hardstone beads were extremely popular, and the bracelet 'Twist', launched by Van Cleef and Arpels in 1962 as part of a complete parure of matching jewels of pearls, gold and hardstone beads entwined together, set an example that many jewellers imitated (see plate 755).

Bangles in the 1960s tended to be designed as wide rigid bands of abstract or naturalistic inspiration mounted in asymmetrical patterns with diamonds and coloured gemstones so as to obtain the jagged and spiky outlines typical of the decade (see plates 805, 810). Other examples, following the success of the *torsade* bracelet, were designed as *bombé* bands decorated with diagonal lines of differently coloured stones, often alternating with gold corded wire (see plate 809).

Typical of the 1960s is a vast production of animal bangles either carved in hardstone, or of textured gold brilliantly enamelled, and always embellished with cabochon or faceted precious or semi-precious gemstones. Inspired perhaps by Cartier's Chimera bangles of the 1920s and by their Great Cats bangles of the 1950s, they assumed the shape of almost any creature of the animal kingdom: elephants, horses, cats, lions, tigers, bulls, etc. Their popularity lasted through the following decade (see plates 812, 813).

In the 1960s the more innovative jewellers such as Andrew Grima produced more abstract bangles set with, or carved from, aggregates of crystals (see plate 804).

The most typical form of bracelet of the 1970s consisted of a band of floral or geometrical motifs of Indian or Islamic inspiration set with diamonds and multicoloured precious and semi-precious gemstones, always mounted in yellow gold. Indian *boteh* motifs and patterns inspired by the decoration of Islamic tiles and carpets were among the favourite decorative devices used by Van Cleef and Arpels in the 1970s and were widely and abundantly copied and imitated (see plates 814, 815).

Other popular bracelets of the 1970s were designed as large, chunky chains of oval, circular or lozenge-shaped links, lavishly set with brilliant-cut diamonds, mounted in yellow gold and sometimes embellished with coloured gemstones (see plate 816).

Plate 817. A gold coin bracelet by Bulgari, late 1970s. Bulgari started a big fashion for setting ancient coins in jewels which was widely imitated throughout the 1980s.

Plate 818. A pair of diamond wristwatches, one by Ebel and one by Sandoz, typical of the 1960s in the small round dials, the use of white gold and the simplicity of the outline.

Plate 819. A gold, diamond, lapis lazuli and sapphire bracelet/watch by Piaget, c.1970. The design appears to be transitional in the employment of amorphous marine motifs from the 1960s — so reminiscent of Andrew Grima's work — and bold, strong colouring typical of the following decade.

Wristwatches

In the 1960s, ladies' gemset wristwatches did not lose the popularity achieved in the 1950s and continued to be characterised by rather sober and restrained designs. The most typical wristwatch of the period consisted of a fairly small dial, usually circular, surrounded by a border of brilliant-cut diamonds, on a strap of very fine white gold mesh. More expensive examples, intended exclusively for evening wear, consisted of small circular dials within diamond-set floral or foliate borders attached to a diamond line bracelet (see plate 818). These designs are very similar to those typical of the 1950s; what makes them 1960s rather than 1950s are the jagged and spiky outlines of the thin

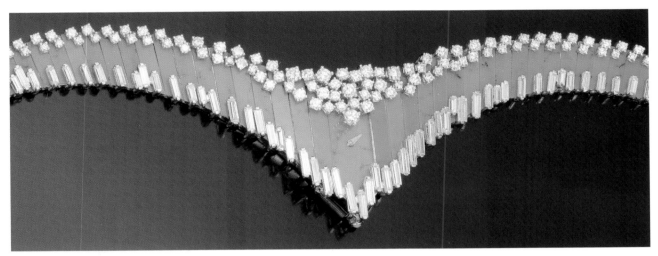

Plate 820 A turquoise matrix and diamond bracelet/watch 'Acapulco' by Chopard, c.1969. An extraordinary design, almost emblematic of jewellery design in the second half of the 1960s.

bracelets and the diamond borders around the dials; obtained by the use of marquise- and pear-shaped diamonds in the typical beaded claw-setting.

Towards the end of the decade many jewellers and watchmakers experimented with bolder, more daring and innovative designs. Andrew Grima was commissioned by Omega to design a collection of wristwatches which became, in his hands, fantastic, sculptural creations where the dials were either seen through a gemstone or were concealed by one, and the bracelets assumed monumental size. Piaget, Chopard and Patek Philippe designed wristwatches more to adorn the arm than to be used as timepieces: wide, asymmetrical bracelets set with plaques of brightly coloured hardstones within diamond borders, their minute dials camouflaged within the design; or wide chain bracelets of gold links, encrusted with precious stones, and with large, hardstone dials (see plates 819, 820).

The most typical lady's wristwatch of the 1970s favoured the same large dials; they were usually round, or square with rounded corners, often made of a plaque of hardstone or closely pavé-set with small diamonds. The borders of the dial consisted either of simple diamond surrounds, or more elaborate and colourful combinations of carved hardstones and diamonds. The straps were usually of yellow gold worked in a variety of mesh or basket-weave linking, but bracelets made of carved hardstone links alternating with gold links were not unusual (see plates 821, 823).

Jewellers occasionally incorporated small watches in their gemset bracelets and disguised their little dials under hinged covers (see plate 824). Conversely, famous Swiss watchmakers, having perceived what the Middle Eastern market was asking for, and at the same time sensitive to the influence of traditional Indian jewels on jewellery design of the 1970s, produced bracelet/watches of yellow gold and diamonds, where the design of dials and bracelet links so often showed Islamic inspiration (see plate 822).

Plate 821. A gold, onyx and diamond bracelet/watch by Cartier, c.1970.

409

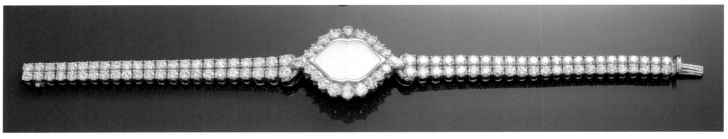

Plate 822. A gold and diamond bracelet/watch by Audemars Piguet, early 1970s. Note the Islamic influence in the ogive scrolls of the dial.

Plate 823. A typical pair of dress watches of the mid-1970s by Patek Philippe. Note the yellow gold throughout and the use of carved hardstones, probably worked in Idar Oberstein.

Plate 824. A bracelet watch by Gérard, late 1970s. The ever popular torsade motif is here used as a vehicle for a watch. Note the exclusive use of circular-cut diamonds mounted in yellow gold.

Rings

The popularity of rings reached an all-time height in the 1960s and 1970s. Fashionable women wore several of them at the same time, and often more than one on the same finger.

The great novelty of the 1960s in ring design is the mounting of the central, larger stone of a cluster in a raised setting above the others. The designs were aimed at creating, with the use of pointed stones such as pear-shaped or marquises, the typical splintered, jagged effect so typical of the decade (see plates 825, 827).

Ballerina mounts were also popular, where the central stone was mounted within an undulating border of diamonds (see plate 825). The traditional *solitaire* diamond ring lost its appeal in favour of three-dimensional clusters.

Rings of lesser intrinsic value tended to favour the use of large cabochons or pearls, encaged in elaborate gold work or surrounded by small diamonds in gold designs reminiscent of the moon's surface or of sea-worn rocks (see plate 826). Jewellers moulded yellow gold in abstract shapes, reminiscent of the bed of the sea or crystal forms, and studded it with variously coloured gemstones thus creating large, effective and eye-catching rings (see plates 828, 829). Crystals, and crystal aggregates mounted as rings are also a typical feature of the 1960s — a fashion which remained in favour well into the next decade (see plate 831).

Very popular in the 1960s and 1970s was also the *boule* ring, first designed by Van Cleef and Arpels in the mid-1930s, and reinterpreted in many different ways through the following decades. A *boule* shaped ring was designed by Van Cleef and Arpels with diagonal rows of pearls, gold beads and hardstone beads to accompany the bracelet and the necklace in their popular 'Twist' parure in 1962 (see plate 755). The 1970s versions, almost invariably set in yellow gold, tended to make use of fairly large, often precious coloured stones

Plate 825. A ruby and diamond cluster ring, c.1960. A variation of the popular 'ballerina' mount, the baguette and brilliant-cut diamonds set in an undulating design.

Plate 826. An opal, diamond and gold ring by Chaumet, Paris, 1960s. Note the textured gold.

Plate 827. A sapphire and diamond cluster ring, 1960s. Here the step-cut Ceylon sapphire is placed at the centre of a cluster of marquise-shaped diamonds in typical 1960s fashion. Very little setting metal is visible.

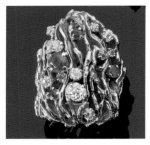

Plate 828. A gold, ruby and diamond ring in the manner of Charles de Temple, late 1960s.

Plate 829. A gold and diamond ring composed of textured gold prisms and cushion-shaped diamonds. A style made popular by Grima and of the 1960s. This example however, was made in 1975.

Plate 830. A ruby, emerald and diamond boule *ring by Van Cleef and Arpels, c.1970. A re-working in yellow gold of a design which started in the mid-1930s although rubies, emeralds and diamonds would not have been a combination of stones fashionable at that time.*

Plate 831. A chalcedony nodule encrusted with a growth of minute quartz crystals mounted as a ring with a pearl and diamonds by Gilbert Albert, c.1970. Typical of Albert's production is the employment of precious stones and natural crystal forms in the same jewel. The fashion for employing unworked crystals had been started in the 1960s, notably by Andrew Grima.

Plate 832. A gold and crocidolite ring, by Kutchinsky, early 1970s, of entwined hoop design. Rings of entwined hoop design were very popular in the decade, either carved in hardstone or entirely pavé-set with diamonds.

Plate 833. A gold and diamond ring by Van Cleef and Arpels, New York, c.1970. Lion mask rings, pendants and earclips enjoyed great popularity in the first half of the 1970s and were much imitated.

in effective chromatic combination (see plate 830).

Cluster rings remained popular in the 1970s: more formal in design than in the previous decade, they favoured the use of baguette diamond surrounds and yellow gold mounts. The great popularity of carved hardstone jewels in this decade prompted the creation of numerous rings of sculptural design set with materials such as coral, lapis lazuli, crocidolite, onyx and ivory, and carved in numerous different shapes — entwined rings, half-moons, diamonds, etc. — all embellished with small diamonds (see plate 832).

Bibliography

Anderson, B.W., *Gem Testing,* London, 1980.

Becker, V., *Art Nouveau Jewellery,* London 1985; *Antique and Twentieth Century Jewellery,* London, 1980 and 1987; *The Jewellery of René Lalique,* London, 1987; *Antique and Twentieth Century Jewellery,* London, 1980.

Bury, S., *Jewellery Gallery Summary Catalogue,* Victoria and Albert Museum, London, 1983.

Cartlidge, B., *Twentieth-Century Jewelry,* New York, 1985.

Evans, J., *A History of Jewellery 1100-1870,* London, 1953 (new edition 1970).

Gabardi, M., *Les Bijoux de l'Art Déco aux Années 40,* Paris, 1980.

Gere, C., *Victorian Jewellery Design,* London, 1982; *European and American Jewellery,* London, 1985.

Gere, C., Rudoe, J., Tait, H., Wilson, T., *The Art of the Jeweller, A Catalogue of the Hull Grundy Gift to the British Museum,* London, 1984.

Gere, C., Munn, G., *Artists' Jewellery, Pre-Raphaelite to Arts and Crafts,* Woodbridge, 1989.

Gübelin, E.J., Koivula, J.I., *Photoatlas of Inclusions in Gemstones,* Zurich, 1986.

Hinks, P., *Nineteenth Century Jewellery,* London, 1975; *Twentieth Century Jewellery 1900-1980,* London, 1983.

Flower, M., *Victorian Jewellery,* London, 1951

Fontenay, E., *Les Bijoux Anciens et Modernes,* Paris, 1887.

Les Fouquet, Bijoutiers & Joailliers à Paris, 1860-1960, Musée des Arts Décoratifs, Paris, 1983.

Medvedeva, G., Platonova, N., Postnikova-Loseva, M., Smorodinova, G., Troepolskaya, N., *Russian Jewellery 16th-20th Centuries from the Collection of the Historical Museum, Moscow,* Moscow, 1987.

Munn, G., *Castellani and Giuliano, Revivalist Jewellers of the Nineteenth Century,* London, 1984.

Nadelhoffer, H., *Cartier: Jewellers Extraordinary,* London and New York, 1984.

Neret, G., *Boucheron: Four Generations of a World-Renowned Jeweller,* Paris, 1988.

Proddow, P., Heale, D., *American Jewelry, Glamour and Tradition,* New York, 1987.

Raulet, S., *Art Déco Jewelry,* Paris, 1984.

Raulet, S., *Van Cleef and Arpels,* Paris, 1986.

Snowman, A.K., *Carl Fabergé,* London, 1980.

Scarisbrick, D., *Jewellery,* London, 1984.

Vever, H., *La Bijouterie Française au XIXe Siècle,* Paris, 1908.

Ward, A., Cherry, J., Gere, C., Cartlidge, B., *The Ring from Antiquity to the Twentieth Century,* London, 1981.

Webster, R., *Gems, Their Sources, Description and Identification,* revised by B.W. Anderson, London, 1983.

continued

Additional Bibliography to Chapter Nine

Cerval, M. de, *Mauboussin,* Paris, 1992.

Grima, Retrospective, Catalogue of an Exhibition, London, 1991.

Mascetti, D., Triossi, A., *Earrings from Antiquity to the Present,* London, 1990.

Ormesson, J. d', Gere, C., Becker, V., Vreeland, D., *Jean Schlumberger,* Milan, 1991.

Van Cleef & Arpels, Catalogue of an Exhibition, Paris, 1992.

Approximate Guide to Relative Values at Auction

The following list of prices has been included to give a broad outline of the relative values of items in this book. The object of their inclusion is purely to enable the reader to form a judgement on the relative value of one piece against another. The values on which this list is based were originally established in 1994 in pounds sterling and they have been converted to US dollars using a conversion factor of $1.50 to £1. They should not, therefore, be taken as offering current auction prices. It should also be borne in mind that these figures can be severely affected by condition, quality of stones, the importance of a particular auction and the excitement which it generates. The economic situation is also relevant, as are small changes in fashion. The list is a guide to relative values in a field where there can never be absolute prices.

Plate 39. $7,500 – $10,500
Plate 40. $1,500 – $6,000
Plate 41. $22,500 – $30,000
Plate 42. $3,000 – $4,500
Plate 43. $1,200 – $1,500
Plate 44. $22,500 – $30,000
Plate 45. $30,000 – $45,000
Plate 46. $4,500 – $7,500
Plate 47. $18,000 – $22,500
Plate 48. $1,500 – $2,000
Plate 49. $600 – $900 (pair)
Plate 50. $3,000 – $4,500
Plate 51. $30,000 – $45,000
Plate 52. $60,000 – $90,000
Plate 53. $15,000 –$22,500 (top); $1,500 – $2,000 (bottom)
Plate 54. $10,500 – $15,000
Plate 55. $300,000 – $375,000
Plate 56. $6,000 – $7,500
Plate 57. $3,000 – $4,500
Plate 58. $7,500 – $10,500
Plate 59. $3,000 – $4,500
Plate 60. $3,000 – $4,500
Plate 61. $1,800 – $2,000
Plate 62. $4,500 – $6,000
Plate 63. $4,500 – $6,000
Plate 64. $4,500 – $6,000
Plate 65. $6,000 – $9,000
Plate 66. $7,500 – $10,500 (top); $4,500 – $6,000 (bottom)
Plate 67. $12,000 – $15,000
Plate 68. $9,000 – $12,000
Plate 69. $3,000 – $4,500
Plate 70. $6,000 – $7,500
Plate 71. $6,000 – $7,500
Plate 72. $79,200 (8. 10.87)
Plate 73. $3,000 – $4,500
Plate 74. $6,000 – $9,000
Plate 75. $4,500 – $6,000

Plate 76. $3,000 – $4,500
Plate 77. $1,200 – $1,800
Plate 78. $2,000 – $3,000
Plate 79. $1,500 – $2,000
Plate 80. $10,500 – $15,000
Plate 81. $300 – $500
Plate 82. $1,500 – $2,000
Plate 83. $4,500 – $7,500
Plate 86. $300,000 – $375,000
Plate 87. $9,000 – $12,000
Plate 88. $15,000 – $22,500
Plate 89. $30,000 – $45,000
Plate 90. $30,000 – $45,000
Plate 91. $6,000 – $9,000 (top); $2,000 – $3,000 (bottom)
Plate 92. $75,000 – $105,000
Plate 93. $1,800 – $2,000
Plate 94. $1,500 – $2,000
Plate 95. $1,500 – $2,000
Plate 96. $15,000 – $22,500
Plate 97. $6,000 – $9,000
Plate 98. $3,000 – $4,500
Plate 99. $22,500 – $30,000
Plate 101. $13,500 – $16,500
Plate 102. $6,000 – $9,000
Plate 103. $600,000 – $900,000
Plate 104. $15,000 – $22,500
Plate 105. $7,500 – $10,500
Plate 106. $12,000 – $15,000
Plate 107. $225 – $375
Plate 108. $6,000 – $15,000
Plate 109. $12,000 – $15,000
Plate 110. $4,500 – $6,000
Plate 111. $22,500 – $30,000
Plate 112. $12,000 – $15,000
Plate 113. $1,500 – $2,000
Plate 114. $1,200 –$1,800
Plate 115. $15,000 – $22,500
Plate 116. $15,000 – $22,500

Plate 117. $18,000 – $22,500
Plate 118. $4,500 – $6,000
Plate 119. $10,500 – $15,000
Plate 120. $3,000 – $4,500
Plate 121. $4,500 – $6,000
Plate 122. $3,000 – $4,500
Plate 123. $7,500 – $10,500
Plate 124. $3,000 – $4,500
Plate 125. $4,500 – $6,000
Plate 126. $15,000 – $22,500
Plate 127. $3,000 – $4,500
Plate 128. $2,000 – $3,000
Plate 129. $3,000 – $4,500
Plate 130. $1,200 –$1,800
Plate 132. $30,000 – $45,000
Plate 133. $22,500 – $30,000
Plate 134. $3,000 – $4,500
Plate 135. $1,500 – $2,000
Plate 136. $6,000 –$9,000
Plate 137. $300 – $3,000
Plate 138. $600 – $900 (pair)
Plate 139. $6,000 – $9,000
Plate 140. $7,500 – $9,000
Plate 141. $2,000 – $4,500 (each)
Plate 142. $3,000 – $4,500
Plate 143. $22,500 – $30,000
Plate 144. $12,000 – $15,000
Plate 145. $4,500 – $7,500
Plate 146. $2,000 – $3,000
Plate 147. $12,000 –$18,000
Plate 148. $1,200 – $1,800; $900 – $1,200
Plate 149. $150 – $225 (each)
Plate 150. $3,000 – $4,500
Plate 151. $6,000 – $9,000
Plate 152. $1,200 – $1,800
Plate 153. $1,200 – $1,800
Plate 154. $2,000 – $3,000

Plate 155. $3,000 – $4,500
Plate 156. $4,500 – $6,000
Plate 157. $3,000 – $4,500
Plate 158. $4,500 – $7,500
Plate 159. $4,500 – $6,000
Plate 160. $4,500 – $6,000
Plate 161. $4,500 – $6,000
Plate 162. $6,000 – $9,000
Plate 163. $6,000 – $9,000
Plate 164. $6,000 – $9,000
Plate 165. $3,000 – $4,500
Plate 166. $13,500 – $18,000
Plate 167. $9,000 – $12,000
Plate 168. $2,000 – $3,000
Plate 169. $3,800 – $5,300
Plate 170. $3,000 – $4,500
Plate 171. $9,000 – $12,000
Plate 172. $7,500 – $10,500
Plate 173. $1,800 –$2,000
Plate 174. $600 – $1,200 (each)
Plate 175. $600 – $1,200 (each)
Plate 176. $800 – $1,800 (each)
Plate 178. $90,000 – $120,000
Plate 179. $4,500 – $6,000
Plate 180. $1,200 – $1,800
Plate 181. $3,000 – $4,500
Plate 182. $2,000 – $3,000
Plate 183. $60,000 – $90,000
Plate 184. $2,000 – $3,000
Plate 185. $3,000 – $4,500
Plate 186. $6,000 – $9,000
Plate 186. $1,500 – $2,000
Plate 187. $45,000 – $75,000
Plate 188. $22,500 – $30,000
Plate 189. $22,500 – $30,000
Plate 190. $22,500 – $30,000
Plate 191. $1,500 – $2,000
Plate 192. $4,500 – $6,000
Plate 193. $7,500 – $10,500
Plate 194. $7,500 – $10,500
Plate 195. $3,000 – $4,500
Plate 196. $3,800 – $5,300
Plate 197. $500 –$600 (each)
Plate 198. $1,200 – $1,500
Plate 199. $6,000 – $7,500
Plate 200. $6,000 – $9,000
Plate 201. $6,000 – $9,000
Plate 202. $7,500 – $10,500
Plate 203. $9,000 – $12,000

Plate 204. $30,000 – $45,000
Plate 205. $4,500 – $6,000
Plate 206. $1,500 – $15,000
Plate 207. $22,500 – $30,000
Plate 208. $6,000 – $9,000
Plate 209. $4,500 – $6,000
Plate 210. $2,000 – $3,000
Plate 211. $2,000 – $3,000
Plate 212. $1,200 – $1,800
Plate 213. $225 – $300 (each)
Plate 214. $1,200 – $1,500
Plate 215. $500 – $600
Plate 216. $1,200 – $1,500
Plate 217. $1,200 – $1,800
Plate 218. $2,000 – $3,000
    $1,500 –$2,000
Plate 219. $6,000 – $7,500
Plate 220. $7,500 – $9,000
Plate 221. $15,000 – $18,000
Plate 222. $27,000 – $33,000
Plate 223. $1,500 – $1,800
Plate 224. $1,800 – $2,700
Plate 225. $2,000 – $3,000
Plate 226. $4,500 – $6,000
Plate 227. $9,000 – $12,000
Plate 228. $12,000 – $18,000
Plate 229. $30,000 – $45,000
Plate 230. $4,500 – $6,000
Plate 231. $18,000 –$22,500
Plate 232. $3,000 – $4,500
Plate 233. $1,200 – $1,800
Plate 236. $900 – $1,200
Plate 237. $1,200 – $1,500
Plate 238. $2,000 – $3,000
Plate 239. $1,200 – $1,800
Plate 240. $2,000 – $3,000
Plate 241. $1,200 – $1,800
Plate 242. $12,000 – $18,000
Plate 243. $1,200 – $1,800
Plate 244. $22,500 – $30,000
Plate 245. $12,000 – $18,000
Plate 246. $45,000 – $75,000
Plate 247. $6,000 – $9,000
Plate 248. $6,000 – $9,000
Plate 249. $4,500 – $6,000
Plate 250. $4,500 – $6,000
Plate 251. $9,000 – $12,000;
    $12,000 – $15,000
Plate 252. $4,500 – $6,000

Plate 253. $4,500 – $6,000
Plate 254. $10,500 – $15,000
Plate 255. $10,500 – $15,000
Plate 256. $900 – $1,200
Plate 257. $1,200 – $1,800
Plate 258. $2,000 – $3,000
Plate 259. $800 – $1,000
Plate 260. $15,000 – $22,500
Plate 261. $7,500 – $12,000
Plate 262. $9,000 – $13,500
Plate 263. $12,000 – $18,000
Plate 264. $2,000 – $3,000
Plate 265. $2,000 – $3,000
Plate 266. $1,500 – $2,000
Plate 267. $3,000 – $4,500
Plate 268. $2,000 – $3,000
Plate 269. $6,000 – $7,500
Plate 270. $12,000 – $18,000
Plate 271. $9,000 – $12,000
Plate 272. $30,000 – $45,000
Plate 273. $9,000 – $12,000
Plate 274. $7,500 – $12,000
Plate 275. $10,500 – $15,000
Plate 276. $6,000 – $9,000
Plate 277. $6,000 – $9,000
Plate 278. $9,000 – $13,500
Plate 279. $6,000 – $9,000
Plate 280. $15,000 – $21,000
Plate 281. $18,000 – $22,500
Plate 282. $7,500 – $10,500
Plate 283. $22,500 – $30,000
Plate 284. $18,000 – $22,500
Plate 285. $6,000 – $9,000
Plate 286. $4,500 – $7,500
Plate 287. $4,500 – $6,000
Plate 288. $12,000 – $15,000
Plate 289. $2,000 – $3,000
Plate 290. $6,000 – $9,000
Plate 291. $30,000 – $45,000
Plate 292. $300 – $900 (each)
Plate 293. $2,000 – $3,000
Plate 294. $900 – $1,200
Plate 295. $300 – $500
Plate 298. $7,500 – $10,500
Plate 299. $7,500 –$10,500
Plate 300. $15,000 – $22,500
Plate 301. $22,500 – $30,000
Plate 302. $37,500 – $52,500
Plate 303. $18,000 – $27,000

Plate 304. $4,500 – $7,500
Plate 305. $75,000 –$105,000
Plate 306. $60,000 – $90,000
Plate 307. $18,000 – $22,500
Plate 308. $2,000 – $3,000
Plate 309. $4,500 – $7,500
Plate 310. $18,000 – $22,500
Plate 311. $37,500 – $52,500
Plate 312. $3,000 – $4,500
Plate 313. $3,000 – $4,500
Plate 314. $30,000 – $45,000
Plate 315. $6,000 – $9,000
Plate 316. $4,500 – $6,000
Plate 317. $2,000 – $3,800
Plate 318. $1,500 – $7,500
Plate 319. $60,000 – $90,000
Plate 320. $4,500 – $6,000
Plate 321. $22,500 – $30,000
Plate 322. $15,000 – $22,500
Plate 323. $22,500 – $30,000
Plate 324. $9,000 – $13,500
Plate 325. $18,000 – $22,500
Plate 326. $3,000 – $4,500
    (brooch);
    $3,000 – $4,500 (pendant);
    $6,000 – $9,000 (necklace)
Plate 327. $6,000 – $9,000
Plate 328. $90,000 – $120,000
Plate 329. $4,500 – $7,500
Plate 330. $4,500 – $7,500
Plate 331. $3,000 – $4,500
Plate 332. $9,000 – $12,000
Plate 333. $6,000 – $9,000
Plate 334. $4,500 – $6,000
Plate 335. $500 (each)
Plate 336. $1,200 – $1,800
Plate 337. $1,200 – $1,800
Plate 338. $1,800 – $2,000
Plate 339. $1,800– $2,700 (each)
Plate 340. $2,000 – $3,000
Plate 341. $2,000 – $3,000
Plate 342. $45,000 – $60,000
Plate 343. $1,200 – $1,800
Plate 344. $18,000 – $22,500
Plate 345. $18,000 – $22,500
Plate 346. $2,000 – $3,000
Plate 347. $900 – $1,200
Plate 348. $4,500 – $6,000
Plate 349. $22,500 – $30,000

Plate 350. $600 – $900
Plate 351. $1,800 –$2,000
Plate 352. $900 –$1,200
Plate 353. $7,500 – $9,000
Plate 354. $9,000 – $12,000
Plate 355. $3,000 – $4,500
Plate 356. $3,000 – $4,500
Plate 357. $3,000 – $4,500
Plate 358. $7,500– $12,000
Plate 359. $30,000 – $45,000
Plate 360. $9,000 – $12,000
Plate 361. $4,500 – $6,000
Plate 362. $3,000 – $4,500
Plate 363. $3,000 – $4,500
Plate 364. $7,500 – $10,500
Plate 365. $4,500 – $7,500
Plate 366. $7,500 – $10,500
Plate 367. $22,500 – $35,000
Plate 368. $3,000 – $4,500
Plate 369. $3,000 – $4,500
Plate 370. $1,800 – $2,000
Plate 371. $1,500 – $2,000
Plate 372. $4,500 – $7,500
Plate 373. $2,000 – $3,000
Plate 374. $2,000 – $3,000
Plate 375. $1,800 – $2,000
Plate 376. $900 – $1,200
Plate 377. $900 – $1,200
Plate 378. $1,200 – $1,800
Plate 379. $3,000 – $4,500
Plate 380. $3,000 – $4,500
Plate 381. $900 – $1,200
Plate 382. $3,000 – $4,500
Plate 383. $3,000 – $4,500
Plate 384. $3,000 – $4,500
Plate 385. $1,500 – $2,000
Plate 386. $1,800 – $2,000
Plate 387. $1,800 – $2,000
Plate 388. $225 (each)
Plate 389. $500 – $800 (each)
Plate 390. $6,000 – $9,000
Plate 391. $7,500 – $10,500
Plate 392. $9,000 – $12,000
Plate 393. $6,000 – $9,000
Plate 394. $7,500 – $12,000
Plate 395. $4,500 – $7,500
Plate 396. $30,000 – $45,000
Plate 397. $1,200 –$1,800
Plate 398. $2,000 – $3,000

Plate 399. $1,500 – $1,800
Plate 400. $1,500 – $1,800
Plate 401. $15,000 – $22,500
Plate 402. $4,500 – $7,500
Plate 403. $22,500 – $30,000
Plate 404. $6,000 – $9,000
Plate 405. $2,000 (each)
Plate 406. $2,000 – $3,000
Plate 407. $4,500 – $7,500
Plate 408. $1,500 – $2,000
Plate 409. $1,800 – $2,000
Plate 410. $3,000 – $4,500
Plate 411. $9,000 – $12,000
Plate 412. $4,500 – $6,000
Plate 413. $1,200 – $1,500
Plate 414. $900 – $1,200
Plate 415. $3,000 – $4,500
Plate 416. $27,000 – $35,000
Plate 417. $9,000 – $12,000
    (brooch);
    $1,500 – $2,000 (tiepin);
    eggs, depending on condition
    and inventiveness of design,
    $3,000 – $13,500
Plate 418. $45,000 – $60,000
Plate 419. $5,300 – $6,800
Plate 420. $2,000 – $3,000
Plate 421. $10,500 – $15,000
Plate 422. $6,000 – $7,500
Plate 423. $7,500 – $12,000
Plate 424. $6,000 – $9,000
Plate 425. $15,000 – $18,000
Plate 426. $90,000 – $120,000
Plate 427. $1,200 – $1,800 (each)
Plate 428. $9,000 – $12,000
Plate 429. $1,800 – $2,700
Plate 430. $6,000 – $7,500
Plate 431. $2,000 – $18,000
Plate 432. $12,000 – $18,000
Plate 433. $3,000 – $4,500
Plate 434. $4,500 – $12,000
Plate 435. $900 – $1,400
Plate 436. $9,000 – $12,000
Plate 437. $1,200 – $1,800
Plate 438. $18,000 – $27,000
Plate 439. $30,000 – $45,000
Plate 440. $15,000 – $22,500
Plate 441. $12,000 – $18,000
Plate 442. $4,500 – $7,500

Plate 443. $1,500 – $2,000
Plate 444. $2,000 –$3,800
Plate 445. $3,800 –$5,300
Plate 446. $3,000 – $4,500
Plate 447. $2,000 – $4,500
Plate 448. $150 – $1,200 (each)
Plate 450. $30,000 – $45,000
Plate 451. $30,000 – $45,000
Plate 452. $27,000 – $33,000
Plate 453. $22,500 – $30,000
Plate 454. $45,000 – $60,000
Plate 455. $9,000 – $12,000
Plate 456. $6,000 – $7,500
Plate 457. $9,000 – $12,000
Plate 458. $15,000 – $22,500
Plate 459. $30,000 – $45,000
Plate 460. $75,000 – $105,000
Plate 461. $1,500 – $2,000
Plate 462. $1,800 – $2,700
   (pearl negligé);
   $4,500 – $5,300
   (emerald negligé)
Plate 463. $9,000 – $12,000
Plate 464. $3,000 – $4,500
Plate 465. $3,000 – $6,000
Plate 466. $15,000 – $18,000
Plate 468. $4,500 – $6,000
Plate 469. $60,000 – $75,000
Plate 470. $2,000 –$2,700
Plate 471. $67,500 – $82,500
Plate 472. $4,500 – $9,000
Plate 473. $1,800 – $2,000
Plate 474. $22,500 – $30,000
Plate 475. $4,500 – $6,000
Plate 476. $4,500 – $6,000
Plate 477. $6,000 – $9,000
Plate 478. $3,000 – $4,500
Plate 479. $6,000 – $7,500
Plate 480. $2,000 – $3,000
Plate 481. $6,000 – $7,500
Plate 482. $1,500 – $2,000
Plate 483. $4,500 – $6,000
Plate 484. $3,000 – $4,500
Plate 485. $1,500 – $2,000
Plate 486. $2,000 – $3,000
Plate 487. $9,000 – $12,000
Plate 488. $7,500 – $9,000
Plate 489. $9,000 – $10,500
Plate 490. $18,000 – $22,500

Plate 491. $18,000 – $27,000
Plate 492. $1,500 – $1,800
Plate 493. $22,500 – $27,000
Plate 494. $4,500 – $6,000
Plate 495. $1,800 – $2,700
Plate 496. $6,000 – $9,000
Plate 497. $6,000 – $7,500
Plate 498. $3,800 – $5,300
Plate 499. $2,000 – $3,000
Plate 500. $3,000 – $4,500
Plate 501. $225,000 – $500,000
Plate 502. $30,000 – $45,000
Plate 503. $900 – $1,200 (each)
Plate 504. $1,800 –$2,700
Plate 505. $1,500 – $2,000
Plate 506. $900 – $1,200
Plate 507. $5,300 – $6,800
Plate 508. $12,000 – $18,000
Plate 509. $2,000 – $3,000
Plate 510. $1,800 – $2,700
Plate 511. $12,000 – $15,000
Plate 512. $3,000 – $4,500
Plate 513. $21,000 – $27,000
Plate 514. $3,000 – $4,500
Plate 515. $30,000 – $45,000
Plate 516. $6,000 – $9,000
Plate 520. $75,000 – $90,000
Plate 521. $180,000 – $270,000
Plate 522. $90,000 – $105,000
Plate 523. $52,500 – $67,500
Plate 524. $9,000 – $12,000
Plate 525. $6,000 – $7,500
Plate 526. $45,000 – $60,000
Plate 527. $9,000 – $13,500
Plate 528. $18,000 – $22,500
Plate 529. $15,000 – $18,000
Plate 530. $22,500 – $27,000
Plate 531. $18,000 – $22,500
Plate 532. $7,500 – $9,000
Plate 533. $6,000 – $9,000
Plate 534. $6,000 – $9,000
Plate 535. $180,000 – $225,000
Plate 536. $90,000 – $120,000
Plate 537. $120,000 – $180,000
Plate 538. $18,000 – $22,500
Plate 539. $120,000 – $150,000
Plate 540. Sold in Geneva
   2.4.1987
   for 3,905,000 SF

Plate 541. $45,000 – $60,000
Plate 542. $3,000 – $4,500
Plate 543. $1,500 – $2,000
Plate 544. $300,000 – $500,000
Plate 545. $15,000 – $18,000
Plate 546. $45,000 – $75,000
Plate 547. $22,500 – $30,000
Plate 548. $18,000 – $22,500
Plate 549. $4,500 – $6,000
Plate 550. $2,000 – $3,000
Plate 551. $30,000 – $45,000
Plate 552. $9,000 – $12,000
Plate 553. $12,000 – $18,000
Plate 554. $15,000 – $18,000
Plate 555. $2,000 – $3,000
Plate 556. $27,000 – $35,000
Plate 557. $7,500 – $10,500
Plate 558. $7,500 – $10,500
Plate 559. $9,000 – $12,000
Plate 560. $18,000 – $27,000
Plate 561. $10,500 – $15,000
Plate 562. $7,500 – $10,500
Plate 563. $7,500 – $10,500
Plate 564. $27,000 – $33,000
Plate 565. $4,500 – $6,000
Plate 566. $7,500 –$10,500
Plate 567. $30,000 – $45,000
Plate 568. $45,000 – $60,000
Plate 569. $4,500 – $6,000
Plate 570. $9,000 – $12,000
Plate 571. $2,000 – $3,000
Plate 572. $4,500 – $6,000
Plate 573. $6,000 – $12,000
   (each)
Plate 574. $18,000 – $22,500
Plate 575. $22,500– $30,000
Plate 576. $22,500 – $30,000
Plate 577. $7,500 – $10,500
Plate 578. $6,000 – $9,000
Plate 579. $7,500 – $9,000
Plate 580. $18,000 – $27,000
Plate 581. $22,500 – $30,000
Plate 582. $22,500 – $30,000
Plate 583. $6,000 – $7,500
Plate 584. $22,500 – $35,000
Plate 585. $75,000 – $90,000
Plate 586. Sold in Geneva
   2.4.1987
   for 1,650,000 SF

Plate 587. $7,500 – $9,000
Plate 588. $9,000 – $12,000
Plate 589. $90,000 – $120,000
Plate 590. $9,000 – $12,000
Plate 591. $7,500 – $9,000
Plate 592. $22,500 – $30,000
Plate 593. $7,500 – $9,000
Plate 594. $9,000 – $12,000
Plate 595. $180,000 – $270,000
Plate 596. $180,000 – $225,000
Plate 597. $180,000 – $270,000
   (the bracelet)
Plate 598. Sold in New York in
1987 for $445,000 US
Plate 599. $18,000 – $27,000
Plate 600. $12,000 –$18,000
Plate 601. $15,000 – $22,500
Plate 602. $45,000 – $60,000
Plate 603. $35,000 – $52,500
Plate 604. $7,500 – $9,000
Plate 605. $9,000 – $13,500
Plate 606. $18,000 – $22,500
Plate 607. $9,000 – $12,000
Plate 608. $60,000 – $75,000
Plate 609. $10,500 –$15,000
Plate 610. $4,500 – $6,000
Plate 611. $3,000 – $4,500
Plate 612. $22,500 – $30,000
   (pair)
Plate 613. $22,500 – $30,000
Plate 614. $22,500 – $30,000
Plate 615. $52,500 – $75,000
Plate 616. $7,500 – $10,500
Plate 617. $1,200 – $1,500
Plate 618. $30,000 – $45,000
Plate 619. $22,500 – $30,000
Plate 620. $75,000 – $105,000
Plate 621. $45,000 – $60,000
Plate 622. Sold in Geneva
   2.4.1987
   for 968,000 SF
Plate 623. $45,000 – $60,000
Plate 624. $45,000 – $60,000
Plate 625. Sold in Geneva
   2.4.1987
   for 1,540,000 SF
Plate 626. $30,000 – $35,000
Plate 627. $9,000 – $13,500
Plate 628. $12,000 – $18,000

Plate 629. $1,800 –$2,000 (each)
Plate 630. $3,800 – $5,300
Plate 631. $4,500 – $6,000
Plate 632. $9,000 – $13,500
Plate 633. $2,000 – $3,000
Plate 634. $4,500 – $6,000
Plate 635. $12,000 – $15,000
Plate 636. $900 – $1,200
   (diamond eternity ring);
   $1,800 – $2,000 (triple
   hoop ring)
Plate 637. $7,500 – $9,000
Plate 638. $6,000 – $9,000
Plate 639. $15,000 – $18,000
Plate 640. $7,500 – $10,500
Plate 641. $1,500 – $2,000
Plate 642. $7,500 – $10,500
Plate 643. $9,000 – $12,000
   (each)
Plate 644. $15,000 – $18,000
Plate 645. $6,000 – $7,500
Plate 646. $27,000 – $30,000
Plate 647. $18,000 – $22,500
Plate 648. $9,000 – $13,500
Plate 649. $22,500 – $30,000
Plate 652. $9,000 – $12,000
Plate 653. $4,500 – $6,000
Plate 654. $7,500 – $10,500
Plate 655. $4,500 – $6,000
Plate 656. $7,500 – $10,500
Plate 657. $18,000 – $22,500
Plate 658. $10,500 – $15,000
Plate 659. $12,000 – $18,000
Plate 660. $12,000 – $18,000
   (without ring)
Plate 661. $45,000 – $60,000
Plate 662. Sold in Geneva
   24.1.1987
   for 220,000 SF
Plate 663. $6,000 – $9,000
Plate 664. $7,500 – $9,000
Plate 665. $3,000 – $4,500
Plate 666. $3,800 – $5,300
Plate 667. $9,000 – $12,000
Plate 668. $12,000– $18,000
Plate 669. $12,000 – $18,000
Plate 670. $45,000 – $60,000
Plate 671. $9,000 – $15,000 each
Plate 672. $60,000 – $90,000

Plate 673. Sold in Geneva
   2.4.1987
   for 1,265,000 SF
Plate 674. Sold in Geneva
   2.4.1987
   for 605,000 SF
Plate 675. Sold in Geneva
   2.4.1987
   for 907,500 SF
Plate 676. $22,500 – $30,000
   (necklace); $18,000 – $22,500
   (clip)
Plate 677. $10,500 – $15,000
Plate 678. $150,000 – $225,000
Plate 679. $30,000 – $45,000
Plate 680. $15,000 – $22,500
Plate 681. $7,500 – $9,000
Plate 682. $5,300 – $6,800
Plate 683. $4,500 – $6,000
Plate 684. $4,500 – $6,000
Plate 685. $18,000 – $22,500
Plate 686. Sold in Geneva
   2.4.1987
   for 1,210,000 SF
Plate 687. $30,000 – $35,000
Plate 688. $18,000 – $27,000
Plate 689. $2,000 – $3,000
Plate 690. $15,000 – $22,500
Plate 691. $12,000 – $18,000
Plate 692. $6,000 – $7,500
Plate 693. $4,500 – $6,000
Plate 694. $3,000 – $4,500
   (each)
Plate 695. $12,000 – $15,000
Plate 696. $3,800 – $5,300
Plate 697. $3,000 – $4,500
Plate 698. $4,500 – $6,000
Plate 699. $4,500 – $6,000
Plate 700. $3,800 – $5,300
Plate 701. $12,000 – $18,000
Plate 702. $15,000 – $22,500
Plate 703. $12,000 – $18,000
Plate 704. Sold in Geneva
   2.4.1987
   for 1,540,000 SF
Plate 705. Sold in London
   24.3.1988
   for £81,400
Plate 706. $3,800 – $4,500

Plate 707. $7,500 – $10,500
Plate 708. $4,500 – $6,000
Plate 709. $4,500 – $6,000
Plate 710. $6,000 – $7,500
Plate 711. $3,000 – $7,500
Plate 712. $1,800 – $2,000
Plate 713. $1,500 – $2,000
Plate 714. $1,200 – $1,800 (each)
Plate 715. $7,500 – $10,500
Plate 716. $4,500 – $6,000
Plate 717. $2,000 – $3,000
Plate 718. $3,000 – $4,500
Plate 719. $18,000 – $22,500
Plate 720. $30,000 – $35,000
Plate 721. $22,500 – $30,000
Plate 722. $30,000 – $35,000
Plate 723. $22,500 – $30,000
Plate 724. $9,000 – $10,500
Plate 725. $12,000 – $15,000
Plate 726. $4,500 – $6,000
Plate 727. $30,000 – $45,000
Plate 728. $7,500 – $10,500
Plate 729. $27,000 – $33,000
Plate 730. $9,000 – $12,000
Plate 731. $6,000 – $7,500
Plate 732. Sold in Geneva
    2.4.1987 for 2,090,000 SF
Plate 733. $35,000 – $45,000
Plate 734. $12,000 – $15,000
Plate 735. $6,000 – $9,000
Plate 736. $7,500 – $10,500
Plate 737. $6,000 – $9,000
Plate 738. $6,000 – $9,000
Plate 739. $6,000 – $9,000
Plate 740. $3,000 – $4,500
Plate 741. $3,800 – $5,300
Plate 742. $15,000 – $18,000
Plate 743. $4,500 – $6,000
Plate 744. $6,000 – $9,000
Plate 745. $4,500 – $6,000
Plate 746. $4,500 – $7,500
Plate 747. $6,000 – $9,000
Plate 748. $6,000 – $7,500
Plate 749. $3,000 – $4,500
Plate 750. $6,000 – $7,500
Plate 751. $1,200 – $1,800

Plate 752. $4,500 – $6,000
Plate 753. $6,800 – $8,300
Plate 754. $52,500 – $67,500
Plate 755. $12,000 – $18,000
Plate 756. $52,500 –$60,000
Plate 757. $15,000 – $22,500
Plate 758. $45,000 – $52,500
Plate 759. $6,800 – $8,300
Plate 760. $225,000 – $300,000
Plate 761. $36,000 – $45,000
Plate 762. $30,000 – $45,000
    coral and chalcedony jewels
    $9,000 – $12,000
    chalcedony sautoir
Plate 763. $18,000 – $27,000
Plate 764. $48,000 – $57,000
Plate 765. $5,300 – $6,800
Plate 766. Sold in Geneva 2.4.87
    for: 28,600 SF
    30,800 SF
    28,600 SF
Plate 767. Sold in Geneva 2.4.87
    together with a matching
    bangle for 176,000 SF
Plate 768. $4,500 – $6,000
Plate 769. $18,000 – $22,500
Plate 770. $12,000 – $18,000
Plate 771. $3,000 – $4,500
Plate 772. $60,000 – $75,000
Plate 773. $6,000 – $9,000
Plate 774. $90,000 – $120,000
Plate 775. $60,000 – $67,500
Plate 776. $500 – $600
Plate 777. $4,500 – $6,000
Plate 778. $52,500 – $67,500
Plate 779. Sold in St. Moritz
    19.2.1993 for 872,500 SF
Plate 780. Sold in Geneva
    17.11.1993 for 2,038,500 SF
Plate 781. $3,000 – $4,500
Plate 782. $2,700 – $3,800
Plate 783. $30,000 – $35,000
Plate 784. $4,500 – $6,000
Plate 785. $3,000 – $3,800
Plate 786. $7,500 – $10,500
Plate 787. $52,500 – $67,500

Plate 788. $4,500 – $6,000
Plate 789. $52,500 – $67,500
Plate 790. $9,000 – $12,000
Plate 791. $2,700 – $3,300
Plate 792. $6,000 – $7,500
Plate 793. $3,000 – $3,800
Plate 794. $3,800 – $5,300
Plate 795. $30,000 –$35,000
Plate 796. $3,000 – $4,500
Plate 797. $1,500 – $3,000
Plate 798. $35,000 –$52,500
Plate 799. $2,000 – $3,000
Plate 800. $1,200 – $1,500
Plate 801. $7,500 – $10,500
Plate 802. $15,000 – $22,500
Plate 803. $9,000 – $12,000
Plate 804. $3,000 – $3,800
Plate 805. $5,300 – $6,800
Plate 806. $52,500 – $67,500
Plate 807. $15,000 – $22,500
Plate 808. $30,000 – $35,000
Plate 809. $15,000 – $22,500
Plate 810. $12,000 – $18,000
Plate 811. $18,000 – $22,500
Plate 812. $15,000 – $22,500
Plate 813. $18,000 – $22,500
Plate 814. $22,500 – $30,000
Plate 815. $30,000 – $45,000
Plate 816. $12,000 – $18,000
Plate 817. $3,000 – $4,500
Plate 818. $4,500 – $7,500 each
Plate 819. $9,000 – $12,000
Plate 820. $12,000 – $18,000
Plate 821. $6,000 – $7,500
Plate 822. $12,000 – $18,000
Plate 823. $5,300 – $6,800 each
Plate 824. $35,000 – $52,500
Plate 825. $3,000 – $4,500
Plate 826. $5,300 – $6,800
Plate 827. $45,000 – $52,500
Plate 828. $1,800 – $2,000
Plate 829. $4,500 – $5,300
Plate 830. $15,000 – $22,500
Plate 831. $1,500 – $1,800
Plate 832. $300 – $500
Plate 833. $7,500 – $10,500

Index

NOTE: *page numbers in italics refer to picture captions*